The Power of the Badge

∴

The Power of the Badge

∵

SHERIFFS AND INEQUALITY
IN THE UNITED STATES

Emily M. Farris &
Mirya R. Holman

THE UNIVERSITY OF CHICAGO PRESS

CHICAGO AND LONDON

The University of Chicago Press, Chicago 60637
The University of Chicago Press, Ltd., London
© 2024 by The University of Chicago

Published 2024
Printed in the United States of America

33 32 31 30 29 28 27 26 25 24   1 2 3 4 5

ISBN-13: 978-0-226-83449-8 (cloth)
ISBN-13: 978-0-226-83451-1 (paper)
ISBN-13: 978-0-226-83450-4 (e-book)
DOI: https://doi.org/10.7208/chicago/9780226834504.001.0001

CIP data to come

♾ This paper meets the requirements of ANSI/NISO Z39.48-1992
(Permanence of Paper).

Contents

Foreword and Acknowledgments

One of the most common questions we get when we talk to other academics, journalists, the public, and our family and friends about this project is: what on earth made you start to work on research on county sheriffs? For both of us, our early experiences shaped our interests. Mirya's early life in a rural county in Oregon where the sheriff provided most of the law enforcement taught her lessons about the importance of the office. Growing up on a commune, a mom who ran a domestic violence shelter, and several brushes with the law all reinforced the complex story of sheriffs in rural America. Emily's upbringing in Alabama and interest in the Civil Rights Movement and its legacy led her to wanting to better understand sheriffs' roles in American politics. That her home county was under federal oversight for racial discrimination for her entire time living there (and well beyond, from 1982 to 2017) highlighted the importance of the office and its resistance to change.

In January 2012, we met up in the basement bar of the conference hotel in New Orleans at the Southern Political Science Association conference. Could we figure out a project to collaborate on? We chatted about growing up and why we decided to work on urban politics. But there's so much in local politics outside of cities. Like . . . sheriffs! Maybe a research project on the representation of women and people of color in the office would be something to work on, we mused. "There must be work on this, right?" Mirya volunteered to look for data, Emily for literature. A week later, we had a file named "thoughts on project," which included the line "How much discretion do sheriffs have over local policies—to be determined." Here we are, twelve years later, still trying to answer that question and the many more that have come up during this project.

It is impossible to spend more than a decade on a research agenda and not accrue debts so wide and deep to the many, many people who have motivated, encouraged, and supported us to keep the project alive and well. We want to begin by thanking the more than one thousand sheriffs that took our surveys to help us better understand their office. Without these sheriffs, this project would not be possible. That sheriffs trusted us (sometimes with some skepticism) with their views on a wide range of topics continues to astonish us both. We are very grateful.

A driving motivation for working on this project has been learning about those that the criminal justice system fails to protect or outright harms. Our deepest debts go to those who have paid the prices—in their lives, freedoms, and well-being—of the stories we tell here. We hope that by writing this book, we can bring the smallest slivers of attention and justice. Our struggle to understand sheriffs' unique relationship with guns started after the Sandy Hook shooting and the Constitutional Sheriffs and Peace Officers Association's (CSPOA) reaction to it. We worked on this project across a decade, during which time thousands of mass shootings occurred in the United States, including several that involved small children, such as Uvalde. We hold those children particularly close to our hearts.

We have been incredibly lucky to be aided in our research process through discussions and collaborations with journalists. As sheriffs made news across the country, we benefited from a wide set of conversations with journalists interested in accountability, democracy, and criminal justice. Of particular importance has been a relationship with Maurice Chammah and the Marshall Project. We are thankful to Maurice, Akiba Solomon, Susan Chiba, and others at the Marshall Project for their support of our project and its second survey of sheriffs in 2021. The high quality of work produced by reporters such as Maurice, Alan Greenblatt, Ashley Powers, and others has given us faith in the journalistic process, and we offer our appreciation to those committed to faithfully telling the full story of sheriffs. We are also very thankful for the many nonprofits, activists, and community members dedicated to holding sheriffs accountable.

Several scholars supported this project in a variety of ways. Peter Burns introduced the two of us as the "academic grandchildren" of Clarence Stone and has been an extraordinary mentor for more than twenty years. Mirya's colleagues at Florida Atlantic University and Tulane (and now beyond), especially J. Celeste Lay, Chris Fettweis, Anna Mahoney, Jeffrey Morton, and Menaka Philips, provided support and feedback. Mirya would especially like to thank Christina Xydias, Bethany Albertson, and Shannon McGreggor, who put up with weird and terrifying discussions of sheriffs during our morning writing group. Emily's colleagues at Texas Christian University (and now beyond), especially Max Krochmal, Gabe Huddleston, Jim Riddlesperger, Matt Montgomery, Chip Stewart, Luis Romero, and Amina Zarrugh encouraged the project. We are thankful for the research assistants at FAU, TCU, and Tulane who worked on the project and often went down the sheriff rabbit holes with us. A group of friends and colleagues who kept telling us that this was a cool and important project pushed us to keep going. We would especially like to thank Tiffany Barnes, Salil Benegal, Andrea Benjamin, Becky Bromley-Trujillo, Constantine Boussalis, Erin Cassese, Meredith Conroy, Justin de Benedictis-Kessner, Sam Jackson, Ellen Key, Zoe Nemerever, Kelsey Shoub, Candis Watts Smith, Miranda Sullivan, Jane Sumner, Heather Silber Mohamed, Matthew Thomas, Chris Warshaw, and Christina Wolbrecht for their faith in and enthusiasm for this project. We even thank those who told us this was not an interesting or worthy project; we hope you enjoy the book, despite yourselves. We received a lot of support from friends (and motivation from enemies) on social media. We thank our supporters—here is that book you have been asking about. Now you've got to read it!

Colleagues attending a wide set of talks and conferences gave us considerable feedback. An early presentation at a Southern Political Science Association meeting reassured us that there was something "there" in our work. The 2021 American Political Science Association (APSA) Justice and Injustice mini conference in 2021, and particularly support from Allison Harris, Hannah Walker, and Ariel White and comments from Michael Leo Owens, gave us renewed motivation. Talks at Johns Hopkins, Tulane University Law School, the University of North Carolina's American Politics Seminar, the Minority Politics Online Seminar Series, Appalachian State University, St. Olaf College, Elon University, and the Hobby School of Public Affairs at the University of Houston all provided amazing feedback on elements of the project. Mirya is particularly thankful to her new colleagues at the Hobby School for their enthusiasm for the project.

We would like to thank Sara Doskow, our editor at the University of Chicago Press. This book might not exist at all, and certainly not in as good shape, without Sara. By happenstance, Sara sent us a message wanting to talk about our work about sheriffs about a week after we created a potential outline for a book. We had discussed ideas for a book (or two . . . or three— stay tuned!) many times over the years, but the timing and fit never felt right until our conversation with Sara. Her encouragement and guidance have greatly improved our manuscript, as have the anonymous reviewers who provided feedback. Our friend Kelly Clancy of Epilogue Editing was one of the first people to read and comment on the full draft, and we are grateful for her skills as an editor and her enthusiasm for the project. Thank you to the University of Chicago Press, who believe this kind of work is political science and is worthy of publishing.

Money is a tricky issue in academia; many of us have none of it for research and some of us have more than we can spend. The work of this text was largely free in that it took us just thousands of hours of time. We received an APSA Latino Fund grant early to help us with the first survey, the Marshall Project purchased a National Sheriffs' Association directory for us in 2021, and Arnold Ventures provided funds for us to think and write together. We both benefited from long-overdue sabbaticals to help with research and writing this book and from personal financial security that allowed us to both take a full year of leave at reduced pay. We begged and borrowed to fund research assistants to help with data collection across the life of this project. We estimate that the entire direct research costs of this book are around $7,000, including three writing retreats.

Our professional relationship has gone through a dissertation defense, several new jobs, moves, successes, rejections, a baby, pets, nemeses, mantras, and hundreds of thousands of Google Chats (remember those?), emails, texts, Zoom calls, and snarky Twitter DMs. Mirya is extraordinarily thankful for her relationship with Emily: you always want me to win, even when I don't think I deserve it. I am so lucky to have you as a coauthor and friend. Emily feels very much the same: I am extraordinarily thankful for your collaboration and your mentorship, but most importantly your friendship. Few relationships that emerge out of a night at a New Orleans bar can celebrate such breadth and success, and I am so fortunate to have you in my life.

Mirya would like to thank Zach, who has listened to a LOT of tales about sheriffs in the last two decades. He continues to find my obsessions humorous rather than annoying and does not blink at hours (ahem, days, months, years) of collecting data, writing retreats in faraway lands, or me spending our household's money on things like a crate of sheriff coloring books. My family, friends, and community providing casual tolerance of this project exemplifies how much broad support they have provided. My family is partially (say, 1 percent) to blame for this book: I've been taught to pursue ideas for ideas' sake, that tenacity is a virtue, and that everyone loves a good story. Lambeaux, Marx, and Maggie remind me that there's more in the world than writing. My sweet dog, Nola, sat at my feet for almost the entirety of this project—she always seemed to believe I could do anything. I miss her every day and I'll keep trying to prove her right.

Emily would like to thank her family and friends for their love and support—particularly when it came in the form of "I thought you might find this sheriff story interesting. . . ." My parents' lifelong support has allowed me to follow my curiosities and interests, and I am grateful for their constant loving presence in the journey. Thank you to Loren for his love and partnership. He always encourages me to continue over any large (or small) boulders in the way. Loren and Clara made time and space for this project and provided needed distraction as well. Y'all inspire me and make my life richer in every way possible. Clara helpfully hurried this book along, as I promised her I'd write her a book next. Hopefully the next book takes us down a new rabbit hole, one filled with imagination, some magic, and maybe a unicorn. May we all imagine a better future together.

The Power of the Badge

When Sheriff Keith Cain retired in 2021, he was just shy of completing his sixth elected term as the chief law enforcement officer of Daviess County, Kentucky. Cain had received exceptional accolades in office, including the governor's award for Outstanding Contribution to Kentucky Law Enforcement (twice!), the Kentucky Sheriff of the Year award, the National Sheriffs' Association Sheriff of the Year,[1] and the Buford Pusser National Law Enforcement Officer of the Year.[2] Like many other sheriffs across the country, Cain is a native of the county where he served; he began his career as a patrolman in the sheriff's office in 1974 and worked in the office continuously until 2021 (Pickett 2021). Cain ran unopposed for sheriff in 1998 and faced only two challengers across his next four elections, a common feature in sheriff races in the United States.

Sheriff Donny Youngblood shares many characteristics with Cain including that he is a lifelong resident of Kern County, California, where he has served as sheriff since 2006. Youngblood began working in the Kern County Sheriff's Office (KCSO) in 1972. Unlike Cain, Youngblood and KCSO have been dogged by controversy. From Youngblood being caught on tape saying that it is better financially to kill a suspect than to injure them (Winton 2018), to the office's high rates of killing and injuring suspects (Swaine and Laughland 2015),[3] to investigations and allegations by the ACLU for violating the rights of immigrants (ACLU 2022)[4] and settlements in the courts and with the California attorney general and the Department of Justice (Morgan 2020),[5] Youngblood exemplifies sheriffs who serve long tenures in an office with broad authority and numerous problems.

More than three thousand sheriffs across the United States occupy unique positions in our counties' politics, where voters elect[6] white men,[7] such as Cain and Youngblood, to an office with enormous autonomy and authority. In this book, we argue that the autonomy and authority granted to sheriffs in the United States create an environment where sheriffs rarely change; elections do not create meaningful accountability; employees, budgets, and jails can be used for political gain; marginalized populations can be punished; right-wing extremism flourishes; and reforms fail. Sheriffs occupy an exceptional place in the American political system: they are bureaucrats who hold the legitimate right to harm and kill people, they are influential elected officials with very few checks on their power, and they both set and implement a wide set of significant policies. In essence, in a policy arena where rules and regulations govern violent interactions between people and the state, they hold the power to *create*, *execute*, and *implement* these rules and regulations.

The office of sheriff predates the United States. For sheriffs, these origins are so central to their identity and the importance of the position that the National Sheriffs' Association and state associations routinely produce reports about sheriffs' history, and many sheriffs feature "history of the office" sections on their websites. Although sheriffs quickly point out the deep roots and continuity of their position, these histories largely skip over the role sheriffs played in the maintenance of the status quo, inequality, and white supremacy. Instead, sheriffs often focus on the Judeo-Christian and European origins of the office[8] and highlight their status as elected law enforcement, a feature that is uniquely American. As Sheriff Craig DuMond of Delaware County, New York, writes on the history page on the county's website, the "special designation" of sheriffs means "the Sheriff is often referred to as the 'people's lawman.' It is the Sheriff who answers directly to the people who elect him/her into office rather than the 'government.' This distinction is just as important today as it was in 1634" (Delaware County Sheriff 2022).

The electoral nature of the office shapes who sheriffs are and what they do. It also affects the ability to hold sheriffs responsible for bad behavior or provide accountability for "effectively delivering services to their communities, while treating people fairly, with dignity, and within the boundaries of formal law" (Archbold 2021, 1666). Sheriffs argue that they are held accountable because they answer directly to voters. However, as we will show in this book, sheriffs' elections fundamentally fail as a mechanism of democratic accountability as they allow the same people (that is, overwhelmingly white, conservative men) to hold the office repeatedly with little change, even when misconduct occurs in office. Like many other sheriffs, neither Cain nor Youngblood regularly faced competitive elections, and both regularly ran unopposed. Even after saddling taxpayers with more the $20 million in settlements for wrongful death and other abuses, Youngblood sought and won reelection again in 2022, noting to a reporter that "no one has told [him]" it is time for someone new to be sheriff (Bell 2021). Because most sheriffs serve in their offices as deputies prior to their election, sheriffs oversee their potential political opponents and can potentially control who runs for office given their authority. For example, Youngblood fired his chief deputy after the staff member challenged him in the 2018 election (Arellano 2022), and Cain retired before the end of his term, allowing his handpicked successor to take over the office and run in the next election as the incumbent.[9]

Sheriffs' electoral selection (and its accompanying autonomy) shapes their behavior in office.[10] While sheriffs across the country vary in their responsibilities, almost all sheriffs oversee jails and courthouse security, and many sheriffs serve as the primary law enforcement organization in their county, with investigative and arrest powers. Sheriffs' interests in reelection lead them to increase their authority and decrease or distort their accountability. As we will discuss, sheriffs do this by hiring more employees, diversifying their budget sources, and building new jails. While discussions of policing accountability and scholarly analysis tend to focus on large metropolitan police forces, we suggest more attention ought to be paid to sheriffs and their authority.

Sheriffs occupy a unique position in carceral policymaking: they both participate in the process of making up the rules, policies, and norms that define the edges of the carceral state and engage in the enforcement of those policies. And they make a living from the carceral state: many sheriffs control both how big and/or how full jails are (Littman 2021), and counties can use those jails to extract resources from prisoners, taxpayers, private prison companies, and their state and the federal governments. Sheriffs Cain and Youngblood exemplify how sheriffs contribute to and build on the political economy of the carceral state. Youngblood lobbied for the construction of multiple new jail facilities in his counties where he runs the jails, and both sheriffs increased the number of employees that they supervise and sourced funds and materials from state and federal governments to increase their offices' capacity. Both counties also developed novel ways to raise money from those jailed—for example, the Daviess County Detention Center generated $522,000 in 2019 from fees and charges levied against those in jail, including $305,000 in charges for services and $195,000 from charging those incarcerated for using the telephone (Vera Institute 2022).

Sheriffs' autonomy and authority afford the men who hold this office exceptional power: they both set policy and then enforce that policy, including in areas that disproportionately affect marginalized populations. So, we argue that when sheriffs hold negative views about a population, they then can set policy that punishes that group, producing inequality in how law enforcement treats marginalized groups from county to county. Variations across counties can mean that victims of sexual or domestic violence in some counties receive social services while others do not[11] or that Black motorists are unfairly targeted for traffic violations in some places and are not in others. In Kern County, Sheriff Youngblood provided jail access for Immigration and Customs Enforcement (ICE) so that they could quickly retrieve any person of interest, while other counties limited their cooperation with ICE.

The combination of sheriffs' individual autonomy and their authority provides an environment where far-right extremists can recruit eager sheriffs to believe that their office wields seemingly unlimited power and autonomy (even more than the United States president, one group claims). In our current era of polarization and intra-federal conflict, the consequences of radicalization are broad reaching and troubling, especially as right-wing extremist sheriffs mobilize around efforts to oppose and refuse to enforce gun safety laws and COVID restrictions and mobilize around efforts alleging election fraud. The recruitment and radicalization of sheriffs into these anti-government extremist views builds on and takes advantage of the autonomy and authority of the office and its unique role in the federal system.

If sheriffs are unresponsive to calls for change, produce inequalities through their biased views, and endorse extremism, then what can we do to reform the office? In this book, we trace central attempts at reform, focusing on how characteristics of the office often mean that sheriffs sidestep broader efforts at changing law enforcement. Both Cain and Youngblood pushed back against the idea of reform, arguing that their office simply needs to do a better job developing deep relationships with the community: Cain told *Kentucky Law Enforcement Magazine*, "If we're working every day to engage the community in a positive way and build relationships with them, when we do make mistakes—and we will as long as we recruit from the human race—the community will be better suited to forgive us" (Cain, quoted in Foreman 2016). And Youngblood similarly notes that the reputation of the sheriff and his employees shapes their relationship with the community (Arellano 2022).[12] In this way, sheriffs resist calls for comprehensive reform, instead focusing on immutable factors like their relationships with the community.

Ultimately, sheriffs themselves are resistant to reform because it points to problems with the office itself and the individuals who hold it. If law enforcement is flawed, so are these men, as their identities are tied to being sheriff. Cain saw his career as exemplifying a "servant's heart" (Pickett 2021): "It's more than a profession. It's certainly more than a paycheck. It's more than even a passion. I firmly believe that just as a priest or pastor is called to the ministry, law enforcement officers are called to law enforcement" (Foreman 2016). Similarly, Youngblood mused, "At the end of the day, this is my community and I love it. I am still at my desk at 7 o'clock in the morning. . . . I'm proud to be a part of this community" (A. Bell 2021).

We use sheriffs like Cain, Youngblood, and others in this book as a lens to contribute to scholarship on local politics, American political development, federalism, political behavior, sociology, criminal justice, public administration and policy, and political extremism. Through a deep focus on this single unique office, we bring new data and insights to central questions across these fields. Studying sheriffs thus allows us to examine where there are continuities with broader patterns in criminal justice and how these patterns take on locally specific forms in the office of sheriff. We suggest that the design of the office—and the individuals who serve in it—challenge central tenets of democracy. Our work engages with the robust body of scholarship that has examined the problems with democracy and elections in local politics, particularly the ways that local elections fail to hold elected officials accountable and the ways that local bodies fail at representation (Burns 2006; de Benedictis-Kessner 2017, 2018; Schaffner, Rhodes, and La Raja 2020; Kirkland 2021; Anzia and Bernhard 2022). Tracing the evolution of the office of sheriff and connecting it to the broader history of policing in the United States allows us to better understand the deep roots of these inequalities (Trounstine 2018, 2008; Francis and Wright-Rigueur 2021; Francis 2014; Fortner 2016), as well as the potential for—and limits on—change.

Sheriffs are "site and agent of carceral policymaking" (Littman 2021, 866), participating deeply in both the creation and reinforcement of the United States' obsession with imprisonment. We build on two bodies of scholarship in demonstrating the importance of sheriffs in these systems: those scholars who describe the institutional roots of the United States' incarceration problem (Gottschalk 2016; Gunderson 2020; Zimring and Hawkins 1999, 1995) and those who focus on the political economy of incarceration, the role of race and markets, and how policing shapes the behaviors and beliefs of race-class subjugated communities (Soss, Fording, and Schram 2011; Page and Soss 2021; Weaver, Prowse, and Piston 2019; Soss and Weaver 2017; Muller and Schrage 2021).

No academic text in more than a hundred years has focused closely on sheriffs, nor have broader research projects on law enforcement, criminal justice, or elections considered sheriffs' combination of autonomy and authority. We suggest that sheriffs represent key fundamental tensions in politics in the United States: that popular ideas of the elected office rarely match the realities, that racism and nativist sentiment sit at the core of American politics, and that even as some places change, path dependency and institutional lethargy shape much of what is politically possible, despite efforts at reform.

Evidence

In the book, we draw on several core sources of data and information. For much of the text, we rely on information provided to us by sheriffs on two surveys that we conducted in 2012 and 2021 and a broad set of companion data we gathered from other sources on the sheriffs who took the surveys. Each survey contains the responses of more than five hundred sheriffs who resemble the demographics of sheriffs overall in the United States. These surveys should *not* be taken as panels: we did not survey the same group of sheriffs nine years apart, but instead surveyed two samples of the entire population of sheriffs in 2012 and 2021.

We first surveyed sheriffs in 2012 at the beginning of our research into the office. In early 2021, Maurice Chammah, a staff writer and reporter at the Marshall Project, approached us with a proposal to work together to do another survey. The Marshall Project, which is a nonpartisan, nonprofit organization that "seeks to create and sustain a sense of national urgency about the U.S. criminal justice system" (Marshall Project 2022), paid for the costs of purchasing a directory of sheriffs from the National Sheriffs' Association. We then worked together to develop a survey instrument with items that were consistent with our first survey and included questions of interest to Chammah and the Marshall Project. We received human subjects approval for both surveys: the 2012 survey was evaluated by the Florida Atlantic University Institutional Review Board and the 2021 survey was evaluated by the Tulane University and Texas Christian University Institutional Review Boards. In 2021, we retained full control of the raw data and responses to the survey and provided cross tabs and de-identified information to the Marshall Project, per our agreement with the Marshall Project, our human subjects approval, and the consent we received from the sheriffs who participated in the surveys.

For each survey effort, we started with the full population of county sheriffs and attempted to email each sheriff.[13] This proved to be difficult. Although the National Sheriffs' Association maintains a directory of sheriffs and updates it each year,[14] the directory had incomplete or incorrect data in both 2012 and 2021. For each survey effort, we updated the directory through phone calls and web searches, including sheriffs' websites, social media accounts, media reports, and state-level directories.

All available data suggests that the sheriffs who completed our surveys

TABLE 1.1. Survey counties

Measure	2012 survey counties	2021 survey counties	US counties overall
Average county % vote for Obama in 2008	38%	36%	38%
Average county % vote for Biden in 2020	33%	36%	38%
Average of county population (2010)	54,490	57,261	61,474
Average median household income (2010)	45,134	45,097	43,244
Average county % White (2010)	82%	82%	79%
Average county % Latino (2010)	7%	8%	8%
Average county % Black (2010)	7%	7%	9%
Average county % rural (2010)	23%	23%	23%
Share of the land owned by state or federal government (2022)	15%	16%	13%

Note: Data from the US Census Bureau, the MIT Election Archive, and Headwaters Economics. See Data and Methods appendix for more information.

are similar to sheriffs overall, and the counties they represent are similar to counties in the United States. In both 2012 and 2021, the counties represented by sheriffs in our survey look very similar to the average US county (see table 1.1).

Our research also features the construction and analysis of large databases of information about sheriffs, including their gender, race, social media handles, website biographies, and media coverage. In 2012 and 2015, we constructed databases of the gender and race of all sheriffs in the United States and analyze this data throughout the book, but especially in chapter 2. In 2021, we also took a random sample of 15 percent of the total US sheriff population and collected information on the key issues facing sheriffs' offices, their websites and social media activity, and media coverage of their offices. We draw qualitative information from this dataset and our collection of news stories involving sheriffs over the decade we worked on this project, including identifying sheriffs to feature in vignettes in the book.

To examine who runs as a candidate in sheriff elections, we rely on the California Election Data Archive (Bernhard and de Benedictis-Kessner 2021), which provides the names and stated occupations of all candidates for local office in California from 1996 to 2020. California is the only state to provide such information about candidates for local office in a comprehensive form over time. We hand code the occupations of all candidates for sheriff in this data to understand patterns of who runs for the sheriff's office and combine this data with administrative information, including the number and salaries of employees of each sheriff's office.

We supplement the original data we have collected with materials from the Law Enforcement Management and Administrative Statistics, the Census of Law Enforcement, the Census of State and Local Law Enforcement Agencies, jail data from the Vera Institute, and reports and data from the Department of Justice, the Bureau of Justice Statistics, the Centers for Disease Control, the US Census Bureau, and datasets compiled by nonprofit and media organizations like the *Washington Post*'s Police Shooting Database, Mapping Police Violence, the Sentencing Project, and more. Details of these sources and the data we use from them can be found in the Data and Methods appendix.

That sheriffs serve at the county level aids in our supplemental work in many ways, as a wide set of additional information about crime, population, demographics, and politics is available at the local level (Nemerever and Rogers 2021). Yet, sheriffs' jurisdictions are often far more complicated than just serving at the county level, in part because of the variety of coverage over incorporated or unincorporated spaces in counties. Sheriffs serve all people who live in their counties. But sheriffs' domain as the primary law enforcement agency in a county extends only to unincorporated areas (where 40 percent of the US population lives) or those towns and cities that have contracted their law enforcement services to the sheriff. Incorporated areas with small populations are more likely to contract their services to sheriffs. This results in sheriffs covering a large share of incorporated areas: in 2020, more than 75 percent of cities have fewer than five thousand residents, and more than 40 percent have fewer than five hundred residents (US Census Bureau 2020). In many other cities and towns, the sheriff sometimes has concurrent law enforcement duties, meaning that the sheriff's deputies have the full power to pursue and arrest individuals but share those duties with a local police department. A visual depiction of a county with these overlapping forms of power is available in the Data and Methods appendix. In a select set of jurisdictions, sheriffs do not possess law enforcement powers but instead provide only services like running the jail, courthouse security, and serving warrants and evictions. We consider the sheriff's domain to be the county overall, given that the sheriff (at minimum) provides jail, warrant, and courthouse services in the vast majority of counties and can oversee a much broader set of services.

We made ethical choices about the presentation of information in this book. For sheriffs who filled out our survey, we guaranteed them confidentiality, which means that we do not and cannot connect any sheriff's individual responses on the survey to their identity. We made this decision to encourage sheriffs to be as honest as possible with us and to recruit a large sample of sheriffs. Because of this promise we made, when we use data from either survey, we provide no identifying information about the sheriffs themselves. We do identify individual sheriffs when they are quoted from other sources, including interviews in media or social media outlets, social media, news coverage, or radio shows or YouTube videos (see Data and Methods appendix for a map of every county/sheriff mentioned by name in the book). When we quote sheriffs from the survey, social media, or their own writings, we provide their exact responses, including their use of capitalization, word choice, and spelling and grammar, and we do not use *[sic]* to indicate misspellings or grammatical mistakes; if it is in a quote, that is how the sheriff reported it directly to us, errors and all. The book addresses issues of violence, white supremacy, racism, misogyny, and inequality. As we believe that it is important that people know what sheriffs do and say, we provide exact quotes whenever possible, even when some might find material to be offensive. Because sheriffs are overwhelmingly men (99 percent in 2012 and 98 percent in 2021), we use he/him pronouns to discuss sheriffs in general, except if we are talking about a particular sheriff who is a woman. Throughout the book, we use the common terms *law enforcement* and *criminal justice*, though we draw attention to the challenge posed by the lack of actual legal enforcement or justice within these systems.

Despite their presence in almost every county in the United States and the central roles they play in law enforcement and criminal justice, we know much less about what sheriffs do (or do not do) and the roles they fill; the lack of an "empirical examination" means that "folk knowledge has been accepted as fact" about sheriffs (Decker 1979, 97). At minimum, we aim to provide some remedy to this oversight through this book's examination of the legal and practical responsibilities and roles of the sheriff. But challenging "folk knowledge" also requires engaging in some skepticism about the information that sheriffs themselves provide to us and the public. Throughout the book, we intersperse information from sheriffs themselves about how they view their motivations, challenges, and daily activities with administrative data, media accounts, and our own observations of sheriffs' work.

Looking Ahead: Plan of the Book

We begin with an investigation of the history of the office of the sheriff in the United States. In chapter 1, we use a political development approach to examine the key moments in sheriffs' history, focusing on path dependency: "At any given moment, the different rules, arrangements and timetables put into place by changes negotiated at various points in the past will be found to impose themselves on the actors of the present and to affect their efforts to negotiate changes of their own" (Orren and Skowronek 2004, 11). Like others, we focus on key points of conflict as a means of examining when change does and does not occur (Peters, Pierre, and King 2005). In short, sheriffs have the authority and autonomy that they have today because of actions in the past. We make the argument that sheriffs have long been involved in the maintenance of the status quo, racial institutional orders (King and Smith 2005), and class inequality (Piston 2018) in the United States in their efforts to shape and expand the carceral state.

In chapter 2, we focus on the electoral nature of the office and compare it to other offices. We draw on what sheriffs articulate as core to the office: the continuity and electoral nature of American sheriffs. But when placed against any standard for democratic accountability, sheriffs' elections fail. In the chapter, we detail the uncompetitive nature of sheriff elections, where sheriffs enjoy extremely high rates of uncontested elections and incumbency reelection. We then argue that this can be directly traced to the shallow pool of candidates that run for the office and that sheriffs manipulate this pool to keep it shallow. A consequence of this is an extremely unrepresentative set of sheriffs in terms of gender, race, race and gender, ideology, partisanship, or broad political preferences.

Elections do not shape just who holds the office but also how sheriffs behave in office. In chapter 3, we apply the expectation from political science that elected officials seek reelection above all other ends to sheriffs' behavior as the manager of their staffs and as someone who oversees a budget and a jail. We focus on how sheriffs navigate managing their employees, budgetary challenges, and overseeing a jail not just as simple bureaucratic tasks but also as opportunities and challenges the sheriff faces in cultivating reelection. Sheriffs are not just managers dealing with shortages of quality applicants for jobs in their offices but also direct supervisors of the population most likely to present a serious challenge on the ballot. Sheriffs are not only bureaucrats negotiating budgets with county commissioners but also elected officials who seek to increase their capacity every year as a tool for ensuring reelection. And they are not just jail wardens passively supervising prisoners but elected officials viewing their jails as both problematic and as resource-generating opportunities. In expanding their sources of revenue, sheriffs rent out jail bed space, seize assets from those accused of crimes, and generate increasingly large amounts of their budget from fees and charges levied on those incarcerated in their counties (Swenson 2010; Ryan 2020; Kang-Brown and Subramanian 2017). To understand sheriffs' behavior, we suggest that looking to the political dynamics of the office is key.

In chapter 4, we argue that sheriffs' unique role in both creating and enforcing policy centers the sheriffs' own attitudes in shaping law enforcement decisions. This can create widespread inequality across counties and be particularly harmful for marginalized groups. We focus on three policy areas—intimate partner violence, racial profiling in traffic enforcement, and immigration enforcement—as examples of how sheriffs' attitudes influence the policy choices of their offices. Given the lack of change in who holds the office of sheriff, we also show that these attitudes and that the relationship between sheriffs' individual attitudes and policy choices are stable across the past decade. As a result, women, Black people, and immigrants are subject to unequal treatment by law enforcement across counties, with policies dependent not necessarily on demand or need but on what a particular sheriff thinks about a marginalized population.

In chapter 5, we examine how sheriffs' negative views about marginalized populations overlap with an anti-federalism orientation developed in a constellation of right-wing extremist views, including disruptive political behavior aimed at restoring "some imagined (but not necessarily imaginary) past" (Jackson 2019a). Although sheriffs have a great deal of autonomy already within the federal system, they often resist *any* attempts to constrain their behavior, with right-wing extremism fueling these views. In this chapter, we detail how sheriffs increasingly identify with right-wing extremism and the consequences for their engagement in enforcement activities. Sheriffs who endorse right-wing extremist views express a deep unwillingness to enforce federal and state laws, including gun control and COVID mitigation. Currently, right-wing sheriffs are actively recruiting more sheriffs and incorporating bogus concerns about elections fraud into the into their extremist movement, and we argue this poses challenges for the operation of American democracy.

Chapter 6 concludes the book by reflecting on how we got to this point in the United States and the possibilities for a different path in the future. In considering reform, we ask: to whom are sheriffs responsible? And for what are sheriffs responsible? In evaluating these questions, we examine both what sheriffs themselves say and what we have observed in our more than decade-long study of the office. We consider the ways that previous reforms have tackled pieces of these questions and the possibility for changes and future work moving forward.

CHAPTER ONE

Filling in an Incomplete
History of Sheriffs

In 2021, individuals incarcerated in Morgan County Jail told the local paper that they had to beg family for commissary money to buy food to avoid eating the nutritionally inadequate and "gross" meals provided by Sheriff Ron Puckett (Sheets 2021).[1] This was not the first, second, or even third time that those imprisoned in the jail had complained about sheriffs' allotment of meager food (Whitmire 2018).[2] Prior Morgan County sheriffs Ana Franklin and Greg Bartlett both faced federal judges for complaints over their spending of the jail's food funds (Nossiter 2009). Thanks to an antiquated Alabama law, Sheriffs Franklin and Bartlett personally pocketed the jail's surplus meal profit, amounts that exceeded hundreds of thousands of dollars over the years.[3] Sheriffs Barlett and Franklin earned nicknames as part of resulting scandals: Sheriff Bartlett was Sheriff Corndog because of those in jail testifying that they ate corn dogs twice a day for weeks after Bartlett and a neighboring sheriff split the $1,000 cost for an eighteen-wheeler full of corn dogs, and Sheriff Ana Franklin was the Car Lot Sheriff from when she personally loaned $150,000 of the jail food budget to a corrupt car lot business (Remkus 2018). Investigations dating back to 1891, 1907, 1911, and 1915 found similar issues of Alabama sheriffs personally profiting off food allowances and jails (Harris 1972). A political columnist covering the events in 2018 noted this ongoing pattern in history: "I'm looking back in our archives at the same story, written again, and again and again" (Whitmire 2018). In 2019, Alabama legislators finally tightened restrictions on the food fund law,[4] but complaints over the quality of food in jail persist.

How has the office of sheriff evolved over time? As demonstrated by the Alabama sheriffs and their choices about feeding inmates in jail, change is often slow in the history of sheriffs. In many ways, sheriffs and their offices still resemble their origins, and many sheriffs focus on their long history as important to understanding the office. Sheriffs often highlight their origins and histories on their websites and social media. For example, the Morgan County Sheriff's Office Twitter bio focuses on the office's origin: "The Morgan County Sheriff's Office was established February 6, 1818 and has a long history of protecting and serving the citizens of Morgan County!"[5] On Facebook, the sheriff's page provides a history of the office copied from the National Sheriffs' Association and notes, "The Morgan County Sheriff's Office can trace it's roots to 1816, when the Treaty of Turkey Town was signed. This lead to the formation of Cotaco County on February 6, 1818 (later named Morgan County)" (Morgan County Sheriff's Office 2020).[6] Many other sheriffs and sheriff associations across the United States similarly draw attention to the long history of the office. The Alabama Sheriffs Association website recounts the medieval English history of the office ("at least as far back as 1066") through its colonial roots in America, concluding with "most importantly, the office of sheriff has not lost the dignity it has enjoyed since its inception. Like their Middle Ages counterpart, a sheriff today continues to hold the respect and admiration of the citizens they protect" (Alabama Sheriffs Association 2022).

Yet, the histories sheriffs present are often incomplete. Missing in Alabama's history are the stories of sheriffs who sold and leased enslaved people (*Macon Republican* 1853; *NPR* 2008), joined and led the Ku Klux Klan (Rogers and Pruitt 2005), colluded with lynching mobs (*New York Times* 1933; NAACP 1919), led campaigns of racialized violence against organized labor (Kelly 2001), killed Black men in custody (*New York Times* 1953), and organized posses to put down "race-riots" (*New York Times* 1960). Absent are the sheriffs who went to jail for violating federal law, beating prisoners, and willfully neglecting their duty (*New York Times* 1929; *New York Times* 1970; WTOK 2019). Missing is Alabama's arguably most (in)famous historical sheriff and former president of the National Sheriffs' Association, Dallas County Sheriff Jim Clark, who was a "virulent racist"[7] and notoriously clashed with civil rights activists in Selma.[8] Perhaps unsurprisingly, sheriffs' own historical versions of the office gloss over or omit these histories and instead focus on different moments in time.[9]

Sheriffs instead point to the British and colonial origins of the position as they tell their office's history, often to set up its importance and uniqueness in law enforcement. They point to the history of the office extending back prior to the tenth century in medieval England and its importance in the Magna Carta (NCSA 2022).[10] The office of sheriff moved with the British to the colonies, but here the paths diverged, as sheriffs in the United States survived well beyond their English roots. While the office of High Sheriff in England has devolved into a weak symbolic position, sheriffs in the United States transformed into an elected office that we argue deeply shapes the form and function of local policing and law enforcement throughout US history.

When Attorney General Jeff Sessions, a former US senator from Alabama, praised sheriffs and referenced the "Anglo-American heritage" of the office at the National Sheriffs' Association 2018 conference, the audience and the public interpreted that history in different ways. While a Justice Department spokesperson defended the phrase as a reference to shared legal heritage between the United States and England, others in the public connected his statement to the unstated role of sheriffs in history who violently enforced white supremacy. Here, we focus on both histories to show how the office establishes its authority and autonomy over time.

In this chapter, we agree with sheriffs: their office's history is important. Yet, the histories presented by sheriffs and their associations are anemic versions of the role that sheriffs have played in the development of the United States and, in particular, its inequality. In what follows, we aim to provide a remedy to those absences by using tools from American political development. We examine durable shifts (Dilworth 2010) in the autonomy and authority of the sheriff's office in US history. We focus on points of change for sheriffs, local government, and law enforcement in the United States, attempting to understand how (or if) sheriffs changed their behavior or office to reflect these broader patterns. To develop this history, we reviewed primary and secondary accounts, relying on newspaper articles, reports, and contemporary scholars of the points in time of our interest. We also draw heavily from sheriffs' own accounts. Our aim is not to provide a fully comprehensive history of the office of sheriff, which has received limited historical scholarly attention, nor is it to detail all the points where the power or status of the office changes, but to focus on the broad moments of change and patterns in how the office has engaged with power, established authority and autonomy, and reinforced existing racial and societal hierarchies.

As we trace the history of the office, we focus on characteristics that are consistent across time in the United States: the elected nature of the office, the reliance on self-funding through fees and taxes, and the pervasive nature of inequality, particularly the enforcement of institutionalized racial inequality (King and Smith 2005). Understanding the key points of change, power, and authority in the history of the office provides a richer context to sheriffs today. We use American political development approaches, following Orren and Skowronek (2004, 11), who argue, "At any given moment, the different rules, arrangements and timetables put into place by changes negotiated at various points in the past will be found to impose themselves on the actors of the present and to affect their efforts to negotiate changes of their own." By engaging with how key moments in US history influenced the office, we can understand both a more complete view of these moments and how they may impact the position of sheriff today.

The Norman and Anglo-Saxon Sheriff to the Colonial Sheriff

The office of sheriff can trace its origins as far back as at least tenth-century[11] Norman England, and the shire-reeve (or "county" and "guardian") was "The King's Steward" who served to enforce the king's laws and protect the Crown's interests in local areas (W. A. Morris 1918; Howard 1889). These sheriffs were expected to use violence to protect the king's interests: "The Norman sheriff was in a peculiar sense a royal agent and he ruled the county with an iron hand" (Howard 1889, 310). While the shrieval office's original purpose was to serve royalty, officers were soon seen as representing other members of the aristocracy in the area, and sheriffs grew in power (Sharpe 2016).[12] During the writing of the Magna Carta, sheriffs acted as both advisers and participants. Indeed, the Magna Carta frequently mentions the sheriff, and a number of its clauses relate to the duties, office, or restrictions of the sheriff (Holt, Garnett, and Hudson 2015). The sheriff held a central and essential role in local political control, making decisions about military, financial, and judicial issues, leading one early scholar of police administration to posit, "The whole plan of local government in England, and to a somewhat lesser extent in this country also, once centered about this office" (B. Smith 1933, 38).

When British colonists came to the Americas, so did the office of the sheriff, first appearing in Virginia as early as 1634 "without momentous change" (B. Smith 1933, 42). In England, the office evolved into "a dignified and gentlemanly non-entity" (Moley 1929, 28). In comparison, the office in the United States slowly transitioned to deriving authority from popular mandate through direct election (Falcone and Wells 1995). The move was purposeful, as the colonists saw a royally controlled sheriff as an imposition of power from the British Empire, especially because "persons of means were sometimes able to influence" who received appointment to sheriff (Greenberg 2005, 23).[13] These interests, combined with the weak remote influence of the Crown and "the widespread enthusiasm for local population election . . . gradually wore away the ancient tradition" of appointed sheriffs (B. Smith 1933, 44). As a result, colonial assemblies and later states shifted the sheriff from a Crown-appointed individual to someone selected via election by voting members of the local population.[14] Here, sheriffs could act independently, given the near complete absence of any supra law enforcement agencies (Friedman 1994; Gottschalk 2016).

The sheriff in the colonies grew in power to the point that a historian noted, "No other single officer in the county exercised such plenary executive and administrative powers as did the colonial sheriff" (Wager 1928,

9–10). Sheriffs also served as tax collectors; the combination of law enforcement and taxation power meant that sheriffs appeared in early colonial and
state constitutions, with the state granting the officeholders a wide range of
powers. Thomas Jefferson would remark in a letter that the sheriff was "the
most important of all the executive officers of the county" (Jefferson 1905).
As states wrote their constitutions, they dictated the creation of the office of
the sheriff.[15] In newly created states, sheriffs were designated as "the executive officer and one of the most important functionaries of the county" (Howard 1889, 392). As a result of their status as one of the first public officials,
legal historians have noted that sheriffs could thus "develop their role with
little opposition from competing organisations or officials" (Gullion 1992,
1152). Consequentially, sheriffs were able to elevate the position of the office,
extending their power and responsibility in these newly formed counties.

From colonial times forward, many sheriffs managed jails. The evolution
of various systems of jails in the US in no way resembles a "planned" enterprise, leading to wide variations in how sheriffs ran them (Mattick 1971). In
doing so, sheriffs participated (often eagerly) in shaping these systems to
be economically powerful, even as they failed at the goal of rehabilitation
(Meskell 1998). One major path toward economic profitability was contract
prison labor, where sheriffs leased jail populations to private contractors
(Gildemeister 1977), a practice that continues today in many jails (Zatz
2020; ACLU and Global Human Rights Clinic 2022). Early sheriffs often
drew a salary directly from the funds raised by the economic profits of the
jail, tying the office to the political economy of incarceration.

Sheriffs during the early 1800s also created power in the form of the
office's ability to command the posse comitatus (which translates to "the
power of the county"), or to call upon non-deputized men in the community to serve under the sheriff, particularly in times of emergency. The ability to call up a posse is rooted in the office's English roots, where places
lacked centralized police forces and sheriffs had few (if any) staff and relied
on local men to enforce laws. In the United States, states and local governments again granted sheriffs this power, which they used readily to engage
in social control by suppressing mobs and policing enslaved people. The
courts regularly granted sheriffs extensive power to command a posse: "His
[position is] largely a discretionary one. In all times of great emergency,
or in a crisis of unusual danger, the limits under which his discretion may
be exercised have been held by the courts not to be fixed."[16] The power to
raise a posse and compel men into its service stood out as remarkable to
both Alexis de Tocqueville (1835) and Henry David Thoreau (1849), who
viewed posses as both coercive and communitarian. Sheriffs used posse
power throughout history to hunt down escaped enslaved people, quell la-

bor uprisings, and enforce Jim Crow laws (P. C. Burnett 1997; Kopel 2014). For example, one political science professor noted in 1922 that "it happens occasionally even today, when labor disorders occur, that business men are suddenly required to do police duty in emergencies" (Porter 1922, 167), with the sheriff deputizing "company men" to break up labor disputes.

Sheriffs, Slavery, Reconstruction, and Jim Crow

Sheriffs' histories focus on the founding of the office and then either completely ignore or downplay the role that sheriffs played in upholding slavery and white supremacy. Many sheriffs' offices and associations simply supply key dates to demonstrate their long history. For example, the Maryland Sheriffs' Association asserts that the office's "proud heritage of service" extends to 1634 "when the first Sheriff's Office in America was established in St. Mary's County." While these early sheriffs were appointed, "since 1776, with the exception of a period between the War of 1812 and 1867," all sheriffs have been elected (Maryland Sheriffs' Association 2022). A history of the sheriff's office in Atlantic County, New Jersey, skips from the construction of the first jail (as their website states, "Every good Sheriff deserves a jail") in 1840 to a history of the "modern" office, starting in 1932 (Atlantic County Sheriff's Office 2022).[17] Recall the Alabama Sheriffs Association's historical assessment that "the office of sheriff has not lost the dignity it has enjoyed since its inception." This simplistic early view of the history of the office is in stark contrast with a broad set of evidence of sheriffs' engagement with the enterprise of enslaving people and maintaining, creating, and reinforcing systems of white supremacy.

For much of the early years of slavery in the United States, "the control and discipline of slaves were considered the responsibility of any free and responsible citizen" (Greenberg 2005, 34), but some political offices (including sheriffs) were given specific powers to help enforce the systems of enslavement. In the South, slave patrols emerged and then evolved into what a sociologist called "some of the earliest public law enforcement in the United States" (Carlson 2020, 28). In the North, watch and ward committees, composed of volunteers loosely organized by neighborhood or geographic area, engaged in the work of reinforcing white supremacy by expelling or coercing Black people in their communities to move or self-segregate (Greenberg 2005).

Sheriffs were deeply and continuously involved in the surveillance, control, and abuse of Black people from early points of colonial history to the modern conception of the office. In the South, sheriffs were regularly tasked with organizing slave patrols and controlling enslaved people more generally in rural areas—for example, in Virginia in 1663, the colonial assembly gave sheriffs control over enslaved persons and the responsibility to return those who ran away through "whatever force appeared necessary" (Hadden 2003, 28; Cope 1973). Other states followed suit; in 1757, Georgia's Colonial Assembly wrote the first formal patrol law and assigned sheriffs the duty of controlling enslaved persons in rural areas (B. Wood 2007; Yanochik 1997). South Carolina's extensive and regressive slave code[18] required runaway enslaved people be turned over to the sheriff within four days of capture (H. M. Henry 1914). Court proceedings from the colonial era routinely depict sheriffs arresting individuals for escaping their enslavers, including arresting free Blacks and refusing to release them, even when provided with evidence of their legal status (H. M. Henry 1914).[19] In Northern states, sheriffs often served as the primary institutional organizer of the watch committees that would work to capture individuals who might have been enslaved (Greenberg 2005; Orren 1998). The role of sheriffs in enforcing laws that restricted the movement of enslaved Black people continued after the US founding and often served as the basis for fugitive slave acts passed by state legislatures.[20] Sheriffs actively took part in patrols[21] and held those people captured by the patrols in their jails. Given that sheriffs had to pay for their office with fees and fines, the monetary incentives associated with catching, reprimanding, and selling the enslaved incentivized sheriffs' participation in the recapture of enslaved persons.[22] In some states, the sheriffs' capacity as tax collectors further embedded them in the enterprise of enslavement, as the office was directly responsible for collecting poll (or head) taxes, including those charged on the enslaved (Rogers and Denham 2001; Thornton 1978). These poll taxes often served as a sheriff's major source of income.[23] Free Black persons who did not pay taxes could be arrested by the sheriff and hired out for labor in states across the South; the sheriff could then keep the wages paid for this labor (Sawers 2017), incentivizing the sheriff to identify free Black persons who were unable to pay their poll or property taxes.

The end of the Civil War and the beginning of Reconstruction produced efforts at the national, state, and local levels to change the power of sheriffs as well as who held the office of sheriff. In the discussion leading up to the Civil Rights Act of 1866, Republican representatives noted the need to protect Black Southerners from sheriffs, as the officials would take away the arms of Black residents of their county immediately prior to white lynching efforts (Leddy 1985). Racist behavior by sheriffs formed an underlying justification for the right to individually possess firearms after the Civil War, as Black Southerners needed to be able to protect themselves from sheriffs and their posses (Halbrook 2013).

Immediately following the Civil War, formerly enslaved African Americans ran for and won a wide set of local, state, and national offices in the South, including serving as sheriffs (Berlin 2010; Hahn 2005). In research documenting the locations and offices of Black lawmakers during Reconstruction, historian Eric Foner (1993) counts forty-one Black sheriffs, a number exceeded only by county commissioners and registrars in local leaders; Black sheriffs held offices in thirteen counties in Mississippi (Hahn 2005). The election of "black sheriffs, school board officials, and tax assessors in plantation regions . . . symboliz[ed] the political revolution wrought by Reconstruction" (Foner 2013, 159).

Black Southerners saw the election of Black candidates to local offices, particularly the sheriff, as key to changing the South after the Civil War. As a historian of the Black Reconstruction experience notes, "Although sheriffs, magistrates, county commissioners, and registrars might appear to be less consequential officeholders, they in fact represented the formal linchpins of the postemancipation South's emerging political order" (Hahn 2005, 221). The importance of these offices was represented by Black communities sometimes electing their own sheriffs as alternative local law enforcement leaders to bypass white Southerners who would not recognize legal changes (Hahn 2005; Foner 2013). Foreshadowing the emerging era of Jim Crow, Black sheriffs or Northern Republican white sheriffs often saw their dictates ignored by white residents or derailed by white judges through violence or intimidation (Barnes 1998). For instance, in Vicksburg, Mississippi, white mobs violently attacked and killed approximately three hundred Black citizens supporting Warren County Sheriff Peter Crosby, a Black sheriff who had been forcibly removed from office on false charges (Crosby 2005).[24] In other places, Black sheriffs were run out of town, such as Sheriff John M. Brown, the first Black sheriff of Coahoma County Mississippi, or charged with inciting violence when Black-white conflict emerged in their counties (Schnedler 2021).

During Reconstruction, violent white supremacist militias, including the Ku Klux Klan (KKK), emerged in the South to replicate the racial violence of slavery and slave patrols (Hadden 2003). The existence of these vigilante groups (Bateson 2021) allowed for law enforcement to follow the Civil War Amendments and Northern demands while still reinforcing the existing racial order. As a result, "policemen in Southern towns [could] carry out those aspects of urban slave patrolling that seemed race-neutral but in reality were applied selectively" (Hadden 2003, 218). The role of keeping the peace (and reinforcing racial order) in rural areas in the South fell to sheriffs. "Nearly always white and male, and overwhelmingly Democrat," these sheriffs served as "linchpins in the maintenance of white supremacy and its class-based and race-based privileges" (T. Moore 1997, 50). The counties that elected Black sheriffs during Reconstruction often returned swiftly to electing white sheriffs with the end of Northern oversight. These new sheriffs were often members of the Ku Klux Klan or other local white supremacist organizations (Barnes 1998). As support for Reconstruction at the federal level ended, white supremacist efforts to suppress the Black vote in the South often involved sheriffs, including arming men via posse powers to intimidate or harm Blacks trying to vote (Hahn 2005).[25] Sheriffs were responsible "to make certain that black voters didn't get into the voting booth at all" (T. Moore 1997, 53).

Violence allowed for the maintenance of white supremacy in the South, and sheriffs played a pivotal role in facilitating that violence during the Jim Crow era. Sheriffs allowed, encouraged, and aided white mobs' lynching of Black people (Fairlie 1920; T. Moore 1997; Blackmon 2009). For instance, following the 1930 lynching of George Grant, a forty-year-old Black man shot to death in his cell following accusations that he killed a sheriff deputy, Sheriff Tom Poppell of McIntosh County, Georgia, told a reporter, "I don't know who killed the Negro and I don't give a damn" (J. Harris 1930). Sheriffs regularly "put at risk for lynching" any Black person accused of a crime and allowed mobs to take Black people from their custody in jail (Hahn 2005, 428). In their documentation of lynching cases from 1889–1918 (Francis 2014), the NAACP noted that victims were "taken from the Sheriff without resistance by a mob" or that a "mob broke into the jail" to kill a Black victim (NAACP 1919). J. P. Walker, one of the suspected leaders of the lynch mob that murdered Mack Charles Parker in Pearl River County, Mississippi, in 1959, was later elected sheriff in 1963 (Smead 1988; *Jet Magazine* 1959).[26]

Not every sheriff participated in or facilitated lynching: for example, some sheriffs protected Black Floridians from lynch mobs and offered rewards for the apprehension of people who participated in the murder of Black people in their communities (Shofner 1981; NAACP 1919). Other sheriffs tried to prevent lynchings: the NAACP focused on Sheriff Sherman Ely of Allen County, Ohio, as the face of a national campaign that rewarded public officials who prevented lynchings (Bernstein 2006).[27] A South Carolina sheriff, W. H. Hood of Chester County, was praised for working with the governor to prevent a lynching mob and protect a Black man arrested and jailed for murdering the sheriff's father (Beck 2015). Some other sheriffs who opposed white supremacist violence were driven from their offices and run out of the county (Foner 2013). To try to stop sheriffs from taking part in lynchings, states passed laws during this time threatening removal from office if someone was lynched while in their custody. Nonetheless, sheriffs had a reputation among Black communities as facilitators and participants in a racist and crooked justice system (T. Moore 1997).

Sheriffs also used incarceration as a tool for social control of Black Southerners through the enforcement of Black Codes and convict leasing (Mancini 1996).[28] Shortly after the end of the Civil War, Southern states adopted a variety of Black Codes that limited the mobility, rights, and freedom of Black residents (A. Davis 1998; Blackmon 2009). Sheriffs "function[ing] as labor recruiters for planters" enthusiastically embraced their role in enforcing these laws (Wiener 1979, 981). For example, in Mississippi, Black residents with "no lawful business or occupation" were fined fifty dollars a day; if someone could not pay this fee, they could be hired out to local white businesses by the sheriff, with the sheriff pocketing a portion of the wages earned by the laborer (Cohen 1991).[29] Some sheriffs would collude with planters or business owners facing labor shortages to arrest Black residents of the county for petty charges and then force them into convict labor (Oshinsky 1997). As the convict labor system evolved to provide peonage to the penitentiary system, "all of which clearly were institutional descendants of slavery" (A. Davis 1998, 76), sheriffs continued to benefit directly from the criminalization of Blackness.

Sheriffs and Westward Expansion

Sheriffs helped the imperial expansion of the United States west of the Mississippi River. Throughout early expansion, counties were often the first level of government created, and with that came the establishment of the office of the sheriff to execute laws (G. E. Howard 1889, 412; Prassel 1972). As Americans expanded west, sheriffs were designated as the main (or only) law enforcement officials and tasked with keeping the peace, maintaining jails, and assembling and controlling posses, as well as often protecting the courthouse, assembling jurors for trials, and collecting taxes, for which they usually received a percentage of proceeds.[30] While these activities were largely bureaucratic, studies of westward expansion regularly note the violent nature of the office—for example, a 1969 report on the causes of violence on the frontier noted that "the truth is, the lawman was as closely associated with violence as the outlaw" (Franz 1969, 103).

On the frontier, sheriffs often served as the first and sometimes only law enforcement representatives as settlers engaged in community violence during this time, particularly violence against Black, Native American, and Mexican American communities (Obert 2018).[31] Much of the violence carried out in the name of white supremacy in the West was facilitated by both the presence of sheriffs and their low level of resources, capacity or interest in managing violence (Carlson 2020).[32] The "legal" violence included arresting, shooting, or killing nonwhite residents, including on Native American reservations where sheriffs' offices were not supposed to have legal authority (McGrath 1987). For example, in Gila County, Arizona, a sheriff deputy (accompanied by a posse) shot an Apache on a reservation without cause. The coroner did not conduct an inquest, and the deputy continued to serve under the sheriff (Hayes 1968). Even when prosecutors did indict sheriffs or their deputies for shooting people, juries rarely found them guilty of the crimes (McKanna 1997).[33] Sheriffs gained particular notoriety in westward expansion because of their role in tolerating, permitting, or at times collaborating with vigilantes (R. M. Brown 1969). In some circumstances, sheriffs themselves were suspected to be involved in illegal activities, such as Sheriff Henry Plummer of Beaverhead County, Montana, who was hanged in his office's gallows by vigilantes for suspicion of leading his own road gang.[34]

Community posses were central to the racist violence of the time; sheriffs would raise a group of white men in the community to seek fugitives, those accused of crimes, or anyone accused of an affront to white supremacy. Sheriff Pat Garrett of Lincoln County, New Mexico used the office's posse power to chase after the notorious outlaw Billy the Kid. Sheriffs today often point to raising and controlling a posse as a key role of the office, as the sheriff's website of Maricopa County, Arizona, points out: "The concept of a Sheriff's Posse began during the territorial days of the old west. When the rule of law was threatened in a community, the Sheriff (or Marshal) authorized private citizens to help him re-establish order. Collectively, these deputized private citizens formed the Sheriff's posse. After the threat was eliminated, the possemen ended their temporary law enforcement duties and returned to their private lives. In 1912, the Arizona State Constitution recognized and defined a Sheriff's legal authority to organize posses" ("Posse History" 2022).

Sheriffs regularly "connived with vigilantes" (R. M. Brown 1969, 170); at times they would lose control of posses (or choose not to try to control them) or would actively fan local vigilante violence. Following a sheriff's arrest, a mob would often form and demand the immediate release and hanging of the prisoner. Sometimes sheriffs tried to intervene to allow for the regular carriage of justice, but they also permitted or escalated the violence. In Douglas County, Nebraska, a crowd, drawn to watch a legal public execution, began to agitate around lynching a Black man currently held in the jail for a minor crime. The sheriff, John Boyd, reportedly said, "If I had my way, and was not sheriff, I would furnish the rope to hang the wretch" (McKanna 1994, 70). Sheriffs were often "happy to have a nefarious bad man disposed of quickly, cheaply, and permanently by a lynching" (R. M. Brown 1969, 147), especially if that lynching helped the sheriff maintain control over Black, Mexican, and Native American populations.[35]

Sheriffs' roles in promoting community violence, encouraging vigilantism, and reinforcing white supremacy in communities in the West represents both the power and the powerlessness of the office. Sheriffs' authority was only as good as the respect the community gave the office. Sheriffs often came from local white elite groups, either hired by landowners and business leaders or owned land and businesses themselves (R. M. Brown 1969). In turn, "virtually any male could become a deputy sheriff . . . especially if he had connections with the sheriff" (McKanna 1997, 43), meaning that the entire office was composed of individuals selected for who they knew rather than their interest in law and order. For instance, one of the most iconic Western photos of gamblers and gunfighters included the sheriff of Ford County, Kansas, and his undersheriffs Wyatt Earp and Bat Masterson (who later became sheriff himself) as part of the Dodge City Peace Commission.

With the increased stability of white order in the West in the later 1800s and early 1900s, sheriffs moved into a new form of vigilante justice: efforts to quell union organizing by laborers across the country. As a historian of guns and violence notes, "Private corporate interests . . . operated in a context in which the traditional, local law enforcement institutions rather than the military were the most important locus of coercion in the United States" (Obert 2018, 212). From miners organizing in Colorado to lumber workers in Washington, sheriffs regularly sided with business owners and engaged in or permitted violence against striking or organizing workers.[36] In Everett, Washington, the Snohomish County sheriff Donald McRae and 200+ vigilantes beat striking union members with clubs and bats as they arrived on the boat from Seattle; the sheriff and others eventually fired weapons at the workers, killing five and wounding more than twenty (P. Taft and Ross 1969). Sheriffs engaged in similar actions during strikes or union actions on railroads, in coal and copper mines, and in mills and oil refineries, often serving as "leader[s] in the campaign against the union" (P. Taft and Ross 1969, 240). One newspaper described a "human slaughter" in Luzerne County, Pennsylvania, after Sheriff James Martin and his deputies shot and killed nineteen and wounded thirty-eight immigrant strikers in a Lattimer coal mine (G. A. Turner 2002, 11).

Sheriffs used their posse and appointment power to aid companies in suppressing unions. During a coal strike in Las Animas County, Colorado, in 1913–14, Sheriff James Grisham deputized all of the coal mine guards, thus granting them the authority to use force legally against the striking workers; twenty-one people were killed, including miners and their wives and children (McKanna 1995; 1997).[37] Sheriffs in other locations appointed deputies (with salaries paid for by the offending company) as private police to union bust (P. Taft and Ross 1969). In 1936, Sheriff Logan Jackson deputized citrus orchard guards and issued a "shoot to kill" order against striking Mexican migrant farm workers in Orange County, California (G. Thompson 2016).[38] Rarely, sheriffs would broker agreements between the striking workers and the employer; in Bayonne, New Jersey, Hudson County Sheriff Eugene Francis Kinkead arrested both the leader of a strike and guards that worked for the oil refinery after a deadly confrontation, noting that he did not like "the methods of wealth in employing gunmen and toughs to shoot defenseless men and women, any more than I like the methods of strikers destroying property" (Fitch 1915, 414–15).

Political Reforms and Sheriffs

In the Northeast, the emergence of urban police forces, political conflicts between political machines and progressives, and demographic change all changed the power of sheriffs, particularly in rapidly urbanizing areas. That most Northeastern states adopted state police agencies that had full law enforcement powers further eroded the power of the sheriff in the region (Musgrave 2020).

As the US population spread west and the country became increasingly urbanized, local political conflict shaped sheriffs' powers. In the Northeast, sheriffs regularly served as cogs in urban political machines, engaged in patronage, and reinforced existing political power structures (Ansell and Burris 1997). In New York, sheriffs involved in political patronage used the office to extract hundreds of thousands of dollars in fees and fines; the sheriff of each borough of New York City was paid a salary in the range of $12,000 but also was entitled to half of all fines and fees collected. In 1914, the sheriff collected just under $50,000 in fines, the equivalent of close to $1.3 million in today's dollars (*New York Times* 1915). Grover Cleveland, the only sheriff to later serve as president of the United States, left office with an estimated $25,000, the equivalent of $600,000 in today's dollars, thanks to fees during his two-year term as Erie County, New York sheriff from 1871–1873 (Wickser 1947). In Boston, Chicago, and Philadelphia, the sheriff's office was an important patronage position used by the political machines (Trounstine 2008; Gillette 1973).

When progressives and those opposed to political machines sought to diminish their power, sheriffs were a target of legislation and state control. In New York, the state legislature removed sheriffs' ability to extract personal funds from fines and fees (*New York Times* 1915). Similarly, in Illinois and Vermont, state legislatures passed laws that limited sheriffs' powers, removed the financial benefits of the job, and looked to sever the position from the political machine. As a result, sheriffs in urban areas that experienced conflict between machines and progressives (which was the case for many large cities in the Northeast and Midwest) are today much weaker offices than their counterparts in rural places in those same states or urban areas that were not similarly experiencing machine-progressive challenges.

These changes had deep consequences for the interactions between Black people and sheriffs in urban areas in the Northeast and Midwest. White communities focused their racist efforts on creating and enforcing segregation in communities (Trounstine 2018), particularly as Black communities swelled during the Great Migrations (Grant 2019). The level of segregation then allowed for segregated provision of services, including policing. But as the Black population increased in these city centers (Grant 2019), sheriffs' power simultaneously diminished in these rapidly urbanizing Northern and Midwestern cities that developed their own policing. As a result, sheriffs in these regions became primarily rural law enforcement leaders, removed from the segregated urban environment where crime concentrated (Muhammad 2011). While accounts of Black experiences in the early 1900s in the American South and West often reference sheriffs, they are nearly absent from Black discussions of life in urban areas of the Northeast and Midwest as a result.

Liquor, Cars, and Guns

Three developments in the early twentieth-century United States changed the office of the sheriff: the availability of the automobile, Prohibition (the legal ban of alcohol), and a dramatic increase in gun-related violence (Carlson 2020). As one dissertation on the history of gun control notes, "In the twenties a new type of crime began. Robberies of banks and the use of guns by criminals became much more common. A spectacular crime wave replaced the calm period of the late nineteenth and early twentieth centuries. In these good old days, a policeman's gun was merely a symbol of office, never fired, and sometimes even nonfunctional" (Leddy 1985, 215). In more urban areas, these changes meant that police became the "regulators of morality."[39] In rural areas of the country, where sheriffs had already enforced morality in their communities for more than a century (Thacher 2020), the advent of automobiles, alcohol, and guns often had a major impact on the jobs of sheriffs.

Increased accessibility of automobiles led to a shift toward the regulation of traffic, the ability of police to move quickly (and the accompanying quick movement of those escaping the police), and the movement of crime across a broader area. As a treatise on rural crime noted in the 1930s: "The sheriffs . . . are thereby confronted with novel situations which they are ill-prepared to combat. The coroner finds himself engaged in conducting investigations into homicides committed by professional gun-men, and the untrained justice of the peace is forced into the unfamiliar role of dispensing justice to total strangers" (B. Smith 1933, 5). As we discuss further in chapter 4, traffic enforcement continues to allow sheriffs, and law enforcement more broadly, to overpolice Black and Latino drivers (Shoub 2022).

Cars also became lethal weapons during this era. Protecting sheriffs and their deputies from being killed in car accidents or by individuals using cars as weapons became a focus of sheriff associations and policy and remains a major priority even today (Barker et al. 2021). These are rational fears: in most years, crashes and being struck by moving vehicles while on foot have been the leading causes of death for all police officers in the United States; this held true until COVID became the leading cause of death in 2020 and 2021 (CDC 2021; Treisman 2022).[40]

The national Prohibition of alcohol in 1920 and the repeal in 1933 (Maveety 2018) additionally reshaped law enforcement in the United States. Sheriffs had long been involved in the local regulation of alcohol in the United States, from enforcing rules for taverns to checking licenses to refusing to enforce early state efforts at Prohibition (Thacher 2020; Clubb 1856). By the time the national coordinated campaign for Prohibition began in earnest in the late 1800s, organizers recognized sheriffs' lax attitude toward Prohibition and attempted to institutionalize and incentivize enforcement (McGirr 2015; R. Hamm 1995; Rogers and Denham 2001). For instance, sheriffs could pocket the fees and fines levied from those arrested for alcohol-related issues.

Sheriffs faced competing pressures in enforcing Prohibition. On one hand, sheriffs could use their power to extract fees and bribes from those engaged in the production, sale, or serving of alcohol. Temperance organizations regularly complained that sheriffs allowed "the bootleggers, the gamblers, and the houses of illfame to operate openly" (McGirr 2015).[41]

As political scientist V. O. Key notes in his treatise *Southern Politics* (1949, 235n), "The allocation of authority for prohibition enforcement makes this sheriff's post extremely important and the campaign for this office one of the hardest fought in county politics. In some counties the legitimate fees of the office mount up and outside the genuinely dry counties supplementary revenues are available." V. O. Key goes on to note that Prohibition had "created conditions in some counties where the sheriff's office is more lucrative than that of the supreme court justices of the United States," concluding, "Common gossip makes [this] estimate overly modest."

Forces also pushed the other direction: sheriffs' role in social control and white supremacy naturally aligned with the aims of Prohibition and the groups involved in pushing for alcohol bans. Members of the Klan, which was deeply involved in the advancement of anti-alcoholism and "enforced" a wide set of Prohibition policies (Blee 2009; Pegram 2008), often worked as a sheriff posse to assist in raids or recruiting sheriffs to participate in their own organized raids (McGirr 2015; Gordon 2017). The *Fiery Cross*, the Klan's publication in the 1910s and 1920s, regularly references the involvement of sheriffs in raids of stills (Blee 2009; Gevitz 1986). Those involved in Prohibition often assured sheriffs that "the officials will find the Klan a wonderful ally" (Young 1938, 136). As with slavery, financial incentives encouraged the cooperation of sheriffs: jail and courthouse fees laid upon those arrested for alcohol provided a lucrative set of funds for sheriffs (McGirr 2015). The intertwined nature of racism and social control meant that those arrested for liquor law violations were disproportionately Black. Prohibition sufficiently institutionalized policing, allowing for a shift of race control from "popular justice and white mobs to legal institutions and the police" (Adler 2015, 43).

Dramatic increases in access to reliable firearms also shifted the role of sheriffs in the early 1900s, as did gun crimes directly associated with Prohibition. During this period, the National Rifle Association (NRA) became an advocate for the police carrying pistols and receiving training in firearms (Carlson 2020). Sheriffs soon followed, although many sheriffs did not offer service weapons to their deputies until professionalization efforts in the latter half of the twentieth century. As gun laws changed in the late 1980s and 1990s, many sheriffs largely supported common sense gun reform; for example, the National Sheriffs' Association supported the assault weapons ban passed by Congress in the early 1990s (R. Yardley 1991). As the possession of guns has increased in the private population in the United States, sheriffs have responded in kind, increasing the number, size, and caliber of weapons they use and control. The concern about firearm violence is rooted in deaths of law enforcement agents; in 2019, for example, of the fifty-four "felonious" deaths (i.e., not accidental), forty-eight were killed by firearms (LEOKA 2019). Yet, as we detail in chapter 5, this changes in the 2000s, as sheriffs hold increasingly radical attitudes about gun rights and regularly engage in coordinated efforts to defend gun rights.

Professionalization, Civil Rights, and the Twentieth Century

Writing in 1950, O. W. Wilson, an early author of modern policing, wrote, "Lack of uniformity in current policing practices . . . raises questions as to the relative merit of the widely divergent methods" (Cohn 1978). Indeed, policing in the United States by 1950 offered wildly disparate levels of professionalization and modernization. Some cities had modernized their police forces, increasingly relying on technology and analytics to watch what worked and what did not in the pursuit of criminals. Sheriffs' deputies and police forces were "largely poorly trained, poorly equipped, and, until the 1960s, uniformly white" (Taylor 2018, 316).

Across the 1960s and 1970s, police would be pushed toward professionalization after racist and cruel actions by police officers who beat and killed Black people spurred urban unrest in several cities (Schrader 2019). These professionalization efforts included increased standards for hiring, pay rates, and the hiring of full-time officers, and the institutionalization of a wide set of formal procedures within the office. During this period, police officers also began to unionize in earnest (Klein 2014). The goal, as Schrader (2019, 602), a scholar of race and policing, writes, was that "police would better serve to legitimize the liberal state by enacting violence, or its threat, with fairness and without bigotry. That project was never completed, but it was the dominant approach among police for decades. It remains the dream of many police leaders today."

Sheriffs, particularly in rural areas, were far more reluctant participants in these professionalization processes. Across rural America, sheriffs' offices in the 1950s, 1960s, and 1970s pursued the same criminal justice strategies as they had used in the early 1900s. Underinvestment in the office and jails, high levels of incumbency in who held the position, and a fidelity to tradition all stymied efforts to improve their offices (B. Smith 1933; Cohn 1978; Sitton 2000). The core characteristics of the sheriffs' office itself were antithetical to the push for professionalization: an office funded by fees, a deep attachment to white supremacy and racism, a reliance on social control for authority and power, and the elected nature of the position.[42] As Sitton (2000, xi) notes in his study of Texas sheriffs, "Rural and small-town Texas around 1950 was a strange, often violent, complicated place, where nineteenth-century life-styles persisted, blood ties held, racial apartheid remained rigidly enforced, and sheriffs play the key role in keeping the lid on things."

Sheriffs themselves noted the long effort of professionalization for the office. By 1969, Sheriff Don Genung of Pinellas County, Florida,[43] writes, "Step by step for many years the Sheriffs of Florida have been moving toward the goal of professionalization in law enforcement. We abolished the fee system of financing law enforcement, with its inherent evils. . . . We have strengthened criminal laws, developed modern communication networks, helped create minimum standards for law enforcement officers, enhanced law enforcement training opportunities. . . . All this is history." Noting that the 1968 Omnibus Crime Bill would provide "millions of dollars in federal funds for improvement of local law enforcement," Sheriff Genung feared sheriffs would face an ultimatum: "Law enforcement will move forward—with us or without us—and, if we fail to move with it, we must be prepared to see the Sheriff's job degenerate to that of a jail keeper and a process server."

Sheriffs' role in maintaining white supremacy in the South, where the office controlled vast resources and white men held the position for decades, further limited efforts at professionalization. The power of the sheriff was particularly important in supporting the status quo in rural counties. Rural Southern sheriffs often were the most resistant to the idea of professionalization, arguing that they lacked the resources or staff to make updates to their jails, train their deputies, or adopt new methods of law enforcement (Handberg 1984; Handberg 1982). In North Carolina, efforts by pro-business leaders to reform policing to attract business focused specifically on sheriffs (Taylor 2018) and led to the governor appealing to sheriffs that as *state* officers, they were duty bound to "treat everyone alike" because they had to enforce state law (Hodges 1956). In Mississippi, sheriffs stymied reform in multiple ways as the state association (and individual sheriffs) lobbied against "enhancing Mississippi law enforcement, and for reforming state government more generally" (Mickey 2015, 207).

Sheriffs played significant roles in resisting the Civil Rights Movement, including well-known efforts such as jailing riders during the Montgomery Bus Boycott and assaulting civil rights leaders in Selma (Benn 2006; McWhorter 1989; *NBC News* 2004). These well-known cases were not exceptions: sheriffs across the South participated in a wide set of violent, racist acts to suppress civil rights and maintain white supremacy (Ward 2018; SPLC 2014b). As T. Moore (1997, 50) notes in his analysis of race and the Southern sheriff, "Because of their wide powers and multiple roles, sheriffs played a particularly notable role in the [South's] racial history."[44] For instance, long-serving Sheriff "Lummie" Jenkins of Wilcox County, Alabama, was described both as "notoriously cruel" to civil rights activists and as a "modern day hero" (or, a "god or a monster") to other residents during his eight terms in office (Marvar 2018). When Martin Luther King Jr. organized a voting rights march in Wilcox County in 1965, white officials stopped the regular route of a ferry that would have been the quickest way to connect to the Black community in Gee's Bend to their destination. Sheriff Jenkins said, "We didn't close the ferry because they were black. We closed it because they forgot they were black" (Marvar 2018; Jett and Gentle 2018). Civil rights leaders would avoid specific sheriffs and viewed sheriffs as members of the white supremacist system. Later, sheriffs, their families, and their supporters would engage in revisionist history to portray these men as simply doing their job, going as far as to sue media outlets for libel based on coverage of sheriffs' bad behavior (Edmondson 2019).

Sheriffs used their power to engage in violent repression of Black people in their communities.[45] Sheriffs such as Alabama's Jim Clark reveled in perpetrating violence against civil rights activists in the 1960s and actively reinforced existing Jim Crow and white supremacist systems. When asked about his violence toward protesters (in particular, punching civil rights activist C. T. Vivian in the face on camera) in Selma, Alabama, Clark was "unsure" if he had struck Vivian: "If I hit him, I don't know it. One of the first things I ever learned was to not hit a n----- with your fist because his head is too hard" (*New York Times* 1965). He later told a reporter in 2006, "Basically, I'd do the same thing today if I had to do it all over again" (Fox 2007). Sheriffs rarely faced consequences for their violence toward Black communities. For instance, in Lake County, Florida, four African American men (known as the Groveland Four) were wrongfully[46] accused of raping a white woman. One of the accused was killed by a sheriff's posse of one thousand white men who shot him over four hundred times, and the other three were beaten to coerce confessions. After a new trial was ordered, Sheriff Willis McCall shot two of the defendants, killing one and injuring the other, as he was transporting them. McCall was never indicted (G. King 2018).

Other sheriffs actively supported white members of their communities who were engaging in racist violence. Tallahatchie Sheriff Clarence Strider supported the defense of a group of white men on trial for murdering Emmett Till in Philadelphia, Mississippi, including shaking hands with the defendants after their not-guilty verdict ("Sheriff Clarence Strider" n.d.). His son later told a reporter, "He got 'em arrested, carried 'em to jail, went before the grand jury, they got an indictment and tried 'em in a court in front of his peers and they turned 'em loose. So I don't see how they keep wantin' to bad name the sheriff and his job because he couldn't convict them. He wasn't on the jury" ("Sheriff Clarence Strider" n.d.). Sheriffs commonly applied so-called "race-neutral" laws in ways that limited the accountability of whites and punished their county's Black residents.

The passage of federal civil rights legislation, particularly the Voting Rights Act, upended some elections in the South, although many racist sheriffs continued to serve long after. In Macon County, Alabama, Lucius Amerson was elected in 1966 as the first Black sheriff in the South since Reconstruction, followed by new Black sheriffs in Tennessee in 1978 and Georgia in 1984 (T. Moore 1997; Bond 1969). In 1993, 2.9 percent of sheriffs in the South were Black, concentrated in counties where Black voters were a large share of the electorate; in his examination of the representation of Southern Black sheriffs, Moore notes, "The low rate of black office holding among county sheriffs in the South is an indication of how stubborn racial domination of political institutions can be, and an indication both of how far the region has come and how far it still has to go" (T. Moore 1997, 58). As we discuss in the next chapter, this pattern persists nationwide: when Snohomish County, Washington, elected John Lovick in 2007, he was the first Black sheriff to hold office west of the Mississippi River since 1900.

The 1970s and 1980s also gave rise to mass incarceration in the United States, driven in part by the war on drugs and a deeper investment in incarceration as a tool (if not *the* tool) for addressing crime. The "law and order" rhetoric of the times and its racial undertones were used to penalize people of color and marginalized communities in the expanding carceral state that perpetuated both overpolicing and underprotecting certain groups. Sheriffs participated in these efforts in a wide variety of ways. As sheriffs controlled jails and the rise of mass incarceration increased the demand for jail space, sheriffs directly benefited from a renewed emphasis on building carceral facilities and capacity. This was also a continuation of longer trends of placing the carceral state at the center of their office's activities, now managing the consequences of the country's legacy of racial and class inequalities. We discuss these trends in much more detail in chapter 4.

Posse Comitatus Movement and "Constitutional" Sheriffs

Most sheriffs' offices eventually adopted many of the core components of professionalization, including uniform standards for hiring deputies, increase in employee pay, and adopting more systematic procedures for jail management, crime investigation, and traffic stops (Struckhoff 1994; Weisheit, Falcone, and Wells 1994). Yet, the period following represented a key point of deviation between sheriffs' offices and police departments, particularly between rural sheriffs and urban police. As urban police increasingly professionalized, with the presence of internal affairs and rules and regulations around hiring (Rushin 2017, 2016), sheriffs were often exempt from or slow to adopt these changes. This resistance was buoyed by rural counter-majoritarian and extremism that emerged in the 1970s and 1980s, particularly in the American West.

The resurgence and evolution of white supremacist, anti-government, and firearms-focused militia movements shaped sheriffs' behavior, and the emergence of the Posse Comitatus movement was particularly impactful, which we discuss more in a later chapter. Accounts differ as to whether Bill Gale[47] or Henry Beach, a former army lieutenant colonel or a former dry cleaner, actually founded the Posse Comitatus movement, which focused on the "power of the county."[48] Support for white supremacy, Nazi Germany, the Ku Klux Klan, antisemitism, and a firm belief that the county sheriff held the ultimate legal authority in the United States were central to the movement (Stock 1996; Levitas 2004). While sheriffs had long trumpeted the constitutional nature of their office (Decker 1979; B. Smith 1933), the false idea spread through the right-wing extremism (RWE) community that this office was somehow *more* constitutional than others, with extremist writings calling sheriffs "the only legitimate law enforcement officer" (H. Howard 1989). Although antigovernment, RWE continued to center the sheriff as the acceptable government official because of his potential as a protector of individual constitutional rights and ability to interpose between citizens and the federal government. The "county movement," aimed at returning political control to local leaders, emerged concurrently in the 1980s and 1990s and also centered the office of the sheriff (Chaloupka 1996).

As these ideas circulated in far-right environments, the issue of gun control provided an opportunity to further mobilize some sheriffs to their cause. In 1992, the passage of the Brady Bill instituted a variety of mechanisms of gun control policy including a provision that required "local chief law enforcement officers" (CLEOs) to perform background checks on handgun purchases. Sheriffs Jay Printz (Ravalli County, Montana) and Richard Mack (Graham County, Arizona), recruited by the National Rifle Association, sued, challenging the constitutionality of this provision. The Supreme Court, in *Printz v. United States*,[49] overturned the CLEO prevision of the law, ruling that Congress does not have the power to compel CLEOs to perform a federal task. The decision, where the court broadly focused on the relationship between Congress and CLEOs, gave a boost to far-right extremism among sheriffs. Richard Mack took this determination—that

Congress cannot compel state actors to perform an action for the federal government—to continue the right-wing movement's efforts to recruit sheriffs to their causes (Jackson 2020).

Mack lost reelection, but he became active in the anti-government Patriot Movement and one of the "most popular speakers on the Tea Party circuit" as he espoused the Posse Comitatus view of sheriffs as "constitutional" officers (Burghart and Zeskind 2010). Mack went on to participate in the founding of the Oath Keepers, an RWE militia movement (Jackson 2020), and form his own group, the Constitutional Sheriffs and Peace Officers Association (CSPOA). "Constitutional sheriffs" promote a view that sheriffs are constitutional officers designated as the chief law enforcement officer in some state constitutions. This designation, sheriffs argue, means that they single-handedly must defend the US Constitution and their state constitution, including from the federal government when it engages in behavior that they see as unconstitutional. In recent years, this has led to conflicts over enforcing state gun control measures, COVID restrictions, and election security. We discuss the specific pattern of right-wing extremism among sheriffs in detail in chapter 5, with a detailed history of the movement's origins, changes, and current implications.

Sheriffs Then and Now: Moving Forward

As these key points of history show, sheriffs' autonomy and authority connect to the office's history and how sheriffs have navigated key moments in US history. As the office evolves, its historical connections, and their problems, remain in many ways.

Take, for instance, the Los Angeles Sheriff's Department (LASD),[50] which is the largest law enforcement agency in the country, and the roots of this power run directly toward a deep history of incarceration (Hernández 2017). The county's billion-dollar jail system "imprisons more people than any other city in the United States, which incarcerates more people than any other nation on earth" (Hernández 2017, 1). It is tempting to view the jails, which are directly controlled and operated by the Los Angeles sheriff, as the product of the broader rise in mass incarceration across the US. But, as noted by Hernández (2017), a professor of history, African American and Urban studies, the roots of these incarceration patterns extend far back in the county's history. In 1905, the *Los Angeles Times* reported "Our cussedness has increased in proportion to our population," while declaring the jail inadequate, and biographies and accounts of Los Angeles sheriffs from the early 1900s are full of discussions of jails at or above capacity.

When the (now former) Los Angeles County sheriff Alex Villanueva appeared on Fox News's *Hannity* program in 2021, he was quick to remind viewers of the history of his office: "The origins of the L.A. County sheriff department date back to 1850. This was literally the Wild West." The sheriff then continued: "Fast-forward 171 years, it's becoming the Wild West again. The difference that tamed the Wild West was the sheriff: The sheriff's department, law and order, structure, a civil society." The sheriff continued, "Again, we're going to wind back the clock in history here; the sheriff's department, we are going to reassert authority and order and we are going to take care of business."

Such rhetoric is at odds with Villanueva's original campaign for office in 2018, which pledged to expel federal immigration authorities from the jail, install body cameras, launch a "truth and reconciliation" commission, and engage in a "massive shakeup" of command in the department to break down path dependency (Lau 2018). During his campaign, while promising reform, Sheriff Villanueva told his supporters, "This is a rare moment in history, where we not only have the opportunity but the courage and the responsibility to challenge an existing power" (Lau 2018).

Villanueva won the election as the first candidate to unseat an incumbent LA sheriff in over one hundred years and took office to tackle the long-standing problems of violence and corruption in the department (Anania 2020; Tobar 2011). The list of scandals in the Los Angeles Sheriff's Department is long, including issues with jail management, violent white supremacist gangs and subgroups in the LASD, use of force, police killings, civil rights violations, and financial mismanagement (M. Davis 2006; Escobar 1993; Davis and Wiener 2021; Castle 2021). The US Department of Justice investigated civil rights violations and corruption in the department and its jails,[51] eventually charging and convicting former sheriff Lee Baca of felony obstruction of justice and lying to the FBI.[52]

But Villanueva's tenure as sheriff turned out not to be the progressive shakeup he described; indeed, Democrats in Los Angeles suffered a "rude shock" at the sheriff's behavior (Sheets 2022). Villanueva's closure of investigations into misconduct, his refusal to address gangs within the department, his defiance of subpoenas, and his threats against reporters (K. Brown 2022; Levin 2020, 2021; Lau 2019; Tchekmedyian 2021a) all point to a deep path dependency, where sheriff after sheriff continues the same patterns of corruption, civil rights violations, and racism. In response to the widespread and long-term problems in the LASD, Los Angeles County created several commissions including the Kolts Commission (1992)[53]; a Special Counsel (1993–2014); the county Office of Independent Review (2001–14); the Citizens' Commission on Jail Violence (2012)[54]; the county Office of Inspector General (2014); and the Civilian Oversight Commission (2016–current). Thus far, such attempts to control, reform, and fix the Los Angeles Sheriff Department have not been successful. When Villanueva lost to Robert Luna, a Long Beach police chief also promising change in 2022 (Sheets 2022), advocates for reform expressed cynicism about the possibility of reforming the office (Stoltze 2023; Reed 2023).

As we progress through this text, we will come back to common themes of change and continuity, autonomy and authority, and the role of white supremacy and inequality in shaping the behavior of those in the office. In the next chapter, we consider the ways that elections shape the office, including who becomes sheriff and how representative sheriffs are of their counties and the US overall. Chapter 3 evaluates what sheriffs do today in the context of their positions as elected officials, including their formal and assumed powers, how they manage staff, and the role of sheriffs in maintaining jails. In chapter 4, we focus on the power of individual sheriffs to shape specific policies: domestic violence and violence against women, racial profiling through engagement like traffic stops, and immigration enforcement. In chapter 5, we again take up a discussion of the evolution of sheriffs' anti-federalist attitudes, starting with Posse Comitatus through today's Constitutional Sheriff movement. With these evaluations, we show the importance of considering where and how policy change occurs among sheriffs and, in the final chapter, the challenges of reforming the office.

CHAPTER TWO

Electing Sheriffs

Tarrant County, Texas, is home to the city of Fort Worth, a diverse community of two million people, and Sheriff Bill Waybourn, first elected in 2016. Waybourn initially secured victory in a Republican primary runoff against Dee Anderson, the county's five-term Republican incumbent sheriff. While Anderson campaigned on his management, Waybourn ran on a platform emphasizing improving deputy morale and with the endorsements of local law enforcement agencies, a local Tea Party group, and conservative backers like Chuck Norris and the widow of "American Sniper" Chris Kyle (Waybourn 2016). After his election, Waybourn actively pursued a national conservative profile, including frequent appearances on right-wing media. Appearing before Trump's White House lectern in full uniform and cowboy hat, Waybourn championed his jail's new partnership with federal immigration enforcement and warned that immigrants released from custody are "drunks" who "will run over your children," prompting calls for his resignation (Fernández 2019).

Voters in Tarrant County returned Waybourn to office for another term in 2020, despite criticism of Waybourn's divisive politics and an increasing number of problems with his management of the local jail. The Tarrant County jail temporarily lost certification in 2020 after a spike of in-custody deaths (eighteen people in Waybourn's first term[1]), and detention officers in the jail have faced charges of assault while on duty and falsifying government records (Suarez 2020; Dallas News Editorial Team 2021).[2] Even as the county supported Joe Biden, Waybourn won reelection in 2020. Waybourn is not the first Tarrant County sheriff to win reelection after controversy: in 1996, Tarrant voters reelected Sheriff David Williams as he faced a lawsuit for creating a "God Pod" in the jail that forced evangelical Christianity on those in custody and complaints that he focused too little on his primary responsibility of the county jail (Clarke 2002; E. Moore 2001).[3] Voters reelected Waybourn over his Democratic challenger, Vance Keyes, a Black police captain in Fort Worth who ran on a reform platform (Chammah 2020b). Since Waybourn's reelection, concerns over the alarming conditions of the Tarrant County jail continue, with an additional thirty-one deaths in custody in the two years since his reelection (Manna 2022a).

Both the 2016 and 2020 sheriff elections in Tarrant County show the impact of elections on the office. The sheriff's office is the only local law enforcement office uniformly selected via popular election. In this chapter, we examine that uniqueness: we explore the nature of sheriff elections and the individuals who serve as sheriffs across the United States. Sheriffs themselves argue that the office is special because of its long history and because the sheriff is the only directly elected law enforcement officer in the United States. While sheriffs are right—they are unique!—we argue that the electoral nature of the office does not function as a democratic check on sheriffs and their behavior. We first document who sheriffs are and the interest from sheriffs in defending the electoral component of their office and the arguments they make as to why elections are so important in setting their office apart from other offices. We then show that sheriff elections fall short of the lofty aim sheriffs articulate: these elections are uncompetitive, and the pool of potential challengers is shallow (and kept shallow by sheriffs themselves), and these limit voters' ability to make informed decisions—or decisions at all—about who holds the office. In conclusion, we discuss how sheriffs represent a broader set of problems associated with using elections as a mechanism for accountability, particularly given the low levels of information that voters hold about sheriffs.

Who Are Sheriffs?

Sheriff Waybourn shares many characteristics with past sheriffs in Tarrant County and across the country: he is a Republican with extensive law enforcement experience, including serving as a police chief in a small town in Tarrant County. And like every sheriff in Tarrant County before him, Waybourn is a white man.[4] The average sheriff in our studies is a white (92 percent of sheriffs) man (98 percent) who worked in the office (78 percent) and attended high school (56 percent) in the county he now represents. To begin this chapter, we first focus on the characteristics of sheriffs, including their gender, race, background, partisanship, and ideology. Nationally, more than 90 percent of sheriffs are white, and 98 percent are men. This differs from the US overall, communities in which they serve, other elected offices, and members of their own staff. Sheriff Waybourn is also more conservative than Tarrant County, where Beto O'Rourke (D) garnered more votes than Ted Cruz (R) in the 2018 Senate race and Joe Biden edged out

Donald Trump in 2020. Using responses from our surveys and partisan affiliations on the ballot, we document that sheriffs are more ideologically conservative and more Republican compared to the communities where they serve. We then show that sheriffs collectively are becoming more conservative and Republican over time and are aligning less and less with their communities in ideology.

Gender and Race

One of the most notable observations of the office of sheriff and its occupants is that white men are grossly overrepresented in the office of sheriff (see table 2.1). Women make up slightly more than half of the US population overall and represent 11 percent of full-time employees who work for sheriffs; *only 2 percent of sheriffs are women.* Women comprised 20 percent of Congress, which arguably has a much higher barrier to entry than sheriffs' offices, 32 percent of mayors of large cities, and 24 percent of local prosecutors (Who Leads Us 2019; CAWP 2018). And white people hold a disproportionate share of positions in sheriffs' offices: *over 92 percent of sheriffs are white.* Like gender, sheriffs' racial diversity is far lower than sheriffs' employees or elected officials in Congress. If we examine sheriff candidates, these patterns continue: nearly 97 percent of candidates are men and 92.5 percent are white. Thus, sheriffs are unrepresentative largely in part

TABLE 2.1. Gender and racial makeup of sheriffs

	Sheriffs	Sheriff candidates	Sheriff's employee	Congressional representatives	US population
Gender					
Women	2%	3.2%	11.4%	20.5%	50.5%
Men	98.0	96.8	88.6	79.5	49.5
Race					
Asian American	0.1	0.2	0.03	3.2	6.0
Black	5.2	4.8	6.7	10.5	12.4
Hispanic	2.5	2.2	5.1	8.0	18.7
Native American	0.2	0.3	0.04	0.7	1.1
White	92.1	92.5	80.6	77.5	61.6

Note: Sheriff and sheriff candidate data from Who Leads Us (2020) and author verification. US population data from 2020 US Census. Employee data from LEMAS (LEMAS 2016). Congressional data from CAWP and Pew (Schaeffer 2019).

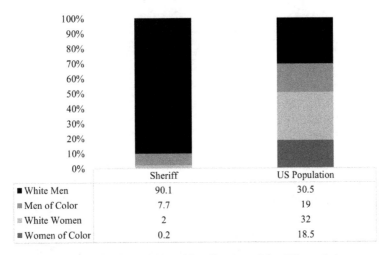

	Sheriff	US Population
■ White Men	90.1	30.5
■ Men of Color	7.7	19
■ White Women	2	32
■ Women of Color	0.2	18.5

FIGURE 2.1. Gender and race of sheriffs, compared to US population

Note: Sheriff data from Who Leads Us, verified and corrected by the
authors; US population data from the US Census (2020).

because the supply of candidates who are not white men is extremely low,
an intentional product of a system designed to resist change.

These patterns persist when we examine the intersection of race and
gender: while white men are 90 percent of sheriffs, they comprise only 30
percent of the US population overall (see fig. 2.1). Women of color are 18.5
percent of the US population but 0.2 percent of sheriffs. The lack of women
of color in office is again not simply because they run for office but then fail
to get elected; white men made up 89.6 percent of sheriff candidates in 2018
(Who Leads Us 2020). White men represented 92.2 percent of unopposed
candidates who ran in 2018. In comparison, white men made up just under
70 percent of prosecutor candidates in 2018 (Who Leads Us 2019).

The history of people of color and women (and especially women of
color) becoming sheriff is generally one of extraordinary circumstances. As
we discussed in chapter 1, post-Reconstruction efforts in voting rights and
election led to the election of Black sheriffs across the South in the second half of the nineteenth century. Jim Crow and racism soon diminished
and then decimated the number of Black sheriffs serving in office by the
early 1900s, creating spans of more than a hundred years between Black
sheriffs in some counties. For instance, in 1869, Fort Bend County, Texas,
elected Walter Moses Burton.[5] In 2020— over 150 years later—Fort Bend
elected Eric Fagan as its second Black sheriff (Modrich 2021). In Laramie,
Wyoming, Sheriff Aaron Appelhans was the first Black sheriff in the state's
131-year history when elected in 2021. In our data, which spans 2012 to 2018,

TABLE 2.2. Sheriffs' gender and race, 2012 and 2018

	2012	2018
Women	1.7%	2%
Men	98.7%	98%
Asian American	0%	0.1%
Black	4%	5.2%
Hispanic	2.5%	2.5%
Native American	0.4%	0.2%
White	93.1%	92%
Women of color	0.01%	0.2%
White women	1.3%	2.%
Men of color	6.7%	7.7%
White men	90.5%	90.1%

Note: Sheriff demographic data collected by the authors in 2012 and from Who Leads Us (verified and corrected by the authors) in 2018.

the percentage of non-white sheriffs increased just 1 percent over that time (see table 2.2).

Less than 2 percent of sheriffs in the United States are women; in 2021, sixteen states had no women as sheriffs. The share of women increased 0.3 percent between 2012 and 2018 (a total of five more women) while the share of women of color increased from 0.01 percent to 0.2 percent (a total of four more women of color).[6] The first women sheriffs typically came to the position because of the death of their sheriff husbands (Schulz 2004).[7] The *New York Times*, in describing Clara Senecal, New York's first woman sheriff, who had been appointed to the position of Clinton County sheriff in 1926 after her sheriff husband died, described her as follows: "Mrs. Senecal is slightly more than 50 years old, well preserved, and of fine appearance. She was standing at the side of the late sheriff's casket when she was told the Governor Smith had announced her appointment" (*New York Times* 1926). These patterns continued throughout the twentieth century, with widows taking over the office or wives of sheriffs running because their husbands were not allowed to run for an additional term.[8] In 1922, an Arkansas newspaper published the headline "Woman sheriff on job,"[9] echoed nearly a century later when Utah elected its first woman sheriff in 2017.[10] Women of color serving as sheriffs are even more rare, with the first Black woman elected sheriff in 1992 (Jacquelyn H. Barrett of Fulton County, Georgia). In comparison to another local office that is dominated by white men— prosecutors—the *stickiness* of lack of diversity among sheriffs is quite remarkable. For example, the Campaign for Reflective Democracy found a 34 percent increase in the share of women (from 18 percent to 24 percent) prosecutors from 2015 to 2019. There has not been a similar change among women running for or holding the office of sheriff.

What does the dramatic underrepresentation of women and people of color as sheriffs mean in terms of how sheriffs behave in office? Research on electing women and people of color to legislative and executive office outside of law enforcement (for example, as mayors, legislative representatives, or governors) argues that their representation matters as the descriptive representation of traditionally marginalized groups shapes the policies produced by those governments (McBrayer and Williams 2022; Holman 2015; T. Osborn 2012; Dittmar, Sanbonmatsu, and Carroll 2018; Farris, Holman, and Sullivan 2021). But research within policing presents more mixed evidence: while police violence and racism often prompt calls for replacing white leaders with Black or Latino leaders (Shoub and Christiani 2022), only some research finds that the representation of non-white leaders translates to policy decisions or outcomes (Shoub et al. 2020, 487; Baumgartner, Epp, and Shoub 2018; Shoub and Christiani 2022; Shoub 2022; B. W. Smith 2003). Similarly, calls for more women in policing often follow national attention on police violence, but the research on how women as the heads of policing agencies might shape policy choices or outcomes is often quite muddy (Gunderson and Huber 2022; Shoub, Stauffer, and Song 2021; Meier and Nicholson-Crotty 2006). For example, political scientists Gunderson and Huber (2022) examine the effect of women in the police force, finding little evidence that their presence changes the rate of reports or closures of sexual assault because they are "Blue first and foremost."

At the core of the arguments for the effect of electing women and non-white sheriffs is that descriptive representation will lead to substantive representation. The effects of electing fewer white men as sheriffs on the activities of the office is an open question, with few opportunities for assessment: the low numbers of women and sheriffs of color limit the methodological approaches available for evaluating whether electing these individuals to the office matter in terms of policy outcomes. One possibility is that race and gender are simply shortcuts for broader political identities, with women and people of color expressing more support for the Democratic Party and for liberal ideological commitments (Ondercin 2017; Benegal 2018; White and Laird 2020; Holman, Podrazik, and Mohamed 2020). In this context, we might simply examine these attitudes directly, rather than descriptive representation. To do so, we next look at sheriffs' self-identification within party identification categories, their ideological stances, and their party affiliation on the ballot.

Sheriffs' Partisanship and Ideology

Partisanship operates as a core (if not the core) political cue for individuals supporting policy, voters selecting candidates, and elected officials engaging in work in office (Campbell et al. 1960; Kalmoe and Mason 2022; Ondercin and Lizotte 2021; de Benedictis-Kessner 2021; 2022; Bernhard 2022). On both the 2012 and 2021 survey, we asked sheriffs for their individual placement on a five-point party measure (Strong Democrats, Democrats, Independents, Republicans, Strong Republicans), a five-point ideology scale (Very Liberal, Liberal, Moderate, Conservative, Very Conservative), and which party they "represent as sheriff," with Republican, Democrat, nonpartisan, or other as options. Table 2.3 provides the breakdown of these categories.

Sheriffs are overwhelmingly conservative Republicans. The most common categories for sheriffs' politics are Republican partisanship, conservative ideology, and Republican on the ballot. Only *one single* sheriff on our 2021 survey identified as very liberal, and five total sheriffs identified as liberal. While twenty percent of sheriffs identify as a Democrat or report that they ran as a Democrat for office, less than one percent of sheriffs identify as liberal. Observational data from every sheriff candidate who won office in 2018 aligns with our party on the ballot data: of the 1,220 sheriffs up for election in 2018, 54 percent of the winning candidates were Republicans, and 26 percent were Democrats. Prosecutors have a similar partisan composition, both in terms of who holds the office (54 percent Republican, 29 percent Democrats) and who runs as candidates (52 percent Republican, 30 percent Democrats) (Hessick and Morse 2020), although some evidence would suggest that prosecutor candidates are changing more rapidly than are sheriffs (Who Leads Us 2019).

While sheriffs' ideology and partisanship correlate with their populations' preferences, sheriffs are still much more conservative and Republican

TABLE 2.3. Sheriff partisanship and ideology, 2012 and 2021

Partisanship		Ideology		Party on the ballot	
Strong Democrat	1%	Very liberal	0%	Democrat	22%
Democrat	22	Liberal	1	Republican	66
Independent	10	Moderate	42	Nonpartisan	9
Republican	47	Conservative	43	Other	2
Strong Republican	20	Very conservative	13		

Note: Data from 2012 and 2021 surveys. Table includes percentages for all sheriffs who reported partisanship, ideology, and their party on the ballot.

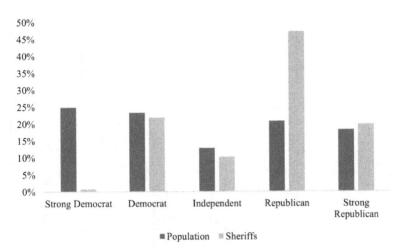

FIGURE 2.2. Sheriff and population partisanship (2021)

Note: Sheriff partisanship from 2021 survey. Population partisanship from 2018 and 2020 CES data, selecting only those respondents who live in counties where we surveyed a sheriff.

than their counties. On both the 2012 and 2021 surveys, we asked sheriffs to provide their partisanship and ideology. Understanding how sheriffs compare to their populations requires some careful data work, as many sheriffs represent counties with small populations who are not routinely surveyed about their partisanship and ideology. We use three measures: a measure of partisanship calculated from aggregating large public opinion surveys together so we can compare the share of people in each county represented by sheriffs that identifies into each partisan category, the share of the county that voted for Barack Obama in 2012 (to accompany our 2012 survey data) and Joe Biden in 2020 (to accompany our 2021 survey data), and a measure of the ideology of the population in each county calculated by political scientists Tausanovitch and Warshaw (2013; 2022).[11] All three of these measures are discussed in more detail in the Data and Methods appendix. Finally, we examine sheriffs' attitudes about Presidents Trump and Biden, compared to nationally representative samples of Americans. In the Results appendix, we provide additional comparisons, including the overlap between ideology and partisanship for sheriffs and the population, a correlation matrix of the population's views and sheriffs' views, and sheriffs' partisan affiliations on the ballot compared to state legislators.

Partisanship: Sheriffs are far less likely to be strong Democrats and far more likely to Republicans compared to the population in the counties they represent (see Fig 2.2). Take the sheriffs we surveyed in 2021: just under 25 percent of people who live in those counties identify as strong Democrats;

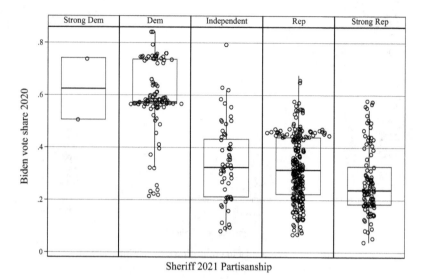

FIGURE 2.3. Sheriff partisanship (2021) and Biden vote share in county (2020)
Note: Sheriff partisanship from 2021 survey; Biden vote share
in 2020 from MIT's Election Data Archive.

only one percent of sheriffs do. And while 39 percent of the population in
these counties identifies as either Republicans or strong Republicans, two-
thirds (67 percent) of sheriffs identify as Republicans or strong Republicans.

We next compare sheriffs' partisanship and party on the ballot to the
voting patterns in their county in figure 2.3. Here, we focus first on a comparison between the share of the county that voted for Biden in 2020 and
the sheriffs' responses on the 2021 survey (see Results appendix for the
2012 data). Here, the boxes represent the median and standard deviation
of distribution of votes for Biden in the counties, by the partisanship of the
sheriff. We see that the average vote for Biden in counties where the sheriff
is a strong Democrat (63 percent), Democrat (58 percent), Independent
(34 percent), Republican (33 percent), and Strong Republican (26 percent)
reflects the sheriffs' partisanship, with relatively wide variations. For example, sheriffs who identify as strong Republicans represent counties that
voted for Biden in wildly ranging rates from 11 percent to 71 percent. We see
similar patterns looking at sheriffs who answered our 2012 survey and voted
for Obama (see appendix figure A2.2).

Ideology: These patterns continue when we look at ideology but with an
even larger rightward skew among sheriffs. In our 2021 survey results, only
a single sheriff identified as very liberal, compared to 10 percent of the US
population, and only five total sheriffs (1 percent of the sheriffs surveyed)

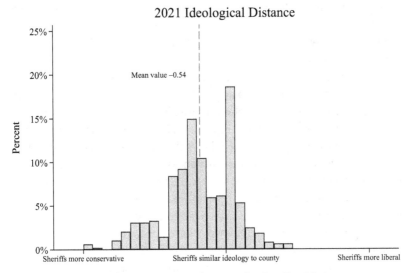

FIGURE 2.4. Ideological distance between the sheriff and their county

Note: Figure depicts the difference between the sheriff's ideology and the ideology of the county that they represent. See Data and Methods appendix for more information.

identified as liberal, compared to 19 percent of the population. And while just under 40 percent of the populations of the survey counties identified as conservative or very conservative, almost 56 percent of sheriffs selected as such.

We next take the reported ideology of each county's population, calculated by Tausanovitch and Warshaw (2013; 2022), and subtract that from that county's sheriff's ideology. A score of zero here indicates that the sheriff and the county they represent have the same reported ideology; a negative value means that the sheriff is more conservative than their county; a positive value means that the sheriff is more liberal than their county.[12] For example, if the sheriff's ideology were liberal (or a value of 2) and the county's ideology were conservative (4), this value would be 2, while if a conservative sheriff (2) served in a liberal county (4), the value would be –2. We then present this as a histogram, with percentages in figure 2.4.

On average, sheriffs are more conservative than the counties that they represent, with sheriffs -0.55 more conservative than average, compared to the ideology of their counties. The distribution also reflects the conservative leaning of sheriffs, as the value is negative with a left-hand skew. We find no sheriffs who are at least a whole point more liberal than their counties, while more than 10 percent of sheriffs are more than a whole point on our scale more conservative than their counties.

But such a relationship obscures the extent to which sheriffs may be simply representing the median or mean preference in their counties. It is possible that the skewed partisanship and ideology of sheriffs simply reflect the views and preferences of voters in their counties. In "The Delegate's Paradox," Ahler and Broockman (2018, 1117) argue that "constituencies comprising citizens with idiosyncratic policy preferences are often best represented by politicians who appear ideologically polarized." In this circumstance, a political leader who is more ideologically extreme than their constituents will still be a good representative for the constituents' interests so long as that representative follows the *majority* of their constituents' preferences in the majority of circumstances. So, for example, if a sheriff is very conservative and their county's population is conservative, this distance could be fine if the sheriff regularly engages in behavior that is consistent with the preferences of the majority of their county residents. It is thus entirely possible that moderate levels of preference in the population lead to imbalanced representation among elected leaders.

To examine this, we look at swing counties, or those where Biden won or lost by less than 10 percent (i.e., where Biden's share of the ballot was between 40 and 60 percent) and compare this to sheriffs' own political positions. A third of sheriffs (33 percent) in our 2021 sample represent a swing district. In figure 2.5, we provide a scatter plot of the vote for Biden in each county (with the symbol indicating whether Biden won less than 40 percent of the vote [triangle], 40–60 percent [square], or more than 60 percent [diamond]). We provide a scatter plot of the relationship between the share of the vote received by Biden in the county and the sheriff's partisanship (top pane), ideology (middle pane), and partisan affiliation on the ballot (bottom pane). These comparisons again reveal correlations between sheriffs' partisanship, ideology, and party and the population's preference, but with a rightward bias in sheriffs' representation of their districts' interests. For example, 58 percent of swing counties are represented by a Republican sheriff and 67 percent are represented by a conservative sheriff. And only 1 percent of swing counties—and 1 percent of counties that voted for Biden—are represented by a liberal sheriff.

Location may also matter: in the United States, urban and rural areas increasingly diverge in their political preferences (Huijsmans et al. 2021; Rodden 2019), with populations in rural areas expressing much more conservative views on policy areas, ideology, and partisanship compared to urban residents. Because sheriffs often represent rural areas or primarily provide services to rural fringes of counties with urban and rural areas, their ideological and partisan views may simply be indicative of the populations they represent. However, we see little evidence that partisan or ideological

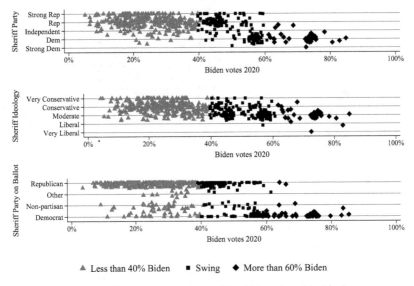

FIGURE 2.5. Swing vote counties and sheriffs' partisanship, ideology, and party on the ballot

Note: Figure depicts the partisanship and ideology of sheriffs from 2021 survey and votes for Biden by county in 2020.

distance between the sheriff and his county is concentrated in urban or rural areas (see Results appendix).

A Growth in Distance

One of the most consistent patterns in sheriffs' partisan and ideological stances is that the distance between sheriffs' and their counties' political preferences have grown from 2012 to 2021 (see table 2.4). When we compare to our 2012 data, we see that sheriffs we surveyed in 2021 are less Democratic and more Republican and conservative in 2021 compared to 2012. Recall that our 2012 and 2021 data are not a panel (i.e., we did not get the same sheriffs to answer both surveys), so this is not that single sheriffs are changing their ideological or partisan positions. Instead, this suggests that through replacement, elections, and *potentially* individual change, we see sheriffs collectively becoming more conservative and more Republican.

We also see the ideological distance between sheriffs and the communities that they represent grew from 2012 to 2021, with sheriffs much more conservative than their communities in 2021 than in 2012 (see figure 2.6).

TABLE 2.4. Sheriff partisanship and ideology, 2012 and 2021

PARTISANSHIP

	2012	2021
Strong Democrat	2%	1%
Democrat	29	22
Independent	20	10
Republican	41	47
Strong Republican	7	20

IDEOLOGY

	2012	2021
Very liberal	0%	0%
Liberal	2	1
Moderate	53	42
Conservative	36	43
Very conservative	9	13

PARTY ON BALLOT

	2012	2021
Democrat	33%	22%
Republican	50	66
Nonpartisan	9	9
Other	8	2

Note: Data from 2012 and 2021 surveys. Table includes percentages for all sheriffs who reported partisanship, ideology, and their party on the ballot.

We again map the distance between the population's ideological position in 2012 minus the sheriff's reported ideological position (left panel) and compare that to the difference between the county's and sheriff's ideology in 2021 (right panel). While sheriffs in 2012 were more conservative than their counties (average ideological distance of -0.16), this distance is larger in 2021 (average ideological distance of -0.54), with a less normal distribution.

The ideological and partisan identities of sheriffs could be impactful on the policies they enact and enforce. Research by political scientists on the partisanship of municipal-level actors like mayors and city council members as well as county commissioners shows that partisanship matters—that is, the budgets of cities and counties change because a Democrat or Republican is elected to office (de Benedictis-Kessner and Warshaw 2020b; 2016). Recent work on prosecutor partisanship and outcomes reliably finds

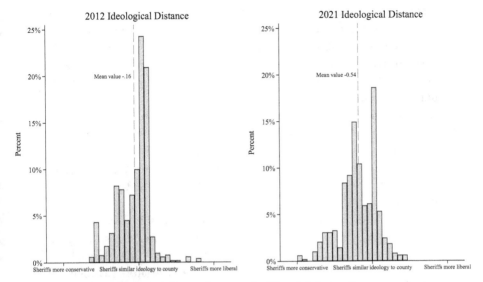

FIGURE 2.6. Ideological distance between sheriffs and their counties, 2012 and 2021
Note: Figure depicts the difference between the sheriff's ideology and the ideology
of the county that they represent in 2012 (left pane) and 2021 (right pane).

that Republican prosecutors prosecute defendants (particularly Black defendants) more and pursue longer sentences (Krumholz 2019; Arora 2018; Yntiso 2022). For example, Yntiso (2022) finds that narrowly electing a Republican prosecutor (over a Democrat opponent) leads to tougher charges, but only in cases involving Black defendants.

But sheriffs may be exceptional in the role of partisanship. For example, Thompson's (2020) evaluation of the effect of electing a Democrat or Republican sheriff on the rate of immigration deportations finds no relationship between partisanship and immigration policy. And our earlier work on immigration (explored more in chap. 4) finds little evidence that partisanship is associated with the immigration policies that sheriffs choose to enforce. Sheriffs themselves often argue that political party is not important in shaping their behavior. One told us, "My office is not motivated by any political party stances. We remain neutral on any perceived biases. Our only mission is to keep working at keeping the community safe and protecting the rights and freedoms. We all realize that there is good and bad in all categories of people." Another sheriff noted, "There is no place for personal or political preferences in the performance of our duties."

Other sheriffs told us that they do not allow partisanship to shape their office's behavior because they provide services to all in their county, no matter the political party: "I serve all of the people in [my county] no matter what their race, creed, gender, religion, sexual orientation, socioeconomic status, or political party affiliation may be and I'm bound by the Constitution to do it!" Other sheriffs dismissed the importance of party: "I believe regardless of which party you belong to we as Sheriff's have a unique responsibility to up hold the law and protect the constitution. we as leaders should be making the RIGHT choices not the Politically correct ones." Others connected these views to whom they view as their constituents: "First is that we serve all of our citizens. Not the fed or the state. Not a political party."[13] A small group of sheriffs, when we asked them about political party, indicated that they had run under both the Democratic and Republican parties in the past.

And yet, the same sheriffs who argue that partisanship does not matter also often place themselves at odds with progressive or liberal state legislators or other government officials. Sheriffs volunteered "Liberal state laws/legislature" and "Anti-law enforcement Liberal legislators" as their top problems; one detailed concerns about progressive tyranny: "Sheriff's Offices nationwide are the best protection against advancing tyranny by state and federal governments. I never used to believe this until I had to personally, as Sheriff, oppose unconstitutional decisions being foisted on this country and state in the interest of progressive ideology."[14]

The contentious relationship that sheriffs have with progressive or liberal government officials is also evident in their views of national politics, where sheriffs' views are out of step with the broader population. In 2021, we asked sheriffs to provide their approval of President Biden and former President Trump. In figure 2.7, we compare this to nationally representative polling data.[15] For both figures, we again show that sheriffs are much more conservative that the American population. For example, while only 1 percent of sheriffs strongly approve of Biden, 34 percent of the population does so, and while more than half (55 percent) of the public strongly disapproved of Trump, only 8 percent of sheriffs does so.

Electing Sheriffs

How is it that sheriffs are so white, male, and conservative? Most sheriffs are selected via a direct election, where registered voters in their county[16] vote on who will be their chief law enforcement officer in a single or run-off election. Most US counties (over 2,700) elect their sheriffs via some version of a partisan election. Sheriffs in five states (California, Louisiana, Minnesota, Oregon, and Tennessee), along with a few counties, hold elections that are

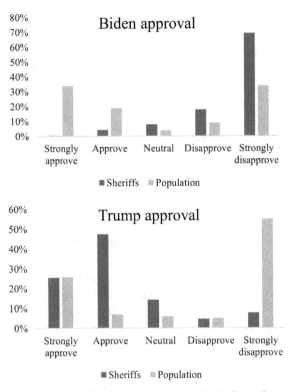

FIGURE 2.7. Sheriff and population approval of Biden and Trump

not direct partisan contests, but only Minnesota, Oregon, and Tennessee have nonpartisan elections.[17] Most sheriff elections are for four-year terms without term limits, which exist for some sheriffs in counties in Colorado and for all sheriffs in Indiana, New Mexico, and West Virginia. Sheriff elections are both on- and off-cycle in that in some states' sheriffs are elected on a ballot alongside presidential candidates (twenty-one states) or at midterm congressional elections (seventeen states). The remainder are in states like Louisiana, where local elections are held off-cycle from federal elections.

Of the characteristics that set sheriffs apart from other local leaders, sheriffs themselves focus closely on the electoral nature of their office, including the origins of their elected office in state constitutions, the long tradition of electing sheriffs, and the accountability afforded via elections. The roots of these elections are found in many state constitutions. Of the forty-six states with elected sheriffs today, thirty-eight states established the office in the original state constitution and another eight states (South Carolina, New York, Tennessee, Louisiana, Virginia, Massachusetts, Maine,

New Hampshire) adopted sheriff elections after statehood (DeHart 2020).[18] Many of these constitutions note sheriffs should be elected. According to sheriffs, the constitutional origins differentiate them from other law enforcement positions. The constitutional origins elevate them from a department to an office and protect sheriffs from sway or control by other local leaders.[19] While sheriffs are factually correct that state constitutions do lay out sheriff as an elected office, these constitutional provisions rarely actually grant sheriffs special powers compared to other county offices or specifically root that power in the electoral nature of the office. Delaware, for example, laid out in their initial state constitution that "the treasurer, secretary, clerks of the supreme court, prothonotaries, resistors, recorders, sheriffs, and coroners shall, by virtue of their offices, be conservators thereof within the counties respectively in which they reside." And Michigan designates a "sheriff, a county treasurer, and one or more coroners, a register of deeds, and a county surveyor" as county offices.[20]

As we have previously discussed, sheriffs emphasize not just that they are elected but that the *tradition* of an election is key to their power. As the National Sheriffs' Association notes, "The first of two important characteristics that distinguish the Office of Sheriff from other law enforcement units is its historical roots" (National Sheriffs' Association 2022). One report for the Florida Department of Law Enforcement remarks, "We have, of course, evolved from a sheriff responsible to a total autocratic form of government to the democratic form of government that we cherish in the United States" (M. L. Hall 2008). Electing sheriffs is important, they argue, because of "national traditions and practices," stability, and continuity of the office (National Sheriffs' Association, n.d.). Sheriffs connect this history to their position and power today. One response to our survey noted that sheriffs in their state "have a proud tradition and are considered the chief law enforcement official in their respective counties." As we mentioned in the previous chapter, many sheriffs produce histories on their own websites and frequently quote Thomas Jefferson asking "where then is our republicanism to be found?" if citizens are denied the chance to elect a sheriff (Jefferson 1905).

Sheriffs argue that there are historical roots to the elected nature of the office; however, the office extends back to the early ninth century in England, where sheriffs were appointed by the king or duke to serve as tax collectors and local enforcers.[21] Sheriffs point to both as claims for legitimacy: the office has a long history reaching back centuries, and elections are a key piece of that history. When Jeff Sessions spoke to the NSA in 2018, he noted this history: "Since our founding, the independently elected Sheriff has been seen as the people's protector, who keeps law enforcement close to and amenable to the people" (Sessions 2018; Washington 2018). Sessions went on to refer to the "Anglo American heritage of the office" (and drew public ire for his phrasing, as discussed in chap. 2) (Vazquez 2018). For the sheriffs, however, the central remark of Sessions' comments was, "We must never erode this historic office." Sheriffs hope that by emphasizing the historical nature of elections, the office will remain an elected one.

Sheriffs posit that elections provide greater accountability for an office that has a great deal of power. In a position paper, the NSA notes, "In our democracy, we should have the right to choose who is to be sheriff. In many counties the sheriff is the single most powerful individual and institution. . . . Citizens should have the freedom to choose their sheriff and direct election is the best means to accomplish that" (National Sheriffs' Association, n.d.). Sheriffs in our surveys echo these sentiments; one wrote that "the office of the Sheriff is the only law enforcement official who answers directly to the voters of their county. It is a critical office in county government," and another argued that "the Office of Sheriff is in the 'purest' category of public service as answering only to the people they serve. A Sheriff is allowed to serve only by the will of the citizens. This is the most important aspect of the Office of Sheriff." Other sheriffs go further in emphasizing their power, as we will discuss more in chapter 5 with the rise of the so-called constitutional sheriffs movement, and one sheriff in our survey argued that the office is the "most important elected position in the United States of America."

Sheriffs believe that elections also keep the office independent of other influences and directly accountable only to voters. The NSA argues, "The sheriff provides a check and balance as an elected county official directly responsible to the citizens that protects from undue influence by members of the county board or by other county officials." These views are echoed by the sheriffs in our surveys; one told us, "Now as a duly elected sheriff I am free from politics. I answer only to the voters who expect this office will follow the rule of law, the constitution and laws of this state and the United States. We walk beneath the banner of public trust. It will not always be easy, but it will always be right."

The NSA regularly produces materials that advocate for the office of the sheriff remain an elected position. In "Preserve the Office of the Sheriff by Continuing the Election of Our Nation's Sheriffs" (National Sheriffs' Association 2015), the NSA argues that sheriffs should remain elected because "in local jurisdictions in which a Sheriff is 'appointed,' there can be a decrease in the quality and continuity in the law enforcement services and administration of a Sheriff's Department. When the Sheriff is subject to the political/economic whims and caprices of a county board/commissioners, etc. as an 'appointed' head of a 'Department' (not an 'elected' Office), local law enforcement often becomes 'politicized' to the public's detriment." Sheriffs pick up this rhetoric; one told us, "Being Elected by our citizens and representing them in public safety matters is my most important role as Sheriff. Being elected and not an appointed Chief having to answer to one mayor allows me to better serve the public." Another sheriff framed the importance this way: "Chiefs of police are many times hamstrung by their political leadership (city council or mayor) and thus are unable to speak out on issues. Thankfully I am elected by the people and have more autonomy and am able to comment on the misguided attempts at police reform."

These are not new arguments from sheriffs: in a 1958 NSA magazine article titled "Appointing Sheriffs Viewed as Sure Prelude to Police State," Sheriff Donald Tulloch of Barnstable County, Massachusetts, argues that those advocating for moving to appointed office "are saying, in effect, that Democracy doesn't work, and in my language, that's a bit on the 'pink' side." Tulloch goes on, "It is my firm belief that such a philosophy [of seeking appointment for sheriffs] is in keeping with the communist abhorrence to filling government offices by free election." Sheriffs are, he writes, "powerful constitutional officers [who] serve as a bulwark against such attempts to weaken democratic governance."

Yet, despite the narratives from sheriffs that elections are both traditionally important and key to the independence of the office, elections can also be deeply problematic. We focus on three ways that sheriff elections fail to provide accountability and independence for the office: sheriff elections are *uncompetitive*, a *limited pool* of candidates means little choice between alternative approaches to running the office, and sheriffs themselves *work to shape (and limit)* who can and does run for the office.

Uncompetitive Elections

Competitive elections are a central component of democratic health (Lindberg 2004). Local political competition produces downstream effects: it can improve service delivery (Moreno-Jaimes 2007), improve the economic health of an area (Pinto and Timmons 2005), and increase political engagement of voters.[22] And competitive elections may reduce bad behavior: "Democracy matters as a safety net against tyranny or corruption" (Stoker 1996, 188).

Federalism is defined by a system of "shared and distinct" powers with both horizontal and vertical checks and balances (Bulman-Pozen 2012; Hinkley and Weber 2021). The autonomy that sheriffs have from other local actors as independently elected officials means the absence of the horizontal checks that traditionally limit an executive's power in other offices or broadly control bureaucracies (Wrightson 1986). For example, while governors can execute policy, state legislatures can check that action; sheriffs have no such legislative equivalent as they set and enforce policy. As a result, the local "checks" on sheriffs in the US federalism system are from voters. But voters are able to engage in such checks only when there are competitive elections between candidates who differ on key stances and characteristics.

Sheriff elections do not meet many of the criteria for competitive elections. Sheriffs often run for office unopposed or without quality opponents. In 2018, 40 percent of sheriffs up for election ran unopposed (Who Leads Us 2020). Zoorob (2022) found that 45 percent of sheriff elections were uncontested across 5,500 elections, including 31 percent of open seats and more than half of sheriff elections with an incumbent. In California between 1996 and 2018, more than half of the races for sheriff were uncontested. We present the average share of the vote received by sheriff candidates in California where there are at least two candidates in the election in a histogram in figure 2.8, which shows that the modal election outcome (by far) is that sheriffs receive more than 95 percent of the vote in California elections.[23] While the rate of electoral contestation for sheriffs is far lower than house elections (where approximately 5 percent are uncontested) or state legislative races (with a 35 percent uncontested rate) (Ballotpedia 2020), sheriff elections look very similar to—and perhaps even more competitive than— other law enforcement–adjacent positions: 70 percent of prosecutor elections, 75–80 percent of local trial judges, 65–70 percent of appellate judge elections, and 33 percent of state supreme court elections are uncontested (Streb, Frederick, and LaFrance 2007; Nelson 2010; Hessick 2018).

Research on other municipal offices shows that low levels of electoral competition have a wide set of political consequences, including distorting representation, leading to the increased importance of powerful groups in the community, and allowing interest groups and lobbyists to access those in power (Anzia 2011; 2013; de Benedictis-Kessner 2017; Trounstine 2013; 2011). In fact, we know far less about the democratic consequences of the lack of sheriffs' electoral competition. But what we do know is that sheriff elections rarely meet the criteria of a "local check."

Sheriffs also enjoy a very high incumbency advantage. Sheriffs serve for longer terms than police chiefs (an average of eleven years for sheriffs compared to four years for police chiefs), run for reelection at extraordinarily high rates, and appear to be protected from national partisan politics (Zoorob 2022; 2020). Studies of the incumbency advantage in Congress

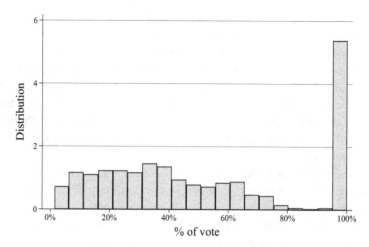

FIGURE 2.8. Share of vote received for each candidate for sheriff
in California, 1996–2018
Note: Elections data from the California Elections Data Archive (CEDA).

and state legislatures point to the ability of incumbents to deter high-quality challengers (Levitt and Wolfram 1997). This "scare off" effect means that quality challengers seek out open seats (or wait for an incumbent to not seek reelection) prior to running (de Benedictis-Kessner 2017). For congressional and state legislative races, this explains only a small portion of the incumbency advantage (Hall and Snyder 2015). We argue that sheriffs are uniquely able to deter high-quality challengers at extremely high rates because the majority of sheriff candidates take a specific pathway to office—one that involves working in the sheriffs' office that the candidate is looking to oversee.

We argue that one principal obstacle to electoral competition for the office of sheriff is a very shallow *eligibility pool of candidates* for sheriff, or the pool of individuals who might be tapped by donors, local political elites, or party leaders to run for office (Crowder-Meyer 2018; Kreitzer and Osborn 2020; Schneider et al. 2016; Sanbonmatsu and Dittmar 2020). While often political ambition is conceived of as an individual choosing to seek office, researchers argue that recruitment is actually one of the key obstacles for diversifying who holds local office (Kreitzer and Osborn 2019). Sheriffs benefit from (and manipulate) a wide set of institutional advantages that reduce the political competition for the job. Some of this relates to where sheriffs serve: low-population counties with a preference for local leadership constrain who can run for office. Formal criteria for service (such as prior law enforcement experience) and informal expectations (such as a deep familiarity with the community) further limit which candidates can run.

A Shallow Eligibility Pool

One potential source of the shallow eligibility pool is that rural communities simply have fewer people eligible to run for office. Electoral competition increases with the size of the office: more than half of elections among small offices are uncontested compared to one in three for sheriffs seeking offices with more employees (Zoorob 2022). Because sheriffs often serve in rural areas with low populations, have deep roots in the community that result in a wide set of connections to individuals (or, as one sheriff noted, "You know, something bad goes on, you feel for everybody because I know all these people"), and rely on informal enforcement of many community standards, candidates with local backgrounds can be advantaged in both seeking office and standing for reelection. The small population in many rural counties further reduces the pool of high-quality challengers and increases sheriffs' incumbency advantages. One sheriff told us, "Rural areas like [my] County are starved for quality leadership in law enforcement are routinely subjected to a revolving door of Office heads which makes it more prone to fail the community."

As an extreme example, take Loving County, Texas,[24] which has the smallest population of any county in the United States at sixty-four people in 2020. In 1944, Edna Reed Clayton was the first woman elected sheriff in both Loving and the state of Texas; she would go on to serve six terms as county clerk (M. B. Jones 2009). Later, Punk Jones[25] would serve as the sheriff for almost thirty years, while his wife served as tax appraiser (M. B. Jones 2009). In the 2000s, Sheriff Dickie Putnam was the husband of the postmaster, who was herself the stepdaughter of a county judge and a niece of a county commissioner (Colloff 1997). The current sheriff, Chris Busse, grew up in Alaska but has been with the Loving Sheriff Office since 2008. Sheriff Busse often ends up in the center of politically powerful families and long-standing feuds in the rural county. Most recently, Loving County judge Skeet Jones (son of former Sheriff Punk Jones) was arrested in 2022 with three ranch hands on charges of cattle rustling (selling stray livestock without properly notifying the sheriff to find their rightful owners) (S. Carroll 2022; Meyer 1993).[26] One of the arrested ranch hands was a former sheriff's deputy who had discussed running against Busse, and when the sheriff then barred him from the county building, there was no one to take out the sheriff's trash, as the former deputy also was the county custodian (Goodman 2022). The Loving sheriff also serves as the county's registrar of voters, and a few days later, Sheriff Busse arrested the judges' son and three others (including a county commissioner) over questions of their residency. In Loving, nearly 40 percent of the county's population works for the county, leaving the sheriff with a complex and personal job.

But the challenges of uncompetitive elections do not happen only in less populated rural areas. Even outside of the smallest county in the United States, the pool of individuals who can or want to become sheriff is very small. Our survey results show all sheriffs (99 percent) have law enforcement experience prior to serving, and most sheriffs (77 percent) worked in their own office as a deputy or jailer prior to running for election. In California, more than 60 percent of candidates have experience in their own office. As an example of a typical career path, Sheriff Mark Milbrandt of Brown County, South Dakota, "started his employment with the Brown County Sheriff's Office in May of 1979 as a part-jailor." In the next year, he moved to a position as a patrol officer and then to the office's "first ever full-time investigator." After a promotion to the chief deputy, he ran for office in 1994 and has served seven terms as sheriff since (South Dakota Sheriffs' Association 2022).

More than half (56 percent) of the sheriffs we surveyed in 2021 went to high school in their current county. Sheriffs highlight their connections to the local community in their bios on websites, in social media, and in campaigns and elections. As one sheriff noted, "I was raised in [my] County, I live in [my] County and I have served the majority of my law enforcement career in [my] County. I want to make [my] County the safest and best it can be especially now in these trying times. This is not just a job, protecting my home county is a personal mission." Sheriffs often tout their connections in their campaigns and promotional materials; the website for Navajo County, Arizona, introduces their sheriff this way: "Sheriff Clouse and his wife Angela, along with their 4 daughters make their home in Snowflake. That makes 7 generations who have lived in Snowflake and he lives on the same block as his great grandfathers did, his roots to Navajo County run deep" (Navajo County, AZ 2022). Another sheriff, when asked why he ran for office, told us, "Born and raised in the county I know the county, the citizens and have a passion to see our county prosper."[27]

That three of four sheriffs emerge out of their own office differentiates the office from other political offices. Even though incumbency effects in state and federal office are incredibly large, only 26 percent of state legislative candidates report a prior political position (Shah, Juenke, and Fraga 2022), and less than 5 percent of candidates for mayor and city council in

California report positions as legislative or local staff. And it is not just that sheriffs gain work experience in the office; sheriffs tap their successors, often retiring before the end of their term so that the next sheriff can gain experience and run as an incumbent in the next election. Sheriffs we surveyed refer to this process as a "natural progression" (a term used by six sheriffs in our survey); as one wrote, "It actually sought me. I was a patrol deputy then promoted to Chief Deputy and after about 4 years in that position the then Sheriff resigned to take a position outside of law enforcement. I was then appointed to serve the unexpired term. After that I have continued to want to serve the community here so I've run for reelection since." Another told us, "I worked my way up the ladder. Patrolman, Deputy Sheriff, LT on night shift, Chief Deputy for 16 years. I was groomed by the Sheriff to take over once he retired." In our 2021 survey, one in five volunteered that they were appointed to office prior to an election or handpicked as a successor when the prior sheriff retired.

If most sheriffs serve in their own offices prior to running and are reelected to office over and over, where exactly would political competition come from? Deputies would have to choose to run against their bosses, facing the very real possibility that they would be fired for the choice.[28] Sheriff Grady Judd from Polk County, Florida, recalled a conversation with the then-sheriff when he was first hired as a deputy. "He said, 'How long are you going to stay with me?' I said, 'All I want to do is be in law enforcement and work for you.' Of course I didn't tell him I wanted to be sheriff because I didn't know how long he wanted to be sheriff—not that I should intimidate him at 19 years of age, but you just didn't say those things" (K. Moore 2022). An internal candidate's likelihood of running for office is highly dependent on whether the incumbent sheriff is in the race. In California, the incumbent running has a big impact on whether a challenger emerges overall, and particularly whether there is a challenger from within the sheriff's own office.

While most successful sheriff candidates may come from their own office, *when* these candidates run is a highly strategic choice. We use the data from California to assess when a challenger is more or less likely to enter into a race, as shown in figure 2.9. As with other results we present in this chapter, we provide predicted probabilities generated from a model that has controls for the county's population and fixed effects for the county. This means that we are estimating the likelihood that a candidate with internal or external experience runs in any election in comparison to other sheriff elections in that county across time. When an incumbent is on the ballot, the likelihood of an internal challenger running for sheriff is 25 percent. Without an incumbent on the ballot, the likelihood of the internal

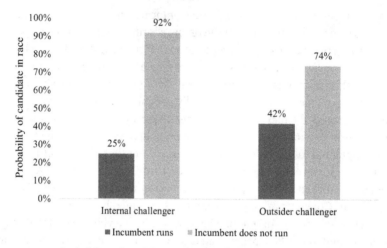

FIGURE 2.9. Probability of candidate with internal or external experience on the ballot
Note: Post-hoc predicted values from model estimating likelihood internal
challenger enters race, with controls for incumbent, population, size of office,
with fixed effects for county. See Results appendix for full results.

candidate running increases to 92 percent. In comparison to other elected offices, this is a very strong "scare off" effect. Outside challengers' behavior is shaped by the incumbent as well, but the difference in likelihood of running is smaller: a 42 percent chance that an outside challenger enters against an incumbent compared to a 74 percent chance without an incumbent.

As part of their routine management, sheriffs have a variety of tools at their disposal to change the likelihood of facing an internal challenger, including keeping dissatisfied employees happy with extra resources. In figure 2.10, we look at the likelihood that an internal challenger runs for sheriff in any election. We find that the probability that an internal challenger emerges is negatively correlated with the sheriff's payroll—that is, in offices where the sheriff's payroll decreased, the probability that a challenger emerges increases (even as we control for whether there is an incumbent, population of county, size of sheriff's office, change in the number of employees in previous year, and change in payroll). These estimates also use fixed effects for county, which means that we are comparing each county to itself over time. In short: in counties where the sheriff has slashed payroll, he is more likely to face an internal challenger. This incentivizes sheriffs to keep the pay. We take up this question again in chapter 3, where we consider the ways that sheriffs might react when an internal candidate emerges as a challenger in an election.

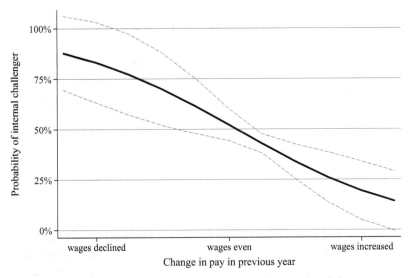

FIGURE 2.10. Probability challenger emerges in California sheriff elections

Note: Post-hoc predicted values from model estimating likelihood internal challenger enters race, with controls for incumbent, population of county, size of sheriff's office, change in the number of employees in previous year, and change in payroll, with fixed effects for county. See Results appendix for full results.

The need to suppress potential opponents from within your own subordinate ranks leads to a wide set of bad behaviors by sheriffs. Deputies running against their bosses have faced accusations of retaliation, demotion for the political competition, or sometimes outright firing. And when sheriffs are sued for retaliation, it is the county that pays the financial settlement, not the sheriff himself (Lerten 2021). Deputies do not even need to actually run for office to face these actions from a sheriff (News8000 2020)—many suffer consequences for simply supporting a sheriff's opponent (Martinez 2021; Paul 2020). After losing an election, sheriffs may seek retaliation: they spend money, fire deputies, run up overtime, and impede the success of their successor (Sheet 2019). Sometimes this bad behavior by the sheriff backfires; several participants in our survey noted that they ran for office after retaliatory behavior by a prior sheriff. As one wrote, "I felt the incumbent had destroyed a once good agency and everyone was scared to run." Another told us, "[I] did not like the past administration's treatment of the citizens of the county or the employees of the sheriff's office."

The Possibility of Change?

Sheriff Charmaine McGuffey grew up in Hamilton County, Ohio, and served for more than thirty years in the Hamilton County Sheriff's Office, rising to the rank of major and commander of Jail and Court Services before eventually seeking office. In many ways, Sheriff McGuffey exemplifies how women sheriffs today follow a similar path to political office as their male counterparts: almost all have law enforcement experience prior to running, and the majority worked in their office prior to election. The election was personal: McGuffey had previously filed a lawsuit against the incumbent sheriff, Jeff Neil, claiming she was fired in 2017 from her position because she is a gay woman, and because she raised concerns over excessive use of force (Avery 2021); eventually, she decided "I can do a better job than" Neil, which gave her the motivation to successfully run against him in 2020 (M. Cramer 2020). In the campaign, she accused him of excessive force, harassment, and zero accountability (McGuffey 2020). McGuffey's Twitter bio (with 2,700 followers) now reads, "Sheriff of Hamilton County, OH. 34-year law enforcement veteran. Committed to accountability, transparency, community engagement, and justice reform."

McGuffey's path to political office came through the Democratic primary, where she defeated Neil by earning the party's endorsement and 70 percent of the vote. Newspaper accounts focused on her criminal justice reform message (Assunção 2020) and anger at Neil, who was registered and running as a Democrat at the time, for attending a Trump rally in 2016 and coordinating with federal Immigration and Customs Enforcement.[29] The degree to which messages like McGuffey's work to oust incumbent sheriffs is in an empirical question with few answers. Political scientists de Benedictis-Kessner, Sides, and Warshaw, who recently examined vote choice for sheriff in twenty-four communities across the country, found "very limited evidence that citizens' views of police, including performance evaluations as well as policy preferences, are associated with voting for . . . sheriff" (de Benedictis-Kessner, Sides, and Warshaw 2022). There is still much yet to learn about how sheriffs campaign and how voters make decisions in sheriff elections. Given the overrepresentation of white men in the office, we also know almost nothing about how voters evaluate gender, race, or sexual orientation of sheriff candidates (Lublin and Brewer 2003).

Since taking office, McGuffey has faced a variety of challenges: she inherited a jail out of compliance with state and national standards and staffing issues that upped overtime and increased the budget. Under her watch, the Hamilton County Sheriff's Office has seen media attention for excessive use of force from a deputy, another deputy arrested for driving under the influence, and the firing of another deputy with a 3Percenters (a far-right anti-government militia) flag on their social media accounts (Cheatham 2021b).[30] The sheriff has also clashed with other political leaders on political issues, testifying against a concealed carry bill that passed the Ohio legislature and about budget issues with the county commission (Planalp 2021). News agencies in Hamilton County regularly publish stories about the sheriff, deviating from the norm across the United States.

What encourages local political competition, and why are sheriffs so immune to it? Local political competition flourishes with robust local political party training for leaders from different groups and organizations, with strong local civic culture, and with the presence of local newspapers, particularly those with political reporters (Rubado and Jennings 2020). These pose problems for political competition for the office of sheriff: sheriffs have been more sheltered from party politics and the nationalization of local politics over the last two decades (Thompson 2020; Hopkins 2018; Zoorob 2020; 2022). Rural areas, where sheriffs are particularly powerful, face high levels of inequality and low levels of infrastructure, social capital, and civil engagement (Kim, Kim, and Altema McNeely 2020; K. J. Cramer 2016; Berlet and Sunshine 2019).

The lack of competition in sheriff elections is indicative of broader themes in American local politics. While in theory democratic elections could provide important mechanisms of accountability, we do not find extensive evidence that elections hold sheriffs accountable. But this is not all that different from the low levels of turnout (Trounstine 2011), lack of information about candidates (Lucas 2022; Holman and Lay 2021; Bernhard and Freeder 2020), and obfuscation by multiple layers of government (Mullin 2008; Dynes 2022) and election timing (de Benedictis-Kessner 2017; Trounstine 2013) that occurs across elected positions at the local level in the United States. That people do not necessarily understand the difference between a police chief and a sheriff likely further inhibits the ability of voters to hold sheriffs accountable for their behavior in office. In this chapter, we have explored who sheriffs are and their elections—next we turn to how the electoral nature of the office shapes their powers and responsibilities.

CHAPTER THREE

Sheriffs' Authority as Elected Officials

K9 Deputy Mako is busy on the job: an Instagram post captures the yellow lab's patrol in Big Pine Key, Florida, with his handler, measuring lobsters, counting catches, and issuing tickets.[1] The Monroe County Sheriff's Office's (MCSO) social media pages cover this activity extensively: if it is July, then Sheriff Rick Ramsay and his deputies (human and K9) patrol for lobster poachers. The sheriff's office issues more tickets for undersized or over-limit catches of lobsters than the rest of the state combined.[2] K9 Deputy Mako frequently stars in other promotional contexts—up on tables with drug busts, among children in the summer through the Sheriff's Office Explorers Program, and serving as a crossing guard to remind drivers to slow down around pedestrians. Even though MCSO is not constitutionally nor legislatively required to offer K9 services, Deputy Mako appears almost as frequently on the office's social media as does Sheriff Rick Ramsay.

Sheriff Ramsay's jurisdiction includes the entirety of the Florida Keys from Key Largo to Key West (13 percent of the landmass of the county), as well as Everglades National Park, which makes up 87 percent of the county but has only seventeen residents. While the county is the largest in total area in Florida, more than two-thirds of the county are open water around the Keys and the base of the state (US Census). And although the year-round population of the Florida Keys tops out at about eighty-five thousand, more than five million visitors come to the Keys each year, meaning Sheriff Ramsay manages a lot of a water and a lot of visitors in the southernmost county in the US. In a YouTube video produced by the Florida Sheriffs' Association, Ramsay says, "I'm blessed to go out, have a nice community where people know me and I go and I just love people, 'Hey sheriff, how you doing sheriff, what's going on, how you doing, you are doing a great job, love what is going on, we love your initiatives' you know it just makes you feel so good that you are actually making these differences."

Sheriff Ramsay appears to be well liked in the Florida Keys community, as he has run unopposed for the last two elections (raising a total of $300 in donations across the 2016 and 2020 elections) and has low turnover in his staff. MCSO maintains seven jails in the county, arrested 876 people in 2019, and has a crime clearance rate of 43 percent, which puts the office a full 20 percent over clearance rates of other similarly sized offices in Florida. Deputies in the office killed two people in the line of duty in the last decade (a low number in comparison to other similarly sized agencies), with the sheriff immediately engaging in outside investigations in both instances. Ramsay detains prisoners for ICE,[3] but he does not publicly espouse anti-immigrant rhetoric, nor does his name appear on any invitation lists for anti-immigrant events organized by right-wing organizations like the Federation for American Immigration Reform (SPLC 2023). When expressing frustration with the Biden administration's efforts to deal with the primarily Haitian and Cuban migrants who regularly land on the county's shores (Craig 2022), Ramsay described the issue as a humanitarian problem and reiterated that immigration was the federal government's responsibility, not his. Sheriff Ramsay, as far as we can tell, has never visited the White House for any event for Obama, Trump, or Biden. He did not sign an antigun control statement that was widely embraced by Florida sheriffs in 2013, and after the Uvalde shooting, the sheriff argued in the local paper for gun safety laws, such as enhanced background checks on all gun purchases. What shapes Sheriff Ramsay's approach in leading Monroe County Sheriff's Office?

To understand offices like Sheriff Ramsay's, we draw on a deep body of scholarship in political science that details the motivations of elected officials to describe how elected officials are driven by a wide set of personal and professional aims. Pursuing these aims requires that officials seek to be reelected to office (Mayhew 1974; Dietrich, Hayes, and O'Brien 2019; Decadri 2021). Our focus on election and reelection as a central motivator for sheriffs departs from many of the existing evaluations of the office, which view sheriffs as pseudo-bureaucratic actors working in a criminal justice system (i.e., Decker 1979; Bromley and Cochran 1999; Doerner and Doerner 2010; Helms 2008; 2007; Helms, Gutierrez, and Reeves-Gutierrez 2016; McCarty and Dewald 2017; Patten et al. 2015; Perez, Bromley, and Cochran 2017; Vardalis and Waters 2010; Cochran, Bromley, and Landis 1999; Cochran, Bromley, and Swando 2002). While we agree with these scholars' descriptions of sheriffs' behaviors, we argue that this bureaucratic behavior should be evaluated as functioning within the environment where sheriffs are dependent on reelection. This chapter offers an assessment of the powers and responsibilities of sheriffs and how those intersect with the electoral nature of the office.

The reelection mandate is true regardless of the malicious or virtuous motivations of someone seeking political office. As scholars studying political succession note, "Except for the rare incumbent who voluntarily steps down, leaders overwhelmingly act as if they want to hold on to power as long as they possibly can" (Bueno de Mesquita and Smith 2017, 708). For example, if a sheriff seeks office because of his interest in creating a safe community, his ability to do so is dependent on whether he can continue to engage in the policies to provide safety. He is thus interested in reelection as a precursor to all these other outcomes of interest. Similarly, if an individual wants to be sheriff because he is interested in being a powerful member of his community and wants to use the office to help his friends and family and further his own fortunes, he also is interested in reelection. After all, he cannot accomplish any of those goals if he loses access to the resources associated with the office.

But seeking reelection for sheriffs is a black box: while we show in chapter 2 that sheriffs enjoy a large incumbency advantage and control their potential future political opposition, we know very little about how sheriffs convince voters to let them keep the office. The literature on the effect of crime rates and criminal justice policy on voting is slim but generally suggests very few connections between actual crime rates and how voters make political decisions. Even though criminal justice is a salient issue in local politics (Hopkins and McCabe 2012), crime rates rarely impact the outcome of local elections (Hopkins and Pettingill 2018). When crime does shape voting, it appears to largely play a role in national voting patterns rather than local—for example, voters hold national parties responsible for criminal justice policy in some circumstances (Drago, Galbiati, and Sobbrio 2020). And in their evaluation of voting for local offices in twenty-four communities, de Benedictis-Kessner, Sides, and Warshaw (2022) find that voters *do not* generally vote for sheriff based on their preferences for criminal justice policy. In an environment where local politics are increasingly nationalized (Hopkins 2018) and voters often hold little direct information about the performance, duties, and capacity of local office (Bernhard and Freeder 2020; Holman and Lay 2021), voters "fail to connect performance with judgments of government" (de Benedictis-Kessner 2018, 1417). Instead, they make decisions about local elections based on the economy (de Benedictis-Kessner and Warshaw 2020a), assumptions about ideology (Holman and Lay 2021), endorsements (Benjamin 2017a; 2017b; 2022; Benjamin and Miller 2019), and the race and gender of local representatives (Holman 2017; Crowder-Meyer, Gadarian, and Trounstine 2015; Crowder-Meyer et al. 2018).

Where, then, does this leave sheriffs, who must seek reelection but may not be evaluated based on how they actually perform in that position? In this chapter, we argue that if reelection is the goal, this is achieved by sheriffs increasing their authority and decreasing their accountability. Authority is key because it helps sheriffs demonstrate capacity for leadership, cultivate a brand and image in the county, and frame the office (and the man who holds the office) as a unique and essential component of the local community. Authority also produces more employees for the sheriff, thus furthering his ability to control his potential political opponents. Decreasing accountability means cultivating a personal relationship with voters (McGregor 2018; McGregor, Lawrence, and Cardona 2017) and suppressing political opposition. The value of increasing authority and decreasing accountability interact in that authority can also help sheriffs stifle electoral competition, reward followers, and build local power structures, and a lack of accountability can help the sheriff expand powers without oversight. In this chapter, we explore sheriffs' powers and responsibilities with their goals of reelection in mind.

Sheriffs' Powers and Responsibilities

We start with the understanding that sheriffs have two sets of powers: those that sheriffs are legally granted with the office (or what we refer to as formal powers) and those that are assumed as components of duties assigned or created (what we call informal or assumed powers). For instance, a state may legally task sheriffs with the formal powers of providing jail facilities. But how the sheriff does that—for example, whether he offers alternative care programs, work release, or job training—are all dependent on a combination of state grants and requirements and the decision of the sheriff or his staff to create new programs. Similarly, a state might grant the responsibility of "preserving the peace," but how exactly he does that is largely up to the sheriff himself.

FORMAL POWERS

In his 1884 treatise on sheriffs, Murfree writes, "The sheriff is, in each of the United States, a constitutional officer, recognized *eo nomine* as part of the machinery of the state government" (Murfree 1884). Because of this, although state legislatures could add or subtract powers from his portfolio of duties, it was, "upon well established legal principles, beyond their powers to circumscribe his common-law functions or to transfer them to other officers" (Murfree 1884). In comparison to city governments, which struggled with state legislative control and limitations on their powers beginning during this time, counties (and sheriffs) did not experience similar constraints (Krane, Rigos, and Hill 2001). Indeed, Murfree (1884) notes that the state legislature "cannot strip [the sheriff] of his time-honored and common-law functions and devolve them upon the incumbents of other offices created by legislative author." In this way, sheriffs have remained remarkably autonomous in the face of broader patterns toward increased oversight and control of local government by state governments.

In many original state constitutions, the office of the sheriff is designated as a core executive office, granted a wide set of powers.[4] Over the twentieth century, state court rulings affirmed the sheriffs' independence, noting that a sheriff "possesses certain common-law powers and duties of which he cannot be deprived by legislature"[5] and that a sheriffs' powers are via "constitutional implication."[6] States amended their constitutions during the twentieth century, but the constitutional powers of sheriffs remained fairly stable. In thirty-five states, the sheriff's office is constitutionally created, which differs significantly from the administrative or legislative origins of most police agencies and local political actors (Falcone and Wells 1995).

States generally task the sheriff with securing courthouse facilities and running jails, as well as broad responsibilities like preserving the peace,[7] arresting individuals committing crimes, and the duty to "prevent and suppress all affrays, breaches of the peace, riots, and insurrections which may come to the sheriff's knowledge."[8] States also grant sheriffs additional law enforcement tasks that range from executing warrants and facilitating work-release programs to handling K9 programs. In some states, sheriffs additionally serve as the coroner or the tax collector.[9] In other states, expanded power for the office is derived from state legislation. This distinction is important as it is far more difficult to change the constitution than to write new legislation in most states; as we discuss in chapter 6, reforms to the office might involve removing certain capacities from the office, but the path to do so is very different across states.

Even within states, sheriffs vary significantly in how much power their offices have, often relative to the size of the constituency and the presence or absence of other police agencies within the county. For example, most highly populated counties in the Northeast and South have separate police agencies who carry out most law enforcement activities, with the sheriff only managing the jail and providing courthouse security. In the West, however, sheriffs often retain significant law enforcement powers—for example, the sheriff's office of Los Angeles County is the largest local law enforcement agency in not just the county but the entire country. Even though cities across Los Angeles County can have their own police agencies, the sheriff's department provides general law enforcement services for forty-two of the cities in the county. In addition, Los Angeles Sheriff's Department provides general law enforcement services for many other local institutions, including courts, schools, hospitals, and public transportation in the county, and all the services for unincorporated areas.

THE OFFICE YOU WANT, NOT THE OFFICE YOU HAVE: SHERIFFS' INFORMAL POWERS

While almost all sheriffs run jails and provide courthouse security, most also engage in a wide set of community activities that fall under the umbrella of "law enforcement" or keeping the peace. Some examples help illustrate these informal powers: Can a sheriff run an annual summer camp for kids? Yes, like MCSO's Explorer Program, many sheriffs do.[10] Rescue injured bald eagles (KCCI 2021)? Yes, sheriffs may also act as game wardens in some places. Limit where people can drive and park in the county because an eclipse can be viewed in the local area and, as Sheriff Scott Berry from Oconee County, Georgia, explains, "There is absolutely no way we can predict exactly how many people will be coming into our county" (Merchant 2017)? Yes, sheriffs often serve as the point person for many local events. Establish a "no-wake" zone in the local lakes (Day 2021)? Yes, sheriffs can make and enforce laws on land, on water, and in the air. The independence and flexibility are hallmarks of the office and make it both interesting and difficult to define.

These assumed powers emerge out of local opportunities: sheriffs buy boats and patrol waterways because they can and because county residents and visitors engage in legal and illegal activities on waterways. *Other sheriffs do not have boats because there are no waterways in their county.* What sheriffs do is deeply shaped by where they serve.[11] But it is not just where the sheriff serves that shapes what he does—sheriffs themselves make decisions about how and where to allocate resources in enforcing the wide set of laws. Sheriff Ramsay and Monroe County Sheriff's Office write more tickets for violations of the laws that protect Florida lobsters because they are granted that power by the county regulations, but also because Ramsay has made a policy decision to invest resources like "extra patrols at boat ramps, bridges and on the water" (Associated Press 2021a) in monitoring Florida lobster harvests.[12] The MCSO also maintains the Sheriff's Office Animal Farm, a facility with more than 150 animals (including lemurs, emus, and a sloth named Molasses, who unfortunately passed of old age in 2022). The Sheriff's Office Animal Farm is located in an open-air area under the jail, staffed by those incarcerated in the jail, and is free for the public to access two weekends a month. The sheriff's office engages the public and portrays a positive community image with the help from creatures such as Hank the armadillo, June Carter the opossum, and BamBam the alpaca.[13]

As one might suspect, running an animal sanctuary is not listed among the duties of sheriffs in Florida, nor are neighborhood cleanups hosted by Sheriff Ramsay and his landscaping truck. Sheriff Ramsay's proactive presence in the community is strategic, as outlined in the MCSO 2020 annual report, where the sheriff promotes his adoption of the "broken windows theory"[14] of crime with his philosophy of "Cleaner Safer Streets, is Cleaner Safer Neighborhoods" (MCSO 2022). Sheriff Ramsay focused the idea that these activities are connected to a broader landscape of crime prevention in a 2017 video to new staff: "It's a proven fact that cleaner neighborhoods are safer neighborhoods. That's why you'll see the sheriff's office out doing community clean-ups . . . not just focusing not just solely on crime prevention or crime investigation, but quality of life. Trying to make people's lives that much better. And with this, we are able to prevent crime from occurring. It is critical to have the citizens know us, like us, trust us."[15]

Like many sheriffs, Sheriff Ramsay recognizes that his job requires reminding the public about what a sheriff is and does. From social media posts on Facebook (74,000 followers), Twitter (20,000 followers), and Instagram (574 posts in the last three years) to a frequently updated blog, to a deputy who writes for a small Key West newspaper,[16] the MCSO works to frame and control how people see the office and the daily work of its deputies. Sheriffs' offices work to make their presence in the community more visible. Sheriff deputies hand out to children's coloring books, stickers, and badges with the sheriff's name. The sheriff's office in Orange County, Florida, rolls out its mobile video game theater with eleven large screens to better connect with kids in the community (Parham 2022). Sheriff Tony Thompson of Black Hawk County, Iowa, rides a donkey while playing basketball in a high school gym for a sober after-prom party fundraiser.[17] While sheriffs often connect efforts of involving the community as part of a broader public safety plan, these efforts have an additional, typically unstated, goal: they assist with sheriffs' reelection. Sheriffs work to form an image of their offices in voters' minds by engaging in image management for their office.

Sheriffs as Managers (of Their Political Competition)

To carry out their powers, managing people is a core responsibility of sheriffs. Many of the responsibilities of the office of sheriff involve hiring, train-

TABLE 3.1. Size of sheriff's offices (2020)

	Number of officers	Percent of sheriffs' offices	Annual per office operating budget
500+ sworn officers	38	1.3%	$479,402,054
250–499	78	2.7	$94,596,311
100–249	241	8.3	$34,209,969
50–99	347	12.0	$12,963,505
25–49	635	22.0	$5,535,108
24 or fewer	1549	53.6	$1,852,730

Note: Data from LEMAS (2020)

ing, and supervising employees. In 2020, more than 360,000 full-time law enforcement employees worked for sheriffs' offices (LEMAS 2020). More than a third of all full-time law enforcement employees, including 25 percent of all sworn law enforcement officers (or those who carry a firearm and badge and have full arrest powers) and more than half of civilian law enforcement officers work for a sheriff (LEMAS 2020). There is enormous variation in the size and function of sheriffs' offices, with offices ranging from having one full-time employee (usually the sheriffs themselves) to more than twenty thousand employees. Over half of sheriffs supervise small offices with fewer than twenty-five employees, and approximately three-quarters of offices have fewer than fifty employees (see table 3.1). Even though more than half of sheriffs' offices have less than twenty-five employees, these offices still collectively employ more than fifteen thousand sworn officers (LEMAS 2020).

When we asked sheriffs about their central challenges in the office, many focused on staffing, with 43 percent of sheriffs in 2012 and 58 percent in 2021 mentioning staffing issues as a core concern. In our surveys, issues with staffing, including hiring, retention, training, and culture, are the most common challenges noted by sheriffs; one simply wrote, "Under-staffed, under-staffed, under-staffed." This was echoed by a variety of responses focused on recruitment and retention of trained staff. Here are some of the responses we received:

- Inability to retain well trained deputies due to wage/economic issues.
- Unable to get qualified and applicants that have the skill and qualities to the job
- COMPETENT EMPLOYEES
- Less interest by quality individuals for careers in law enforcement.
- Lack of good applicants [because of the] current culture.

FIGURE 3.1. Sheriffs' office share of county employees and payroll
Note: All sheriffs' offices. Data from the Census on Local Governments.
See Data and Methods appendix for a more detailed discussion.

Sheriffs often focus on the issues of hiring qualified individuals, especially at the salaries offered by the office. One sheriff noted that "all employees are paid below poverty level making it hard to attract quality employees. When a person can better provide for them self and family on government assistance then by working for [my office]." This echoes complaints that sheriffs regularly present to county commissioners in requests to increase their budgets—for instance, in 2021, Sheriff Jeff Cope of Lyon County, Kansas, requested a 10 percent increase in funding for the law enforcement, jail department, and emergency management budgets and told county commissioners, "We've got to do something with our wages. We're just not attracting the quality applicants that we need" (DeLoach 2022).

When we look at the actual data on the share of county employees that sheriffs manage and the payroll associated with those employees, sheriffs' share of employees and payroll of counties have increased from 20 to 25 percent from 1994 to 2020 (see fig. 3.1).

Sheriffs frequently cite low pay as a major challenge to the office; as one told us, "Preparing for the future to continue being competitive in one of the lowest paying fields." Like Sheriff Cope, Sheriff Ed Brady pleaded with Henderson County, Kentucky, commissioners to raise pay as deputies were leaving for better paying jobs in nearby agencies, noting the range of starting pay was $39,000–$52,000 at other agencies, compared to his office's starting pay at $39,000 (Smith 2020). In some offices, losing just one deputy can have a large impact: in another Kentucky county, the resignation of one of the four deputies in the Owen County Sheriff's Office made local news when the deputy cited low pay and lack of benefits as his reason for leaving (Haines 2018).

Elected managers: The role of sheriff as an employee manager is deeply complicated by the electoral nature of the office. As we noted in chapter 2, the overwhelming majority of sheriffs have law enforcement experience, and most served in their own office prior to their election. This makes for unique elections: for each sheriff, there is a high likelihood that he is currently supervising his political competition. This creates a particular set of incentives for sheriffs as they make choices about who gets a job, receives training, or is promoted.

Sheriffs emphasize the democratic accountability associated with their office. In the context of electoral offices, competitive elections function as the main source of accountability. As Carter and Nordstrom (2017) point out, "Democracies behave differently than dictatorships because elections allow citizens to hold leaders accountable for their policy choices." But what if an elected leader has the capacity to shape the pool of potential challenging candidates because he oversees most of them? We show that sheriff elections are rarely competitive, incumbent sheriffs serve for multiple terms (often for decades), and sheriffs frequently resign before they leave office so that they can select their successor. As we discuss in chapter 2, one reason that sheriffs enjoy an office that appears to be democratic, and yet is not by any definition of the term, is that sheriffs control the pool of their political competition by directly managing those individuals who might one day challenge them for their job.

What kinds of incentives does this create for sheriffs? We present two scenarios and provide data to demonstrate how sheriffs engage in accountability reduction through management. Each assumes that the sheriff wants to retain his job and knows that qualified political competition is a challenge to his continued position and that the political competition is most likely to emerge from his own staff.

Scenario 1—keep your staff satisfied: A staff that is satisfied in their positions and happy with their boss, and that feel there is opportunity for growth within the organization, will be less likely to challenge the sheriff electorally. In this scenario, a sheriff will want to invest heavily in training employees, will lobby for higher pay and benefits for his existing employees, and will reward high-achieving individuals with more power and leadership. When challenged by someone in his own office, the sheriff should *increase pay and training* to make his employees happier and more loyal.

Scenario 2—keep your staff undertrained and undercompensated: If the jobs in a sheriff's office are frustrating to the staff, this presents a potential challenge to the sheriff electorally. In this scenario, sheriffs will keep pay

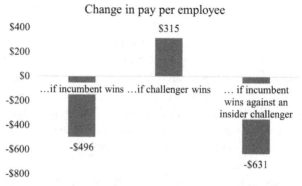

FIGURE 3.2. Change in pay per employee for sheriffs' offices
by the outcome of elections in California
Note: Data from Sheriffs in California; CEDA and Census of Governments.
Challenger characteristics coded by authors. Fixed effect (county)
regression models. See Results appendix for full models.

low, punish dissenters, and limit the potential for growth. These sheriffs
will also promote from within but not necessarily promote high-achieving
individuals. Loyal staff do not need to be particularly well trained, but they
do need to be compensated in various ways, including through resources
such as weapons, cars, and K9 dogs. The sheriff will often retire before the
end of his term to appoint his successor, thus assuring that a loyal member
of his staff is rewarded.

To test the likelihood of these two scenarios, we turn back again to the
data from California on who runs for the office of the sheriff. Here, we focus on two dependent variables: the number of employees and the pay per
employee in the sheriff's office. For each, we again use the Census of Local
Governments data on the number of employees and payroll and look at the
change in the total number of employees and the pay per employee. Payroll
data is standardized for inflation, so all funds are in 2020 dollars. We look
at the change in payroll from a point during the incumbent sheriff's tenure
and one to two years after the election in question. We use county fixed effects to make sure we are measuring the change *within each county*.

In figure 3.2, we present the change in pay per employee if the incumbent sheriff wins, if an internal challenger wins, and then the interaction
between if the incumbent sheriff wins after being challenged by an internal
challenger. Sheriffs' offices where the incumbent sheriff wins against an insider challenger reduce their per-employee spending by more than $600,
whereas if the challenger wins, he increases the per-employee spending by
more than $300.

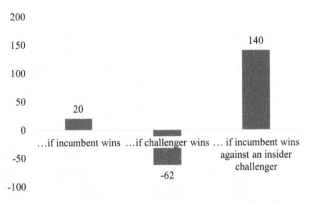

FIGURE 3.3. Change in number of employees for sheriffs' offices by
the outcome of elections in California
Note: Data from Sheriffs in California; CEDA and Census of Governments.
Challenger characteristics coded by authors. Fixed effect (county)
regression models. See Results appendix for full models.

Perhaps this is due to the sheriff simply cutting employees. In a world
where the sheriff doubts the loyalty of his employees, an election might
lead to a purge of the non-faithful. But instead, what we see (fig. 3.3) is a remarkable *growth* in the number of employees when an incumbent sheriff is
challenged by an insider candidate. Taken together, these two pieces of evidence suggest a workforce control story that is most consistent with sheriffs
attempting to grow the number of employees they have (thus spending and
extending their capacity) but not to pay them well, thus not attracting tal-
ent that might become challengers. In this way, sheriffs use their workforce
management tools to discourage accountability.

THE COUNTY'S "LARGEST HOTEL":
OPERATING A COUNTY JAIL

The United States incarcerates more people than any other nation; while
research often focuses on the remarkable growth of the prison population
across the latter half of the twentieth century, a similar growth occurred in
the jail population (Gottschalk 2006; 2014). Indeed, if we counted only the
local jail population, the United States would still top global incarceration
rates (Hernández 2017). These jails are run by sheriffs: 85 percent of sheriffs
operate more than 2,800 jails in the United States. Of the fifty largest jails
in the United States, forty-seven are under the control of elected sheriffs.[18]
Cumulatively, sheriffs oversee a daily jail population of more than seven

hundred thousand individuals, with more than ten million individuals admitted to a jail in a single year (Zeng and Minton 2021). In comparison to state prisons (where the majority of the population is supervised outside prisons through parole or community supervision), only a small fraction (5 percent) of those under the supervision of sheriffs are supervised outside of jail (Zeng and Minton 2021; Kluckow and Zeng 2022; Deng 2020). Running these jails requires funding, staff, and policies; for example, sheriffs report an average of thirty-two employees that work in the jail.[19]

What is a jail, and how does it compare to a prison?[20] While prisons are often distinguished from jails by the length of term that the imprisoned serves (with prisons holding individuals for longer periods) and the severity of the crime (with prisons holding those charged with felonies), the reality is that many jails hold individuals (some accused of or serving time for felonies) for long periods of time. The Bureau of Justice Statistics differentiates between the two by calling the jail population those "held in confinement facilities operated under the authority of a sheriff, police chief, or city or county administrator" while the prison population are those "in a long-term confinement facility run by a state or the federal government" (Kluckow and Zeng 2022, 2). Most individuals awaiting trials who are not released on bail (or cannot afford bail payments) are held in jails. In many states, jails can hold those serving sentences of less than a year. In comparison, the prison population is largely made up of those serving sentences usually for felonies and for periods of longer than a year. These characteristics are reflected in the populations in sheriffs' jails: in 2019, 34.5 percent of the population of jails were being held prior to conviction, compared to 65.5 percent post-conviction. The severity of crimes also reflects the short-term nature of jails: 23.2 percent of those in jail in 2019 were incarcerated for a misdemeanor crime (Zeng and Minton 2021).

Sheriffs' responsibility for jails has deep roots in the history of the office—in the United States, sheriffs have always run jails, and many sheriffs and sheriff associations provide histories of the earliest jails built in their county or state. State statutes regularly refer to sheriffs as the "keepers" of the jails (Gershowitz 2016), a duty that requires sheriffs to "take charge and custody of the prisoners lawfully committed and keep them until they are discharged by law."[21] For example, in Nevada, the state names the sheriff as the "custodian of the jail in his or her county, and of the prisoners therein, and shall keep the jail personally, or by his or her deputy, or by a jailer or jailers appointed by the sheriff for that purpose, for whose acts the sheriff is responsible,"[22] and Arkansas dictates "the county sheriff of each county in this state shall have the custody, rule, and charge of the jail within his or her county."[23]

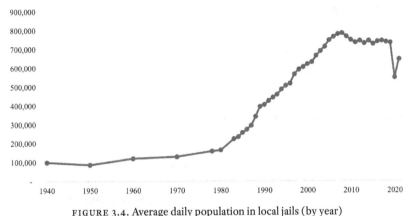

FIGURE 3.4. Average daily population in local jails (by year)
Note: Vera Institute, Prison Policy Initiative, Census Bureau, and Bureau of Justice Statistics
Corrections Statistical Analysis Tool. Figure presents the average daily population in local jails.

Sheriffs have been central actors in the growth of incarceration in the
United States (Littman 2021). Looking at the size of the jail population in
the United States over time, we see enormous growth from 1980 forward, a
leveling off in the 2000s, and a drop associated with COVID in 2020 (see fig.
3.4). However, the jail population increased again in 2021 since this COVID-
related drop. The increase in the jail population reflects a growing number of individuals who are held in pretrial detention, which has increased
threefold since 1970 (Kang-Brown and Subramanian 2017).[24] Sheriffs frequently note that changing standards frustrate their ability to oversee the
jail; one sheriff responding to our survey framed it as such: "Jail—Unfunded
statutory mandates from the State legislature," and another complained of
"poorly thought out legislation about the jail."

The centrality of jail management to a sheriffs' duties, the populations
served, and interactions with other agencies vary across states and even
within a state. While urban sheriffs often only run the jail and provide courthouse security, for rural sheriffs, the jail is but one of many responsibilities.
The sizes of jails reflect these realities and the populations served: more
than a third of sheriffs supervise jails with a daily population under fifty individuals, with 5 percent of sheriffs managing large facilities with a daily jail
population of more than one thousand individuals.

Urban and rural sheriffs also manage different populations in their jails.
The share of the population held in jails pretrial varies for rural (68 percent)
and urban (60 percent) sheriffs, as does the share of the population held
for misdemeanor crimes (26 percent for rural, 22 percent for urban). And

TABLE 3.2. Jails in the United States, 2019

	Fewer than 50	50–99	100–249	250–499	500–999	1000 or more
Number of jails	991	504	642	348	215	150
Share of jails	35%	18%	23%	12%	8%	5%

Source: Bureau of Justice Statistics, Census of Jails 2015–2019

rural sheriffs report much higher rates of holding individuals for federal, state, or tribal authorities (27 percent) compared to urban sheriffs (11 percent). The urban-rural divide of "renting" jail beds to other authorities are particularly pronounced in the US West and South, and particularly in the two states with the highest rate of incarceration—Louisiana and Kentucky (Kang-Brown and Subramanian 2017).

Louisiana stands out because the number of people held in local jails by sheriffs has exploded in the last thirty years, largely because of a federal court order that required Louisiana to reduce overcrowding in their state prisons. Rather than release prisoners or build more prisons, Louisiana began paying sheriffs a per diem for housing; this saves the state money because sheriffs receive less than half a per diem rate as compared to the cost per day for the state to hold someone in a prison. Sheriffs then constructed more jails to hold prisoners for the states. As Gottschalk (2016, 37) writes in her evaluation of the political economy of incarceration, "This quasi-public solution is a win-win situation for state and local budgets and huge loss for inmates" given the low quality of care in these jails.

Sheriffs regularly note concerns with old jails that lack modern functionality. Sheriffs routinely struggle with aging buildings and face issues with securing funding for jail maintenance; one complained on our survey of "a jail that was built in 1974." We also heard about jails out of compliance with the Americans with Disabilities Act, facilities that do not match more modern ideas of jails (where inmates are often held in groups rather than single cells), a lack cameras and other security measures, and high upkeep costs. Sheriffs regularly note that their jails do not meet current standards: one noted that "my jail has no sprinkler system," and another bemoaned "old ways of doing things in an old jail." One sheriff wrote on our survey that he was "in dire need of a new jail."

Communities thus foot the bill for the construction of a new jail. Sheriffs will often ask for a new jail with a capacity far exceeding that of the previous jail because of the "jail-bed market" (Kang-Brown and Subramanian 2017). When sheriffs encounter community pushback, they often package the jail expansion with mental health care and drug rehabilitation services; these packages are "publicly promoted as the community's best solution to these problems" (Mai et al. 2019). This incarceration-as-care is what James Kilgore (2014) refers to as "carceral humanism," or the strategy of remaking law enforcement agencies into social service providers while simultaneously reducing direct funding to social service agencies.

Running for office while running a jail: Jails are a political obstacle for sheriffs to navigate. The daily work of running a jail is incompatible with an elected leader seeking reelection, in part because they are politically unpopular. After all, being a jailor does not net sheriffs that electoral support that is needed to continue to hold the job and often produces a wide set of problems that might complicate reelection campaigns. As a scholar noted in the 1980s, "The only type of vote a sheriff is likely to receive as a result of his jail responsibilities is a negative one—caused by an untimely escape, disorder, or inmate death" (J. A. Thompson 1986, 112).[25] As a result, sheriffs seek alternative benefits from jails, including financial benefits, expanding the workforce, and using the jail to justify the carceral state. These incentives mean that sheriffs seek ways to increase the number of individuals in their jails, to increase the size of their jails, and to increase the budgets for their jails.

Although those in jail are often of the sheriff's constituency (in that they may live in the county and may be eligible to vote), the jail population is also simultaneously unlikely to be the constituency that a sheriff worries about pleasing electorally. The personal contact between individuals in the jail and the sheriff is termed "custodial citizenship" (Lerman and Weaver 2014b; Walker 2020) and can provide clear lessons to individuals about the functions and fairness of governing structures in their communities (Lerman and Weaver 2014a; Weaver, Prowse, and Piston 2019). While much of this work focuses on those convicted of crimes, these patterns likely extend more broadly: Brayne (2014, 383) finds that "individuals who have been stopped, arrested, convicted, or incarcerated are less likely to interact with institutions that keep formal records, such as hospitals, banks, employment, and schools." Those in jail vote at lower rates (White 2019) and are often disenfranchised through a variety of mechanisms, not limited to a broader dissatisfaction with the political and justice systems (Manza and Uggen 2008; Walker 2014) and legal barriers that stop those convicted of felonies from voting (Morris 2021). Sheriffs thus see inmates not necessarily as potential voters but as subjects whose existence increases and complicates their workload.

Jails also represent a key point of tension between sheriffs and other county leaders. As we have previously discussed, while sheriffs have an enormous amount of autonomy in the decisions they make, they are typically dependent on the local county commission for funding. As a result, sheriffs can spend only the money granted to them by the commission or funds that they raise themselves. Because the county commission is also interested in reelection, they want to spend funds on those items that voters will appreciate and recognize. That might include funding programs and services that directly benefit those with the most power in the county, such as local business leaders, or those the majority of the county agrees deserve support, such as education or park facilities (Schneider and Ingram 1993; Kreitzer, Maltby, and Smith 2023; Kreitzer and Smith 2018). Not only are those in jail not powerful (Lerman and Weaver 2014b), but residents view them as undeserving of policy support (Kreitzer and Smith 2018). Thus, even if a sheriff wanted to spend lots of money on improving conditions in his jail for those incarcerated, he would run up against the hurdle of obtaining that funding from the county commissioners.

The characteristics of the populations in county jails further limit the likelihood of counties spending funds on jails, particularly those experiencing mental health crises or those with substance abuse issues, both of which are populations that the general public is traditionally uninterested in assisting through tax funds (de Benedictis-Kessner and Hankinson 2019; Kreitzer, Maltby, and Smith 2023). As one sheriff noted, "We are a small community with limited resources and our jail ends up housing folks who need Psychiatric help, not jail." Another told us, "Jail is not the answer in a lot of cases and we have no where to house them who are not able to function in society but yet are not necessarily criminals."[26] Sheriffs connect these mental health issues to changes in funding for mental health facilities ("There are less beds for those in need [of mental health care] now than there was 20 years ago"), drug problems in their communities (as one sheriff put it, "Generational welfare and drug and alcohol abuse that leads to mental health issues"), and interpersonal violence, abuse, and neglect. Sheriffs regularly estimate that between 20 and 25 percent of the jail population is incarcerated due to mental illness (Carroll 2016)[27] and another 25 percent due to substance abuse issues.

Jails—and inmates—also provide an additional concern for sheriffs because of the litigious nature of incarceration in the United States (Gunderson 2020). The National Sheriffs' Association notes that "jails are one of the most litigious and largest liability concerns a sheriff faces." The report *Sheriff's Guide to Effective Jail Operations*, issued by the Department of Justice, notes, "Given public safety concerns and the high potential for liability associated with incarceration, the operation of the jail is undoubtedly one of the sheriff's most critical duties" (Martin and Katsampes 2007, vii). Among the sheriffs who publicly report civilian complaints (approximately 10 percent of sheriffs), the jail is the overwhelming source of concern for citizens.

Yet sheriffs are often reluctant to get rid of jails. Sometimes this reluctance is couched in concern about not having a jail costing the county more; as one sheriff noted, "Our jail is closed . . . so we have to haul prisoners 44 miles one way to house them. This takes Officers away from patrol where they are needed, but we are mandated by State to house the prisoners." Another sheriff noted that the lack of a local jail changes their arrest patterns: "We either don't put people in jail that normally would be or if we have to transport a bulk of our prisoners to [another] County," which might run as much as $900 in transportation costs. But given the high costs of maintaining their own jail, it is difficult to assess whether the costs of transportation would outweigh those of actually running a jail.

The conditions of confinement in jails are opaque (Deitch 2009b; 2020). The United States lacks a cohesive system of oversight and instead primarily relies on federal courts as reactive responses to harmful conditions. Scholars note a variety of approaches that could include oversight in multiple forms of regulation, audits, accreditation, reporting, legislative, investigation and/or monitoring (Deitch 2009a). A 2010 report concludes, "Formal and comprehensive external oversight—in the form of inspections and routine monitoring of conditions that affect the rights of prisoners—is truly rare in this country" (Deitch 2009b). By 2020, there were more oversight bodies in the (still) patchwork system of jail oversight, including both state offices, such as the Washington State Office of the Corrections Ombuds, created in 2018, and local offices, such as the Delaware County Jail Oversight Body in Pennsylvania in 2019. But still, jail conditions are a challenge to assess.

Budgets as Capacity

Sheriffs receive funding from a wide set of sources, including (but not limited to) local property and sales taxes, state sales and income taxes, intergovernmental transfers from state and federal governments, fines and fees leveraged on those within the criminal justice system, fees on those outside the criminal justice system (such as for gun permits), direct fundraising in their communities, and grants from public and private sources. The diversity of sources of revenue for sheriffs may seem a bit like a tangled mess: how do you expect one person, generally not trained to manage a large budget, to handle such a broad set of resources? But also contained within this complexity are opportunities for sheriffs to expand their authority without decreasing autonomy.

As we have mentioned, concerns about budget cuts are a common talking point from sheriffs themselves. When Virginia considered changing the funding structure for local law enforcement in 2022 as a part of efforts at criminal justice reform, sheriffs reported that they would lose half their staff, if not more. "Law enforcement is a core service that cannot be compromised," Sheriff Charles Jett (Stafford County, Virginia) reported to the *Washington Times* (2022). In our survey, sheriffs report that funding limitations mean that sheriffs "seem to be reactive not proactive" and complain of "tight financial times where we can not work on projects we feel would benefit the community. We have been and are somewhat limited on our ability to be proactive." Sheriffs also connect issues with funding to the ability to hire staff to engage the public: "Funding is not sufficient to make the necessary changes, buy equipment or have additional personnel to make changes that would help the community." In this way, a lack of funding limits the ability of the sheriff's office to be a "learning organization" or an organization that is capable of adapting to new challenges, collects data to understand patterns and is actively involved in revising its own practices. Sheriffs also connect the staffing issues we discussed above directly to broader economic issues: "Budget/Revenue which relates to manpower, 50 percent of staff laid off in past two years." When we look at which sheriffs report funding issues, there are no clear patterns in these responses: sheriffs ask for more money when crime goes up as well as when crime declines, when the population grows or contracts, and when arrests go up or down.

Conflicts with county commissioners over budgets and funding are common, although not all sheriffs have conflictual relationships with other county-level elected officials. In a survey of 107 sheriffs, a quarter reported that they would cooperate with county officials to cut their budgets in a budget crisis, while others respond that they would resist through various efforts, such as making public appeals or formal litigation (LaFrance 2012). For instance, in a dramatic move, when Breathitt County, Kentucky, commissioners delayed the sheriff's budget, Sheriff John Hollan laid off all his deputies (Roberts 2020). After the sheriff's actions, the county approved the budget, plus additional funding to hire another deputy (M. Berk 2020).[28] We argue that the lack of clear oversight by the county commission over sheriffs and sheriffs' views of the office of sheriff as autonomous and with broad authority means that sheriffs are less inclined to cooperate with county commissioners when conflict arises. And because sheriffs themselves claim ownership over their office and become an embodiment of their office, any attempt to remove resources thus becomes a personal blow to the sheriff. When the commissioners of Starr County, Texas, cut Sheriff Rene "Orta" Fuentes's budget by $400,000, the sheriff responded with a public statement that began with a personal appeal: "I have been a humble public service of ALL Starr County residents for over 37 years and have always gone above and beyond to ensure the safety of the community" (D. Hendricks 2017).

Sheriffs often receive attention from the media and other government officials on budget issues. For instance, Representative Ted Poe, testifying before Congress about a visit to Sheriff Arvin West in Hudspeth County, Texas, highlighted the sheriff's budget concerns:

> Now, Sheriff West doesn't have much of a budget. In fact, he has such a small budget that he really doesn't have any vehicles. It's hard for me to understand how a sheriff's department can operate without vehicles, but here's what he does and many of the other sheriffs along the Texas-Mexico border. When they capture a drug dealer, they confiscate his vehicle, and by law they're allowed to keep that vehicle after they go through the proper channels to seize it. So most of his vehicles have come to the sheriff's department with the behest of the drug dealers. And so they're driving drug dealer vehicles, SUVs, very nice vehicles that they have confiscated from drug dealers. And those are the vehicles, the patrol vehicles, most of them trucks, pickup trucks or SUVs so they can patrol up and down this entire county. They've even seized an 18-wheeler and put the sheriff's logo on it. You know, I admire people like Sheriff West, the sheriffs along the border who will do what they need to do to secure the dignity of the United States. (CRO 2007)

Sheriffs in some counties, particularly very rural areas of the United States, do experience significant budget constraints. In Eastern Kentucky, where the local government is deeply in debt and the economy is struggling, Martin County sheriff John Kirk posted on Facebook after the county cut his budget by $75,000: "Law enforcement as we have known for the last four years will not exist. WE ARE BROKE . . . LOCK YOUR DOORS, LOAD YOUR GUNS AND GET YOU A BARKING, BITING DOG. If the Sheriff's office can't protect you, WHO WILL?" Sheriff Kirk and Martin County are not alone in their situation: In 2021, more than a third of sheriffs noted that issues associated with funding or budgets were one of their top concerns as sheriffs. And this is not just a recent problem. In 2012, federal funds associated with timber lands that had made up a large portion of Josephine County, Oregon's budget dried up (Templeton 2013). The sheriff's office, unable to convince local voters to fund the gap via initiative, dramatically cut their employees—from sixty-seven to three. As a result, most calls to 911 would be directed to call the nonemergency line. But a lack of staffing for the nonemergency line meant that those calls were not answered or were placed on hold for an extended period (Parfitt 2019). Even clear emergencies were not addressed: with no law enforcement on duty at night or on the weekends, emergency calls went unanswered, including for domestic violence and sexual assault (Templeton 2013). Gil Gilbertson, the sheriff at the time, issued a statement advising people to leave the county: "The Sheriff's Office regretfully advises that if you know you are in a potentially volatile situation (for example, you are a protected person in a restraining order that you believe the respondent may violate), you may want to consider relocating to an area with adequate law enforcement services." While voters in the county eventually approved a short-term public safety levy, those funds have now run out, and Josephine County's current sheriff, Dave Daniels, is again facing cuts (J. King 2021).

But these experiences are the exception, not the rule. Most sheriffs' budget requests are honored by their county commissioners. In many ways, this relationship between county commissioner and sheriff resembles Niskanen's (1975) classic understanding of bureaucrats as budget maximizers: sheriffs are rationally motivated to seek larger and larger budgets as money is a form of power for the office. Sheriffs have significant information control over the costs and capabilities of the office (Simard 2004; Patty and Turner 2021). Indeed, because sheriffs generally *only* need to request approval from the county commissioners for the budget but control all other policymaking decisions, this reduces accountability further by narrowing the scope of review (I. R. Turner 2018). Again, we turn to looking at the data from California, where we find that sheriffs who are reelected successfully increase their payroll budget in the following year, while insiders and outsiders have a reduced payroll budget (see fig. 3.5).

Most sheriffs are not entirely dependent on the county for funding, as many seek out alternative sources for revenue that they control (Freese 2018). Sheriffs are not unique in this activity, but we argue that they are more incentivized to do so than other law enforcement officers. In their work on predatory financial costs of criminal justice, Page and Soss (2021, 291) note, "Over the past 35 years, public and private actors have turned US criminal justice institutions into a vast network of revenue-generating operations." This is true: increasingly, the cost of interacting with the criminal justice system carries a financial penalty, with the burden laid squarely on those who typically cannot afford small and large fees. Yet, the practice of attaching financial penalties to interactions with the criminal justice system

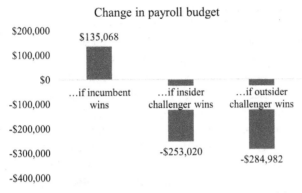

FIGURE 3.5. Changes in payroll budget after elections in California
Note: Data from elections in California, source: CEDA and Census of
Governments. Challenger characteristics coded by authors. Fixed effect
(county) regression models. See Results appendix for full models.

is not new for sheriffs. As we noted in chapter 1, sheriffs have long been
responsible for raising their own revenues from fees and fines, with specific
fees that sheriffs should receive from the criminal justice system sometimes
even laid out in state constitutions. From colonial times on, "Sheriffs typically derived their income from local fees paid for serving court papers and
housing prisoners" (Greenberg 2005, 23). It was not until 1957 that sheriffs
in Florida received a budget; prior to this point, they raised their entire
funds from fees and forfeitures (Florida Sheriffs' Association 1957). The reliance of sheriffs on nontax revenue sources continues today: more than 40
percent of sheriffs report that their offices make money off user fees, compared to just 20 percent of police departments (LEMAS 2013). In Vermont,
sheriffs are still able to increase their own salaries by providing contracted
services to other governments and private companies, with some nearly
doubling their salaries (Freese 2018).[29]

Sheriffs also seek out direct funds from state and federal agencies, particularly around immigration and increased incarceration (Norton and Kang-
Brown 2018). For example, a press release from US Representative Henry
Cuellar, a Democrat from south Texas, about how he had secured more
than $2 million in federal funds (for a total of more than $21 million over
the past fifteen years) for "border security," specifically referenced the local
sheriff: "I want to thank Starr County Sheriff Rene Fuentes, as well as the
local, state, and federal officers for their commitment to helping to secure
our southern border" (Youngentob 2021).

Sheriffs regularly fundraise for specific causes, accept donations from local businesses (Douglas 2021), and use civil asset forfeiture as a tool for purchasing equipment. In civil asset forfeiture, law enforcement agencies seize funds and property from those who interact with the criminal justice system. A small part of this revenue is obtained after a criminal conviction, but law enforcement agencies acquire the majority of their forfeiture revenue from civil asset forfeiture, which does not require a conviction for a crime (Mughan, Li, and Nicholson-Crotty 2020). Seizures by sheriffs' offices account for more than a third of total revenue from civil asset forfeiture, and a higher share of sheriff offices (compared to police departments) report some share of revenues from asset forfeiture (LEMAS 2013). Sheriff Fuentes from Starr County, Texas, argued that his office "depends on forfeiture funds for all safety equipment, tires, uniforms, and even supplemental vehicle repairs" (D. Hendricks 2017).

Yet, as Mughan and colleagues (2020) find, sheriffs have electoral incentives to *not* seize property through civil asset forfeiture; the practice is wildly unpopular with the public, with just 17 percent supporting it (Ekins 2016), and electoral incentives push sheriffs toward both seizing lower levels of assets and resisting state and federal incentives aimed at increasing civil asset forfeiture (Mughan, Li, and Nicholson-Crotty 2020). These patterns are reflected in our survey data: in 2021, more than half of sheriffs either agreed or strongly agreed that "Asset forfeiture is only appropriate after a conviction," and many more chose the option "Protecting the rights of innocent citizens from having their assets be improperly seized" (70 percent) as more important than "Seizing the assets of criminals so they cannot profit from crime" (30 percent).

Yet, sheriffs also note the importance of civil assets in keeping their offices afloat financially. In Martin County, Kentucky, assets seized offer small opportunities to make money to fill patrol cars with gasoline or pay for equipment repairs. In 2019, a truck (a 2001 Silver Toyota Tacoma SR5) seized after a drug bust was sold via sealed bids; this provided enough income to pay for office supplies and toilet paper (Lowe 2019; Jarvie 2019). In another county, the sheriff's office paid for equipment (including body-worn cameras) through auctioning off a property seized via civil asset forfeiture during a drug arrest. Another sheriff told us, "Let the people that do the offenses pay for the equipment, and we've been able to buy patrol rifles, pistols, a lot of different equipment that we wouldn't have been able to buy otherwise." In South Carolina, an expansive civil asset forfeiture law has allowed Sheriff Chuck Wright (Spartanburg County) to seize millions of dollars of money, cars, and goods, including a watch worth $50,000 (Cary 2019).

Sheriffs' struggles with funding are particularly important when it comes to funding the jail. Here, sheriffs fund the jail directly from those incarcerated within it, primarily from two sources: from the inmates themselves and by renting jail space to other local, state, and federal law enforcement agencies. Many sheriffs charge people for being in jail. The most common of these extractions is via telephone services (Wagner and Jones 2019), but prisoners are also charged for items from the commissary, for health care, and a base service fee. The Monroe County Sheriff's Office discussed at the beginning of this chapter proclaims, "Incarceration should never be free and the Sheriff's Office is always looking for ways to offset the cost to taxpayers of operating its facilities. Total jail related fees collected from inmates for 2020 were $261,204" (Monroe County Sheriff's Office 2020).[30] Many sheriffs contract the management of these funds out to a subsidiary organization, which often guarantees some base set of funds to the sheriff. As a result, inmates often pay large markups on goods at commissaries or overpay for services like telephone calls to their families (Fernandez 2022). In Orleans Parish, Louisiana, Marlin Gusman, the former sheriff, defended charging twenty-one cents per minute for phone calls. When asked to justify these costs, the sheriff noted that money from these calls went "into the jail at a time when we are strapped for cash, where we just took care of getting stable funding, doubling employee pay. So we would have to find that from somewhere" (Sledge 2020). The sheriff had raised $2 million from these calls.

Many sheriffs raise large portions of their budgets by charging other governments for holding individuals in jail. In Broadwater County, Montana, 46 percent of the sheriff's budget came from housing prisoners from nearby counties without jails. Sheriff Wynn Meehan, who repeatedly has asked the county for more funding, noted, "You can't bank your public safety off what revenue you think you can generate from a jail" (Ambarian 2020). Sheriffs' enthusiastic support of the criminalization of immigration is rooted, in part, because the federal government has long paid large amounts of money to sheriffs for detaining individuals under Immigration and Customs Enforcement (ICE) holds. In this circumstance, an individual arrested (or, in some circumstances, appearing as a witness to a crime or even a victim of a crime) will have their fingerprints sent to ICE for an immigration check. ICE can then ask the sheriff to hold that individual beyond the normal limit of forty-eight hours if they are going to try to deport them and will compensate the sheriff for that hold. In 2022, ICE paid sheriffs somewhere in the range of $90 a day per person that a sheriff held for the agency.[31] Sheriffs can also lease beds in their jail facilities to the US Marshals Service or ICE, as neither agency has sufficient room to house individuals that they arrest. Sheriff Fuentes, in his response to county commissioners reducing his budget, noted that his jail "houses over 270 prisoners with about 60 percent being federal inmates including MS 13 members and others that need constant supervision" (D. Hendricks 2017). Even as federal sources might supplement costs, they also generate expenditures as the jail population of those arrested locally for misdemeanors and those held for the US Marshals demand very different forms of services and security.

The jail-as-revenue source and civil asset forfeiture are two core examples of the importance of finances for maintaining the carceral state. Sheriffs' role in managing jails and engaging in civil asset forfeiture also exemplify sheriffs' role in the broader system of the "criminal justice as revenue racket" where any engagement with the criminal justice system is expensive, often prohibitively so for poor individuals (Page and Soss 2021). Sheriffs, with expensive jails and expansive powers, sit at the center of these patterns as they seek to expand their authority. Indeed, the entrepreneurial nature of sheriffs' budgets encourage them to engage in financing engagement with the carceral state, as that often offers sheriffs opportunities that they believe are unavailable through traditional revenue sources like property taxes.

Conclusion: The County as a Family

Once a month, Sheriff Daniel Guida appears on KLKS, a news and talk radio show in Aitkin County, Minnesota, to give an update on current events in his office. Like Sheriff Ramsay's blog in south Florida, topics range from when FEMA might disperse disaster relief funds after storms swept through the rural county to the sheriff's attempts to fish for crappies, to law enforcement reactions to the Derek Chauvin trial. From 2019 to 2021, conflicts around the construction of a large oil pipeline ("Line 3") through the county and the accompanying outrage from Indigenous communities and environmentalists across the state were a central issue in these monthly chats.

Sheriff Guida's office has financially benefited from the construction of the pipeline. Embridge, the oil company building the pipeline, negotiated an agreement with Minnesota to pay for the security associated with "public safety issues" surrounding with the pipeline (Holtan 2021), which included nearly five thousand hours of security or $355,393 for the sheriff's office (Guida 2021; Hughlett 2022). When his deputies wanted new guns, the sheriff emailed a manufacturer, "I'm hoping the pipeline will give us an extra boost to next year's budget, which should make it easy for me to propose an upgrade/trade to your rifles" (A. Brown 2021b). Water defenders and other protesters often point to this as an example of how the energy company co-opted law enforcement. In a hearing before a Minnesota House of Representatives committee, Native rights activist Winona LaDuke argued that it "created civil rights problems when a Canadian multinational is paying the expenses of your police forces in the state of Minnesota" (T. Walker 2021).

Sheriff Guida publicly denounced much of the opposition against Line 3 and praised the energy company for its outreach efforts (Holtan 2021).[32] The sheriff often challenged the integrity of the protesters, telling one, "Don't tell lies about cops" (A. Brown 2021a) when the protester complained about a helicopter surveilling the protesters. He accused another protester of lying on camera: "One Anishinaabe core value is Gwekwaadiziwin (Honesty) and I hope our interactions can be based on truths" (M. Taft 2021). He also took issue with LaDuke's characterization of Embridge paying for policing protection: "She has this energy and, you know, she believes they're her truth and her truths aren't necessarily my truths. So some of the things that were said, just aren't real" (Holtan 2021). Although Guida repeatedly accused the environmentalists of lying, evidence is not on the sheriff's side: the helicopter did fly overhead, the water defender did not lie, and Embridge did pay more than $350,000 in police protection to the Aikin County Sheriff's Office.

As we have discussed in this chapter, sheriffs engage in a wide set of activities in their communities to cultivate local reputations and remind voters that the sheriff is from the county and of the county. They host "Jail-a-Thons" where community leaders (including the sheriff himself) are "arrested" on Facebook Live and put in jail to raise money, and "Shop with a Cop" programs take a select group of kids on rides with deputies in squad cars to Walmart to pick out Christmas presents. Sheriffs appear on weekly radio shows, write columns for local newspapers, and hold "office hours" on the porch of the jail to allow community members to raise issues of concern without calling the sheriff directly (S. Stewart 2021). As we discussed in chapter 2, sheriffs often tout being from their communities and their connections to others in the county; a "day in the life" newspaper story of a rural sheriff in Virginia noted he starts his day at the local school as there is no school resource officer. The story also mentioned that the sheriff's daughter, son-in-law, and wife all work at the school "and for six Highland Elementary students, Sheriff Neil is also Grandpa Neil" (Jenner 2019).

As sheriffs communicate with their constituents; make decisions about law enforcement, policy, and staffing; negotiate budgets; and run jails, they do so as members of their own communities. That sheriffs often grew up in their communities and served in their own offices reinforces the idea that they are *of* the places that they police. Running for office in 2018, after serving in the office as a deputy since 1994, Guida taped an ad about how he entered the race to serve his family, broadly conceptualized: "I think about my family at home, my wife and kids. Then I think about my family at work…and then I think about my Aitkin county family" (Guida 2018). But not all community members get the same levels of protection. In dealing with those opposed to the Line 3, Sheriff Guida saw them as outside this family; protesters are from "far away" with a "large legal defense fund and hundred dollar bills are flying in just to pay cash bail" (KKIN 2021). Even locals who engaged in protests were seen unfavorably by the sheriff. When a local woman organized a protest where several people were arrested, Guida's office monitored her social media accounts and, several months later, arrested her for aiding and abetting the arrests: "She was asking people to hold space and encourage them to get arrested. And, in that scenario, we kind of believe that you're instigating those people getting arrested" (Marohn 2022). In 2022, Sheriff Guida was reelected, without a challenger.

In this chapter, we have considered the ways that the electoral nature of the sheriff's office constrains their behavior and pushes them toward particular actions. In the next chapter, we evaluate how the autonomy and authority of the office, along with sexist, racist, and nativist attitudes, interact to determine who they hire, and what policies they set. Sheriff Guida describes the job as one that serves everyone: "And, you know, the longer you sit in the Sheriff's chair the more you realize that you were elected to be a servant of the people. And that's just really what we do. We're servants to everybody" (Holtan 2021). But if sheriffs can selectively apply the protection of the law to some groups and not others or engage in efforts to punitively use the law to punish some groups and not others, then they have failed at the duty of providing even and fair access to the rule of law to all members of their community.

CHAPTER FOUR

Inequality from Autonomy and Authority

In the spring of 2016, Sheriff Craig Rowland of Bingham County, Idaho, found himself in hot water. Objecting to legislation passed by the Idaho state legislature that would require policing agencies to send rape kits to the state forensic laboratory for testing within thirty days, Sheriff Rowland told local news that "the majority of our rapes that are called in are actually consensual sex." After public outcry over the sheriff's claim that most rape victims in his county were lying, the sheriff apologized for offending people and wrote in a Facebook post:

> I know that it is hard for victims to come forward on sexual assault cases. I spoke to a rape victim today and told her that I knew it was hard for her to come forward. I want to apologize to anyone who I might have offended with my statement as my main responsibility is to the public's safety and well being and maintaining their trust. I can also say with re-gret that I now know what it is like to be cyber bullied. Not only have I been threatened but so has my family. I hope that this will clear things up a bit. (Boggioni 2016)

Sheriff Rowland again faced public backlash in November 2021 when he stopped a car of girls from a local church youth group with a gun after they left a "thankful turkey" card on the front door of Rowland's home. Investiga-tors reported that the sheriff pulled the girls' chaperone out of the car by her hair while aiming his gun at her and threatening to shoot. The public and other local officials responded with shock and disappointment, particularly following the sheriff's excuse, where he explained, "I've had drunk Indians come to my door. I live just off the reservation, we have a lot of reservation people around us that are not good people" (CBS2 News 2021). Fearing his office might mistreat Native Americans, women, and victims of sexual as-sault in routine interactions, many had called for the sheriff to resign over the years, and he finally did in 2022, following months of pressure.[1]

Does it matter if someone like Sheriff Rowland is in office? We argue yes. In this chapter, we interrogate the connection between individual sheriffs and their offices' policies, investigating whether sheriffs' individual attitudes shape the policies and procedures of their offices. We focus on areas of the law where the targets of the policy have been routinely treated with discrimination and biases, given sheriffs' long history of upholding the status quo and enforcing social hierarchies in their communities, as discussed in prior chapters.

The Connection Between Sheriffs' Views and Policy Outcomes

We examine the influence of sheriffs' attitudes in three policy arenas where their offices have significant autonomy: violence against women, traffic enforcement, and immigration. We chose our three policy domains as they offer sheriffs three potential paths for policy choices: proactive protections offered to crime victims, over-policing by targeting groups via routine patrols, and over-policing by targeting groups via cooperation with other authorities. We trace the evolution of policing approaches in these domains over the past fifty years: for violence against women from a private matter to criminal offense to an area with specialized services and training, for immigration from a civil matter to a federal enforcement issue to a devolution to local policing agencies, and for traffic enforcement from a minor component of the job to a mechanism by which sheriffs' offices engage in proactive effort to theoretically reduce the likelihood of future crimes in an area targeted for state and federal intervention. In doing so, we draw on Harris, Walker, and Eckhouse's (2020, 428) narrative of the 1970s, 1980s, and 1990s as a site of the "proliferation of policies criminalizing behaviors that stem from poverty and poor mental and physical health; steadily growing law enforcement budgets; and the dramatic expansion of prison capacity, the dense archipelago of which constitutes an enduring shift in American politics."

As we trace shifts in these policies over the last decades, we consider what might matter in shaping modern policy in each area, drawing on historical, scholarly, and news sources. For each area, we show via our 2012 and 2021 surveys that some sheriffs' individual attitudes lag behind the evolution of the policy area. We discuss how sheriffs currently make policing decisions in each area, focusing on questions about policy that we draw from administrative records and our surveys. As we have previously outlined, sheriffs' offices vary enormously in their general capacity, and we

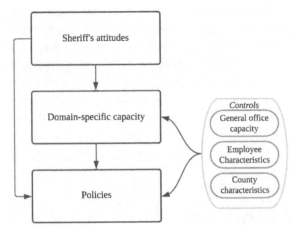

FIGURE 4.1. Theoretical expectations for chapter 4

look at three ways that domain-specific capacity can be defined: the assignment of personnel, specific trainings for employees, and whether employees have skills to serve specific populations. Finally, we consider the ways in which sheriffs' attitudes, as well as the characteristics of their offices and the places they serve, shape these policy choices.

Our theoretical framework is outlined in figure 4.1. As a policy-specific example, we first evaluate what sheriffs think about women's equality and sheriffs' endorsement of myths and misperceptions about domestic violence and sexual assault (*sheriffs' attitudes*). We then document that these views correlate with whether the sheriff reports that his office has personnel training to specifically address violence against women and personnel dedicated to addressing domestic violence (*domain-specific capacity*) and warrantless arrest policies and the requirement that victims be provided services and transportation (*policies*). Through this process, we control for alternatives that might also influence both the domain-specific personnel and policies: the general capacity of the office (such as the total number of employees), the characteristics of the employees more generally (including their gender, race, ethnicity, and training requirements), and the characteristics of the county (including socioeconomic and political variables).

In this chapter, we deviate in approach from much of the work that examines gender, anti-immigrant, and racial biases in policing (Baumgartner, Epp, and Shoub 2018; Shoub, Stauffer, and Song 2021; Gunderson and Huber 2022) in that we rely on survey data to assess *sheriffs' attitudes*, rather than focusing sheriffs' descriptive characteristics. On one hand, this allows us to investigate how and when outcomes vary across sheriffs by their attitudes, rather than their traits. However, this also means that we cannot use some sources of data others use, such as traffic stop reports in North Carolina, as we have a limited number of sheriffs in our survey dataset that report this data. We hope the combination of our approaches and the work by others strengthens collective understandings of the inequalities in policing.

As we have discussed in prior chapters, sheriffs frequently stress their offices' authority and autonomy. We see the consequences of those features: in the three policy areas we look at in this chapter, sheriffs enjoy wide discretion in their offices' application of the law. And we find sheriffs' individual attitudes about the targets of these policies (women, Black people, immigrants) shape their offices' efforts in those domains. It is unlikely that the connection between sheriffs' views and their offices' policies would be so robust if the office had lower levels of authority (especially around the creation and enforcement of policy) and autonomy. Consistent with other work on civil asset forfeiture (Mughan, Li, and Nicholson-Crotty 2020), we do regularly find that sheriffs seem to ignore supra government policies that they do not agree with—for example, even though states vary in whether they explicitly allow warrantless arrests in domestic violence situations, sheriffs' reporting of those policies seems unaffected by state law (Farris and Holman 2015). Sheriffs' attitudes shape the policy choices of their offices and whether those policies align with the policies of supra governments (Farris and Holman 2022; 2023).

Violence Against Women as a Crime in the United States

Sheriff Robert Anderson Strickland of Colleton County, South Carolina, was arrested in November 2019 on a charge of second-degree domestic violence. According to the arrest warrant, Strickland assaulted his girlfriend by punching her repeatedly in the face, took her cell phone to prevent her from reporting the incident and receiving emergency care, and damaged her vehicle as she attempted to leave (Phillips and Kofsky 2020). The sheriff placed himself on paid leave after his assault on his girlfriend, but it was not until his formal indictment that the governor of South Carolina suspended the sheriff from office (Tripp 2019). The sheriff's defense attorney publicly responded that there was no case against his client and questioned why the victim had failed to report the abuse to law enforcement (Ellis 2019), even though her abuser was the sheriff and thus in charge of local law enforcement. Subsequent investigations led to additional indictments against Sheriff Strickland on misconduct charges, including that he coerced a female employee into a sexual relationship, ordered deputies to work on his properties, illegally distributed prescription drugs, among other allegations. The sheriff pled guilty to three charges and was sentenced to one day in jail for the assault charge and five years on probation for misconduct and breach of trust charges (Bartelme 2020).

The ability to report interpersonal violence and have policing agencies do anything at all about it is a recent phenomenon in the United States. For much of the country's history, domestic violence, spousal abuse, and intimate partner violence were viewed as outside the traditional realm of the legal system.[2] Until the mid-1980s, policing agencies typically viewed domestic violence incidents as private concerns outside the realm of legal action, and the classification of these incidents as "disturbances" or "disputes" allowed them to downplay the crimes committed and practice noninvolvement (Buzawa and Buzawa 1993).

The views and policies of law enforcement in the 1960s–1980s reflected the view that domestic violence (and violence against women more generally) was not a concern of law enforcement. Law enforcement officials frequently blamed victims of domestic violence (Schechter 1982). Many held the view that "men have a right to beat and discipline their wives" (MacManus and VanHightower 1989). A 1967 police training manual by the International Association of Chiefs of Police promoted a nonarrest policy that explained, "In dealing with family disputes, the power of arrest should be exercised as a last resort." Police dispatchers believed that domestic violence cases would not proceed to trial and wasted the department's resources, leading dispatchers to encourage victims to drop charges (Parnas 1967), and offender arrests were rare if the victim was the one who reported the incident (Berk and Loseke 1980). As a result, law enforcement largely treated domestic violence as a noncriminal offense, and if law enforcement became involved, officers primarily relied on limited mediation to address what was viewed as a primarily private family issue.

In the 1970s and 1980s, a broad movement worked to extend the protection of law to women; this included addressing sexual assault, stalking, sexual harassment, and workplace protections of gender equality, as well as challenging the handling of domestic violence claims. Shaped by the legal successes of the Civil Rights Movement and the second wave of feminism, collective action focused on using the state, particularly law enforcement and the courts, to guarantee equal treatment for women (Ake and Arnold 2017). Activists raised public awareness of domestic violence, established resources for victims (including domestic violence shelters and crisis hotlines), and increased demands on legislators and law enforcement to address the violence (Hafemeister 2010). Women successfully sued local law enforcement for failing to protect them from spousal abuse.[3] Other class-action lawsuits successfully argued that law enforcement agencies denied women equal protection under the law by refusing to enforce domestic violence policies. Their efforts, combined with growing public pressure, eventually led to new legislation as well as new policy approaches by law enforcement (Mutpfay 1997).

Grassroots organizing and legal activism persuaded Congress to pass the 1994 Violence Against Women Act (VAWA), which addressed the inadequate and uncoordinated effort by law enforcement in prosecuting domestic violence (Nourse 1996; Rivera 1996). VAWA and the subsequent renewals of the act provided federal funding for investigations of violence against women and imposed mandatory restitution for victims (Weissman 2012). Following the federal government's lead, most states and many local jurisdictions strengthened their domestic violence policies, funded local programs, and encouraged law enforcement to take a larger role in combating domestic violence crimes.

Advocates, academics, and policymakers in the 1980s and 1990s also focused on a variety of new law enforcement mechanisms to address violence against women. These approaches aimed to reduce recidivism among domestic violence offenders and to limit the bodily harm and death of domestic violence victims. One significant policy, developed out of the Minneapolis Domestic Violence Experiment, advocated a mandatory arrest of domestic violence offenders. In the Minneapolis Experiment, Sherman and Berk (1984) randomly assigned officers to employ different tactics in cases of domestic violence: to either arrest, advise, or force the perpetrator to leave for an eight-hour period. The researchers found that a mandatory arrest policy led to lower rates of recidivism. These findings prompted widespread adoption of mandatory arrest policies by many state and local agencies. Subsequent studies, however, failed to find equally compelling results from mandatory arrest programs and a recent meta-analysis concludes that mandatory "arrest did not limit the likelihood of another offense being committed during the follow-up periods and likely did not have a deterrent effect on [domestic violence] offenders" (Hoppe et al. 2020, 1). Additional policies to address domestic violence developed out of advocacy and research, including training law enforcement in how to approach domestic violence calls, requiring the provision of information or social services to victims and allowing warrantless arrest in intimate partner violence instances.

The movements to recognize and remedy violence against women face pushback from a variety of sources. Intersectional feminists rightfully argue that the feminist anti-violence advocates engaged in "carceral creep" where "successes against an initially unresponsive criminal justice system evolved into collaborative relationships" with law enforcement (M. E. Kim 2020, 251). Over time, these collaborations grew to cultivate a generation of carceral feminists or anti-violence advocates who allowed and encouraged the expansion of the criminal justice system and the criminalization of poverty, particularly among women of color (M. E. Kim 2018). That these anti-violence movements occurred at the same time as the rise of neoliberalism in the United States (Weaver 2016; Rottenberg 2013), the Reagan Reconstruction (Bostdorff and Goldzwig 2005), and the decimation of most federal funds for local social services (Clark and Clark 1992), particularly relating to mental health care (Marmor and Gill 1989), encouraged the carceral focus of anti-violence advocates. Others note that the women's rights movement directly contributed to the rise of the modern carceral state (Gottschalk 2016).

Approaches to reducing cases of domestic violence remain contested in the public sphere. In the 2010s, the politicization of gender issues (Ondercin 2017) and a move toward explicit misogyny among Republicans (Cassese and Holman 2019; Holman and Kalmoe 2021) moved combating violence against women from an issue largely ignored (but vaguely supported) by both parties to one owned by the Democratic Party. While Congress reauthorized the Violence Against Women Act in 2000 and 2005 with overwhelming bipartisan support, the 2011 reauthorization stalled until 2013 due to criticisms from conservatives who objected to the act overall or disliked expansions of protections to LGBT, indigenous, and immigrant victims. The Violence Against Women Act expired in 2018, and its reauthorization faced four years of opposition from Republicans. After passing the House of Representatives in 2019 and 2021 (*HR 1620*) with widespread Democratic and low levels of Republican support but failing to gain a filibuster-proof majority for passage in the Senate, the legislation was reauthorized in 2022 as part of an omnibus spending package.

Domestic violence remains one of the most chronically underreported crimes to law enforcement (Catalano 2012). While domestic violence is no longer understood as a private or personal matter, victims continue to express reluctance to report crimes to law enforcement, in part because of a perception that law enforcement will not believe them or act on their behalf (Catalano 2012; Novisky and Peralta 2015; Westera, Kebbell, and Milne 2016). Distrust of the police intensifies among women of color and trans individuals, who often experience bias and discrimination from the police (Guadalupe-Diaz and Jasinski 2017; Decker et al. 2019; Ritchie 2017).

Today, victims continue to express reluctance to report sexual or domestic violence to law enforcement, often because they fear law enforcement will not believe them or act to protect them (Catalano 2009; Felson et al.

TABLE 4.1. Sheriffs' endorsement of violence against women myths

	Strongly disagree	Disagree	Neutral	Agree	Strongly agree
Many domestic violence victims could easily leave their relationships, but do not	11%	30%	13%	39%	7%
Domestic violence is best handled as a private matter, rather than by the police	50%	44%	4%	1%	1%
Women falsely report rape to call attention to themselves	31%	46%	21%	2%	0%
Women who dress provocatively are inviting sexual assault	40%	39%	15%	5%	1%

Note: Data from 2012 surveys. Modal cells shaded.

2002; Tjaden and Thoennes 2000). But this reluctance also varies from place to place. Prior work suggests that police attitudes are critical in law enforcement's response to domestic violence. Dismissive attitudes and a lack of support for victims of intimate partner violence among law enforcement may help perpetuate a cycle of crime and underreporting, particularly in rural areas, where domestic violence victims tend to evaluate law enforcement's performance lower than victims in urban areas (Barner and Carney 2011; Horwitz et al. 2011; McCarthy et al. 2019). Indeed, law enforcement's negative attitude about victims of domestic violence was used as a justification for passing mandatory arrest laws, which remove law enforcement officers' discretion about arrests (Robinson and Chandek 2000).

When we examine sheriffs' attitudes about women's equality generally and about victims of domestic violence and sexual assault specifically (see Table 4.1), we see that sheriffs hold wildly divergent views. On both surveys, we asked sheriffs the extent to which they agreed with a broad question about women's inequality: "It is really a matter of some people not trying hard enough; if women would only try harder, they could have the same opportunities as men." On a five-point scale where 1 was strongly disagree and 5 was strongly agree, we found remarkable stability across the near-decade between the surveys: a mean score of 2.09 in 2012 and 2.1 in 2021 (the mean matches the mode score, which was 2 [disagree] on both surveys). When we examined misperceptions about violence against women, we found that sheriffs are much more likely to endorse victim blame for domestic violence than for sexual assault, and do not generally agree with the "old-fashioned" idea that domestic violence is a private matter.

Professionalization and Bias in Police Stops

Around two a.m. on January 27, 2021, Sedrick Altheimer was delivering newspapers in Pierce County, Washington, when Ed Troyer, the county's recently elected sheriff, began to follow him in an SUV. After a verbal confrontation where the sheriff cornered Altheimer for driving in and out of driveways, Sheriff Troyer called the police and informed dispatch that Altheimer "threatened to kill me," prompting a massive police response, with more than forty police and sheriff cars rushing to the scene. According to testimony from a Tacoma police officer, Troyer later told police he was not threatened by Altheimer. Sheriff Troyer insisted the incident had "nothing to do with [Altheimer] being Black," but an independent investigation called by the county council found the sheriff exhibited "improper bias" (Brunner and Kamb 2021a; Moran and McDowell 2021). Following the incident, the Washington State attorney general filed criminal charges against the sheriff for false reporting, and Altheimer filed a lawsuit against the county for damages due to emotional distress from "racial profiling, false arrest and unnecessary use of excessive force of this man whose only crime was 'being a black man in a white neighborhood.'"[4] Sheriff Troyer was eventually found not guilty of filing a false report (Brunner 2022b), even as an investigation by a former US attorney (authorized by the county) found that the sheriff violated policies on bias-free policing (Brunner and Kamb 2021b). At the same time these events were playing out, three Black deputies in the Pierce County Sheriff's Office won a settlement for over $1 million in June 2022, accusing the office of pervasive sexism and racism in hiring, management, and promotion practices (Adams 2021), and the office faced another lawsuit from a deputy in 2022 with additional accusations of sexism (Ramirez 2022).

The altercation between Troyer and Altheimer represents an unfortunately common experience for Black and Latino Americans, particularly Black men: routine activities like delivering newspapers are viewed with suspicion and result in engagement with the carceral state. Racial targeting by the state has been a constant since the start in the United States. In the 1970s, 1980s, and 1990s, police began to employ a high-contact strategy of policing that maximized interactions between the police and civilians; these interactions were meant to send a message to criminals that the police were always watching, and were central to pattens of mass incarceration (Tyler, Rasinski, and McGraw 1985; Shoub et al. 2020). Encouraged to stop anyone who might be behaving suspiciously, police officers increasingly relied on racial, ethnic, and gender stereotypes (Weber et al. 2014; Schneider and Bos 2014; Pettit and Gutierrez 2018) to target potential criminals (Epp, Maynard-Moody, and Haider-Markel 2014). For instance, a 2012 Department of Justice investigation found the "most egregious racial profiling in the United States" in Sheriff Joe Arpaio's office in Maricopa County, Arizona, where "Latino drivers are four-to-nine times more likely to be stopped than similarly situated non-Latino drivers" by deputies (Perez 2011).

This shift in law enforcement practices, from a reactive approach that engaged with individuals after a crime was committed to a proactive strategy aimed at preventing future crimes, also provided expanded opportunities for sheriffs, particularly white sheriffs (Bulman 2019), to see swaths of their communities as potentially under suspicion (Baumgartner, Epp, and Shoub 2018; Tyler, Jackson, and Mentovich 2015). One of the principal consequences of this change was the increase of nonvoluntary contacts where "the police now more frequently approach members of the public with an attitude of suspicion and distrust as they search for signs of criminal character and future criminal behavior (e.g., 'a regulatory gaze')" (Tyler, Jackson, and Mentovich 2015, 604).

Sheriffs played a central role in the development of "proactive policing" through traffic stops, seizing control of rural roads, developing "drug courier profiles," and stopping any driver who fit a particular profile, a "needle-in-a-haystack strategy" (Baumgartner, Epp, and Shoub 2018, 8). Of particular importance to the development of this policing strategy was Bob Vogel, a state-trooper-turned-sheriff who spent enormous time and resources trying to stop drug couriers from crossing his rural county. When judges threw out his various busts on account that he lacked probable cause before conducting a search, Vogel responded by identifying the myriad of ways that the Florida vehicle code granted discretion to any law enforcement officers (D. A. Harris 2003; Vogel 2001), although he denied that race or ethnicity played a role in his choices about what issues might lead to an individual being pulled over. Vogel would eventually decide not to seek reelection as Volusia County sheriff in 2016 because of widespread complaints about his management and law enforcement choices, but his approach survived. For example, he notes in his book (Vogel 2001) that he successfully inspired the Drug Enforcement Agency's Operation Pipeline, a program where sheriffs and highway patrol agents trained other law enforcement officers to "sharpen their perceptiveness of drug couriers" (DEA 2004).

Throughout the 1990s, as the incarceration of Black and Hispanic men soared, legal advocacy organizations filed a series of lawsuits against state law enforcement agencies for disparate treatment (Baumgartner, Epp, and Shoub 2018). In response, the US House passed the Traffic Stops Statistics Act, which required law enforcement to collect a wide set of data to document—and potentially remedy—racial profiling. Because of robust opposition by law enforcement groups, the bill never passed the US Senate (D. A. Harris 2020). But more than twenty state legislatures would pass anti-racial-profiling legislation over the next decade (Baumgartner, Epp, and Shoub 2018; Harris 2020). Widespread publicity and reactions to the police killings of Black men in the 2010s, including Michael Brown in Ferguson, Missouri, and Walter Scott in North Charleston, South Carolina, would lead to new legislation from some states to address racial profiling in policing, but national policing reform, targeting problems such as racial bias and use of force, repeatedly failed to pass in Congress. National attention to policing violence increased dramatically in the summer of 2020 following the murder of George Floyd by a police officer in Minneapolis, Minnesota, and advocacy organization and activists continue to press for meaningful national, state, and local solutions to policing accountability. Throughout all of this, little attention has been paid specifically to sheriffs during these conversations, except for a few high-profile sheriffs in places such as Los Angeles, California.

Today, sheriffs continue to engage in this strategy of policing through traffic stops. When his office was identified as one of the agencies in Texas that issued the most tickets, Sheriff Bryan Beavers of Kaufman County, Texas, said, "We're trying to find the criminal element. The only way to find people (committing crimes) is when you stop them for a violation of law and do interviews on the side of the road" (Dexheimer and Barned-Smith 2021a). Sheriffs in our survey also referenced these patterns, defensively; one wrote, "Although I am rural, one of the major Interstate Highways runs through my county. We interact with few minorities that are not interstate related. When we do, we treat them with respect, like everyone and try to treat them as there is no difference, when in actuality, we probably treat them better than others." Sheriffs also defended racially biased rates in policing, as one sheriff told us in 2021:

Law enforcement is blamed for the end result of a broken system. We arrest minorities at a higher rate than whites because they commit crimes at a higher rate. We don't ask race when our 911 dispatcher takes a call. We respond. Minorites commit more crimes, I believe, because of their environment (ie. quality of schools, income, growing up in a violent environment). Our legislators our to blame for this—not law enforcement. An individual is a product of their environment. Not an easy fix. We need to funnel resources into these poor communities—better schools, good jobs and most importantly a safe environment. This means more officers and community policing in these areas. Survey individuals in crime stricken areas. Contrary to the defund the police movement these individuals want more law enforcement—not less. Sadly the vocal 7 or 8 percent of the population is stearing policy for the whole Country. Additionally, we incarcerate in the U.S. at one of the highest rates in the world—yet have the one of the highest recidivism rates. We need to change the whole mentality of an individual from birth. Respect of others and their beliefs.

Sheriffs' personal attitudes shape how their offices engage in traffic regulation as a tool for social control. Legally, the courts granted law enforcement offices broad discretion in using traffic stops in this way. The Supreme Court bolstered the practice in 1996 when they ruled in *Whren v. United States* that a police officer could use any traffic violation, however minor, to stop and investigate someone. And while reform efforts have led some states (including Oregon and Virginia) and local governments to restrict the kinds of traffic violations that law enforcement can use to pull a vehicle over (i.e., Oliver 2020; Palmer 2020), the majority of law enforcement offices, including sheriffs', retain this power.

The result of these practices is biased outcomes: law enforcement agents stop Black and Hispanic drivers more frequently than white drivers (Pierson et al. 2020; Shoub et al. 2020). Once stopped, police search vehicles driven by Black and Hispanic drivers, particularly men, more often (Shoub et al. 2020). Racial differences disappear at night, as officers cannot easily ascertain the race of the driver (Grogger and Ridgeway 2006; Pierson et al 2020). These interactions have deadly consequences for Black and Hispanic drivers (Laurencin and Walker 2020; Streeter 2019). Several of the high-profile cases of police shootings and abuse in the 2010s featured traffic stops as the initiating event: Sandra Bland's failure to signal a lane change, Daunte Wright's registration tag, and the broken taillights of Philando Castile and Walter Scott offered police officers the opportunity to stop—and kill—these individuals (Dexheimer and Barned-Smith 2021b).

These disparities are the cumulative consequence of a wide set of racial biases that have been institutionalized into law enforcement systems. The differences persist even as racial profiling itself (or "the use of race or ethnicity . . . by law enforcement officials as a basis for judgment of criminal suspicion" (Glaser 2006, 3) has been the source of much scrutiny and efforts at reform, particularly by state legislative efforts. As political scientists Baumgartner, Epp, and Shoub (2018, 19–25) explain, racial disparities could potentially emerge out of four causes: differential criminality between white and Black members of the community (which does not bear out to scholarly scrutiny), the persistence of "old-fashioned" racism among

TABLE 4.2. Sheriffs' racist attitudes

	Strongly disagree	Disagree	Neutral	Agree	Strongly agree
I am fearful of people of other races (2021)	0%	0%	3%	30%	66%
White people in the US have certain advantages because of the color of their skin (2021)	23%	38%	18%	17%	3%
Racial problems in the US are rare, isolated situations (2021)	4%	32%	26%	33%	4%
I am angry that racism exists (2021)	1%	4%	15%	51%	28%
The police should be able to take race or ethnicity into consideration as a factor in traffic stops (2012)	63%	27%	9%	1%	0%

Note: Data from 2012 and 2021 surveys. Modal cells are shaded.

a smaller group of officers, implicit biases among a larger group of officers, or institutional practices that produce racial disparities.

We shift the focus and ask: could an individual sheriff's racism (both "old-fashioned" and newfangled) be the source of institutional differences? To answer this question, we examine sheriffs' views on race, particularly using the Fear, Institutional Racism, and Empathy scale (DeSante and Smith 2020a; 2020b; 2020c), as presented in table 4.2. Here, like with the violence against women myths, we see wide variation in the responses based on the measurement of underlying concepts. Sheriffs report a very low level of fear (question 1) and high levels of empathy (question 4) but are less likely to endorse either of the institutional racism questions (questions 2 and 3). A final question that we added (and is not a traditional measure of the FIRE scale) is whether the sheriff agreed with the statement "The police should be able to take race or ethnicity into consideration as a factor in traffic stops." Here we find broad disagreement, with more than 90 percent of sheriffs strongly disagreeing or disagreeing.

The Criminalization of Immigration

In the summer of 2014, Sheriff Paul Babeu of Arizona's Pinal County drew controversy for publicly revealing the location of detained unaccompanied minors accused of illegally crossing the border, which sparked a series of local immigration protests aimed against the federal government. Babeu explained, "Local residents have every right to be upset and to protest. Our federal government has failed to enforce any immigration laws" (Pfeiffer 2014).[5] Echoing Babeu's frustration, a coalition of sheriffs' organizations in the Southwest described the immigration crisis as "spiraling out of control" (Coalition of Sheriffs Organizations 2014), and so did the National Sheriffs' Association, asserting the role of sheriffs in immigration: "Sheriffs have no desire to become Federal border agents; however, until the Federal government provides the necessary resources, manpower, and equipment needed to secure the borders, the responsibility for protecting their communities falls to the nation's sheriffs" (National Sheriffs' Association 2013). Emboldened by the Trump administration's anti-immigrant agenda, sheriffs actively pursued their offices' collaboration with Immigration and Customs Enforcement (Cenziper et al. 2021). But since Biden took office, sheriffs have resumed their concerns about the federal government's border protection—for instance, Sheriff Brad Coe of Kinney County, Texas, described his county as being "under siege" from unauthorized immigrants, leading his office to coordinate with a militia group at the border and even take it upon himself to personally drive four apprehended immigrants back to the port of entry (Gleason 2021; KSAT 12 2022).[6]

Historically, charged debates have dominated immigration policymaking in the United States, particularly in periods of large-scale immigration (Simon 1995). Following World War II and the Civil Rights Movement, the federal government enacted significant immigration reform with the Immigration and Nationality Act of 1965, which set forth the modern federal immigration framework and expanded the foreign-born population in the United States. Meanwhile, the organization of the labor market and the limited available entry for low-skilled migrants led to an increase in the number of undocumented immigrants in the United States, from an estimated two to four million in 1980 to approximately 10.5 million in 2017 (Massey, Durand, and Malone 2003; Stenglein and Kamarck 2019). Frustrations over unauthorized immigration have continued as a potent force in recent political debates.

Sheriffs frequently emerge as the public face in local immigration debates in their communities. Some sheriffs, such as former sheriff Joe Arpaio of Maricopa County, Arizona, and Sheriff Terry Johnson of Alamance County, North Carolina, have attracted national attention for charges of racism and nativism and are often seen as controversial and polarizing figures in their immigration efforts. Protesters objected to Sheriff Arpaio and his office's engagement in immigration raids, where deputies went door to door in neighborhoods and workplaces to check immigration status. Department of Justice officials have investigated both Sheriff Arpaio and Sheriff Johnson for illegally targeting Latinos in their law enforcement activities. Sheriff Johnson argued that the Department of Justice's case against him for civil rights violations was a manifestation of the Obama administration's "war on local law enforcement" (Zucchino 2012). Lower-profile sheriffs, such as Sheriff Sam Page of Rockingham County, North Carolina, and Sheriff Rick Jones of Butler County, Ohio, also vocally opposed efforts to reform federal immigration policy, which, in their view, have done too little to strengthen border security and immigration enforcement (Morse 2013).

Previous immigration reforms to address issues associated with unauthorized immigration include the Immigration Reform and Control Act of 1986, which granted amnesty to a group of unauthorized immigrants and increased employer sanctions and Border Patrol support, and a series of laws in the 1990s focused on restrictions of public benefits, streamlined procedures for deportation, and increased border security. Two national efforts in 1996 began to shift or devolve immigration enforcement to state and (mostly) local law enforcement: the Antiterrorism and Effective Death Penalty Act, which allowed local law enforcement to engage in civil immigration action, and the Illegal Immigration Reform and Immigrant Responsibility Act (IIRIRA), which authorized training of state and local law enforcement in federal immigration enforcement through the 287(g) program. Beginning in the 1990s, states and localities devised a variety of policies in dealing with immigration issues, including requirements for state and local law enforcement officials to check the immigration status of individuals suspected to be undocumented during their routine enforcement activities. Following the terrorist attacks on September 11, 2001, Congress further strengthened border enforcement and deportation efforts and consolidated these efforts into the Department of Homeland Security (DHS), which coordinated closely with local policing agencies via two programs: 287(g) and Secure Communities.

The 287(g) program, which derives its name from the authorizing section in the IIRIRA legislation, empowers local law enforcement to assist in immigration enforcement through memoranda of agreement (MOAs) between the federal government and state and local law enforcement agencies. In the program, the MOAs have allowed officers in local law enforcement to receive training for the identification and processing of undocumented immigrants and to deputize local officers in their immigration enforcement duties with the coordination and cooperation of federal immigration authorities (Vaughan and Edwards 2009).

In the late 2000s ICE began aggressively expanding a newer program to increase domestic deportation capacity: Secure Communities, whereby local law enforcement could run the fingerprints of any individual through FBI and Department of Homeland Security databases, primarily when an individual entered a jail. Federal immigration agents then could decide to issue a detainer, asking local law enforcement to hold suspected immigration violators for federal authorities to investigate. Secure Communities was replaced by Priority Enforcement Program from 2015 to 2017, reinstated by President Trump in 2017, and ended again by President Biden in 2021, although the data-sharing practice largely remains, known now as the Criminal Apprehension Program.

Immigration enforcement poses a unique political challenge, particularly for local law enforcement agencies. While local policing agencies traditionally have enjoyed significant support in their efforts to prevent crime and apprehend criminals, there is considerably less consensus over the proper role of local sheriffs and police in enacting and enforcing immigration policy (Chand 2020), and the issue has come up in sheriffs' elections. In a handful of recent sheriff elections in Georgia and North Carolina, activists focused on the sheriffs' involvement in the 287(g) program as a central concern. In 2018 in Mecklenburg County, North Carolina, a local organizer explained their ultimately successful effort to replace Sheriff Irwin Carmichael: "We feel like the best way to get rid of the program is to get a new sheriff, somebody that understands that the program is not working" (Speri 2018).

Activists and scholars point out that the enforcement of immigration violations may risk undermining local law enforcements' efforts at communication and collaboration with immigrant communities and lead to racial profiling (Waslin 2010; Rodriguez, Muzaffar, and Nortman 2010; Romero and Serag 2004; Gardner and Kohli 2009; Gutierrez and Kirk 2017). For instance, a study looking at the sheriff's office in Frederick County, Maryland, showed an increase in the arrests of Latinos following the implementation of a 287(g) program (Coon 2017). Frederick County sheriff Chuck Jenkins, in his fifth term in office,[7] continues to support the program, even after settling lawsuits of racial profiling and wrongful detention (Keller 2021). According to a 2022 report by the ACLU, 59 percent of sheriffs participating in 287(g) agreements have records of making anti-immigrant statements, and 65 percent have records of a pattern of racial profiling and other civil rights violations. As we mentioned in chapter 3, ICE renewed an agreement with Sheriff Bill Waybourn of Tarrant County, Texas, despite numerous deaths in custody and lost certification from the Texas Commission on Jail Standards (*Dallas News* 2021; H. Jones 2020).

TABLE 4.3. Sheriffs' restrictive and nativist immigration attitudes

	Year	Strongly disagree	Disagree	Neutral	Agree	Strongly agree
Federal spending on tightening border security and preventing illegal immigration should be increased	2012	2%	1%	12%	46%	39%
	2021	1%	1%	8%	20%	70%
In routine patrols, law enforcement should be allowed to inquire about a person's citizenship status	2012	1%	6%	23%	44%	26%
	2021	6%	17%	35%	27%	14%
Irish, Italians, Jewish, and many other minorities overcame prejudice and worked their way up. Today's immigrants should be able to do the same without any special favors	2012	2%	6%	26%	47%	20%
	2021	2%	7%	28%	45%	17%
Immigrants today take advantage of jobs and opportunities here without doing enough to give back to the community	2012	3%	26%	33%	28%	10%
	2021	7%	26%	40%	20%	7%

Note: Data from 2012 and 2021 surveys. Modal cells are shaded.

To measure sheriffs' restrictive and nativist views on immigration and toward immigrants, we asked four questions on both the 2012 and 2021 surveys (see table 4.3). Most sheriffs agreed that federal spending on border security should be increased across both surveys; in 2021, 70 percent strongly agreed. Fewer sheriffs agreed in 2021 that law enforcement should be allowed to inquire about a person's citizenship status during routine patrols, with the modal response as neutral compared to being in agreement in 2012. In questions assessing the sheriff's personal views about immigrants, attitudes remained consistent across sheriffs in 2012 and 2021: the majority believed today's immigrants should be able to overcome prejudice and work their way up without any special favors and were neutral toward the statement "Immigrants today take advantage of jobs and opportunities here without doing enough to give back to the community."

What Shapes Policy Choices by Sheriffs' Offices?

Central to our argument is that sheriffs' sexist, racist, and nativist attitudes will be related to the policies that they choose for their offices. To test this argument, we examine the relationship between these attitudes and domain-specific personnel and policy choices. We describe these further next.

Domestic Violence: Sheriffs' offices are regularly the first point of contact in situations involving violence against women. Almost all sheriffs' offices report addressing domestic violence incidents (90 percent). And while sheriffs' offices used to lag behind local police departments in offering specialized services to domestic violence victims (Farris and Holman 2015), more recent evaluations indicate that sheriffs are equally likely to have a specialized unit to handle intimate partner violence and to have staff who have received training to provide services to victims of domestic violence and sexual assault (LEMAS 2013; 2016; 2020).

Data from our surveys suggests that variation emerges from within sheriffs' offices on policies around arrests, the provision of domestic violence services, and training for deputies. To understand the role that sheriffs' attitudes might play in shaping responses to domestic violence, we turn to our survey. On both the 2012 and 2021 surveys, we ask if any deputies received specialized training to address interpersonal violence, with 77 percent of sheriffs on both surveys indicating their deputies had received this specialized training.[8] On the 2012 survey, sheriffs provided if their office had "a policy or procedural directive" for the mandatory arrest of individuals in three domestic violence situations: violating a domestic violence restraining order (68.9 percent), misdemeanor domestic violence (62.7 percent), and felony domestic violence (81.6 percent). We also asked if their officers must advise victims of domestic violence of their legal rights and medical options (86 percent) or provide transportation to services (64 percent).

Racism in traffic stops: To understand the role that sheriffs' attitudes might play in shaping racial profiling, particularly in routine law enforcement efforts like traffic control, we again look at personnel and policy choices. We examine two measures: reported staff in sheriffs' offices that handle traffic direction, control, and investigations, as well as the share whose officers receive training to address racial profiling. Overall, 91 percent of sheriffs report staff who handle traffic control, and 95 percent have staff who handle traffic investigations. A smaller but still substantial share of sheriffs' (85 percent) report staff with training to address racial profiling. On the 2021 survey, we asked sheriffs whether they have "a policy or directive" that that "Forbid[s] officers from using race or ethnicity in traffic stops,

TABLE 4.4. Immigration checks by points of contact with the sheriff's office

	2012	2021
Interviewed as a crime victim, complainant, or witness	26%	19%
Stopped for a traffic violation	26	22
Arrested for DUI/DWI	67	65
Arrested for a nonviolent crime	79	72
Arrested for domestic violence	87	75
Arrested for a violent crime	88	75

Note: Data from 2012 and 2021 surveys

questioning, or arrests," with approximately three-fourths (73 percent) of sheriffs reporting such a policy.

Immigration enforcement: To look at personnel and policy choices of sheriffs when it comes to immigration policy, we look at sheriffs with 287(g) agreements and when sheriffs reported to us that their officers typically check immigration status. The number and scope of 287(g) agreements have varied under different presidential administrations: beginning in 2002 under George W. Bush and expanding up to 72 local law enforcement agencies with agreements and then down to 35 under Obama, the program reached a historic high of 150 during the Trump administration. Despite Biden's campaign pledge to terminate agreements made during the previous administration, Immigration and Customs Enforcement (ICE) had 142 active agreements as of November 2021, the time of the 2021 survey, of which 93 percent (132) were with sheriffs' offices (ICE 2022; CRS 2021).

Given that sheriffs can be the avenues via which Immigration and Customs Enforcement agents access information on immigrants, our surveys asked, "When your officers encounter individuals who might be unauthorized immigrants in each of the following situations, do they typically check their immigration status with Immigration and Customs Enforcement?" We find a consistent pattern of responses between 2012 and 2021 but find fewer sheriffs reporting cooperation in 2021 than 2012 (table 4.4). For example, while a quarter of sheriffs reported checking the immigration status of those interviewed as crime victims, complainants, or witnesses, only 19 percent reported to do so in 2021, and it was similar with those arrested for violent crimes: 88 percent in 2012 and 75 percent in 2021. A couple of factors may explain this shift downward among sheriffs. Depending on the county, ICE's reimbursements for the daily detention of individuals may not exceed the costs accrued by the county. Some counties, such as Prince William

County, Virginia, ended their 287(g) agreement partially over budgetary concerns (Gathright 2020). In other counties, interagency agreements with ICE can provide desired revenue; Plymouth County, Massachusetts, has billed ICE for more than $109 million since 2003.[9] Additionally, some states such as California, Illinois, and Washington have passed laws that restrict cooperation with ICE, although several sheriffs have resisted these policies and found ways to continue collaborating with ICE. And finally, sheriffs also may be wary of taking on the legal risk of cooperating with ICE, as courts have established that detention of someone beyond their release date may violate their Fourteenth Amendment rights (ILRC 2016).

While we expect that sheriffs' individual attitudes about targeted groups will relate to their offices' personnel and policy choices, alternative factors could also play a role. The first and most central possibility is that sheriffs' sexist, racist, and anti-immigrant attitudes are simply proxies for ideology and partisanship. Increasingly, Americans have sorted into parties with very different views about gender, race, and immigration (M. R. Holman and Kalmoe 2021; Mason 2018; Cassese and Holman 2019; Silber Mohamed 2017), and we may be simply identifying a connection between partisanship and ideology and policies. Yet, research, including our own, suggests that partisanship is *less* impactful for sheriffs' policy choices than in other offices (Farris and Holman 2015; 2023; D. M. Thompson 2020), and our work in chapter 2 suggests sheriffs' partisanship (at least) is a poor proxy for their broader attitudes. We include partisanship and ideology as controls to assess this possibility.

Characteristics of the sheriff's office can also influence the policies and procedures of that office. For example, the number (if any) of women deputies influences how violence against women policies are implemented at the county level (Meier and Nicholson-Crotty 2006); gender imbalance in the ranks of law enforcement agencies may be a potential source of bias against engaging in domestic violence prevention (Sherman et al. 1992). The representation of Black officers reduces racial disparities in traffic stops (Christiani et al. 2021). And the presence of Latino officers and leaders shapes immigration policy (Varsanyi 2010). We thus control for the characteristics of the deputies who work in the office.

Sheriffs themselves focus extensively on capacity as an impediment to their office's ability to update rules and procedures, engage in training, and modernize. For example, some sheriffs have vocally resisted reform efforts as cost-prohibitive for their office. Following the passage of a criminal legal system reform bill in Illinois, Sheriff Darby Boewe of Edwards County wondered how the county could afford the costs of the now-required body cameras, remarking, "This county can't even afford to provide health insurance for me or any of its employees" (B. Williams 2021). We drill down on general capacity as an important component of whether sheriffs have been able to "catch up" with changes in criminal justice approaches over the last decade. Overall, smaller sheriffs' offices are less likely to have personnel dedicated to domestic violence, to hire bilingual officers, or to report their employees have received training to address violence against women, immigration, or racial biases. Yet, we consistently find that sheriffs' individual attitudes shape the personnel and policy choices of their office beyond these general capacity arguments.

Capacity certainly drives whether a sheriff's office has personnel dedicated to domestic violence, as is clear once we examine the personnel and directives for sheriffs by the size of the office. Among sheriff's offices with more than one hundred employees (approximately 12 percent of all sheriffs' offices), almost all have some personnel dedicated to domestic violence issues, while half of sheriffs' offices with less than one hundred employees do so. We see similar patterns in table 4.5 in whether the office has written directives relating to domestic violence: 96 percent of sheriffs' offices with one hundred or more employees have a written directive, compared to 89 percent of those with fewer than one hundred employees.

We see similar patterns for traffic enforcement, racial profiling training, and bilingual employees (see table 4.6). On racial profiling, we see

TABLE 4.5. Domestic violence personnel in sheriff's offices by office size

	Under 100 employees	100 or more
No personnel	65.2%	7%
Special unit with part time personnel	6.6	46.1
Special unit with full-time personnel	28.2	28.2

Note: Data from LEMAS (2020)

TABLE 4.6. Share of sheriff's offices with traffic enforcement, training to address racial profiling, and bilingual employees

	Traffic control	Training to address racial profiling	Bilingual employees
Overall	*91%*	*85%*	*52%*
More than 100 employees	85%	93%	89%
100 or fewer employees	93%	83%	39%

Note: Data from LEMAS and CESLLEA

the emergence of a domain-specific gap: sheriffs with fewer employees are more likely to report that they engage in traffic control but less likely to report their employees have received racial profiling training. In comparison, in larger offices, more offices have employees that are trained in racial profiling than engage in traffic enforcement. And the same pattern again emerges when we look at bilingual employees: while about half of sheriffs' offices have bilingual employees overall, nine of ten large offices have at least one bilingual employee; the number is closer to four in ten for smaller offices.

These patterns suggest that capacity may be a central driver of both domain-specific personnel and policies and procedures. As such, we use data from the Census of Local Governments, LEMAS, and our survey to control for the total number of sworn employees and nonsworn employees and the average daily number of inmates in the county jail. We take a log of this value.

Community characteristics may also potentially influence sheriff attitudes in these domains. While domestic violence incidents do not relate to specific demographics, research suggests that law enforcement may pay more attention to domestic violence in low income or economically distressed communities (Margolin, Sibner, and Gleberman 1988). At the same time, research also suggests that law enforcement often fails to protect poor women, who are more vulnerable to domestic violence situations because they lack economic resources to leave their abusers (Zorza 1992). We thus control for the county median household income. The racial composition of the community shapes the rate that law enforcement engages in racial profiling (Baumgartner, Epp, and Shoub 2018); we thus control for the share of the community who are Black. Immigration is a more salient issue in communities with more immigrants (Collingwood and O'Brien Gonzalez 2019), where sheriffs might either react with more efforts to provide services (shaping the presence of bilingual employees) or be more interested in strict enforcement. We control for the share of the population who are immigrants. We also include the percentage of votes received by Obama in 2012 for analysis of 2012 and Biden in 2020 for analysis of 2021 as a measure of the county's general liberalism, as ideological liberalism correlates with women's rights (Holman and Kalmoe 2021) and anti-racism (Benegal 2018).

The Relationship Between Attitudes and Personnel and Policy

We first look at the likelihood that there are employees in the sheriff's office with domain-specific knowledge and training and then examine the likelihood that the sheriff's office has a set of policies relating to domestic vio-

TABLE 4.7. Personnel and policies of interest

Area	Personnel	Policies
Violence against women	Deputies received specialized training to address interpersonal violence	Mandatory arrest of individuals
Racial profiling and traffic	Training to address racial profiling	Forbid[s] officers from using race or ethnicity in traffic stops, questioning, or arrests
Immigration	Percent of personnel who are bilingual	Do they typically check their immigration status with Immigration and Customs Enforcement?

lence, racial profiling, and immigration. Table 4.7 details these personnel and policies. For each, we then consider whether the sheriffs' individual attitudes about the targets shape their offices' personnel and policies, with controls.

We start by looking at personnel choices. Here, we would expect a weak relationship between the sheriffs' individual attitudes and personnel training and knowledge, given that sheriffs' employees themselves could seek out this training, or it could be provided or mandated by a supra government— that is, state or federal government. As a reminder, we present differences across our key attitudinal measures, where we distinguish between positive and negative views of the target group as post-hoc predicted probabilities. Here, positive views include the following: sheriffs do not believe women just need to try harder to achieve equality, they do not endorse racist views, and they hold expansive and positive views toward immigration and immigrants. Negative views include the following: sheriffs see women as just needing to try harder, endorse racist views, and endorse restrictive and nativist immigration views.

We find consistent relationships between the sheriffs' views of target groups and the presence of personnel who possess skills associated with providing higher quality services to that target group (see table 4.8). For example, while almost all sheriffs who report positive views of women's equality report having deputies trained to address interpersonal violence, fewer than three-quarters of those sheriffs with negative views report similar trainings. We see similar gaps in racial profiling training and the share of sheriffs who report any bilingual employees.

TABLE 4.8. Sheriffs' views and domain-specific personnel

Personnel	Sheriffs' views of target group	
	POSITIVE	NEGATIVE
Deputies trained to address interpersonal violence	99%	72%
Deputies trained to address racial profiling	94%	81%
Percent of personnel who are bilingual	72%	46%

Note: Data from 2012 survey (attitudes) and LEMAS 2016 (policies). Only includes those sheriff offices where the sheriff in 2012 was still in office in 2015/2016 during the LEMAS survey. Predicted values generated from the results of a full model with controls for sheriff ideology, partisanship, and education, office capacity, and demographics and political characteristics of the county. See Results appendix for full models.

Sheriffs' Attitudes and Office Policies

How do sheriffs' attitudes relate to their office policies toward the target groups? Table 4.9 presents the probability that a sheriff's office has policies about domestic violence, racial profiling, and immigration, generated from a model with full controls. Here we see strong relationships between sheriffs' views and the policies in their offices, with particularly large substantive effects for the immigration policy question; among those with positive views of women, these offices provide more services to victims (8 percent more likely), have mandatory arrest policies (16 percent), and allow warrantless arrests (14 percent). Similarly, lower levels of racist views are correlated with increased probability of forbidding officers to use race or ethnicity (10 percent more likely), and lower anti-immigrant views are associated with a very large difference in having policies about when to check immigration status.

We then examine data from both 2012 and 2021 on the relationship between sheriffs' attitudes toward immigrants and immigration and their offices' choices to check immigration at a variety of points of interaction with the public. As we show in figure 4.2, sheriffs who hold less tolerant attitudes toward immigration and immigrants are more likely to check the immigration status of potentially unauthorized immigrants at every contact point, with a *widening* gap between sheriffs who view immigrants favorably and those who do not as we move from 2012 to 2021.

TABLE 4.9. Sheriffs' views of target group and office policies

	SHERIFFS' VIEWS OF TARGET GROUP	
	Positive	Negative
Deputies provide services to victims of domestic violence	77%	69%
Any mandatory arrest policy for domestic violence	79%	63%
Allow warrantless arrests in misdemeanor domestic violence	86%	72%
Forbid officers from using race or ethnicity in traffic stops, questioning, or arrests	96%	86%
Advise officers when to inquire about immigration status and how to report	78%	21%

Note: Data from 2012 and 2021 surveys. Predicted values generated from the results of a full model with controls for sheriff ideology, partisanship, and education, office capacity, and demographics and political characteristics of the county. See Results appendix for full results.

Conclusion: The Impact of Individual Attitudes

In this chapter, we have focused on three policy areas where a history of biases and discrimination, and a patchwork of state and federal policy efforts, have provided an opportunity for sheriffs: they can make choices about who gets protection from the law and who is targeted by the law. We show that for each policy area, the sheriffs' individual attitudes about the target of the policy (women, Black people, immigrants) relate to personnel choices and policies and procedures. The substantive effect of these attitudes changes across issues, but the effects are consistent: if the sheriff does not like your group, he structures hiring, training, and policy in his office to punish you.

The three policy areas that we discuss in this chapter represent areas where the protection of the law can be unevenly provided to individuals based on their gender, race, and ethnicity. Most constituents will not experience domestic violence, immigration checks, or racial profiling. As Baumgartner, Epp, and Shoub (2018, 3) note, for most people, "police behavior seems normal, respectful, and appropriate." For the targeted group, however, the choice of the sheriff's office to provide protection or not (in case of domestic violence) or engage in enhanced scrutiny (in the case of

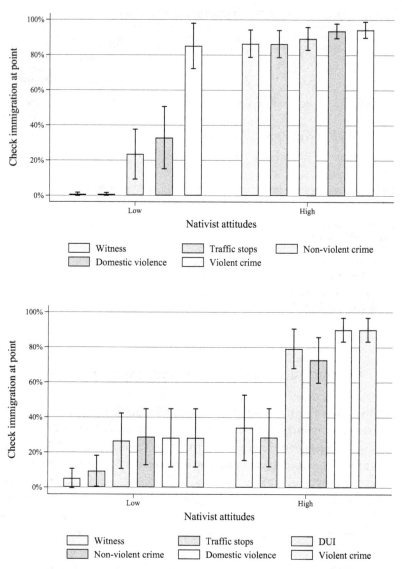

FIGURE 4.2. 2012 (top) and 2021 (bottom) relationships between immigration attitudes and immigration check policies

Note: Data from 2012 and 2021 surveys. Predicted values generated from the results of a full model with controls for sheriff ideology, partisanship, education, office capacity, and demographics and political characteristics of the county. See Results appendix for full models.

immigration and traffic stops) can dramatically change the course of an individual's life.

Our work on racial profiling also provides needed information about how racial profiling works in nonurban communities. The work on heavily policed Black communities in the United States focuses nearly exclusively on the experiences of urban neighborhoods and their interactions with police departments. From a deep evaluation of a Philadelphia neighborhood (Goffman 2015) to a myriad of studies of blocks and neighborhoods in New York City and Chicago (Clear and Frost 2013; Ba et al. 2021; Geller and Karales 1981) to studies of large urban police departments and sheriffs' offices (Pierson et al. 2020), much of the work that documents the current nature of policing, particularly racial biases in policing, completely ignores sheriffs' offices.

Of particular interest for us is the changing nature of immigration policy in the sheriff's office and the deepening effects of nativism on those policy choices. Moving from 2012 to 2021, we see that fewer sheriffs are checking the immigration status of individuals, but the effect of anti-immigrant attitudes increases in substantive effect onto those choices. Some of this may reflect the uneven challenge posed by immigration itself. Given that patterns of immigration vary dramatically from place to place, sheriffs face a variety of challenges when it comes to immigration enforcement in their counties, and sheriffs' offices vary significantly in their resources available to deal with immigration concerns. Illustrating the lack of resources some sheriffs' offices face, Brooks County, Texas, one of the poorest counties in Texas with one of the nation's busiest Border Patrol checkpoints, has only four deputies in the office, and only one is dedicated to immigration emergencies (Saslow 2014). The unequal distribution of immigration issues and availability of office resources at the local level in the United States further suggests variation may occur in sheriffs' and their offices' approaches to immigration policy and enforcement.

In between our two surveys, cooperation with the federal government on immigration issues became a central component to sheriffs' election campaigns, particularly in the urban South as we mentioned in North Carolina and Georgia. In Durham, North Carolina, an outside challenger campaigning on a promise to stop cooperating with Immigration and Customs Enforcement via leasing beds in the county jail won against the incumbent. And in Gwinnett County, Georgia, the sheriff's office went from running immigration checks on more than twenty thousand individuals to severing ties with ICE completely after the county elected a new sheriff, Keybo Taylor, on an immigration reform ticket. In nearby Cobb County, Craig Owens did the same, ending the sheriff's fourteen-year participation in the 287(g) program (Kass 2021). These changes suggest that it is possible to change the sheriff and thus change the policy.

These changes come amid a broader shift emerging in the relationship between sheriffs and the federal government, defined increasingly by conflict for some sheriffs as we will discuss in the next chapter. We observe this conflict down in south Texas, where immigration and its related challenges are a salient issue for sheriffs. For Sheriff Arvin West, doing his job of keeping the peace meant his office used to regularly smell like weed. Hudspeth County, Texas, is home to the "checkpoint to the stars," a US Border Patrol checkpoint that screens for drugs and other illegal substances and regularly busts famous people like Willie Nelson, Fiona Apple, and Johnny Cash (Reinart 2013). Alongside the celebrity busts, the checkpoint regularly seized various amounts of marijuana from people crossing the US-Mexico border into the United States, making it one of the busiest checkpoints in the 2000s and early 2010s.[10] Sheriff West's jurisdiction over Hudspeth County is a challenge of capacity: the office has 14 deputies to patrol more than 4500 square miles of desert; each person arrested for only drug charges must be driven 75 miles away for federal booking. In addition to the border checkpoint, West provides law enforcement for just over 3000 residents of the county, which was known at one point as the location of one of the biggest sludge dumps in the United States (J. Yardley 2001).

The Border Patrol and Sheriff West are caught: the checkpoint relied on the sheriff to hold those arrested, and the sheriff was dependent on federal dollars to run his jail and office. Yet, as the Border Patrol increased the number of low-level drug arrests in the early 2010s (up 300 percent from 2009 to 2012), they also decreased the amount of money they gave to the county to handle these arrests. As a result, in 2015, Sheriff West began refusing any checkpoint cases involving marijuana and, instead, renting out beds in his jail to other jurisdictions who pay more than Border Patrol (J. Burnett 2015). Sheriff West explained: "We're arresting people for the federal government at my local taxpayers' cost, and that ain't right for them to burden this cost. They're not going to pay. We're not going to play" (Becker and Schulz 2013). Now, the checkpoint busts only half the number of people it did in 2012–down to 916 busts in 2019 (or a paltry 493 in 2021) from more than 2100 in 2012 (US Customs and Border Patrol 2022).

West's standoff with Border Patrol is far from the only time he has come into conflict with the federal government. He in active in the vocal set of sheriffs advocating for shifting immigration reform ("'Scarborough Country' for June 19" 2006). In 2006, while testifying about border issues in front of the US House of Representatives Homeland Security Committee, West said the representatives were "dumbasses" if they accepted everything that Border Patrol told them.[11] And in 2016, West's relationship with a navy intelligence officer who tried to set up a militia training camp in the remote county became national news; West also appointed several navy intelligence officers as reserve deputies (Whitlock 2016). Sheriff West also appeared (alongside Alex Jones, Richard Mack, and Randy Weaver, among others) in *Revelation: Dawn of Global Government*, a film about how "The American Republic, Christian faith and liberty are rapidly being destroyed by a Trojan horse of globalism."[12]

CHAPTER FIVE

The Radicalization of County Sheriffs

After a five-day hospitalization for COVID-19 in summer of 2021, Sheriff Bob Songer of Klickitat County, Washington, returned to work eager to challenge pandemic restrictions (Associated Press 2021b). Having called the governor an idiot for requiring masks (Brynelson 2021), Songer had adamantly refused since the start of the pandemic to enforce state masking policy and other pandemic orders. As a self-described constitutional sheriff, with connections to far-right groups (Tanner 2021), Songer threatened to arrest government officials he believed to be acting unconstitutionally during the pandemic, prompting a rebuke by Klickitat County commissioners (Bertram 2021).[1] Challenging COVID-19 restrictions was not the first time Songer had asserted his extreme views and clashed with other officials: in 2018, Songer was one of the Washington sheriffs who vocally opposed initiative 1639, a gun safety measure, which included enhanced background checks and raised the legal age to twenty-one to purchase semiautomatic rifles (Kaste 2021). Songer explained his opposition as a constitutional sheriff: "My job as a sheriff is to throw bad guys in jail, but it's also to protect the constitutional rights of citizens of our county. I follow the rule of law when I believe it's constitutional."[2]

In this chapter, we examine how sheriffs like Songer have radicalized over the last half century through right-wing extremists' efforts to recruit sheriffs into their ideologies of anti-government extremism, white supremacy, and nativism. Unlike the individual attitudes held by sheriffs in chapter 4, these efforts to radicalize and empower sheriffs emerge from specific mobilization efforts, both on the part of general right-wing extremist organizations, including anti-federal militias and white supremacist and nativist groups, and from sheriff-centered organizations including former sheriff (of Graham County, Arizona) Richard Mack's Constitutional Sheriffs and Peace Officers Association (CSPOA) (Tsai 2017; Chammah 2020a). These efforts have led to the alignment of attitudes and preferences between sheriffs and extremists on issues such as guns and COVID-19.

Right-Wing Extremism and County Sheriffs

Where do these views come from, and why are sheriffs at the center for right-wing extremist (RWE) movements? In answering, we provide a broad overview of the key events from the last fifty years of RWE organizations focusing on sheriffs and their connections to the movement. We then trace the rise and power of the CSPOA in guiding what sheriffs think about the federal government, American identity, and racism and nativism. Using quantitative and qualitative data from our surveys, we detail RWE attitudes among sheriffs, including the finding that a large share of sheriffs holds extremist views.

Does it matter if a large share of sheriffs in the United States express RWE attitudes? In short, yes. We demonstrate that RWE sheriffs now have radical beliefs about a wide set of policy attitudes, including firearms regulations, COVID-19 mandates, and the January 6th insurrection, all of which present a central threat to the rule of law, federalism, and efforts to provide equality. In each area where RWE leaders have been active, sheriffs' attitudes align. As election denialism has propagated in the United States, we conclude by discussing how sheriffs with RWE attitudes have been activated around the issue and perpetuate conspiracy theories and misinformation.

A HISTORY OF RIGHT-WING EXTREMISTS' CENTERING OF SHERIFFS

While sheriffs had long trumpeted the constitutional nature of their office (S. Decker 1979; B. Smith 1933), right-wing extremists in the 1970s actively promoted the pseudo-legal idea that the office of sheriff was somehow *more* constitutional than others. Drawing revisionary inspiration from the medieval Anglo-Saxon practice[3] of a sheriff calling on a posse of men to keep the peace (Kopel 2014), right-wing extremists in the 1970s loosely organized into a Posse Comitatus (Latin for "power of the county") paramilitary movement. Rooted in conspiratorial beliefs of white supremacy and antisemitism, followers asserted that the county sheriff held the ultimate legal authority under the divinely inspired US Constitution and rejected the legitimacy of the federal government, particularly the federal income tax (Stock 1996; Levitas 2004). The movement was founded by retired army lieutenant colonel William Potter Gale, who was motivated into politics as he viewed federal efforts to enforce civil rights legislation as an example of the illegitimacy of the government (Levitas 2004). He sought an office whose authority was, in his mind, legitimate, could be controlled by white citizens, and could be used to resist the power of the federal government; he focused on the county sheriff. Gale's ideas were then further popularized by Henry Beach, who printed the *Posse's Blue Book*, featuring a sheriff's star on the front.[4]

The *Blue Book* argued that "the county has always been and remains to this day, the TRUE seat of the government for the citizens who are the inhabitants thereof. The County Sheriff is the only legal law enforcement officer in these United States of America" (Gale 1971, capitalization in original).[5] In language that is mimicked by sheriffs today, the *Blue Book* noted "his oath of office is to uphold, preserve, and defend the constitution of the United States and the State in which his County Exists. He may be required to do no less and no more than in the performance of his official duties." Posses were urged to take custody of any government officials who violated the Constitution and publicly hang those officials as an example. As the Posse Comitatus leaders died and followers engaged in violent standoffs with law enforcement, the movement eventually fell apart (Levitas 2004; Durham 2006).

Even as the organization faded, the ideas from the Posse Comitatus movement evolved as other right-wing movements continued to center sheriffs. These movements included sovereign citizens (Sullivan 1999), Aryan Nation activists (M. S. Hamm 2002), Christian nationalists (Dobratz and Shanks-Meile 2000; M. S. Hamm 2002), and a variety of Patriot and militia groups. For instance, Randy Weaver, an RWE with ties to the Aryan Nations who was directly involved in the Ruby Ridge standoff, ran for sheriff of Boundary County, Idaho, in 1988 on the platform of the "primacy of the county" and that the sheriff had the authority to refuse to enforce federal laws (S. A. Wright 2007; Bock 1995). Extremist writings called sheriffs "the only legitimate law enforcement officer" and specifically referenced that sheriffs could protect citizens from overreach (Howard 1889). In the 1980s and 1990s, sheriffs took a central role in "the county movement" (Chaloupka 1996) and the "radical localism" movements (Barkun 2007; 1997), a loose confederacy of RWEs with "a highly romanticized version of the past" (Barkun 1997, 218) aimed at returning political control to local leaders.

RWE focused in on anti-federal and anti-government efforts, eventually moving to "direct most of their violence against the federal government and proxies in law enforcement" (Perliger 2012, 4). Anti-government extremists included those who oppose interactions with the global political order (particularly the "New World Order"), any involvement in the United Nations, and a general view that the federal government's natural inclination is to erode individual constitutional rights. Resistance to the federal government expanded particularly in the west, through opposition over environmental regulations and the regulation of federal lands in the Sage Brush Rebellion movement. Sheriffs, who often sided with local opposition to federal environmental protections or refused to enforce limited access to federal lands, were heralded as legitimate political actors (Nemerever 2021). Even though sheriffs are members of both the government and law enforcement, extremists continued to accept and elevate the legitimacy of the office. Oklahoma City federal building bomber Timothy McVeigh himself espoused pro-sheriff views while holding vigil in Waco during the Branch Davidian standoff, telling a reporter that "only the local sheriff had the proper authority to serve warrants" to the Branch (S. A. Wright 2007, 163, quoted in trial transcripts).

ORGANIZING CONSTITUTIONAL SHERIFFS

Sheriffs today often focus on the importance of their office in state constitutions, referring to their office as a "constitutional office." Legally, the placement of the office of sheriff in state constitutions has important implications, as several state courts and the US Supreme Court use this to classify the office as an organ of the state, rather than a local office (*Mcmillian v. Monroe County, Alabama* 1997). This distinction matters in a variety of ways but is particularly important to establishing that sheriffs have autonomy beyond other local actors, who are constrained by state law (Dillon 1911). And while the idea that sheriffs are constitutional officers has gained favor in the past fifty years, sheriffs in the late 1800s and early 1900s also espoused these ideas.

Primed for resistance following years of centering by right-wing extremists and their own interpretations of their office, sheriffs found an opportunity to assert their constitutional authority with the 1992 Brady Handgun Violence Prevention Act. In the Brady Act, Congress temporarily required sheriffs to perform background checks for handgun purchases until the creation of a national background check system. A lawsuit funded by the National Rifle Association, two sheriffs (Jay Printz, Ravalli County, Montana; and Richard Mack, Graham County, Arizona) successfully challenged Congress's ability to compel them to execute federal law. In a 5–4 decision in *Printz v. United States* (1997), Scalia wrote for the majority that the Brady Bill violated the Tenth Amendment, explaining that congressional action cannot compel state officers, such as sheriffs, to execute federal laws under a system of dual sovereignty.

Though the US Supreme Court ruled that Congress could not compel *any* state actor to execute federal laws, Mack interpreted the decision to broadly suggest that sheriffs had a unique ability to resist any efforts at all by the federal government. Drawing on his connections with right-wing extremists, Mack began actively circulating his ideas. By 2021, sheriffs were repeating Mack's interpretation; as one sheriff told us in an open-ended response to our survey, "There has already been a case in the Supreme court in the 80's that ruled that a county sheriff has more authority in their county than the federal government. the 10th amendment of the US Constitution covers federal overreach. As a nation we need to get back to the principles that formed this country."

THE EMERGENCE OF THE CONSTITUTIONAL SHERIFFS AND PEACE OFFICERS ASSOCIATION

After losing reelection for sheriff in 1996, Mack used his notoriety as a complainant in *Printz* as a springboard into a career as a speaker and self-published author in the anti-government, Patriot, and Tea Party movements. Despite reportedly not owning a gun prior to his election as sheriff, Mack became a lobbyist for Gun Owners of America, a gun rights organization with ties to right-wing extremists active in the militia movement (Banks 1995). Mack developed a network with numerous right-wing extremists, including tax protesters, conspiracy theorists, militia activists, and white supremacists. For instance, Mack wrote the foreword to Randy Weaver's 2002 book on the Ruby Ridge standoff, and in 2009 Mack served as a founding member of the Oath Keepers (Jackson 2020). Mack continues to work closely with extremists, including protesting alongside militia members in standoffs with the federal Bureau of Land Management in Nevada and Oregon and on the right-wing speaker circuit, including a 2021 tour alongside antisemitic and conspiracy theorist Robert David Steele, who believed 9/11 and COVID-19 to be hoaxes, part of an elite plot to seize global power. Recently, Mack has repeated election fraud conspiracy theories, including endorsing a debunked documentary about fraud in the 2020 election and organizing sheriffs to intervene in elections.[6]

Following a series of failed attempts to win elected office and a resurgence of the anti-government RWE movement following the election of President Obama, Mack formed the Constitutional Sheriffs and Peace Officers Association (CSPOA) around 2009–10. CSPOA is a network of self-described "constitutional sheriffs" who promote their office as the ultimate protector of the Constitution. An organization rooted in RWE views of the sheriff's office dating back to the Posse Comitatus movement (ADL 2021), CSPOA encourages sheriffs to refuse to enforce laws they believe to be unconstitutional and resist overreach by the federal government.

Mack teaches sheriffs that they have the highest constitutional authority in the United States. The CSPOA's website reads, "The vertical separation of powers in the Constitution makes it clear that the power of the sheriff even supersedes the powers of the President" (CSPOA 2022b). Mack regularly accuses the federal government of tyranny, arguing that county sheriffs are the last line of defense against federal infringement of constitutional rights. CSPOA emboldens sheriffs to resist federal authorities, including promoting a resolution in 2014 that threatened to have federal agents arrested by sheriffs for entering their counties without permission (CSPOA 2014).

Mack claims CSPOA membership, which includes access to a private posse members' website and weekly webinars with Mack for either $11 a month or $99 for the year (CSPOA 2022a) and currently includes up to a tenth of the nation's sheriffs, a quarter of the leadership of the National Sheriffs' Association (Cooper 2019), and more ten thousand members (Kindy 2021), although these numbers are not possible to independently verify. In our 2021 survey data, less than 10 percent of sheriffs reported that they were currently or previously had been members of the CSPOA (in comparison, nearly nine in ten sheriffs indicated they were members of the National Sheriffs' Association).

Beginning in 2012, Mack has conducted trainings for sheriffs and deputies about his deep opposition to the federal government and extreme beliefs on the US Constitution and the country's founding. Mack conducts trainings across the country, including in Tennessee and Montana, where attendees are eligible to receive state-certified continuing education credits. Along with working with current sheriffs, Mack encourages voters to monitor their sheriffs. For example, the CSPOA provides a survey for voters to ask their sheriff about their opposition to the IRS randomly auditing citizens, the United Nations confiscating Americans' guns, and the federal government raiding dairy farmers (CSPOA 2016). Mack's organization offers Constitutional Sheriff of the Year awards (see table 5.1 for a summary of award winners[7] and their individual connections to right-wing extremism), and sheriffs across the country now refer to themselves as "constitutional sheriffs."[8]

Mack and CSPOA's efforts in the 2010s focused substantially on recruiting and training sheriffs around issues of guns, which had been the foundation of Mack's political activism and national reputation. When Obama pushed for national gun control after the Sandy Hook elementary school shooting, the CSPOA recruited more than 450 sheriffs and 19 state sheriff associations to sign statements or be listed as supporters of CSPOA's efforts to oppose federal gun control policy. The CSPOA provided a list of

TABLE 5.1. List of CSPOA award winners

Award	Sheriff	Right-wing extremism connections
2012 CSPOA Interposer	Brad Rogers Elkhart County, Indiana	Threatened to arrest federal Food and Drug agents investigating a dairy farm (R. Schneider 2011); sponsored by Oath Keepers to travel to take part in militia standoff with federal agents at Clive Bundy's ranch in Nevada (Rogers 2014)
2012 CSPOA Lifetime Achievement	Dave Mattis Big Horn County, Montana	Announced a written policy forbidding federal officials from entering his county and exercising authority without his permission (County Sheriff Project 2012)
2012 CSPOA Lifetime Achievement	Joe Arpaio Maricopa County, Arizona	Armed up to 52 different volunteer posse groups; ignored judicial orders and detained immigrants; refused to cooperate with federal investigations (Tsai 2017)*
2012 CSPOA Sheriff of the Year	Glenn Palmer Grant County, Oregon	Called armed militants occupying Malheur National Wildlife Refuge "patriots" and may have leaked federal information to the Ammon and Ryan Bundy (Zaitz 2016; Neiwert 2016); one of the first sheriffs to sign CSPOA's anti-federal gun control legislation letter
2013 CSPOA Sheriff of the Year	David A. Clarke Jr. Milwaukee County, Wisconsin	Called for his constituents to arm themselves; said the federal government is a greater threat than terrorists (SPLC 2013)**
2014 CSPOA Sheriff of the Year	Nick Finch Liberty County, Florida	Released a man*** who had been arrested for carrying illegal concealed weapon (Cotterell 2013); after being suspended for this, Finch successfully fought his suspension on the grounds that the sheriff has the ultimate authority over his own jail (Van Sickler 2018; Powers 2018)
2015 CSPOA Sheriff of the Year	Pamela Elliott Edwards County, Texas	Allegations of intimating Latino voters and ties with militias (Hannaford 2016); appears on cover of Mack's book *Are You a David?*
2016 CSPOA Sheriff of the Year	Dar Leaf Barry County, Michigan	Recruited other sheriffs to seize voting machines in 2020; defended accused militia members arrested in plot to kidnap governor (Agar 2020); currently focused on perpetuating misinformation about voting fraud (Tanner 2022)

(continued)

TABLE 5.1. Continued

Award	Sheriff	Right-wing extremism connections
2019 CSPOA Sheriff of the Year	Bob Songer Klickitat County, Washington	Sent letter to attorney general telling him to stay out of county; told residents to refuse to participate if the ATF came to the county (Goldendale Sentinel 2022; The Dana Show 2022); refused to cooperate with COVID-19 restrictions (Brynelson 2021)
2020 CSPOA Sheriff of the Year	Scott Nichols Franklin County, Maine	Refused to enforce governor's executive order on COVID, stating, "This is not Nazi Germany or Soviet Russia where you are asked for your papers!" (Nichols 2020)

Note: * Arpaio also had numerous accusations of misconduct, including abuse of power, misuse of funds, failure to investigate crime, targeting of reporters and opponents, and civil rights violations. He also described his tent city jail as a "concentration camp" and cost his county more than $100 million in lawsuit payoffs (Attwood 2010; NPR 2021).

** Clarke's tenure in office was noted with numerous allegations of misconduct, including mistreatment and death of those in custody, including the death of someone in custody from "severe dehydration" and the use of restraints on pregnant women (Reilly 2016).

*** The man released by the sheriff would later be arrested for murder (Schweers 2016).

sheriffs and sheriffs' state associations, noting, "Sheriffs have risen up all over our great nation to stand up against the unconstitutional gun control measures being taken. The following is a list of sheriffs and state sheriff's associations from who have vowed to uphold and defend the Constitution against Obama's unlawful gun control measures."

Who were the sheriffs listed, and what were their motivations? While the CSPOA eventually removed the entire list from their website, we were able to access it at several points in time prior to removal and then with the Wayback Machine. We compared the list across 2013, identifying any sheriff or sheriff state association who appeared as supporters on CSPOA's website. We map this in figure 5.1, indicating individual sheriffs or state association supporters in light gray and counties where both the sheriff and state association appeared as supporters in dark gray.

As the map shows, more sheriffs and state associations in the West were listed as supporters of the statement. The American West has served as an incubator for many of the RWE movements that have centered sheriffs, and this connection is evident. At the same time, they are not *confined* to the West: sheriffs and associations across the country were listed as part of the CSPOA statement. For example, the Florida, Georgia, and South Carolina

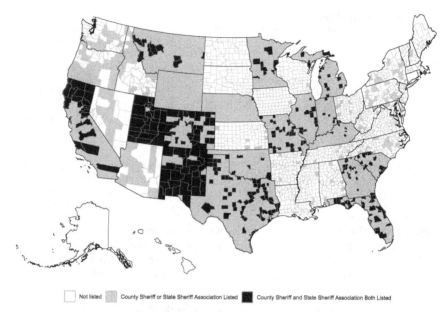

Not listed | County Sheriff or State Sheriff Association Listed | County Sheriff and State Sheriff Association Both Listed

FIGURE 5.1. Sheriffs and sheriffs' state associations listed for CSPOA gun statement
Note: Figure constructed by the authors from data collected from CSPOA website.

sheriffs' associations signed statements, as did sheriffs in the Northeast and Midwest. By 2013, the CSPOA was engaged with sheriffs across the country.

RIGHT-WING EXTREMISM IN SHERIFFS' GUN STATEMENTS

To illustrate the motivations of the sheriffs and sheriff state associations issuing statements, we downloaded each available statement, news article, or social media post (a total of 117 total justifications) from each sheriff and state sheriff's association and coded statements to identify themes consistent with ideas connected to right-wing extremism. An undergraduate research assistant, blind to the research questions in the study, read through 20 percent of the statements and, working with the authors, constructed a coding scheme that identified common themes in the statements. The student then coded the remainder of the statements into that coding scheme and selected the parts of the statement that corresponded with the coding category (see Data and Methods appendix). The messages from sheriffs about their support for the CSPOA and their opposition to gun control efforts track well with broader messages from RWE organizations, including discussions of a violent fidelity to the past, anti-federalism, and nativism.

Violent Fidelity to the Past

A central tenet of RWE is the willingness to take violent action to restore the past or protect a traditional way of living (Jackson 2019a; Campion 2019), often "reflecting a deep sense of nostalgia for the good old days" (Betz and Johnson 2004, 324). Those who subscribe to RWE ideologies often claim they are fighting to return the world to some past, often seeking to reestablish white male power (Wimmer 2002). In the case of sheriffs, the focus is on the "ancient" forms of the office and early points in US history when sheriffs could operate with near complete impunity (T. Moore 1997).

A violent fidelity to the past serves as a common theme in sheriffs' statements about gun rights. For example, the CSPOA statement notes "our country is in great turmoil and a new movement is underway to destroy the principles." These views are echoed by sheriffs: the Utah Sheriffs' Association closes their statement with "we are prepared to trade our lives for the preservation of [the Constitution's] traditional interpretation," and Sheriff Blake Dorning (Madison County, Alabama) wrote, "I took a constitutional oath to defend the Constitution of the United States of America, to defend the Constitution of the State of Alabama, even if it takes my life."

Interposition and Sheriffs' RWE

Anti-government efforts (particularly efforts against the federal government) often sit at the core of RWE efforts. Anti-federalism was the core of the Posse Comitatus and militia movements in the 1980s and 1990s, often initially spurred by the federal government's efforts to improve civil rights or protect the environment (Kopel 2014; Chaloupka 1996). RWE movements generally work against the state, such as the Patriots Movement in the 1990s (Blee and Creasap 2010); this poses an issue for sheriffs as they are themselves members of the government. Sheriffs bypass this tricky situation by placing themselves at the center of opposition to the (federal) government and focusing on the idea that the office of the sheriff has more legitimacy than other offices, a view that emerges from both racist and anti-federalist foundations of American RWE. While sheriffs do widely enjoy discretion in their abilities, so-called constitutional sheriffs assert they have greater legal authority and discretion because of the theory of interposition. In 2019, Mack told NPR, "Sheriffs standing for freedom have the responsibility to interpose—it's the 'doctrine of interposition'—whenever anybody is trying to diminish or violate the individual rights of our counties" (Kaste 2021).

While RWE has emerged as a cohesive identity only recently, sheriffs' engagement in "interposition" has a long history rooted in racism and white supremacy. In *Cooper v. Aaron*, 358 U.S. 1 (1958), a 1958 case involving Arkansas's refusal to comply with mandated desegregation following the *Brown* decision, the Supreme Court rejected the idea of interposition, or that states or lower governments are able to oppose or refuse actions by the federal government that they deem unconstitutional. The strategy of "massive resistance" of southern states to civil rights laws included sheriffs like Dallas County, Alabama's Jim Clark, who famously wore a "Never" button on his uniform regarding integration. Despite the Supreme Court dismissing interposition as a legal strategy, the CSPOA and sheriffs continue to promote the idea. Indeed, the movement likes to "portray itself as a new incarnation of the civil rights movement" (Goldstein 2019) even as their ideas and rhetoric actually sound similar to Civil Rights era sheriffs complaining about voting rights.[9] For example, Sheriff Clark of Dallas County wrote in 1965, "We in Alabama, the victims of this Federally encouraged vendetta, have reached the moment when we will have to fight for our constitutional rights with all the odds against us and only a precarious chance of survival. Though I am but a small-town sheriff, I shall continue to fight for the right foot by foot, step by step, and I will never voluntarily surrender my constitutional guarantees to these illegal judicial edicts" (J. Clark 1965). The interposition view is thus aligned with both a history of racial violence and the current RWE movement (Reid 1956).

Endorsement of interposition and anti-federal views is common among the gun statements from sheriffs in 2013 and from sheriffs on our surveys. The CSPOA encourage sheriffs to distinguish themselves as people who would "uphold and defend the Constitution against Obama's unlawful gun control measures." Sheriff Tim Mueller (Linn County, Oregon) articulated that he would "refuse to participate, or stand idly by, while my citizens are turned into criminals due to the unconstitutional actions of misguided politicians," and the Georgia Sheriffs' Association wrote that they "will aggressively oppose federal or state legislation which infringes upon law abiding citizens' right to bear arms." Sheriffs themselves replicate this language in their responses to our survey, noting that they have a "responsibility to interpose between the overreaching state and my community."

NATIVISM AND RACISM

Right-wing extremism also involves a set of nativist and racist views (Jackson 2019a; Banda and Cluverius 2021; Cluverius, Banda, and Daly 2020), which have been adopted by CSPOA and sheriffs with RWE attitudes. Nativism includes attitudes and actions that reject anything foreign, with a particular emphasis on nonwhite immigrants (Shapira 2013; Jackson 2019b;

Morlin 2017). As we discussed in chapter 4, sheriffs have a central role in immigration enforcement. The CSPOA has long advocated for extremely nativist and anti-immigrant views. The organization's Statement of Views includes nativist views, with the following appearing on their website from 2017 to 2022: "We are a nation of laws, and our immigration laws are not being enforced. Further, immigrants are not assimilating into our culture as they once did. This results in devastating consequences culturally and economically. The vast majority of immigrants today come here illegally, many committing crimes as they do. Administration policies actually encourage people to come here illegally, and the flood of children and thousands of others, including entire villages, that overwhelm our Border Patrol are causing a crisis that cannot be understated." The CSPOA also advocates for sheriffs to "use their authority to protect their citizens from abuse and violation of their rights by the invasion of illegal aliens" and for the protection of the southern border and the deportation of "all illegal aliens caught committing crimes" (CSPOA 2022b).

Like the broader right-wing environment in the US and Europe (Mudde 2019), CSPOA mixes nativism in their messaging and political activities. Listed in the CSPOA Statement of Positions are anti-immigrant and nativist views, such as "County Sheriffs must use their authority to protect their citizens from abuse and violation of their rights by the invasion of illegal aliens," which "are not assimilating into our culture as they once did" (CSPOA 2022b). The CSPOA and individual sheriffs echo racist and nativist stereotypes in their discussions of guns (DeSante and Smith 2020b), writing statements like "Federal politicians are ignoring the inner city violence and recidivists" (CSPOA 2022b). According to the Montana and Michigan Sheriff Association's statements, "family, gangs, drugs" are the causes of violence, not the availability of guns.

National events have further centralized nativism among sheriffs with RWE attitudes. Trump recruited sheriffs as active partners in his nativist policy choices, declaring himself a "big fan" of sheriffs. Trump regularly hosted sheriffs at the White House, attended news conferences with sheriffs, visited their counties, and appointed them to positions in his administration (Ulloa 2020). One of those gatherings was in 2018 as part of a lobbying effort by FAIR (Federation for American Immigration Reform), an anti-immigrant group with ties to white supremacists and eugenicists that has been declared a hate group by the Southern Poverty Law Center (Cenziper et al. 2021). Trump pursued relationships with sheriffs to bolster his claims of "law and order," and sheriffs benefited through the expansion of resources in immigration control. Under the Trump administration, Immigration and Customs Enforcement actively pursued 287(g) agreements, and the arrest rate under 287(g) reached its highest in over a decade in 2019. In 2017, Trump pardoned former Maricopa County sheriff Joe Arpaio of a criminal contempt conviction for defying a judge's order to stop profiling and detaining immigrants (A. Kelly 2017). In 2020, numerous sheriffs endorsed President Trump in reelection efforts (Trump 2020) and joined Trump in his false claims of voter fraud after Trump lost the election. CSPOA more recently has focused in on continuing Trump's claims of voter fraud, with sheriffs promising to investigate the 2020 election results (Stone 2022a; Eisler and Layne 2022).

CSPOA and other RWE organizations like the Oath Keepers and Protect America Now have been successful in shaping sheriffs' beliefs and behavior. In evaluating the role of the CSPOA in the anti-federal land management movement, political scientist Zoe Nemerever (2021, 254) finds that "Constitutionalist sheriffs increase citizens' grievances through anti-federal government position-taking" and that the presence of a constitutional sheriff increased the probability of violence against government officials in Western US states by more than 50 percent. And we find in previous work that sheriffs whose views on immigration align with CSPOA engage in regressive immigration policy and are more likely to check the immigration status of individuals who are victims of or witnesses to crimes (Farris and Holman 2017). Here, we show that RWE attitudes are associated with a wide set of policies that CSPOA engage in recruitment and proselytizing on, including guns, COVID-19 mandates, and the January 6th insurrection.

The Form and Distribution of Right-Wing Extremist Attitudes among Sheriffs

Just how much do sheriffs endorse right-wing extremist views? In our 2021 survey, we set out to measure the level of endorsement through a set of survey questions developed out of our understanding of how RWE has evolved in communities of sheriffs. We measure sheriffs' RWE attitudes through their agreement (on a five-point strongly disagree to strongly agree scale) to seven questions that capture subcomponents of right-wing extremist attitudes: anti-federalism, the use of violence to defend the "American way of life," racism, and nativism (see table 5.2), tapping into items from research on RWE (Jackson 2020), white solidarity and racism (C. D. DeSante and Smith 2020c; Jardina and Piston 2019), and nativism (Farris and Holman 2017). Each question represents a core component of how RWE has emerged and developed among sheriffs over the past half century.

As we discussed in chapter 1, sheriffs have long upheld white supremacy and nativism through their central roles in capturing enslaved individuals (Rogers and Denham 2001; Thornton 1978), enforcing Jim Crow (Fairlie 1920; T. Moore 1997; Blackmon 2009), and lending legitimacy to community violence, particularly violence against Black, Native American, and Mexican American communities (Obert 2018). Over the last half century, sheriffs' views have become increasingly intertwined in more contemporary RWE efforts in the United States with shared foundations in white supremacy and nativism (Jackson 2019a; Perliger 2012). We measure these views through sheriffs' endorsements (or lack thereof) of institutional racism (DeSante and Smith 2020a; 2020b; 2020c) via the question "White people in the US have certain advantages because of the color of their skin." We capture nativist views via questions that capture resentment toward immigrants ("Irish, Italians, Jewish and many other minorities overcame prejudice and worked their way up. Today's immigrants should be able to do the same without any special favors") and views of immigrants as taking more than they give back.

White nostalgia is also a prevalent view among right-wing extremists in the United States and abroad (Campion 2019). As a particular form of racism (and misogyny, see Wilson 2020), white nostalgia is rooted in the belief that the American way of life is under attack and needs to be defended, even if that defense requires force. A central goal of right-wing movements is "to revert fundamental features of the political system to some imagined (though not necessarily imaginary) past state" (Jackson 2019a, 4). RWE sheriff organizations hold positions that sheriffs have a responsibility to be "the upholder, defender, protector and servant to the liberties of the people within the county" (CSPOA 2022b). These views also tap into core views of Christian Nationalists who view the United States as founded as a Christian nation and seek to merge and protect Christian and American identities (Whitehead, Perry, and Baker 2018). For instance, multiple sheriffs have faced public scrutiny for putting Bible quotes on patrol cars or on walls of their headquarters, including Columbus County, North Carolina, sheriff Jody Greene, who explained on Facebook that "I am not scared of much, but I am afraid of burning in Hell" when challenged to remove a Bible verse from the office's wall (Greene 2021).[10]

Right-wing extremism in the United States is also rooted in anti-government views, with right-wing activists motivated to resist efforts by the federal government to collect taxes, protect the environment, and protect civil rights (Jackson 2019a; Pantucci and Ong 2021). Unlike right-wing extremists more generally, however, sheriffs' anti-government views

TABLE 5.2. Components of RWE

Question	Mean response	Subcomponent measure
White people in the US have certain advantages because of the color of their skin. (reverse coded)	3.6	Racism
Irish, Italians, Jewish, and many other minorities overcame prejudice and worked their way up. Today's immigrants should be able to do the same without any special favors.	3.7	Nativism
Immigrants today take advantage of jobs and opportunities here without doing enough to give back to the community.	2.9	Nativism
The traditional American way of life is disappearing so fast that we may have to use force to save it.	2.8	White nostalgia
The federal government should have to get my permission before engaging in enforcement actions in my county.	3.7	Anti-federalism
The sheriff's authority supersedes the federal or state government in my county.	3.5	Anti-federalism
I am willing to "interpose" on behalf of county residents when I believe a state or federal law is unjust.	3.9	Anti-federalism

Note: All questions from 2012 and 2021 surveys.

are decidedly anti-*federalism*. That is, sheriffs believe in government because they are themselves members of the government but manifest their anti-government views as the resistance to supra governments. Contained within this are the veneration of the political sovereignty (Kerodal, Freilich, and Chermak 2016) of the sheriff's office and the endorsement of the sheriff's office itself as the protector of Americans from overreach by these supra governments. We measure these views through three questions that tap into these beliefs, including that the sheriff's authority supersedes that of these supra governments, that "the federal government should have to get my permission before engaging in enforcement actions in my county," and, a view that directly emerges from CSPOA (as we describe later), "I am willing to 'interpose' on behalf of county residents when I believe a state or federal law is unjust."

We generate a single averaged measure to capture the constellation of RWE attitudes.[11] The RWE attitudes scale is right skewed with a mean of

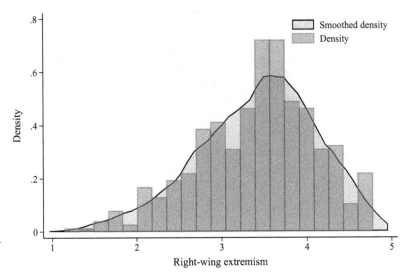

FIGURE 5.2. Distribution of right-wing extremism measure

3.42 and a median of 3.5, indicating a high level of agreement with the measure (see fig. 5.2 for histogram and density of the measure).

We see additional evidence of sheriffs' constitutional interpretation and clashes with other levels of government when we asked sheriffs in an open-ended response to tell us the top three problems facing their offices in both the 2012 and 2021 surveys. Sheriffs expressed concern that the public is not aware of the constitutional nature of the office [one sheriff explained his concern of "making the public aware of the Sheriff's Duties (Constitual)"[12]], as well as the need to push back against infringements of the sheriff's constitutional powers. These concerns include "a growing concern of many in regard to constitutional rights," unfunded mandates and "poorly thought out" legislation from federal and state governments, and "interference by County Administration." Other sheriffs specifically referenced what they see as attacks or "overreach" from state and federal governments; one noted that they had concerns about the "the legislative branch of government attempting to pass and passing unconstitutional laws" as well as "the attempt to do away with the power of the Sheriff. the Sheriff is the last line of defense for the Constitution." Others expressed concern about respect for the office's autonomy: "Inability of other elected officials to respect the authority of Sheriff and allow him to run his office without their constant interference."

Sheriffs also highlighted the constitutional nature of their office in the concluding open-ended question on the survey; one mentioned, "The office of the Sheriff primary responsibility is to defend the Constitution," and another wrote, "We as Sheriff's have a unique responsibility to up hold the law and protect the constitution." Another sheriff explicitly noted that their powers may exceed the state or federal government: "I believe that I am a constitutionally-elected official and, therefore, am not obliged to enforce any executive order, policy, directive or program not covered by the federal or state constitutions." Sheriffs see their role as preventing tyranny; one noted, "Sheriff's are America's last hope and truly stand between the tyrants and our constituencies." Another said, "Sheriff's Offices nationwide are the best protection against advancing tyranny by state and federal governments." Another ended his discussion of the powers of the sheriff with "Respect the Constitution."

GUN POLICY

Do these RWE attitudes matter in shaping sheriffs' policies? Sheriffs' unique role of both setting and enforcing policy would suggest so, particularly in those policy areas where there has been substantial RWE activity, such as gun control. We look specifically at how extremist views correlate with an unwillingness to engage with red-flag laws and background checks. Red-flag orders allow for a family member, health care worker, or law enforcement official to petition for a judge to order the removal of firearms from the possession of an individual who might harm themselves or others. Empirical evidence suggests the presence of these laws results in declines in suicide rates, particularly among men (Dalafave 2020). While a variety of individuals can initiate a red-flag order, the laws are designed to depend on the participation of sheriffs. Law enforcement are regularly involved in the petition to the judge to remove firearms from someone's possession (Blocher 2013; Blocher and Charles 2020). For example, a team of public health scholars found that more than 70 percent of the Extreme Risk Protection Order in Washington originated from law enforcement officers in the first two years of the state's program (Rowhani-Rahbar et al. 2020), and in our evaluation of ERPOs in California, Colorado, and Virginia, sheriffs originated more than 40 percent of ERPOs. After a judge's order, the sheriff is potentially involved again: a law enforcement agency then must take custody of the firearms. This presents another opportunity for the sheriffs' discretion to shape (literally) protection from the law as sheriffs might choose not to petition for a gun seizure or refuse to remove guns from someone's possession. For example, when a gunman with homophobic attitudes killed five people at Club Q in Colorado, news reports noted that he had previously threatened others and would have been eligible to have his weapons removed through an ERPO (Kenney 2022). Bill Elder, the sheriff of El Paso County, Colorado, where the shooting occurred, had previously stated that he would not enforce Colorado's red-flag laws (Riley 2020).

Some sheriffs have been vocal supporters of red-flag laws and sheriffs' engagement in background checks, often with an emphasis on how these laws allow for control over firearms policy to remain in the hands of sheriffs and provide revenue for the office. For example, in Alabama, the state sheriffs' association actively opposed efforts to remove gun background checks from the local level. In a discussion of background checks, Heath Taylor, sheriff of Russell County, Alabama, noted, "The Alabama Sheriffs Association feels that each sheriff knows their constituents and that goes beyond running a background check and seeing who has a felony in their background. We know things that the computer can't tell us. We know things about our citizens. We know who is going through a divorce. We know who is in a bad time. Who may be drinking too much. Who may be abusive but hasn't necessarily crossed the line of a crime. But in our opinion, they don't need a pistol permit (*Alabama Russell County Sheriff Statement on Shall Issue Permits* 2015).

Sheriffs have also been involved in the creation of red-flag laws. For example, sheriffs in Louisiana actively campaigned to expand red-flag laws to include domestic violence. In Lafourche Parish, the sheriff's office flags any individual who is ineligible to possess guns by federal or state law and shares that information with all offices capable of issuing gun-related permits, including Louisiana Fish and Wildlife (Flanagan 2020; Gifford Law Center 2022). Sheriff Craig Webre testified for the creation of a state law that established that sheriffs' offices are "responsible for overseeing firearm transfers and outlined procedures to divest prohibited persons of their firearms" (Louisiana State Legislature 2018). The state adopted the policies of Lafourche Parish and expanded red-flag laws to include domestic violence.

Yet, many other sheriffs have vocally opposed these laws. For example, when Colorado passed a red-flag law in 2019, a wide set of sheriffs called it a "gun grab." Sheriff Steve Reams (Weld County, Colorado) hosted a fundraising event billed as an "American Celebration" with conservative musician and gun activist Ted Nugent to oppose the state's new law that created ERPOs. On stage, Reams characterized the Colorado gun rights situation as dire: "The red-flag bill is just one step towards a really bad path for this state. If we don't fight back hard and we don't fight back strong, we're going to lose this state." Sheriff Reams went on to say, "Essentially what I'm saying is, I won't be an applicant for a red-flag order" (Paterson 2019).

We first examine sheriffs' support for and willingness to enforce a national gun registry. Here, we expect a particularly strong negative relationship between RWE and sheriffs' support for a gun registry, given that CSPOA emerges out of Mack's opposition to this particular piece of the Brady Bill. We use two questions from the 2021 survey. We measure favorability via "Please tell us if you would favor or oppose the following policies related to firearms: A government database that requires the sheriff's participation in maintaining a gun registry and performing background checks," where the mean response was 1.8 (or a modal response of "oppose") on the strongly oppose (1) to strongly favor (5) scale. We then asked if they would comply with such a database if it were "passed into law" with 18 percent of sheriffs indicating that they would comply.

Given the entanglement between CSPOA and gun rights activism, we expect that RWE sheriffs will be less likely to indicate that they favor red-flag laws or be willing to enforce them but anticipate a weaker relationship given that red-flag laws allow sheriffs to retain autonomy and are rooted in activism by sheriffs themselves. We find higher levels of favorability and willingness to enforce. We again measure favorability via the sheriffs' favor or opposition to "A requirement that your office confiscates firearms from people flagged as a danger to themselves or others," where the mean response was 2.9 or "neutral" on the strongly oppose (1) to strongly favor (5) scale. We then asked, "If the following firearms policies were passed into law, would you comply with them? . . . A requirement that my office confiscate firearms from people flagged as a danger to themselves or others." Here, 35 percent of sheriffs indicated that they would comply with enforcement.

To understand the relationship between RWE and views toward a national gun registry and red-flag laws, we then estimate a model where favorability (left) and willingness to enforce (right) serve as our dependent variables and our RWE scale and our central set of controls. RWE attitudes and gun preferences are associated with conservativism and Republicanism in the United States (Banda and Cluverius 2021; Cluverius, Banda, and Daly 2020). These factors are also associated with preferences for gun control (Pearson-Merkowitz and Dyck 2017; Hayes, Fortunato, and Hibbing 2021). Rural residents and police also have stronger preferences against gun control efforts (Carlson 2020; Lynch, Logan, and Jackson 2018; Woldoff, Litchfield, and Sycafoose Matthews 2017). Whiteness and racism are also deeply associated with extremism and pro-gun views in the general population and among the police (Blum 2020; Carlson 2020; Filindra and Kaplan 2017; 2016). We thus control for a variety of variables associated with these relevant controls: capacity, population, percent Black, percent rural, percent Biden vote in 2020, sheriff ideology, and whether the sheriff is a Re-

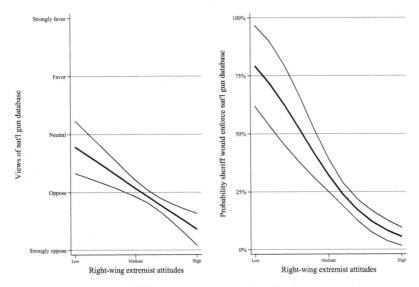

FIGURE 5.3. Right-wing extremism and a national gun registry
Note: Predicted probabilities generated post hoc from models with controls for sheriff
ideology (liberal to conservative), Republican partisanship, county population, the capacity
of the office (including the number of deputies and jail capacity), and the share of the
population who voted for Biden in 2020. Full results available in Results appendix.

publican. We then estimate the substantive effects of the RWE measure on
favorability and willingness to enforce and present those results visually.
Full results for each figure are available in the Results appendix.

As expected, we see a significant and substantively meaningful relationship between RWE and sheriffs' views toward a gun registry and willingness to comply with a national gun registry (see fig. 5.3). Moving from the
bottom of the RWE scale to the top, we see a decline in support for a gun
registry from neutral to strongly oppose. An even stronger effect is found in
the relationship between RWE and willingness to comply with a national
gun registry: a move from the low end of the RWE scale to the high end is
associated with a drop from 75 percent saying they would comply to five
percent.

We find a substantively meaningful and statistically significant relationship (p = 0.014) between RWE and sheriffs' lack of favorability toward red-
flag laws (see fig. 5.4). Moving from the low end of the RWE scale to the
high end of the scale results in a one-point reduction in favorability on the
five-point scale. But where we see a particularly powerful relationship is
between RWE and sheriffs' willingness to actually enforce laws: here, more

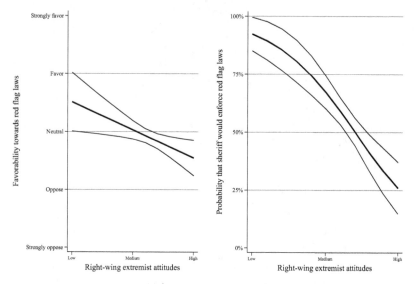

FIGURE 5.4. Right-wing extremism and red-flag laws

Note: Predicted probabilities generated post hoc from models with controls for sheriff ideology (liberal to conservative), Republican partisanship, county population, the capacity of the office (including the number deputies and jail capacity), and the share of the population who voted for Biden in 2020. Full results available in Results appendix.

than 85 percent of sheriffs who are low on the RWE scale are willing to enforce the red-flag laws. For sheriffs high on the RWE scale, only a quarter (26 percent) are willing to enforce red-flag laws.

Does this translate into actual enforcement? In California, Colorado, and Virginia, we examined the court records of ERPO requests by sheriffs, coding the number of requests per 100,000 people (see Data and Methods appendix). While ERPOs vary quite a bit across states (given the variation in the stringency of the laws themselves from state to state), we also see that sheriffs' RWE is strongly correlated with lower rates of ERPO petitions (see fig. 5.5). Across all three states, sheriffs with low rates of RWE file close to twice as many petitions for ERPOs as do sheriffs with high levels of RWE.

RWE AND OTHER POLICIES: COVID-19

Perhaps these relationships should be expected: after all, efforts to recruit sheriffs toward extremism are deeply rooted in gun rights, and the CSPOA has expended significant efforts at tailoring a message around gun rights to appeal to sheriffs. The extent to which these views have moved beyond federal overreach (as we capture with the gun database question)

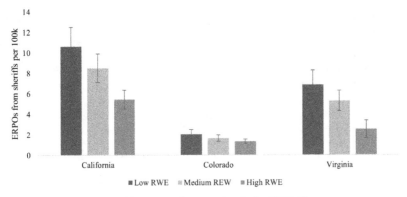

FIGURE 5.5. Extreme Risk Protection Order (ERPO) requests
by sheriffs per 100,000 population

Note: Data collected and coded by authors via state court records systems petition requests.
See Data and Methods appendix for more information and Results appendix for models.

and into broader views on gun policy indicates that CSPOA and gun rights advocates have been successful in these attempts. We also find strong relationships between RWE views and opposition to a national ban on assault weapons, support for allowing the open carry of firearms in government buildings, and the county becoming a Second Amendment sanctuary. Thus, RWE clearly shapes views about firearms in the United States.

But do these views also shape what sheriffs think about other policy areas? We argue yes, for those areas are where the CSPOA and extremists more generally have aligned on policy, including COVID-19 mask mandates and the January 6th insurrection.

As COVID policies spurred RWE activism in the general public (Tripodi 2021), lockdowns and mask and vaccine mandates prompted fierce opposition from RWE organizations, including the CSPOA (Chammah 2020a). Sheriffs vocally resisted mask mandates, articulating RWE-consistent views like anti-federalism with Sheriff Adam Bieber (Shawano County, Wisconsin), who argued that "Health Code orders should never encroach the Constitutional rights of the American people. The Bill of Rights was designed to protect against government overreach." Similarly, Sheriff Mike Herrington (Chaves County, New Mexico) refused to enforce the governor's mandates because "the Sheriff is not a hireling of the State. We do not work for the Governor or the County." Sheriffs' resistance presents a core issue for the enforcement of these mandates; as Sheriff Mark Lamb (Pinal County, Arizona) noted, "The only way these ridiculous and unconstitutional [COVID-related] mandates and orders, which are not laws, are going to continue is

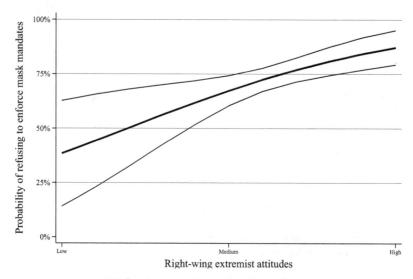

FIGURE 5.6. Right-wing extremism and mask mandate enforcement
Note: Predicted probabilities generated post hoc from models with controls for sheriff
ideology (liberal to conservative), Republican partisanship, county population, the
capacity of the office (including the number of deputies and jail capacity), COVID rates
in the county, and the share of the population who voted for Biden in 2020; only sheriffs
who served in states with mask mandates. Full results available in Results appendix.

if you continue to enforce them." Mack himself referred to masks as "face
diapers" and argued that sheriffs could not be forced to enforce either mask
or vaccine mandates (Mencimer 2021).

But how widely did sheriffs resist COVID mandates? In our 2021 survey,
we asked sheriffs, "What best describes mask mandates in your county?"
Response options included: there were not mask mandates, the sheriff
was not responsible for enforcing them, there were mask mandates and
the sheriff enforced them, or there were mask mandates but the sheriff did
not enforce them. Just under a third of sheriffs (31 percent) selected the
"did not enforce" option. We look at the substantive effects of RWE on the
probability of the sheriff refusing to enforce mask mandates (see fig. 5.6).
We find evidence of a strong substantive relationship: moving from the low
end (38 percent) to the high end (87 percent) of the RWE scale is associated
with an increase of nearly 50 percent in the probability that a sheriff refuses
to enforce mask mandates.

January 6th Insurrection

The radicalization of sheriffs into right-wing extremist ideologies continues today, in part through groups like the Proud Boys, Oath Keepers, and Three Percenters, alongside the CSPOA. These organizations center sheriffs ideologically and count them among their members and their founders (Jackson 2020). Sheriffs also have participated in events that involve threats and violence against federal and state government, including their presences at the January 6, 2021 insurrection and related events. Sheriff Dar Leaf from Barry County, Michigan shared a stage with and later defended militia members charged in a plot to kidnap the governor over her COVID-19 measures and tried to recruit other sheriffs to seize voting machines as part of an election conspiracy theory. Several other sheriffs participated in the January 6th efforts, including National Sheriffs' Association executive committee member Sheriff Chris West from Canadian County, Oklahoma, who attended the "Stop the Steal" rally in D.C. on January 6th, and Sheriff Mike Carpinelli from Lewis County, New York, who used official letterhead to ask for a light sentence for a capitol rioter.

To understand the relationship between RWE and sheriffs' views toward January 6th, we asked sheriffs, "Do you think the following individuals or groups are responsible for the violence at the US Capitol on January 6?" with options including Donald Trump (13 percent), social media companies (40 percent), congressional Republicans who opposed certification of the election (10 percent), Antifa (27 percent), and Joe Biden (9 percent). We again find a strong, significant relationship between RWE attitudes and these views; for example, moving from the low to high end of the RWE scale is associated with decreases in the view of Trump's responsibility from 50 percent to 5 percent and increases in the view of Antifa's responsibility from 7 percent to 70 percent (see fig. 5.7).

In many ways, the January 6th insurrection is consistent with past efforts of constitutional sheriffs to use force against the government; it is just a very different venue. Sheriffs' involvement in the Sagebrush Revolution and in the occupation of Malheur National Wildlife Refuge in Eastern Oregon (Skillen 2020) both represented key points where sheriffs supported individuals engaged in armed rebellion against the federal government. Clive Bundy, a cattle rancher who engaged in an armed standoff against federal agents over grazing fees on federal land frequently references the office of the sheriff, as does his son, Ammon, who led the Malheur standoff.[13] The conflict is not limited to major events: In Piute County, Utah, Sheriff Marty

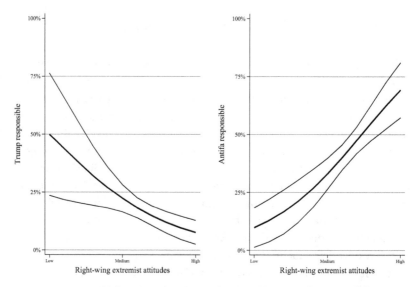

FIGURE 5.7. Right-wing extremism and views of January 6th responsibility

Note: Predicted probabilities generated post hoc from logit models with controls for sheriff ideology (liberal to conservative), Republican partisanship, county population, the capacity of the office (including the number of deputies and jail capacity), and the share of the population who voted for Biden in 2020. Full results available in Results appendix.

Gleave threatened to deputize "every man, woman and child in the county" to arrest federal employees for barring ranchers from federal land where restoration efforts were underway to revitalize aspen growth. Testifying before the Utah state legislature in 2016, Sheriff Gleave noted, "These federal people have no right to be here if you follow (the Constitution)" (Roth 2016). Other sheriffs regularly threaten to deputize citizens in various efforts to repel federal officers (Mcfeely 2022), particularly relating to the Bureau of Land Management. Indeed, sheriffs in our surveys are more likely to comment on the BLM (Bureau of Land Management) than they are to mention BLM (Black Lives Matter).

Following January 6th, sheriffs continue to be active promoters of false claims of voter fraud and other far-right conspiracy theories. For example, Sheriff Chuck Jenkins of Frederick County, Maryland, reported attending a CSPOA and Liberty University seminar and repeated Trump's lie that we will "find out this was the biggest fraud ever played." Sheriff Jenkins ominously proclaimed that "we're at a turning point in this society, where we are good vs. evil, and we have to somehow prevail" (Petrohilos 2021). Mack hosted a press event in Vegas in 2022 promoting election fraud conspiracies with a number of sheriffs, including Sheriff Calvin Hayden from Johnson County, Kansas, and Sheriff-elect Cutter Clinton from Panola County, Texas (Berzon and Corasaniti 2022).

Protect America Now and New Trends in RWE

Another modern evolution of RWE sheriffs is the emergence of the Protect America Now (Pishko 2021) organization led by Mark Lamb, who was elected sheriff of Pinal County, Arizona, initially in 2017 and ran for reelection unopposed. The Protect America Now organization is Lamb, just as CSPOA is Mack, but Lamb's approach to cultivate followers is through a more mainstream path. He (and his office) appeared on a reality television show; he launched a subscription streaming network, American Sheriff Network and wrote a book; and his Instagram account has more than 185,000 followers (as of April 2022) with the bio "God, Family, Freedom. . . . .that pretty much says it all. Oh, and Guns. 🤠."[14]

Lamb has capitalized on a public appetite for a more mainstream version of CSPOA, and he speaks at conferences at Mar-a-Lago and is a vocal supporter of former President Trump. In April 2023, Lamb filed paperwork to run for US Senate in Arizona. While Lamb does not call himself a constitutional sheriff, his positions align with RWE across a variety of dimensions. The description of his book, *American Sheriff: Traditional Values in a Modern World*, asks, "Are you concerned about the direction America is headed? Who is out there in the trenches fighting for our freedom and holding fast to the Constitution on our behalf?" and argues that "Our County Sheriffs are the last bastion of freedom against government overreach on a local and federal level." Lamb's efforts overlap almost entirely with the CSPOA, focusing on guns, immigration, and resisting COVID-19 mandates (Fox News Staff 2021). For example, Lamb regularly appears on news media to criticize the Biden administration's immigration policy (Hanchett 2022).

Beyond his central issues, Lamb's approach also aligns with Mack on what he is selling. Both sheriffs make money off their notoriety. Lamb sells books, T-shirts, and subscriptions to his reality television network. Along with memberships to CSPOA and courses, Mack peddles stickers to protect you from 5G, supplements, and essential oils. Both Mack and Lamb engage in ostensibly philanthropic activities—Mack through participating in a variety of fundraisers, especially for sheriffs in legal trouble, and Lamb through his American Sheriff foundation (AZ Central 2020). Mack's foundation, established as the "only not-for-profit foundation that is truly dedicated to restoring the faith and goodwill between our communities and the men and women that serve as first responders at a time when our Country is divided in its support for Law Enforcement" (American Sheriff Foundation 2022), raises money through donations and raffles, including raffling off an AR15 on Valentine's Day (C. Fernandez 2022). The foundation has repeatedly run into issues around tax filings and spending (Oxford n.d.; AZ Central 2020). These side hustles by both Mack and Lamb may emerge from the precarious position of both leaders: Mack was repeatedly unable to win reelection across multiple counties and offices and was accused of embezzling $350,000 from an anti-vaccine group, and Lamb has faced a variety of legal scrutiny, including a criminal investigation by the attorney general (CBS 5 News 2020).

Despite the questionable financial nature of both men and their organizations, their messages resonate with the public and with sheriffs. As we have shown here, Mack and CSPOA have successfully radicalized a generation of sheriffs to believe that the office has seemingly unlimited power and autonomy. As a result, the office of sheriff, already imbued with a great deal of autonomy and discretion, has become entangled with anti-federalism views. These views stand in the way of a wide set of reforms and policy efforts. Here, we have focused on firearms and COVID-19, but we anticipate similar effects in other areas where sheriffs receive specific signals on noncompliance from RWE individuals and organizations. For example, as CSPOA and Mack increasingly lobby their membership to take action against voting fraud, we expect to see these views proliferate among right-wing extremist sheriffs.

CHAPTER SIX

Sheriffs, Inequality, and the Possibility of Accountability

Oddie Shoupe was first elected sheriff of White County, Tennessee, in 2006. During his twelve-year tenure as sheriff, constituents sued his office more than fifty times (B. Hall 2018a). Multiple lawsuits alleged serious civil rights violations, including allegations of illegal searches (B. Hall 2017), wrongful arrest (B. Hall 2019), excessive force, and other constitutional rights violations, such as the accusation that Shoupe and a local judge were offering inmates a reduced jail sentence if they volunteered to be surgically sterilized (Hawkins 2017). The sheriff's behavior brought national attention when he ordered deputies to shoot rather than "ram" an unarmed man suspected of driving with a suspended license (Lartey 2018). The local prosecutor ruled the shooting to be justified, even when a deputy's body camera revealed the sheriff appearing to boast, "I love this shit. God, I tell you what, I thrive on it" (Hanna and Hartung 2018).[1] Sheriff Shoupe retired in 2018 after he decided not to seek reelection.

Sheriff Shoupe's tenure in office represents many of the fundamental challenges of the policing and legal system in the United States and sheriffs' part in it. Sheriffs and others involved in policing rarely face accountability for misconduct, and previous accountability efforts, such as body cameras and prosecutorial investigations, fail to deliver needed change. As we discuss in the book, sheriffs frequently point to elections as the central tool for their offices' accountability to justify their significant autonomy: if voters are displeased with how sheriffs or their deputies conduct themselves, then voters can just vote the sheriff out. Yet, examples abound of sheriffs accused of heinous behavior being reelected or quietly resigning without consequence. And without consequential reform to the office, the new sheriffs that replace them may continue the same or worse patterns. The democratic process often fails to produce meaningful accountability or change for sheriffs' misconduct. Since White County Sheriff Shoupe's retirement, the office under the leadership new sheriff, Steve Page, has faced a call for a federal investigation into excessive force, following body camera footage allegedly showing a sheriff's deputy repeatedly ordering a dog to attack a suspect, a county settlement in a retaliation lawsuit from former sheriff office employees, and a lawsuit for wrongful death that occurred during an arrest warrant (WTVF 2020; Mojica 2022). In the 2022 election, Sheriff Page's challenger was a former captain in the sheriff's office who had been fired by the sheriff for being "habitually insubordinate," following the captain's overseeing of an internal affairs investigation that criticized the sheriff's response in the dog attack. Page easily won with 3,310 votes to the challenger's 1,587 (K. S. Wood 2022).

Although sheriffs point to their elections as the ultimate accountability mechanism, the White County sheriffs show how little the office changes. Throughout the book, we have challenged this electoral accountability argument of sheriffs, showing that sheriff elections are rarely competitive, as the tenure for sheriffs is longer than other local elected officials and police chiefs; they rarely face competitive challengers in elections; and the pipeline to office is constructed as to limit accountability. As Sheriff W. E. Bozeman of Mitchell County, Georgia, noted of his 22 years in office, "I think they're going to have to vote me out or tote me out" (T. Smith 2015). The lack of electoral or other oversight combined with the decentralized nature of law enforcement in the United States sheriffs creates an office with considerable autonomy and vast and varying powers. As we show in the book, in the sheriff's office, employees, budgets, and jails can be used for political gains, marginalized populations can be punished, and right-wing extremism can flourish. Sheriffs occupy an exceptional place in the American political system, with authority and autonomy that lead to a significant resistance to change and the persistent difficulty of reform.

In this final chapter, we revisit the themes of previous chapters and look specifically at sheriffs and ideas of accountability, or holding law enforcement organizations and individuals responsible for "effectively delivering services to their communities, while treating people fairly, with dignity, and within the boundaries of formal law" (Archbold 2021, 1666). Calls for changes in policing have focused on municipal police departments, often overlooking sheriffs or treating all local law enforcement units as the same. Amid demands for policing reform, we argue that sheriffs deserve particular attention, given what we have shown as their unique position in American politics, local government, and policing. Sheriffs frequently use the unique nature of their office to organize to defeat, alter, or control state and national law enforcement policy and are slow to participate in reform efforts, if they participate at all. We conclude by considering how sheriffs' extraordinary levels of authority and autonomy, combined with low levels of accountability, create persistent opportunities for inequality under the law and challenges in reform.

Where, then, does this leave us? Are there forms of reform and accountability that would work on sheriffs, or that they themselves support? We recap our findings and look for the potential for accountability.

What Do We Know about Sheriffs?

Sheriffs' autonomy and authority, major themes for this book, stem from their ability to both set policy and implement those policies, their elections, the office's long history of independence, and the ability of sheriffs to craft a mythologized view of the office that is selective and insulates them from change. That sheriffs have long been a tool of the enforcement of the carceral state and white supremacy further insulates the office from accountability and change. The very characteristics that make sheriffs resistant to change have also left them vulnerable to right-wing extremism.

In chapter 1, we examine the historical roots of the office, focusing on key points of change for the office and the nation. In doing so, we make the argument that sheriffs have long been involved in the maintenance of the status quo in the United States, from upholding the Crown's interests in early colonial America to serving as a core enforcer for slavery and western expansionism, to fighting labor uprising, to assisting and at times leading the racialized violence of the Jim Crow era, to resisting the professionalization movement. Across the history of the office, incentives have pushed sheriffs (and sheriffs have readily complied) to expand the carceral state, as the office and individuals within the office benefited from the political economy of incarceration. The slow rate of change in the office can be traced to both the power accumulated by those in the office (and their resistance to change) and institutional designs that protect the office.

Chapter 2 moves us forward to today and asks: Who are sheriffs? And do those in office reflect their constituents? Sheriffs today are very white, very male, and very conservative; in each of these ways, they are out of step with their constituents. We document who sheriffs are and their attitudes and compare these patterns directly to their constituents. We then ask: why are sheriffs so out of sync with their constituents? To answer this, we turn to elections as a potential—and failing—tool of democratic accountability. We demonstrate that sheriff elections are highly *uncompetitive* because sheriffs regularly work in their own offices prior to seeking election, sheriffs themselves control the pool of potential political opponents, and sheriffs engage in strategic (and retaliatory) behavior to limit their political opponents.

Thus, the tool that sheriffs point to as making their office highly accountable is really the very thing that serves as a barrier to accountability.

What does this mean for how sheriffs behave in office? In chapter 3, we examine the role that low levels of accountability and high levels of autonomy play in shaping what sheriffs do as law enforcement leaders. We examine their role as managers of people, of the budget, and of the jail as each representing autonomy in unique ways and each as an area where sheriffs' behavior can be directly linked to their election and lack of accountability.

The ability of sheriffs to both set policies and processes and then enforce them means that the preferences and attitudes of sheriffs themselves can easily be translated into policies. In chapter 4, we examine three policy areas with concerns of unequal treatment under the law—violence against women, immigration, and racial discriminatory traffic stops—as venues for examining this connection between attitudes and policy. In each area, we find that sheriffs' individual beliefs about the targeted population (that is, women, immigrants, and Black people) shape their office's policies in those areas. As a result, there is vast inequality in the experiences that marginalized groups have with sheriffs across the country, depending on whether the sheriff has positive views toward a particular group or not.

The relationship between views and policy has been accelerated by a systematic radicalization effort from right-wing organizations and movements, with sheriffs playing a central role. In chapter 5, we discuss the origins, shape, and consequences of the constitutional sheriffs movement, a right-wing extremist movement among sheriffs that advocates the belief that sheriffs have more power than state or federal officials and that sheriffs have a responsibility to "interpose" between supra governments and their constituents. We demonstrate the widespread endorsement of these beliefs among sheriffs and the relationship between these beliefs and views of gun control, COVID restrictions, and the January 6th insurrection.

We next consider next the issues of accountability with the office of sheriff and the options for reform. Officials holding public office in a democratic society have an obligation of accountability to the public. We ask: To whom are sheriffs accountable? And what are sheriffs accountable for?

To Whom Are Sheriffs Accountable?

The expectation of accountability in policing is a more recent development (Rushin 2017), as policing now seen as abusive or as misconduct was considered regular for much of the country's history, as we discussed in chapter 1. Early investigations into policing (e.g., National Commission on

Law Observance and Enforcement 1931) revealed the depth of law enforcement's lawlessness, detailing problems of corruption and brutal and cruel tactics to maintain the status quo of America's racial, ethnic, and class order. For sheriffs, issues of corruption, abuse, and misconduct in the office date prior to its founding in colonial times and remain still a potential for the institutions' function in the enforcement of social control and the status quo. As we discuss in prior chapters, the systemic and disproportionate abuse of Black Americans (and, more broadly, people of color) by sheriffs is a long-standing practice, with serious abuses evident during slavery, western vigilantism, and the Civil Rights Movement, as discussed in chapter 1.[2] And the autonomy of the sheriffs' office today continues to allow sheriffs with racist, xenophobic, and sexist attitudes shape policies that target and harm marginalized members of society, as we demonstrate in chapter 4.

To justify their vast autonomy and powers, sheriffs connect their actions in office to their positions as elected officials in their communities. Although sheriffs frequently point to the office's English predecessor, the office of sheriff in the United States derives its authority from popular mandate through direct election rather than appointment. This institutional change was purposeful, as the colonists saw a royally controlled sheriff as an imposition of power from the British Empire. It was also profoundly important. While the office of high sheriff in England devolved into a weaker, more symbolic position (as the power of the throne also declined), sheriffs in the United States continue to play an important role in local policing, in part because of their electoral connection to the public they serve (Sattler 1992) and because of the expanding carceral state (H. L. Walker 2020; 2014).

While sheriffs contend that elections elevate the accountability the office,[3] we disagree and instead argue that elections afford sheriffs selective and distorted accountability. For most of US history, the right to vote explicitly excluded marginalized groups from the franchise, and those without voting rights were the least likely to receive protection of the law by voting majorities and policing agencies. Take for example Philadelphia, Mississippi, in 1965, where KKK members murdered three civil rights volunteers with assistance from the Neshoba County's sheriff's office. Talking to a reporter following the sheriff's arrest by the FBI for his connection to the slaying, white community members described Sheriff Lawrence Rainey as a "likeable fellow," "a fine man," and "the most cooperative sheriff" the county had ever had (Cleghorn 1965). Rainey's 1963 campaign advertisement for sheriff include the text "Vote for Lawrence Rainey, the Man Who Can Cope With the Situations That May Arise." The newspaper article pointed out that "everyone knew what situations might arise" and went on to describe stories of the sheriff's brutality toward Black community members.

Despite expansions in the right to vote following the efforts of the Civil Rights Movement, who serves as sheriff today remains largely unchanged: as we have shown in chapter 2, sheriffs are overwhelmingly white and male, with some law enforcement background and more conservative than the counties they serve. Their demographics match the highly mythologized image of the sheriff promoted in popular culture: a Western sheriff as a white man in a white hat, protecting a frontier town from threats, or a small-town Southern sheriff seen as one of the most important members of his community (Placide and LaFrance 2014). Sheriffs frequently defend elections as key to their positions in their communities.

One reason for the lack of representation in the office of sheriff is their uncompetitive nature, which benefits incumbent sheriffs, as we show in chapter 2. Sheriffs can serve long tenures, regularly standing for election with little competition. For instance, Sheriff Michael Ashe retired in 2016 after forty-two years as sheriff of Hampden County, Massachusetts, where he never once faced a challenger for reelection and greatly expanded the scope of the sheriff's office.[4] In Tennessee, Houston County sheriff Cullen Talton announced he would not run for reelection at age ninety-one in 2023, having served more than fifty years since being first elected in 1972.

Even when sheriffs face challengers, these are often low-information elections where the traditional path to the office of sheriff is within the office itself. We know little on how voters decide between candidates in sheriff elections, and examples show that voters will reelect sheriffs under indictment or suspicion of misconduct, and many sheriffs can continue to hold office even when under investigation for serious allegations of misconduct. For instance, in 2023 in Franklin County, New Hampshire, voters elected John Grismore, a former deputy in the sheriff's office who had been fired and charged with assault for kicking an individual handcuffed in custody (Ellerbrock 2023). These patterns suggest a segment of voters may reward candidates for misbehavior (or vote for them despite it), similar to the white voters of Mississippi in 1963. Recall Sheriff Joe Arpaio, whom we discuss in chapters 4 and 5, who served as sheriff for twenty-four years and won reelection multiple times, even after the Department of Justice concluded his office engaged in the worst pattern of racial profiling in US history (Kofman 2008). Arpaio styled himself as "America's Toughest Sheriff," and the appeal of sheriffs as aggressive enforcers of punitive policies, often labeling themselves as being "tough on crime" and "law and order" candidates, likely attracts some voters. The racialized policing by sheriffs in the expansive carceral state of today continues to provide sheriffs the legitimacy of state-sanctioned violence against communities of color that harkens back to their roots in maintaining white supremacy.

Issues of reform and accountability do come up in sheriff elections. On our 2021 survey, we asked sheriffs "What were the top three issues in your last election?," and more than 20 percent listed some component of reform or accountability as a central issue in their election:

- "Criminal Justice System reforms (negative impacts of "catch & release" policies)"
- "Dealing with Criminal Justice Reform."
- "RESTORING THE INTEGRITY TO THE SHERIFF'S OFFICE. THE PREVIOUS SHERIFF WENT TO FEDERAL PRISON"
- "Integrity of Office (previous sheriff had been arrested, then acquitted for domestic violence)."
- "Cooperation with ICE. Incarceration rates/racial disparity. Diversity"
- "Diversity (implementing training as well as dealing with pressure from different groups)"
- "De-Escalation training; Transparency; Hiring a more diverse workforce."

Yet, when we asked sheriffs about the top challenges their office faces, very few sheriffs listed efforts at reform. Instead, almost a quarter (24 percent) saw negative effects of state and federal reform efforts as a top challenge. Some focused on how reforms challenge their (perceived) constitutional position. These views range from the more mundane—"Legislation introducing bills to take away some of the Sheriff's responsibilities"—to the extreme: "Higher government arguing among themselves to include our current governor and state staff. Democrats and other parties going against the US constitution when it comes to health care and freedom of choice as no one should tell you to put something in your body or what to wear. That is straight from the books of Hitler in my opinion."

And even as sheriffs acknowledged that reforms were a central issue in elections, they also downplayed or dismissed these interests from their communities. Many sheriffs spoke about state and national overreach (Burns and Thomas 2004; Farris and Holman 2022, 2023). Sheriffs disputed that their constituents' concerns about reform were legitimate: "Unconstitutional mandates by state and federal government that take time to calm citizenry" and "Peoples attitude toward Law Enforcement as a country brought on by the Medea (thank god not in this area very good public support) and mandates."

Other sheriffs framed their responses as challenges associated with capacity, which ranged from concerns about unfunded mandates to the nature of the reforms ("Too many legislative changes too fast") to a reduction of law enforcement capacity: "so many new laws that are trying to tie the departments hands from doing our job correctly." Some sheriffs dislike that changes came from those they see as opposed to law enforcement—"Anti-law enforcement Liberal legislators" and "Over-regulation by outside liberal interests and politicians." Finally, some sheriffs pushed back against the idea of reform entirely, with one sheriff critiquing "A Broken Criminal Justice System that has adopted Marxist social justice theories. . . . Radical Hate spawned by a false narrative stating law enforcement is racist and white supremacist's" and another listing "new state laws restricting new highers, MEDIA!!!" as their top challenges.

Tools for Reform: Elections

If elections are going to be the tool that holds sheriffs accountable, as sheriffs suggest, are there ways to improve the mechanism?

One way may be to improve the pool of candidates and the competitiveness of elections. As we cover in chapter 2, in many states sheriffs are required to have previous law enforcement experience, and as a result many challengers or successors to the sheriffs' position come from within their own office. One reform that may be particularly appealing to those in law enforcement may be a *Law Enforcement Bill of Rights* (LEBoR), which includes (among other protections) "the right [for members of law enforcement] to engage in political activity or run for elective office" (Hager 2015). Some provisions of LEBoRs are criticized for negatively shaping the behavior of sheriffs' deputies and police officers (Dharmapala, McAdams, and Rappaport 2022; Keenan and Walker 2004), but less is known about how these protections might shape the competitiveness of sheriffs' elections or influence the acceptance or implementation of reforms. Do the benefits of a LEBoR outweigh the costs? Other sheriffs voluntarily place any staff member running against them under the supervision of other leaders (such as a nearby county) to reduce the possibility of retaliation or even the appearance of impropriety. There is reason to believe that sheriffs' deputies might need this protection, as sheriffs have retaliated against deputies who run against them. For instance, Sheriff Lenny Gramkow of Bon Homme County, South Dakota, fired the deputy who had run against him one minute after the polls closed when Gramkow lost his reelection bid (878 to 331) in 2018 (Jacobs 2018), and in 2022, Sheriff Jesse Jahner of Cass County, North Dakota, refused to reappoint his challenger as a deputy after he ran against him (Schroeer 2022). But opening the field to more people with law enforcement experience is unlikely to produce much substantive change if sheriffs are just being replaced with others with similar experiences and attitudes.

Activists hoping for greater progressive reform have begun increasingly focusing on recruiting and supporting challengers who are interested in reform for sheriffs' races, mostly in more urban areas (Vankin 2022). A handful of Democratic women sheriffs, including from Charleston County, South Carolina; Orleans Parish, Louisiana; Multnomah County, Oregon; and Fairfax, Virginia, have won election with help from candidate training programs such as Emerge, which helps Democratic women run for office. Campaigns by organizations such as the ACLU and Sheriffs for Trusting Communities have had some limited success in pointing out the failures of sheriffs and targeting particular sheriffs for electoral competition (Lacy 2019). As discussed in chapter 4, Black sheriffs in Georgia and North Carolina successfully ran on more progressive platforms surrounding immigration, campaigning with promises to end racial profiling and their offices' collaboration with ICE (Narea 2020). Sheriff Garry McFadden of Mecklenburg, North Carolina, celebrated his election by cutting a cake frosted with an anti-287(g) message (Spectrum News Staff 2019). These sheriffs' efforts prompted backlash in the North Carolina state legislature, where Republican legislators partnered with the state sheriffs' association to write legislation to force sheriffs' cooperation with ICE; the bill passed the legislature in 2019 and 2021 only to be vetoed by the governor both times (Doran and Bajpai 2022).

Once elected, these reformers often fail to live up to promises, according to activists. For instance, Sheriff David Hutchinson of Hennepin County, Minnesota, a liberal Run for Something–endorsed candidate, ran a campaign that appealed to progressives in 2018 (Run for Something 2018; Perry 2018) but did not run for reelection in 2022 after he was arrested for a DWI following a crash on the way back from a Minnesota Sheriffs' Association conference and was accused of a discriminatory and hostile work environment (Wiita 2022). In Charleston, South Carolina, activists expressed frustration at Sheriff Kristin Graziano's handling of a death in custody, her office's surveillance of activists' social media, and her termination of a Black deputy for not paying student loans (Benson 2021).[5] And as we discuss at the end of chapter 2, in Los Angeles, Sheriff Alex Villanueva ran on a reform and progressive platform in 2018 but became increasingly anti-reform and conservative over his term, clashing with activists, the Los Angeles Civilian Oversight Commission, and the county board of commissioners over numerous issues, including gangs within the sheriff's office, racial profiling, and how his deputies interacted with BLM protesters (Tchekmedyian 2021b; Lau 2019).

Additionally, activists question the premise of a progressive sheriff within the carceral state. While the first woman or nonwhite sheriff is often heralded as a new day within the office (Kramer 2022; Joyce King 2017), descriptive representation alone is not enough to ensure meaningful reform. For example, the right-wing extremist movements, discussed in chapter 5, include both women, such as former sheriff Sharon Wehrly of Nye County, Nevada, and people of color, such as former sheriff David Clarke of Milwaukee County, Wisconsin. Instead, reformers suggest meaningful change must include oversight, institutional changes, investments in initiatives to address the root causes of incarceration, and leadership from professional administrators, rather than new politicians (Kaiser-Schatzlein 2022).

Election-specific reforms might offer a path to increasing electoral competition, including limiting the number of terms a sheriff can run or the total time an individual can serve. Term limits are an interesting case, as many states enacted term limits for sheriffs early in American history because of concerns about sheriffs' ability to personally profit from the office. Today, in three states (Indiana, New Mexico, and West Virginia), the original state constitution stipulates that sheriffs cannot serve more than two consecutive terms. That the office is largely exempt from modern term limit efforts represents an anomaly in many ways. In the 1990s, fifteen states capped the maximum years that elected leaders can serve as part of "good government" reforms (Carey, Niemi, and Powell 2000). Many voters opted for their own versions of these caps for locally elected officials (C. Bell 2011). Yet, most states and localities that adopted term limits for mayors or city councils did not similarly adopt them for sheriffs. The effect of term limits on sheriffs' behavior is entirely unknown. Research on term limits in legislatures finds that they failed as a good government reform as they reduce the time that legislators spend on writing legislation, committee work, and votes (Carey et al. 2006; Fouirnaies and Hall 2022; Holman and Mahoney 2023). But if reformers are interested in a less effective sheriff's office, term limits might be a path toward reducing the power of the office.

Other ballot reforms like approval voting, eliminating closed primaries that often are the primary location of electoral competition, and ranked choice voting might offer the opportunity for new candidates to emerge in sheriffs' elections and to disrupt the high levels of incumbency effects that sheriffs enjoy (Lausen 2008; Santucci and Scott 2021; Santucci 2018; Collins, Lucero, and Trounstine 2020). Other voting reforms like universal vote-by-mail, same-day registration, or eliminating identity requirements could also stimulate a broader, more representative group of voters to participate in sheriff elections (Bonica et al. 2021; Southwell 2009; Grumbach and Hill 2022). While a broad swath of research has examined these kinds of reform on candidate emergence and voting behavior, the effect on highly uncompetitive elections like sheriffs is yet to be explored.

Tools for Reform: Civilian Review

More recent demands for citizen involvement in policing decisions often focus on civilian oversight boards. Civilian oversight boards are a locally created mechanism, staffed by civilians and appointed by local elected officials or via nomination by groups (such as neighborhoods, community organizations, or police unions) (Fairley 2020; Briggs 2017). Some boards require that (current or retired) law enforcement sit on these boards. Boards vary greatly in their powers and responsibilities: some are simply advisory boards whose members provide policy recommendations around law enforcement questions while others are investigative and/or adjudicatory, meaning they can evaluate misconduct and punish behavior, including recommending termination. The most powerful boards can set police policy, such as requiring officers be trained in alternatives to use of force or mandating the implementation of body cameras.

Although sheriffs frequently point to the community connections and legitimacy they gain from elections, few sheriffs support oversight of their office from civilian boards. When we asked sheriffs about the creation of civilian oversight boards, only 2 percent of our sample supported this reform. Sheriffs' resistance to local oversight is reflected in the very low occurrence of county-level oversight boards.[6] More than 85 percent of large police departments have some version of an oversight commission or board (LEMAS 2016). In comparison, only a handful of counties have implemented this oversight tool (Ban 2020). Currently, fewer than forty counties have oversight boards specifically aimed at sheriffs' offices; of those, only fourteen have any actual investigative power.[7]

Those boards that do exist for sheriffs' offices typically have very limited powers. For example, some sheriffs can decline the recommendations of their board or manage the direction of the board by appointing members (Toohey 2021). In 2020, the California state legislature passed AB 1185, which authorized counties to create a sheriff oversight board and/or an inspector general, either by board of supervisor action or vote of county residents (Vankin 2021). As of 2022, only six counties had adopted civilian review boards, and several sheriffs across California dismissed the need for such a board. In 2017, a member of the Sacramento sheriff's office shot and killed Mikel McIntyre, an unarmed Black man in mental crisis. After public outcry focused on creating an oversight board after the sheriff refused to release records, the sheriff called the implementation "a solution in search of a problem" (Rhee 2021; CBS Sacramento 2020). In Solano County, supervisors agreed with their sheriff against an oversight board, even despite recent scandals in the office, including a lawsuit alleging deputies brutally beat Nakia Porter, a Black woman, until she was unconscious during a traffic stop (KTVU 2021), and allegations of far-right extremism support among deputies (S. Morris 2021). As we discussed in chapter 1, county supervisors in Los Angeles established an oversight board in 2016, but former sheriff Villanueva largely ignored the board's requests for information (Dugdale 2021), refused to appear before the board (Tchekmedyian 2021a) or to answer subpoenas (J. Henry 2021), and repeatedly issued public statements defying the board's ability to regulate his behavior, calling the commission's efforts an "abuse of power" (Tchekmedyian 2021b). Recently, a judge ruled that the former Los Angeles sheriff will not face contempt hearings for defying subpoenas from the oversight board (Blakinger 2023).

Sheriffs often actively work to limit the possibility and power of civilian oversight boards. When the state legislature in Virginia was debating legislation to enable civilian oversight for sheriffs, John Jones, executive director of the Virginia Sheriffs' Association, argued sheriffs already have civilian oversight: "Sheriffs as elected constitutional officers are constantly under review, and we think the election is the ultimate citizen review board." Sheriffs were successful lobbying the Virginia legislature to remove sheriffs from the initial bill empowering local civilian oversight in reform policies of 2020 (Dujardin 2020).

Tools for Reform: Appointment

If the mechanism of elections and citizen oversight cannot improve sheriff accountability, some instead recommend institutional changes, including the idea of appointing sheriffs. Historically, early sheriffs in England and colonial America were appointed. Later, governors and state actors used the appointment power to circumvent political forces that they disagreed with—for example, in post–Civil War Reconstruction, Republican governors would bypass local elections to appoint sheriffs in communities where opposition to Reconstruction was at its strongest (Powell 2006; Foner 2013). In Louisiana, Republican governors appointed more than a third of sheriffs from 1868 to 1877 (Powell 2006). In several Southern states, attempts to professionalize policing (particularly out of concerns about racial biases) often led to discussions of appointing sheriffs. These attempts failed, often because of powerful state sheriffs' associations and a lack of coordinated support for appointment from deputies (Mickey 2015; Taylor 2018). State sheriff associations and the National Sheriffs' Association continue to vehemently oppose any efforts at appointment and defend elections.

Individual counties rarely attempt to move sheriffs to an appointed office, with most examples occurring in urban counties where the sheriff's power is already limited by a police department assuming most law enforcement powers. Yet, in those discussions, we often see advocates for appointment highlight the very issues we discuss here: the unrepresentative, limited pool of candidates, low visibility of these elections, and the problems with accountability. Only a handful of counties across the country appoint sheriffs.[8] In each of these places, either the mayor or county executives appoint the sheriff. A small number of other places have redesigned the sheriff's office to be more akin to a police department. For instance, in 1974, Riley County, Kansas, consolidated two police departments and the county sheriff into one office of the Riley County Police Department (Riley County Police Department 2021).[9] To prevent other counties from following Riley's lead, Kansas voters approved a constitutional amendment in 2022 requiring the election of sheriffs in all other counties in Kansas (Carpenter 2022).

Recent efforts to move the sheriff from elected to appointed highlight the discussions and conflicts around this decision. In King County, Washington, home to Seattle, the sheriff position has changed back and forth from elected and appointed: the position was elected from 1852–1969 and 1996–2021 and appointed in the interim and since. In 2020, voters approved charter amendments to allow the county council to return to appointing the sheriff and defining the duties of the office.[10] Those in favor of appointing the sheriff argued that by recruiting, rather than electing, a sheriff allowed for a wide pool of candidates with the ability to recruit nationally and would allow those with a greater stake a greater say in the sheriff's selection, as seven of the nine commissioners have unincorporated land in their district where only 11 percent of the county lives (Bick 2020). Finally, appointment would allow for a quicker removal process in the event of problems, rather than a lengthy recall process. Councilmember Girmay Zahilay explained, "An appointed sheriff is more accountable via the checks and balances of other government branches and can be told to communicate and engage with residents more frequently and authentically" (South Seattle Emerald 2022). The elected sheriff at the time (Sheriff Mitzi Johanknecht) lobbied strongly against the charter amendments, creating a group called Save our Sheriffs (endorsed by the National Sheriffs' Association) and framed the amendments as "defunding the police."[11] Following voters' approval of the change, the county council appointed Patti Cole-Tindall as sheriff, who had worked in the office since 2015 and previously worked with county council (King County 2022).

Other efforts to shift the sheriff's office to be appointed have failed. In 2021, Pierce County, Washington (a neighboring county to King County), considered changing the sheriff back to selection via appointment. Like in King, the Pierce County sheriff office had been previously appointed, from 1979 to 2006, following a former sheriff's conviction for racketeering. However, unlike King, the Pierce County Council struck down a measure to amend the office on a 4–3 vote (Donovan 2021), even amid the current elected sheriff, Ed Troyer, facing a criminal state investigation that we discussed in chapter 4 (Plog 2021). The idea of appointments has come up in other places, such as Ramsey County, Minnesota, and Multnomah County, Oregon, but these counties have not moved forward with legal steps to implement the changes (Gray 2020; The Editorial Board 2016). Meanwhile, Cuyahoga County, Ohio, has considered reverting the sheriff back to an elected position, given the frequent turnover in the position (Puente 2023).

The degree to which appointing versus electing sheriffs would shape their behavior is an open question. A limited body of existing research suggests that the mechanism of selection *might* shape how sheriffs behave by comparing sheriffs to police chiefs, who are municipal employees who serve at the appointment of city leadership. While sheriffs must maintain the support of voters, police chiefs must answer to mayors, city council members, or city managers (LaFrance and Lee 2010). With residency requirements in elections, sheriffs are more place-bound, as they are unlikely to move from position to position, while police chiefs can be poached by one city from another or move after being fired or resigning. Additionally, the elective nature of the sheriff's office means that "the sheriff is less insulated from the public than the police chief and lacks the administrative buffer that most municipal departments have" (Wells and Falcone 2006, 60). Some criminal justice scholars theorize that county sheriffs may interact more frequently and intimately with residents than other law enforcement officials because of the political nature of the office and direct citizen accountability through elections (S. Decker 1979; Falcone and Wells 1995; Wells and Falcone 2006). However, with so few appointed sheriffs' offices, as well as the distinct nature of those that are, there is limited opportunity to know its impact. Calls for shifting the selection mechanism for sheriffs usually follow scandal and face serious opposition from sheriffs and sheriff associations.

Tools for Change: Abolition Movement

For some protestors and activists, the persistence of police abuse and violence demands a policy response beyond reform and calls for defunding or abolishing the police and prisons (McHarris and McHarris 2020). Abolition emerges out of a long line of thought from a Black feminist praxis that calls for a process to disband, disempower, and disarm the police (McDowell and Fernandez 2018; Dobchuk-Land and Walby 2021). Advocates point to issues such as the racist origins of police, the failure of law enforcement to solve crimes, particularly crimes against women, people of color, immigrants, and LGBTQ individuals, and the aggressive policing and police brutality in Black communities and other marginalized communities (Vitale 2017; J. E. Cobbina-Dungy and Jones-Brown 2021). Calls for defunding the police typically recommend moving resources from policing agencies to social service, education, or infrastructure organizations (Weaver and Geller 2019) for community initiatives and reliance (Weaver, Prowse, and Piston 2020). While attention to the police abolition movement has focused largely on municipal policing,[12] some have called to defund and even eliminate the sheriff's office and its powers as well (Pishko 2019).

Some activists have called for the reduction of sheriffs' budgets, but few have been successful. For example, in 2020, Shelby County, Tennessee (location of Memphis, Tennessee), efforts to defund the police included flying a plane with a banner that said "Defund Sheriff" (Burgess 2020), and a county commission meeting became heated following unsuccessful proposals to reduce funding for the sheriff's department and reallocate that money to the county's Community Services Division (Dries 2020). In Los Angeles, the sheriff's $3.4 billion budget has been the target of defunding activism efforts, including cities within the county voting to reduce their funding of the department or to eliminate ties entirely (McGahan 2022; Gonzalez 2022). The diversity of sources of revenue and the autonomy of the office that we discuss in chapters 2, 3, and 4 both pose challenges to defunding sheriffs. If sheriffs receive less money from the county commissioners, do they then turn to extracting more resources from those in jail or engaging in more civil asset forfeiture or contracting with the federal government?

Sheriffs themselves have (unsurprisingly) not reacted positively to such calls surrounding their budgets, often arguing that defunding their offices would result in a reduction of services to the community's most vulnerable residents. Often contained within sheriffs' pushback are "carceral humanism" messages (Kilgore 2014), where sheriffs argue that defunding their office will lead to reduction in services like mental health care and drug addiction counselors, even if those are the kinds of services that would receive the funds previously earmarked for the sheriff. Other sheriffs threatened that, if defunded, their offices would no longer be able to train officers in nonlethal force. Very few sheriffs have supported reexamining their budgets and reallocating resources; Sheriff Daron Hall of Davidson County, Tennessee, supported reallocating funds for mental health care in an op-ed: "Thirty percent of those individuals in our facilities suffer from mental illness. You should take 30 percent of our budget, 30 percent of the police budget, the district attorney's, the courts, etc., and dedicate that money to a fully functioning community-based mental health system that actually helps people, doesn't criminalize them" (D. Hall 2020). However, Sheriff Hall's views remain an outlier among sheriffs and their associations.

Also unsurprisingly, sheriffs fiercely oppose abolition of their position. Sheriffs argue that to eliminate their elections or office would require voters to approve either a constitutional amendment or a state constitutional convention, given sheriffs' positions in many of their state constitutions. Connecticut is the only state to ever eliminate county sheriffs completely. In 1960, Connecticut's legislature abolished county government yet kept eight sheriffs as county officials as they were constitutional officers. In 2000, voters approved an amendment to the constitution that abolished the sheriff's office (Hoffman 2000). The change followed an investigation by the attorney general and numerous complaints of sheriffs' unprofessionalism and misconduct, including campaign finance violations, felony corruption conviction, ethics fines, and charges of embezzlement (Zielbauer 2001). The sheriffs' deputy association engaged in a three-year campaign in favor of the measure because they disliked their lack of civil service protection. Not surprisingly, the state's sheriffs themselves resisted the efforts, with their spokesperson calling the attorney general's report "ill-timed, incomplete and inaccurate" (Zielbauer 2001). One sheriff called the ballot measure a "witch hunt" (Weizel 2000). Ultimately, the sheriffs lost: the measure passed with 66 percent support from voters.

With the current political climate, it would be unlikely to find unified support from a state's legislature, attorney general, and governor to abolish the office, as was the case in Connecticut. Additionally, protections of sheriff deputies' employment from the spoils system in most other states[13] removed this constituency as a likely advocate for abolishment. We would expect that sheriffs in many states would also use their state associations to lobby hard against these efforts. For example, the Louisiana Sheriffs' Association has successfully lobbied against measures that are much less radical, including term limits for the office and the decriminalization of marijuana.[14]

One core challenge in the context of abolition is that sheriffs have often *grown* in strength in the context of police department abolition (W. R. King 2014; J. Cobbina-Dungy et al. 2022). Sheriffs often take over the duties from municipal police departments; in some states, the state constitution requires that sheriffs provide law enforcement for the entire county and thus take over when police departments are disbanded (W. R. King 2014). In other states, sheriffs have offered local governments cost savings during times of austerity (Brunet 2015). This trend started in California in the late 1970s as local governments looked for ways to reduce costs after having resources cut from the tax revolts of the 1970s and 1980s (Lowery and Sigelman 1981). In a study of the disbanding of local police departments, one public administration scholar found that many involved in the transition of services to the sheriff's office saw the benefits as "cost savings, greater visibility of sheriff's deputies, a higher degree of professionalism, and increased sense of personal safety" (Brunet 2015). In other locations, sheriffs take over failing police departments. One concern may be that sheriffs' offices may grow in size and funding from these municipal efforts.

For What Are Sheriffs Accountable?

As the goal of any elected official is to win reelection, sheriffs benefit from constraining accountability in elections but also expanding their autonomy in ways that suits them. Sheriffs enjoy wide discretion in their ability to shape their job and determine the scope of accountability. As we discuss in chapter 3, the formal powers of the sheriff are often defined in state constitutions and generally include powers and responsibilities in law enforcement, jail administration, and service to the courts.

There have been some changes to the job of sheriff, particularly as law enforcement underwent efforts at professionalization in the twentieth century, as the Supreme Court set new constitutional demands on policing agencies and the Civil Rights Movement challenged racial discriminatory practices in the criminal justice system (S. Walker 1977; Schrader 2019). Professionalization in the second half of the twentieth century helped to legitimize law enforcement's authority and helped them to organize themselves for their own independence, power, and resources (Henderson 1975). But this new conception of a more professional and sophisticated policing authority also widened the gulf between police and citizens in the second half of the twentieth century.[15] Police departments became large, centralized bureaucracies that were isolated from the public and generally resistant to and defensive about outside control (Walker and Katz 1992). For sheriffs, however, the unique nature of their role as elected law enforcement officers meant they had long viewed their office as an autonomous agent of the state and empowered by authority from the voters. While sheriffs' offices adapted to the changes (particularly larger and more urban offices), sheriffs also had a greater sense of independence from outside influence and resisted changes imposed onto them from other elected leaders from the start.

What the autonomy of sheriffs means in practice is that it is largely up to the individual sheriff to decide. Sheriffs assume many duties in their quest for reelection, and an individual sheriff's views can shape his office's policies. As one sheriff describes his job in our survey, "The Sheriff's Office is not who the NATIONAL media portrays us to be. We in rural America are the next best thing to your mom and dad. We are the protectors, the doctors, the counselor, the teachers and the enforcers of our laws to keep the peace of our community the best we can. We have many hats in rural America." In his sixth term in Jefferson Parish, Louisiana, Sheriff Harry Lee put it this way: "The sheriff of [Jefferson Parish] is the closest thing there is to being a king in the U.S. I have no unions, I don't have civil service, I hire and fire at will. I don't have to go to council and propose a budget. I approve the budget. I'm the head of the law-enforcement district, and the law-enforcement district only has one vote, which is me" (J. Burnett 2006). In short, the autonomy of the office means that sheriffs enjoy discretion to shape the office in whichever ways he wants.

Sheriffs reinforce their autonomy through brand management, or, as some might call it, "copaganda" (Bernabo 2022). Sheriffs are aware of the need to capture the public's attention and shape the narrative around what they do and the role of their office. In considering how he manages public attention, Sheriff Grady Judd of Polk County, Florida, noted, "I lay it out there and tell them the truth and a little entertainment draws their attention to what's important—and that's the story" (Ring 2022). Judd frequently appears on local television in Tampa, selling "Sheriff on a Shelf" figurines[16] or calling a suspect in a Christmas present theft a "Grinch" with "eggnog for brains" (Monahan and DaSilva 2021). Fellow Florida sheriff Wayne Ivey posts on YouTube a weekly "Wheel of Fugitive" video where he spins a wheel with mug shots of wanted fugitives in Brevard county (Brevard Sheriff 2022). Sheriffs seek to maintain their mythologized image in the popular press with radio shows, social media, and true crime shows on A&E Network and even creating their own streaming network (like Pinal County, Arizona's Sheriff Lamb). While the fragmentation of media sources and social media have made it easier for sheriffs to communicate with the public, brand management is not a modern phenomenon. In the 1950s, Sheriff

"Buckshot" Lane of Wharton County, Texas, came to national fame for writing weekly missives to local newspapers with headlines like "5 Fighters 3 Drunks 5 Drunk Drivers, 4 Peace Disturbers, 2 Insane, 1 Misd Theft, 1 Wife Child deserter, 2 Traffic Violations"; these letters and a broader set of escapades landed the sheriff a nine-page photo essay in *LIFE* magazine in 1950 (*LIFE Magazine* 1950).[17]

Tools for Reform: Investigations

One of the significant challenges that sheriffs face in managing both their brand and staff is dealing with misconduct. A detailed investigation into internal investigations for misconduct in Maine sheriff offices revealed large discrepancies between agencies, with some sheriffs reporting high numbers of internal investigations and sanctions and other sheriffs reporting no investigations or simply that they did not keep track of the data (Keefe, Rhoda, and Ferguson 2021). Even when a sheriff's second-in-command faced a months-long investigation for sexual harassment, sexism, and homophobia, the Kennebec County sheriff failed to report his misconduct to a central database, and the deputy faced no consequences (Rhoda 2021).

When sheriffs themselves have engaged in misconduct, others in local, state, and federal governments may investigate, but the process is complex. For instance, local prosecutors and district attorneys may investigate the sheriff, and local courts may attempt to hold the sheriff accountable via traditional judicial mechanisms, but a traditionally cozy relationship between law enforcement and local prosecutors may threaten the possibility of this as path to accountability. Investigations into sheriffs' misconduct can also originate from state officials, although such mechanisms are perhaps surprisingly underpowered in many states. The most common course for state-level investigations of sheriffs is via the state attorney general, but this office lacks investigative or arrest powers in many states, being able to intervene only when requested by other authorities. When Sheriff Ed Troyer was charged with false reporting following a confrontation with a Black newspaper carrier (as we discuss in chapter 4), the governor had to ask the attorney general to investigate (Ferguson 2021). As is common for sheriffs, indictments alone were not enough for his removal from office. Instead, the governor had to suspend him from his post (Melendez 2021).

The Department of Justice (DOJ) can also investigate sheriffs whose offices engage in repeated misconduct or violate federal laws (DOJ 2017). The most intense (and infrequent[18]) form of federal intervention is a consent decree to correct a "pattern or practice" of unconstitutional policing (Rushin

2013). For example, when Marlin Gusman, the sheriff of Orleans Parish, Louisiana, entered into a consent decree because of "unconstitutional" jail conditions, he agreed to eight years of federal monitors of jail conditions, regular reporting to a judge about the conditions of the jail, and, ultimately, building a new jail facility (Sledge 2020). For some sheriffs, the threat of investigation and costly litigation alone can encourage changes, like Escambia County, Florida's sheriff's office changing conditions of confinement after investigation, thus avoiding a consent decree (DOJ 2013).

For investigations into sheriffs' managements of jails, oversight typically comes in the form of the state setting minimum standards for certification to operate and inspections to ensure compliance (Deitch 2020). Standards tend to be minimal and vague and often are written by sheriffs, either as members of regulatory boards such as in Texas or through sheriffs' associations as in Utah. Sheriffs set their own jail regulation in four states: Idaho, Florida, Oregon, and Utah, where these regulations are voluntary and not well enforced. In other states, outside agencies (such as the Texas Rangers and Texas Commission on Jail Standards) are tasked with investigations with varying success (Kanu 2022). Recall Sheriff Bill Waybourn of Tarrant County, Texas, from chapter 2, whose jail has been criticized for the increased number of deaths in recent years, including the death of a baby ten days after being born unsupervised in the jail. The jail temporarily lost certification but criticisms over the management of the jail persist as deaths in the jail continue.

Investigations into bad behavior, no matter the source, have limited effectiveness as a reform mechanism. Misconduct can be frequent—for instance, in South Carolina at least thirteen of the sheriffs in the state's forty-six counties have been convicted of crimes since 2010, and six were sentenced to prison time. Investigations can be slow—for instance, Sheriff Dewayne Redmon of Graves County, Kentucky, was indicted for charges that the sheriff took drugs from a drop box for himself, ran for reelection (even after a judge ruled he was banned from law enforcement activities), and died in office a year later (Shields and Darnell 2018; J. Wright 2018). Reformers widely criticize investigations as a method for addressing law enforcement misconduct because they fail to propel institutional change and suggest the problem is a "few bad apples." Investigations can serve as a tool for remediating the worst behavior or removing sheriffs from office for gross offenses but may produce little to no broader reform. When they do investigate, the federal government tends to target large offices with high-profile incidents of misconduct, such as investigations into the Los Angeles County Sheriff's Department, which resulted in a prison sentence for former sheriff Lee Baca following a federal civil rights and corruption probe sparked by investigations from the *Los Angeles Times*, the ACLU, and a county commission (Winter 2014). Yet, the punishment of a prior sheriff did not seem to result in changes for the Los Angeles office, as the following sheriff also faced serious allegations of unethical conduct, and reports of deputy gangs engaging in violence, corruption, and illegal activities persist (Tchekmedyian 2021b; Goodyear 2022; Sheriff Civilian Oversight Commission 2023).

Tools for Reform: State and Federal Policies

Federal policy efforts to increase policing accountability have dwindled following the summer of 2020's demands for accountability and change following the murder of George Floyd. The proposed federal legislation, stalled after yearlong negotiations for a bipartisan federal effort, would have included several reforms, including collecting better data, altering qualified immunity, and tying federal funding to changes in local policies, such as banning the use of tactics such as no-knock warrants. Sheriffs opposed parts of the reform: "We have grave concerns about the current draft," said Jonathan Thompson, executive director of the National Sheriffs' Association (Wu and Levine 2021). The South Carolina Sheriffs' Association's president criticized the legislation as "de facto defunding the police" (Tobson 2021).

States have engaged in a wide set of policy efforts at oversight over law enforcement, although sheriffs often are excluded or simply do not participate. These attempts typically focus on a particular aspect of sheriff's responsibilities, such as rules and regulations about jails; the finances of local law enforcement; trainings and practices on use of force; profiling and interactions with vulnerable populations; and crisis intervention. States have also passed laws and implemented executive orders that require more extensive documenting of policing operations, including mandating the use of body-worn cameras, protecting rights to record the police, and incentivizing or requiring data collection/reporting practices (Subramanian and Skrzypiec 2017; NCSL 2021). Some recent efforts to allow for more oversight have failed, like in Maine (Keefe 2021), or been written to exclude sheriffs, as mentioned in Virginia.

States can and have pursued reform on multiple tracks at once. When then-governor Cuomo[19] tasked every local law enforcement agency in New York with developing a plan for reform, he also included an enforcement mechanism: failure to do so would risk future opportunities for state funding. In response, fifty-five of the fifty-nine elected sheriffs' offices in the state eventually created and uploaded plans. But compliance with

TABLE 6.1. Reform policies

Does your office have in place any of the following directives for officers, either as a written policy or as a procedural directive?	Share indicating yes
Limit the use of no-knock warrants	66%
Ban chokeholds or strangleholds	44%
Prohibit shooting at a moving vehicle	74%
Require officers to intervene to stop another officer from using excessive force	49%
Do you favor any of the following policies?	
Give a civilian oversight board the power to investigate and discipline misconduct by your deputies	2%
Create a federal government database to track law enforcement officers who have been accused of misconduct	34%
Make it a crime for police to use chokeholds or strangleholds	8%
Require law enforcement to be trained in nonviolent alternatives to deadly force	57%

Note: 2021 survey data

planning is not the same thing as compliance with engaging in reform. These plans range from 4 pages (Lewis County) to 417 pages (Tompkins County). Sheriff Derek Osborne's plan in Tompkins County included establishing alternatives to the police for nonviolent crimes and mental health crises, wraparound health and human services delivery, and the creation of "a Tompkins County Public Safety Review Board." In his reelection bid, Sheriff Osborne[20] noted that his efforts in the first term included "policies beyond accreditation standards, to include: Duty to Intervene, Equitable Policing, Interactions with Transgender & Gender Non-Conforming Persons, and Responding to Incidents Involving Emotionally Disturbed Persons" as well as the demilitarization of police uniforms, transparency in policies, use of force statistics, complaint procedures in eleven languages, and more stringent hiring standards (Osborne 2022).

On the 2021 survey, we asked sheriffs about the adoption or willingness to support common reform policies with fairly high levels of affirmative response (Campaign Zero 2016; 8 can't wait 2022). As we show in Table 6.1, almost three-fourths of the sheriffs indicated that their office already prohibits their deputies from shooting at a moving vehicle, and almost half require that officers intervene to stop the use of excess force by a fellow law enforcement officer. When we inquired about the degree to which sheriffs favored some of the policies highlighted by reformers, more than half indicated that they would support a requirement that law enforcement receive training on nonviolent alternatives to deadly force, and a third supported the creation of a federal database to track law enforcement officers accused of misconduct. Other policies are far less popular: only 8 percent of sheriffs support criminalizing chokeholds, and as we mentioned above, 2 percent favor the creation of civilian oversight boards.

Although sheriffs do not seem opposed to most of these policy choices, the degree to which shifts in these policies would change outcomes is an open question. One organization, 8CantWait, argued for the adoption of eight policies most associated with reduction in police violence in the aftermath of George Floyd's murder. The 8CantWait policies were adapted from examining police shootings in the one hundred largest cities in the United States.[21] As a reminder, more than half of sheriffs' offices employ fewer than 25 sworn officers, and only 4 percent of sheriffs oversee more than 250 employees. This suggests that additional research is needed to understand how smaller sheriffs' offices and police departments engage in misconduct, especially violence toward individuals, and what policies might shift those behaviors. And data provision from activist groups focuses almost entirely on city-based adoption of these efforts with only a few sheriffs' offices listed on their website. Sheriffs themselves express skepticism about many of the central reform efforts. Take, for example, one sheriff who told us:

> I think "choke holds" have been over blown. It can be trained and be useful in some situations . . . the LVNR [lateral vascular neck restraint] or shoulder pin as taught by PPCT [pressure point control tactics] is just fine when trained on and used properly. I see NYPD was instructing officers to not place any weight on the subject's back. . . . I'm not sure how you wrestle with and fight with someone and then place handcuffs on them, but not put any weight on their back or chest area. Like anything in law enforcement, you have to stay in the "reasonable" arena and I think there has been a knee jerk reaction to some use of force incidents around the US that affect us all.

Sheriffs regularly argue that they lack the capacity or funds to adopt reforms, such as body cameras or mental health care in jails. For example, in Washington State, sheriffs pushed back against reform legislation enacted in 2021 that limited the ability of law enforcement to respond to individuals in crisis. Rural sheriffs noted practical concerns, as limitations of staffing and resources mean that their office is the only first responder in the community. Sheriffs also express frustration about the resources that their offices control and their ability to keep up with changing standards for law enforcement. Forty-two percent of sheriffs in our 2021 survey listed funding as one of their top challenges. Sheriffs note few resources for improvement or to address specific issues in their communities:

- "The costs to maintain quality equipment, training and staff keeps going up, faster than revenue"
- "Budget. Very rural with little tax base. No money for training or improvement"
- "Funding is not sufficient to make the necessary changes, buy equipment or have additional personnel to make changes that would help the community."

In some communities, sheriffs have been effectively defunded for decades because of a lack of a funding base. In chapter 3, we discuss Martin County, Kentucky, and Josephine County, Oregon, where the sheriffs' offices in both counties have been de facto defunded at points in time. Yet, these moves have not been accompanied by a shifting of funds to alternative service providers like social workers as the Defund the Police movement might hope; instead, the money is simply just not there, resulting in no services at all for the residents of these counties.

Tools for Reform: Funding

One of the primary policy tools that local, state, and federal governments have over sheriffs is spending power. The federal government uses funding mechanisms to incentivize reform, typically in the form of conditions on contracts or grants.[22] DOJ awards grants to sheriffs and can then monitor those grant recipients to ensure they are not engaging in illegal discrimination (DOJ 2021).[23] For instance, the DOJ was able to more easily investigate Sheriff Joe Arpaio of Maricopa County, Arizona, for discriminatory policing practices targeting Latinos precisely because Sheriff Arpaio's office had received a large federal grant that gave investigators access to records and materials (DOJ 2011). The federal government also attempts to shape the behavior of sheriffs via threats to retract resources. To promote vaccination against COVID-19, the Biden administration mandated vaccinations for all federal contractors via an executive order, which included sheriffs who had ICE contracts with the federal government (*Stevens and Hildenbrand v. US*, 2021). Sheriffs pushed back against these efforts: in this circumstance, two Ohio sheriffs sued the administration, saying they would give up their ICE contracts rather than risk losing deputies who did not want to be vaccinated (WTVG 2021). Other sheriffs opted to give back COVID-related relief funds because of concerns about the ability of the federal government to use those funds to then force the sheriff's office to engage in other behaviors; Bonner county, Idaho sheriff noted, "I will not follow applicable federal statutes, regulations, and executive orders of President Joe Biden or his administration" (Keith 2021).

The path forward for accountability remains challenged.

Implications and Directions for Future Work

The material in this book is far from a complete picture of the politics, policies, and outcomes of associated with sheriffs in the United States. Despite the importance of sheriff elections, we continue to know very little about what sheriff elections are like, how sheriffs campaign, and how voters make decisions about who will be their sheriff. Many sheriffs reported to us that they spend very little on their campaigns, particularly in their later terms. Does that mean that there simply is not a campaign for the office? How do voters make decisions in these extremely low information electoral environments? We also know very little about the consequences of sheriff elections. In his academic study of the relationship between sheriffs' partisanship and cooperation with ICE, D. M. Thompson (2020) uses close elections as a mechanism for study. Other research in progress finds that sheriffs who are leaving office reduce their arrest rates, providing suggestive evidence that elections do shape sheriffs' behavior. But when and how elections might change the law enforcement experience of a county is a question that remains open; we hope future research will engage in this work.

Our work has relied very heavily on journalistic investigations of sheriffs, and we are incredibly grateful for the work that reporters across the United States have done to hold sheriffs accountable.[24] The decline of local news (Darr, Hitt, and Dunaway 2019; Gentzkow, Shapiro, and Sinkinson 2011; Nielsen 2015) threatens our society-wide ability to hold sheriffs accountable for their bad behavior. But local media also can play a role in amplifying mistruths from sheriffs, especially when local media rely on the sheriffs to provide information and are reluctant to damage those relationships.

When Meeks (2020) evaluated how the media covers sheriff elections, she found little in-depth coverage or accountability. Research on the relationship between local media and sheriffs and how this shapes investigations and accountability would be welcome, as would evaluations of how the decline and nationalization of news have shaped sheriffs' behavior and accountability. We also observed that sheriffs increasingly serve as a news source in their communities through their Facebook pages, which are full of emergency warnings about weather and natural disasters (Burns and Thomas 2015; Downing and Myers 2020), as well as often serving as a form of a community bulletin board. How does the sheriff stepping into a vacuum left by a retraction of local news shape trust in the office and accountability? What will happen if or when Facebook is no longer available or easy for sheriffs to use?

While we speculate about the differences between sheriffs and police chiefs, particularly around the mechanism of appointment versus elections, we do not truly know how a change in selection and accountability might shape sheriffs' behavior. Using case studies of the few counties that have moved back and forth between appointment and election (such as King County, Washington) might provide researchers the opportunity to understand how elections do or do not shape sheriffs' behavior. Similarly, examining how sheriffs change their behavior when powers are removed from their office might provide reformers the opportunity to understand which kinds of concrete defunding and deauthorization efforts are the most successful.

We come out of this project deeply concerned about the long-term consequences of right-wing extremism and constitutional sheriffs. Constitutional sheriffs such as Barry County, Michigan, sheriff Dar Leaf have been involved in supporting those engaged in violence against the government, and CSPOA president Richard Mack has publicly endorsed election fraud conspiracies. The ability of local democracy to withstand these efforts is in question, and more research is desperately needed. Our work also calls attention to the dearth of knowledge that political scientists have about rural politics (but see excellent work by Nemerever and Rogers 2021; Hochschild 2018; Cramer 2016) and asks: how can we know more about local politics outside big cities? As we consider the ways that US democracy is threatened today (Kalmoe and Mason 2022), understanding the roots of some of these attitudes in rural America demands additional consideration.

What Can Be Done?

We close the book with one more sheriff. Kim Stewart is an anomaly among sheriffs for many reasons. She is the first woman sheriff of Doña Ana County, New Mexico, the county's first openly gay sheriff, and the only sheriff that we can identify who mentions the potential of abolishing the office (Gumprecht 2018). Stewart, who had been an investigator with the county's internal affairs division (and sued the county as a whistleblower after she was fired for a $1.6 million settlement) had previously investigated the sheriff in power and decided she was "going to do what [she] could to prevent him from returning to office" (Cook 2022). Since taking office, Stewart has filled vacant positions, hiring more than forty deputies, modernized the computer equipment, and renegotiated several major contracts (Garcia 2022). She also told us,[25] "Sheriff candidates should have to meet certain education and experience levels or abolish the office entirely" and has said "The cowboy hat and the six-shooter on their hip tells me so much about their mindset. . . . More of us need to speak out and say, 'This doesn't represent us'" (Chammah 2022).

Stewart's campaign website states her "long-held belief that government cannot be responsive to the needs of the community without its own house first being in order" (K. Stewart 2022). Her Facebook campaign page features pictures of her dog, comments on the legalization of marijuana that start with "Happy 4/20," and swipes at her opponent for being a DINO (Democrat in Name Only). She also details a list of more than two hundred accomplishments during her first term that include items like withdrawing from Operation Stonegarden, a Homeland Security program that provides funds to local law enforcement agencies to "secure the United States' borders along routes of ingress" (Homeland Security 2022; Nichanian 2018). The Doña Ana County Sheriff Office's (DACSO) cooperation with Homeland Security had been renewed under Stewart's predecessor, Sheriff Enrique "Kiki" Vigil, who had been very vocal and aggressive about his opposition to immigrants in the county.[26]

In many ways, Stewart is the sheriff that some reformers want. She is working on the county jail accreditation process, updated the office's policies to be in line with state and national court rulings, reformed the deputy promotion process, and her office now accurately reports more information to the FBI. But she is not the sheriff that advocates for defunding the police or abolitionists want. Despite Sheriff Stewart's skepticism about the office, she ran for reelection in 2022 to "finish the job she started,"[27] including proposing "a bold budget," increasing the number of staff, and modernizing the office (Cook 2022). Sheriff Stewart is thus expanding the size of and reliance on policing in her community as she works to increase efficiency and fairness. And Stewart admits the office still faces problems, particularly following the arrest of a deputy accused of sexually assaulting a woman he arrested (Garcia 2023).

In this book, we have detailed a wide set of problems with the elected office of sheriff: elections largely fail to hold sheriffs accountable; sheriffs support and expand the carceral state, may engage in civil rights violations and discrimination without meaningful reform, endorse right-wing extremism, and re-create a unequal past where women, people of color, and especially women of color were punished rather than protected by the law. What, then, is the solution to the problem of sheriffs? As we consider whether the office should and can be reformed, the focus on the "white hats" or individuals who might save the office in their local community suggests we just have to find someone "guilty of incredible credentials, impeccable character, and indisputable concern and innovation" (Fredericks 2020).

But does this reliance on good individuals offer a true opportunity to reform the office? After all, for every potentially good sheriff we examine in this book, there are an equal or larger number uninterested in reform, intent on holding onto the office long after change is needed, or engaged in explicitly immoral behavior, and the institution itself perpetuates and accelerates these patterns. For every Sheriff Stewart or Sheriff Cain, we have a Sheriff Youngblood, "Corndog" Barlett, Songer, or Shoupe. So, do we seek more Sheriff Stewarts in our communities and put more resources into creating fair and justice policing? Or do we defund and abolish? The status quo is untenable, but the path forward requires difficult choices, many of which sheriffs themselves will actively fight.

Data and Methods Appendix

In the book, we draw on several core sources of data and information. For much of the text, we rely on information provided to us by sheriffs on two surveys that we conducted in 2012 and 2021. Each survey contains the responses of more than 500 sheriffs who resemble the demographics of sheriffs overall in the United States. For each survey, we started with the full population of sheriffs and attempted to email each sheriff. This in itself proved to be difficult. While the National Sheriffs' Association maintains a database of sheriffs and updates it each year, the database had more than 20 percent missingness in 2012 and 35 percent in 2022. We used web searches, including of sheriffs' offices, social media accounts, and media reports, as well as state-level directories to supplement the directory each year. When we emailed the sheriffs, we looked for correct emails for any emails that bounced back to us as undeliverable.

2012 American County Sheriff Survey: Identifying those sheriffs with a valid email address in the National Sheriffs' Association directory, in state sheriff association directories, or online through web searches, we constructed a directory of 2,838 sheriffs and contacted every sheriff in the constructed directory to participate in an online survey via email in the fall of 2012. As a follow-up, we mailed postcard invitations to all sheriffs with valid mailing addresses if they had not responded to the survey a month after the online invitation. Just under one-fifth (556, 19.5 percent) of the sheriffs for whom we had any contact information participated in the survey.[1]

2021 American County Sheriff Survey: We started with the National Sheriffs' Association directory, which contained email addresses for 1,770 sheriffs. For all sheriffs missing email addresses, we used state sheriff association directories and internet searches to fill in information, resulting in 3,005 email addresses. We emailed these sheriffs in November 2021, with repeated follow-up email reminders. For any email that bounced back as undeliverable, we engaged in another round of internet searches to identify alternative contact information. Over a fifth (576, 21.5 percent) of the sheriffs for whom we had email addresses took the survey.

The average county that a sheriff in the survey represents is generally less demographically diverse than the average US county. The white population is 78 percent in both the average US county and the average county in the survey. Sheriffs in the survey also have a slightly smaller percentage of foreign-born residents. The sheriffs who completed the 2012 survey represent counties that have a lower population than the US average, with a lower population density.

All available data suggests that the sheriffs who completed our surveys are similar to sheriffs overall and the counties they represent are similar to counties in the United States. In both 2012 and 2021, the counties represented by sheriffs in our survey look very similar to the average US county, as we present in table M1.

TABLE M1. Survey counties

Variable	Measure	Source	2012 survey counties	2021 survey counties	US counties overall
Obama vote 2008	Average county % vote for Obama in 2008	MIT Election Archive	38%	36%	38%
Biden 2020	Average county % vote for Biden in 2020	MIT Election Archive	33%	36%	38%
Population	Average of county population	Census	54,490	57,261	61,474
Income	Average Median Household Income, 2010	Census	45,134	45,097	43,244
% White	Average county % White, 2010	Census	82%	82%	79%
% Latino	Average county % Latino, 2010	Census	7%	8%	8%
% Black	Average county % Black, 2010	Census	7%	7%	9%
% Rural	Average count % rural	Census	23%	23%	23%
% Public land	Share of the land owned by state or federal government	Headwaters Economics	15%	16%	13%

Observational Data on Sheriffs

We also collect observational information directly about the sheriffs, in-cluding their gender, race, social media handles, website biographies, and media coverage. In 2021, we also took a random sample of 15 percent of the total US sheriff population and engaged in robust internet searches about each sheriff, collecting information on the key issues of their office, their so-cial media activity, and media coverage of their office. To examine elections and candidates for sheriffs' offices, we rely on the California Election Data Archive, which provides the names and stated occupations of all candidates for local office in California from 1996 to 2020. We hand code the occupa-tions of all candidates for sheriff in this data (643 total candidates across the years) into one of four categories: incumbent, internal challenger, local external challenger, and a miscellaneous category.

In 2012 and 2015, we constructed databases of the gender and race of all sheriffs in the United States. These databases were constructed by the authors and a trained research assistant, who looked at photographs, me-dia coverage, and personal accounts to identify the gender and race of 94 percent of sheriffs in the United States in 2012 and 87 percent of sheriffs in 2015. In 2021, we also took a random sample of 15 percent of the total US sheriff set and engaged in robust internet searches about each sheriff, in-cluding documenting their gender and race. See figure M1 for each sheriff

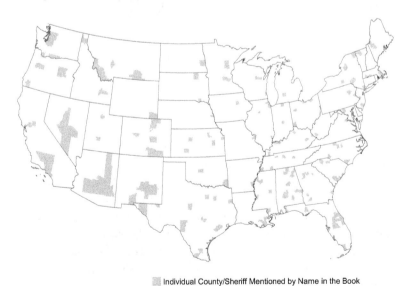

▨ Individual County/Sheriff Mentioned by Name in the Book

FIGURE M1. Sheriffs/counties discussed by name in book

and/or county we mention by name in the book. Please note that this does not include the sheriffs who took either the 2012 or 2021 surveys to preserve their confidentiality.

Partisanship and Ideology of Counties

We use three measures to evaluate partisanship and ideology:

1. A measure of partisanship calculated from aggregating large public opinion surveys together. Here we incorporate data from the 2012, 2014, 2016, 2018, and 2020 Cooperative Elections Study (previously the Congressional Cooperative Elections Study [CCES]) to estimate the share of each county that falls into one of five partisan categories.
2. The share of the county that voted for Barack Obama in 2012 (to accompany our 2012 survey data) and Joe Biden in 2020 (to accompany our 2021 survey data).
3. A measure of the ideology of the population in each county calculated by political scientists Tausanovitch and Warshaw (2013; 2022), who pool together large surveys of the American public and use Bayesian Item-Response and multilevel regression and poststratification, which incorporates respondents demographics and geography to estimate the ideological preferences of each county, even when counties have low populations or are not frequently surveyed.

Administrative Data

We supplement the original data we have collected with materials from the Law Enforcement Management and Administrative Statistics (LEMAS 2013), the Census of Law Enforcement, the Census of State and Local Law Enforcement Agencies, jail data from the Vera Institute, and a variety of reports and data from the Department of Justice, the Bureau of Justice Statistics, the Centers for Disease Control, and the US Census Bureau. That sheriffs serve at the county level aids in our supplemental work in many ways, as a wide set of additional information about crime, population, demographics, and politics are available at the local level.

In chapter 3, we draw on data from the Census of Governments data on employees and payrolls of local governments. We use data from the Survey of Public Employment & Payroll in 1994, 1997, 2002, 2004, 2007, 2008, 2010, 2011, 2012, 2013, 2014, 2015, 2016, 2017, 2018, 2019, and 2020.

Studying Counties

That sheriffs' jurisdictions directly overlap with county boundaries helps our analyses, as we can draw on a large set of sources of data that also are available at the county level. As we note in the introduction, we are aided in our research efforts by the fact that sheriffs serve at the county level and thus we can draw on a wide set of data on counties in the United States. Sheriffs serve all people who live in their counties, but their role as the primary law enforcement agency in a county extends only to unincorporated areas (which covers approximately 40 percent of the US population) or those towns and cities that have contracted their law enforcement services to the sheriff. Many small, incorporated cities also contract their services to sheriffs. These small cities represent a large share of US cities: 75 percent of cities have fewer than 5,000 residents and 40 percent have fewer than 500 residents (US Census Bureau 2020). In most other cities and towns, the sheriff has concurrent law enforcement duties, meaning that the sheriff's deputies have the full power to pursue and arrest individuals but share those duties with a local police department. A visual depiction of a county with these overlapping forms of power is available in figure M2:

Wright County, Minnesota, has a population of 141,337 people, with 17 cities, 18 townships, and 1 ghost town (Dickinson, abandoned in the 1930s). In the county, the sheriff is the primary provider of law enforcement services in all the unincorporated areas (light gray in fig. M1) and is contracted

Wright County, Minnesota Contract Law Enforcement by Sheriff

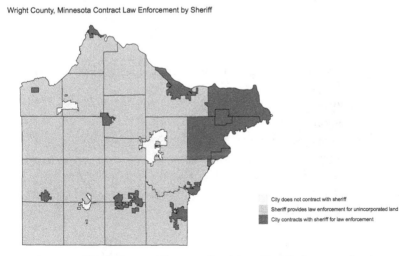

City does not contract with sheriff
Sheriff provides law enforcement for unincorporated land
City contracts with sheriff for law enforcement

FIGURE M2. Wright County, Minnesota, Provision of Law Enforcement Services

to provide law enforcement services for all cities and townships (dark gray) except three: Buffalo (the county seat), Maple Lake, and Howard Lake (white on the map). At the same time, the sheriff (Sean Deringer) and his deputies are able to provide backup or concurrent law enforcement services for these three towns, and those arrested by the municipal police in these towns would be taken to the Wright County Jail.

Survey Questions Used

CHAPTER 2

What party do you represent as sheriff? (2012, 2021)

Where would you place yourself on an ideological scale? (2012, 2021)

Generally speaking, how would you describe your political party preference? (2012, 2021)

Does your family have a background in serving in law enforcement? (2012, 2021)

Did you attend high school in the same county that you now serve as sheriff? (2012, 2021)

Did you work in your county's sheriff office prior to serving as sheriff? (2012, 2021)

Prior to your selection as sheriff, did you work in law enforcement? (2012, 2021)

Do you approve or disapprove of the job performance of the following leaders? (2021)

    Donald Trump

    Joe Biden

CHAPTER 3

Does your office oversee or provide any of the following services? (2012, 2021)

    County jail

    Law enforcement services for tribal lands

    Courthouse security

    Routine patrols of unincorporated areas

    Routine patrols of incorporated areas like cities and towns

Briefly, what do you consider the top 3 problems facing the sheriff's office in your county? (2012, 2021)

CHAPTER 4

How serious a problem are the following issues in your county? (2012, 2021)

Domestic violence

Unauthorized immigration

Does your office have in place any of the following directives for officers, either as a written policy or as a procedural directive? (2012, 2021 for some items)

Advise officers when to inquire about an individual's immigration status and what to report

Forbid officers from using race or ethnicity in traffic stops, questioning, or arrests

Forbid officers from using sexual orientation, gender, or gender expression in traffic stops, questioning, or arrests

Allow warrantless arrests in misdemeanor domestic violence situations

Have you or any of your deputies received specific training in any of these areas? (2012, 2021)

Responding to sexual assault and rape cases

In my opinion, many domestic violence incidents stem from (2012):

The abusers' need for power and control over victims

Alcohol and drug abuse

The victim provoking the abuser

Low levels of income and education

How much do you agree or disagree with the following statements? (2012)

Many domestic violence victims could easily leave their relationships but do not

Domestic violence is best handled as a private matter, rather than by the police

Women falsely report rape to call attention to themselves

Women who dress provocatively are inviting sexual assault

When your officers encounter individuals who might be unauthorized immigrants in each of the following situations, do they typically check their immigration status with Immigration and Customs Enforcement? (2012, 2021)

Interviewed as a crime victim, complainant, or witness

Stopped for a traffic violation

Arrested for DUI/DWI

Arrested for a nonviolent crime, with no prior record

Arrested for domestic violence

Arrested for a violent crime

How much do you agree or disagree with the following statements? (2012, 2021)

> Federal spending on tightening border security and preventing illegal immigration should be increased
>
> In routine patrols, law enforcement should be allowed to inquire about a person's citizenship status
>
> The police should be able to take race or ethnicity into consideration as a factor in traffic stops

How much do you agree or disagree with the following statements? (2012, 2021)

> Irish, Italians, Jewish, and many other minorities overcame prejudice and worked their way up. Today's immigrants should be able to do the same without any special favors.
>
> Immigrants today take advantage of jobs and opportunities here without doing enough to give back to the community.
>
> It is really a matter of some people not trying hard enough; if women would only try harder, they could have the same opportunities as men.
>
> Our society should do whatever is necessary to ensure equal opportunities in this country.
>
> The traditional American way of life is disappearing so fast that we may have to use force to save it.

Which of these two statements comes closer to your own views—even if neither is exactly right? (2021)

> Our country has made the changes needed to give blacks equal rights with whites
>
> Our country needs to continue making changes to give blacks equal rights with whites

How much do you agree or disagree with the following statements? (2021)

> I am fearful of people of other races
>
> White people in the US have certain advantages because of the color of their skin
>
> Racial problems in the US are rare, isolated situations
>
> I am angry that racism exists
>
> Women seek to gain power by getting control over men
>
> Women exaggerate problems they have at work

CHAPTER 5

How serious a problem are the following issues in your county? (2012, 2021)

> Overreach by State and Federal Government

There are several national groups that have sheriffs as members. We'd like
to know much you personally support the positions of these groups.
Are you or have you ever been a member of any of the following
groups? (2021)
> Constitutional Sheriffs and Peace Officers Association (CSPOA)
> National Sheriffs' Association
> Protect America Now
> Oath Keepers

Which best describes mask mandates in your county? (2021)
> There have not been any mask mandates that applied to my county
> There were mask mandates but I chose not enforce them
> There were mask mandates and I enforced them
> There were mask mandates but I was not responsible for enforcing
> them

How much do you agree or disagree with the following statements? (2012,
2021)
> The sheriff's authority supersedes the federal or state government in
> my county
> I am willing to "interpose" on behalf of county residents when I
> believe a state or federal law is unjust

Which of the following statements comes closest to your overall view of
gun laws in this country? (2012)
> Gun laws should be MORE strict than they are today
> Gun laws should be LESS strict than they are today

Which do you think is more important? (2012)
> Controlling gun ownership
> Protecting the right to own guns

Please tell us if you would favor or oppose the following policies related to
firearms: (2021)
> A requirement that your office confiscates firearms from people
> flagged as a danger to themselves or others
> Allowing people to open carry firearms in government buildings in
> your county
> A national ban on assault-style weapons
> A government database that requires your participation as sheriff in
> maintaining a gun registry and performing background checks

If the following firearms policies were passed into law, would you comply
with them? (2021)
> A government database that requires the sheriff's participation in
> maintaining a gun registry and performing background checks
> My county becoming a Second Amendment sanctuary county

A requirement that my office confiscate firearms from people
flagged as a danger to themselves or others
Do you think the following individuals or groups are responsible for the
violence at the US Capitol on January 6? Select any that you think are
responsible. (2021)
Donald Trump
Social media companies
Congressional Republicans who opposed certification of the
election
Antifa
Joe Biden

CHAPTER 6

Does your office have in place any of the following directives for officers,
either as a written policy or as a procedural directive? (2021)
Limit the use of no-knock warrants
Ban chokeholds or strangleholds
Require officers to issue a particular number of tickets or make a
certain number of arrests
Prohibit shooting at a moving vehicle
Require officers to intervene to stop another officer from using
excessive force
Do you favor any of the following policies? (2021)
Give a civilian oversight board the power to investigate and
discipline misconduct by your deputies
Create a federal government database to track law enforcement
officers who have been accused of misconduct
Make it a crime for police to use chokeholds or strangleholds
Require law enforcement to be trained in nonviolent alternatives to
deadly force
How much do you agree or disagree with the following statements? (2021)
The federal government should be able to investigate claims made
about my jail
All law enforcement officers should be required to wear body cams
during patrol
Would you support removing any of the following duties from your office
to other trained non–law enforcement professionals? (2021)
Crisis intervention, such as responses to mental health
Addressing homelessness
Traffic enforcement

Statements from CSPOA and Sheriff Organizations

Mack and CSPOA recruited and compiled a list of sheriffs who opposed the gun control restrictions in 2013–14. The CSPOA provided a list of 487 individual sheriffs and 18 state sheriffs' associations who signed onto the statement, noting: "Sheriffs have risen up all over our great nation to stand up against the unconstitutional gun control measures being taken. The following is a list of sheriffs and state sheriff's associations from who have vowed to uphold and defend the Constitution against Obama's unlawful gun control measures."

Some sheriffs simply signed onto the full CSPOA statement (see section 5A.1), while other sheriffs or state sheriff associations crafted their own statements. In the spring of 2013, we downloaded each available statement, news article, or social media post (a total of 117 justifications). We then subsequently checked it several times using the Wayback Machine and downloaded any new justifications. The list contained the names of sheriffs and their counties, and for some sheriffs it also contained a link to their statement or social media post about opposing gun control, or to local media stories. For any sheriff where there was a broken link, we searched for any information about their stance, using a combination of the Wayback Machine and internet searches. CSPOA also published a separate list of state sheriffs' associations that had produced their own statements; we supplemented this with internet searches for each state association's stance on gun control at the time, collecting a total of twenty-three statements from state associations. We inductively coded the statements with the assistance of a trained undergraduate research assistant into categories that correspond with elements of RWE (anti-federal views, willingness to defend the American way of life, and nativism and racism). We provide example statements below from the CSPOA, from several state sheriff associations, and from several individual sheriffs.

MEASURING PREFERENCES FOR GUN POLICY

We use a multilevel regression and poststratification (MRP) model (Warshaw and Rodden 2012; Tausanovitch and Warshaw 2013; 2022) to measure preferences for gun policy at the local level. We used a two-stage process to estimate the MRP model. First, we estimated a hierarchical logistic choice model for gun policy, with predictors at three levels: the individual (where we include random effects for the respondent's gender, education, race, and age); county (with fixed effects for the county's median income, percent urban, and vote for Biden in 2020); and state (with random effects for region). From this model, we identify the share of individuals in any given county who would take a pro–gun rights position in all possible combinations of age categories, race, gender, and education. In the post-stratification stage, we then match this with information from the US Census to compare our estimates with the actual distribution of population in each county. By matching the estimates of each population group's preference for gun rights to the distribution of that population in each county, we obtain an estimate of the county's support for gun rights.

Extreme Risk Protection Orders

Using existing scholarship as a guide, we used existing sources of data and petitioned courts in California, Colorado, and Virginia to provide us with any petitions for Extreme Risk Protection Orders (ERPO). Information about the subject of the ERPO was redacted (including their names, addresses, and behavior that prompted the ERPO), leaving information about who filed the ERPO. We chose these three states as they have centralized systems for order processes, compared to other states like Washington, which require that you individually visit each county court to examine the ERPOs in person.

Results Appendix

Chapter 2

TABLE A2.1. Sheriff's education

	2012	2021
High school	14%	13%
Some college	35%	32%
AA	18%	19%
BA	23%	24%
MA+	9%	13%

Note: 2012 and 2021 surveys.

TABLE A2.2. Supplemental table to figure 2.4

	Internal challenger
Change in number of employees	2.053
	(3.103)
Change in employee wages	−3.777*
	(2.264)
Population	−0.00007
	(0.00008)
Observations	221
Pseudo R^2	0.118

Note: Logistical regression with county fixed effects. Standard errors in parentheses.

* $p<.1$, ** $p<.05$

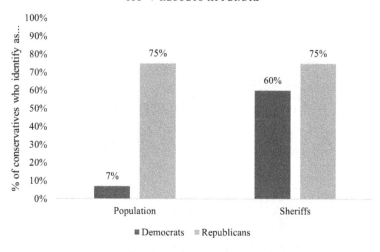

FIGURE A2.1. Overlap between conservative ideology and partisanship (2021)

We see remarkable differences in the degree to which ideology and partisanship align among sheriffs and the population (fig. A2.1). When we compare the share of conservatives in the population who identify as Democrats or Republicans to the same overlap among sheriffs, most people (75 percent) in the population who identify as conservative identify as Republicans and few people (7 percent) who identify as conservatives are likely to also identify as Democrats. While the same share of Republican sheriffs identifies as conservative as in the general population (75 percent), more than half (60 percent) of sheriffs who identify as conservative also identify Democrats.

When we compare sheriffs' partisanship with the vote share in the counties they represent (fig. A2.2) in 2012, we see again correspondence on the tails of the distribution, but not through the middle. But we see that the distance between county vote and sheriff partisanship is less extreme compared to the Biden (2020) and partisanship (2021) comparisons in chapter 2.

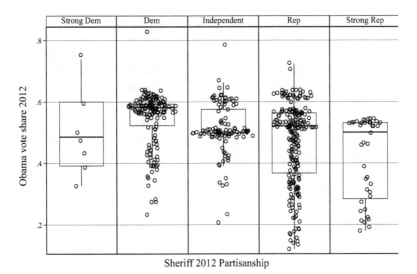

FIGURE A2.2. Sheriff partisanship (2012) and Obama vote share (2012)

While the Republican Party has won an increasingly large number of state legislative seats (up to 53 percent in 2022 from 44 percent in 2010), the share of sheriffs who run on a Republican ticket is still larger. Sheriffs are nearly 20 points less likely to run as Democrats compared to state legislators. As figure A2.3 shows, while 16 percent of sheriffs run on nonpartisan tickets (Crawford 2022), these sheriffs *also* identify overwhelmingly (85 percent) as Republicans on our 2021 survey.

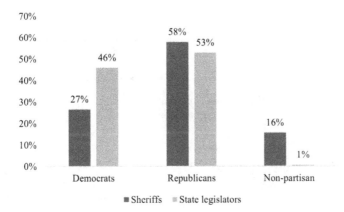

FIGURE A2.3. Sheriff and state legislator partisan affiliation on the ballot

URBAN AND RURAL SHERIFFS

We do not see clear patterns that would indicate that rural or urban sheriffs are more or less politically aligned with the identities of their counties. In figure A2.4, we provide the overlap between sheriffs' partisanship and the share of the population in a county that is urban (from the US Census). We further designate which counties voted for Trump (triangle), were swing (square), and voted for Biden (diamond). The share of the county that is urban is evenly distributed across the partisanship of sheriffs. In figure A2.4, we also show the overlap between the ideological distance (that is, the ideology of the sheriff minus the ideology of the county) and urban population. Here, again, there is no discernable pattern, with smaller and larger ideological distances spread across urban and rural counties.

QU: sho
this refe
be to fig

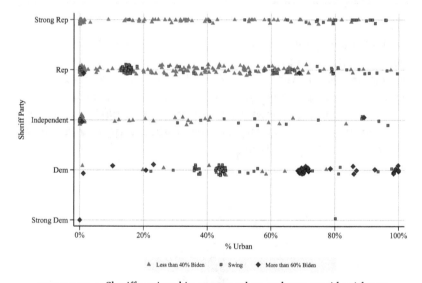

FIGURE A2.4. Sheriff partisanship, percent urban, and 2020 presidential vote

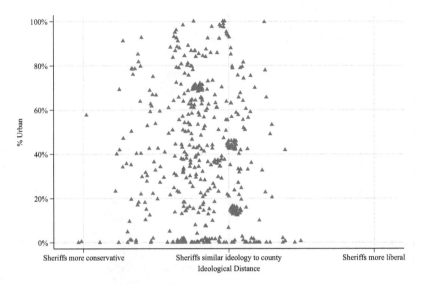

FIGURE A2.5. Ideological distance and percent urban

Chapter 3

TABLE A3.1. Results to accompany figures 3.2, 3.3, and 3.5

	Change in pay per employee	Change in number of employees	Change in overall payroll
Incumbent wins, internal challenger	631.506** (100.045)	19.945 (16.683)	135,067.963 (73,705.421)
Incumbent wins	−495.513* (283.090)	−61.899** (28.641)	−250,020.009** (59,803.044)
Challenger wins	315.001** (102.467)	141.306** (40.321)	−284,981.981** (64,912.121)
Observations	252	252	248
R^2	0.2058	0.0670	0.0763

Note: Standard errors in parentheses

* $p<.1$, ** $p<.05$

Chapter 4

TABLE A4.1. Percent of offices in 2012 with deputies receiving specialized trainings

First responder	75.8%
Victim assistance	90.7%
Evidence collection	93.2%
Victim interview protocol	81.9%
Protecting victim rights	73.6%
Other training	9.2%

TABLE A4.2. Results to accompany table 4.8

	Deputies trained to address interpersonal violence	Percent of personnel who are bilingual	Deputies trained to address racial profiling
Sheriff's views of target group	−0.142* (0.019)	−1.372* (0.727)	−0.065* (0.032)
Office capacity	−0.002 (0.015)	4.135* (1.540)	0.026 (0.027)
Population	−0.864* (0.211)	8.973 (21.587)	−0.224 (0.370)
% Black	0.562* (0.129)	−0.711 (11.440)	−0.237 (0.212)
% Rural	−0.562* (0.071)	14.609 (8.487)	0.258 (0.148)
Obama vote 2012	−0.155 (0.831)	33.915 (142.251)	−2.399 (2.631)
Sheriff party identity	−0.041 (0.061)	−6.515 (6.368)	−0.251* (0.118)
Sheriff ideology	0.032 (0.078)	−12.222 (7.537)	−0.035 (0.138)
Sheriff education	−0.299* (0.065)	8.242 (5.821)	0.153 (0.107)
Believe women's equal opportunities	−0.007 (0.014)		
% Latino		0.567* (0.125)	
Constant	0.999* (0.213)	15.503 (20.647)	0.942* (0.349)
Observations	217	226	236
R^2	0.2837	0.1671	0.0508

Note: Standard errors in parentheses

* $p<.05$

TABLE A4.3. Supplementary results for table 4.9

	Deputies provide services to victims of domestic violence	Allow warrantless arrests in misdemeanor domestic violence	Advise officers when to inquire about immigration status and how to report	Forbid officers from using race or ethnicity in traffic stops, questioning, or arrests
Sheriff has negative views of target group	-0.167* (0.057)	-0.169* (0.071)	-0.817* (0.233)	0.250* (0.82)
Office capacity	-0.170* (0.023)	-0.068 (0.200)	0.110 (0.167)	-0.067 (0.271)
Population	1.866* (0.346)	-0.179 (2.556)	-1.141 (2.206)	5.048 (3.295)
% Black	-0.111 (0.204)	0.792 (1.364)	-0.578 (1.051)	-1.230 (1.367)
% Rural	-0.257* (0.105)	-0.987 (1.133)	-0.883 (0.994)	0.462 (1.401)
% Biden 2020	1.275 (1.237)	0.946 (1.346)	1.607 (1.036)	-1.304 (1.605)
Sheriff PID	0.180* (0.086)	0.487 (0.849)	0.862 (0.722)	0.647 (1.067)
Sheriff ideology	0.159 (0.114)	0.601 (1.044)	1.882* (0.880)	0.747 (1.312)
Education	0.029 (0.098)	-0.091 (0.124)	0.114 (0.102)	0.122 (0.166)
% Latino	-0.012 (0.020)		0.006 (0.011)	
Constant	-1.419* (0.326)	1.226 (2.539)	0.612 (2.327)	-1.844 (3.298)
Observations	523	354	385	352
R^2 / Pseudo R^2	0.1520	0.0169	0.0796	0.0482

Note: Standard errors in parentheses

* $p < .05$

TABLE A4.4. Results to accompany figure 4.2 (2012 data)

	Witness	Traffic stop	Nonviolent crime	Domestic violence	Violent crime
Nativist attitudes	2.225*	2.223*	1.104*	1.139*	0.359
	(0.287)	(0.279)	(0.238)	(0.242)	(0.294)
Office capacity	−0.103	−0.352	0.416*	0.418*	−0.013
	(0.236)	(0.230)	(0.180)	(0.194)	(0.231)
Population	3.937	6.864*	−1.800	−2.458	4.956
	(3.422)	(3.339)	(2.693)	(2.886)	(3.543)
% Black	−2.856	−3.131	−0.855	−1.394	−1.128
	(1.930)	(2.031)	(1.359)	(1.479)	(1.684)
% Rural	1.614	1.386	−0.176	−1.411	2.363*
	(0.942)	(0.881)	(0.776)	(0.855)	(1.101)
Obama vote 2012	−16.426	−12.535	−8.849	−1.865	−3.691
	(12.121)	(11.741)	(8.012)	(8.804)	(9.866)
Sheriff party identity	0.384	1.045	0.267	0.092	2.068*
	(0.772)	(0.774)	(0.671)	(0.712)	(0.801)
Sheriff ideology	−2.911*	−3.084*	−2.803*	−3.170*	−3.177*
	(0.993)	(0.972)	(0.857)	(0.890)	(1.121)
Sheriff education	−0.622	0.254	−1.425*	−1.211	0.276
	(0.858)	(0.839)	(0.671)	(0.716)	(0.876)
Percent Latino	−0.031	−0.005	−0.002	0.001	0.000
	(0.019)	(0.015)	(0.012)	(0.014)	(0.014)
Constant	−9.814*	−13.763*	3.018	4.317	−1.775
	(3.297)	(3.319)	(2.648)	(2.787)	(3.427)
Observations	390	402	385	425	429
Pseudo R^2	0.3070	0.2890	0.1120	0.1368	0.0923

Note: Standard errors in parentheses

* $p<.05$

TABLE A4.5. Results to accompany figure 4.2 (2021 data)

	Witness	Traffic stop	Nonviolent crime	Domestic violence	Violent crime
Nativist attitudes	0.751*	0.450	0.628*	1.044*	0.923*
	(0.314)	(0.295)	(0.231)	(0.254)	(0.270)
Office capacity	−0.348	−0.013	−0.113	−0.067	−0.163
	(0.222)	(0.221)	(0.163)	(0.173)	(0.193)
Population	1.273	−2.935	−0.299	−1.334	0.356
	(2.867)	(2.843)	(2.171)	(2.282)	(2.529)
% Black	2.300	1.209	1.852	2.961*	2.721
	(1.284)	(1.220)	(1.081)	(1.341)	(1.484)
% Rural	0.660	0.097	−0.201	0.029	−0.249
	(1.305)	(1.194)	(0.971)	(1.046)	(1.137)
% Biden 2020	−0.392	−1.445	−0.985	−1.198	−1.951
	(1.485)	(1.409)	(1.054)	(1.111)	(1.176)
Sheriff PID	−1.262	−2.123*	−1.427	−1.676*	−1.563
	(0.951)	(0.898)	(0.737)	(0.802)	(0.877)
Sheriff ideology	−0.560	0.294	1.516	1.263	0.399
	(1.152)	(1.095)	(0.878)	(0.953)	(1.036)
Education	−0.187	−0.155	−0.025	0.041	0.036
	(0.136)	(0.128)	(0.099)	(0.108)	(0.119)
% Latino	−0.017	−0.005	0.012	0.001	−0.005
	(0.018)	(0.014)	(0.012)	(0.012)	(0.013)
Constant	−5.271	0.377	−2.522	−2.521	−1.874
	(2.994)	(2.872)	(2.262)	(2.424)	(2.686)
Observations	297	306	332	338	341
Pseudo R^2	0.0976	0.0815	0.0667	0.1151	0.0904

Note: Standard errors in parentheses

* $p < .05$

Chapter 5

5A1: CSPOA STATEMENT ON GUN CONTROL

It's Time To Stand And Be Counted

The Right of Self Defense for all individuals is a God-given unalienable right that precedes our country's foundation and all government institutions. Our Founders believed this right was so vital that they unanimously declared it as part of the Bill of Rights. Their reference to the Militia within the Second Amendment is not a contradiction, as Founding Father George Mason stated, "I ask sir, what is the Militia? It is the whole people. To disarm the people is the best and most effectual way to enslave them." This principle had nothing to do with hunting or target shooting, but had everything to do with liberty.

Whereas, our country is in great turmoil and a new movement is underway to destroy the principles that made America great in the first place and,

Whereas, President Lincoln warned us that if America were ever to be destroyed, such destruction would come from within and,

Whereas, Federal politicians are ignoring the inner city violence and recidivists, and are proposing registration and confiscation aimed at law abiding citizens and,

Whereas, such statutes will only make criminals out of citizens who are neither criminals nor have the intention of committing any crimes whatsoever and,

Whereas, the Supreme Law of the land expressly forbids gun control in America,

Therefore, in keeping with the Oath we each swore to protect and defend the United States Constitution and the Constitution of our State, and to do our duty to preserve the rights of the people we work for, we, the Sheriffs of America, do hereby declare and make it known, that we will oppose and disallow, any and all attempts to further erode the rights of the citizens of our counties and parishes. Accordingly, we oppose the current gun control scheme being proposed and any attempt to register gun owners or their firearms. In fine, the rights of the people to keep and bear arms Shall Not Be Infringed.

Please fill in the blanks with your name printed below and the county and state you represent, and then sign in the space provided.

I,_____, Sheriff of_____ county/parish State of_____. Signed_____
OR
NO, I will not participate and believe we should have more gun control.
_____(Please initial)

5A2: STATEMENT FROM THE UTAH
SHERIFFS ASSOCIATION

The Honorable Barack Obama
President of the United States of America

The White House
1600 Pennsylvania Avenue, NW Washington, DC 20500

Dear President Obama:

We, the elected sheriffs of Utah, like so many of our fellow Americans, are literally heartbroken for the loved ones of the murdered victims in Connecticut. As Utahans, we are not strangers to this kind of carnage—one of the latest being the 2007 Trolley Square murders wherein nine innocents were gunned down—five losing their lives.

We also recognize the scores of other recent domestic massacres, which have decimated countless honorable lives. As Americans, we value the sanctity of life. Furthermore, similar to our inspired Founders, we acknowledge our subservience to a higher power.

With the number of mass shootings America has endured, it is easy to demonize firearms; it is also foolish and prejudiced. Firearms are nothing more than instruments, valuable and potentially dangerous, but instruments nonetheless. Malevolent souls, like the criminals who commit mass murders, will always exploit valuable instruments in the pursuit of evil. As professional peace officers, if we understand nothing else, we understand this: lawfal violence must sometimes be employed to deter and stop criminal violence. Consequently, the citizenry must continue its ability to keep and bear arms, including arms that adequately protect them from all types of illegality.

As your administration and Congress continue to grapple with the complex issue of firearm regulations, we pray that the Almighty will guide the People's Representatives collectively. For that reason, it is imperative this discussion be had in Congress, not silenced unilaterally by executive orders. As you deliberate, please remember the Founders of this great nation created the Constitution, and its accompanying Bill of Rights, in an effort to protect citizens from all forms of tyrannical subjugation.

We respect the Office of the President of the United States of America. But, make no mistake, as the duly-elected sheriffs of our respective counties, we will enforce the rights guaranteed to our citizens by the Constitution. No federal official will be permitted to descend upon our constituents and take from them what the Bill of Rights—in particular Amendment 11—has given them. We, like you, swore a solemn oath to protect and defend the Constitution of the United States, and we are prepared to trade our lives for the preservation of its traditional interpretation.

5A4: STATEMENTS FROM INDIVIDUAL SHERIFFS

Blake Dorning, Madison County, AL

The federal authorities can try to enforce it. I'm the Sheriff of Madison County. I took a constitutional oath to defend the Constitution of the United States of America, to defend the Constitution of the State of Alabama, even if it takes my life. That is my position.

As long as you are a law-abiding citizen, then I don't see a problem with law-abiding citizens being able to arm themselves however they so choose. Our people in our communities and homes need not fear that the Sheriff of Madison County or his deputies would come to their homes and make an attempt to disarm them. It will not happen under my watch.

Gil Gilbertson, Josephine County, OR
(one of the first signatories on the CSPOA statement)

As the elected Sheriff of this County, I am saddled with the duty, as well as responsibility, to uphold the Constitution and protect those people who placed their trust in me to do what is right.

I believe in our Constitution and all it stands for. We, you and I, are sworn to protect and defend our Constitution as required through the "Oath of Office." This same Constitutional form of government provided us with the most privileged, and envied, country in world history.

Someone once said our country would collapse from within, without a shot being fired. No nation in the world can do more damage to the United States than we can inflict upon ourselves. We are keenly aware of just that by the accelerated pace in which our central (federal) government is usurping the Constitution. This lends itself to a much broader discussion, but for brevity sake I remain focused upon the Second, and Tenth Amendment issues. It is so typical of the "big brother" mentality to punish the masses, for the heinous crimes committed by a few despicable individuals.

The Constitution, and Bill of Rights, guarantee liberties to the people. These documents, as you know, cannot be whisked to the side by regulation or executive order. According to these documents, the Executive and Judicial branches were to have NO lawmaking powers. The question then becomes how is it "executive" orders can be enforced as if they were laws?

As such, any rule, regulation, or executive order repugnant to the constitutional rights of the citizens of this County will be ignored by this Office, nor will this office, or the citizens, allow enforcement of unconstitutional activities by federal officers.

We refuse to participate, or allow our law-abiding citizens to be criminalized through constitutionally repugnant actions by misguided intentions or politicians.

5A3: STATEMENT FROM THE SOUTH CAROLINA SHERIFFS' ASSOCIATION

In response to the many inquiries regarding the recent tragic events in Connecticut and California, and the ensuing public dialogue concerning "gun control" or "restrictions", the forty-six elected sheriffs of South Carolina, who are the acknowledged public safety authority within their respective counties, will comply faithfully to their Oath of Office to, "preserve and protect and defend the Constitution of this State and of the United States."

As South Carolina's constitutional law enforcement authority, we remain focused on solutions. The authority of the Office of Sheriff is derived from the State's constitution and the people who have entrusted us with our office. That document and the statutes of the State bind us together as a people. At a time when those who are governed have less trust in those who govern, it is important that we hold steadfast and focus our attention and efforts on not what divides us, but on what binds us together as a State and Nation.

Further, as constitutional officers of the state of South Carolina and locally elected, our authority to enforce any law extends only to the laws and statutes of South Carolina and the ordinances of our respective counties. We do not possess the authority to enforce any federal law or presidential order.

Garrett Wiggins, Routt County, CO

The question has been asked of me on many occasions and a lot more often since the recent shootings around our country, "What is your position regarding gun control"?

The following paragraphs document my personal belief and position as an American citizen and also in my official capacity as the Sheriff of Routt County regarding gun control or any new or proposed legislation.

- I will support new state and federal legislation and enforce laws under my authority that will: "keep firearms out of the hands of criminals, the mentally ill, any person addicted to controlled substances, individuals convicted or under a restraining order, and convicted felons."

- I support legislation and laws that establish greater or enhanced penalties and minimum sentencing standards for criminals convicted of crimes which use a firearm and other dangerous weapons to commit criminal behavior.
- I support legislation which holds accountable, an individual illegally in possession of a firearm, who sells a firearm to someone who commits an illegal or criminal act with said firearm. (Black market sales)
- I support legislation which gives access to data regarding mentally ill or mentally unstable individuals who present a danger to themselves or others, to those officials responsible for conducting background checks for firearm sales.
- I support Colorado's concealed carry laws and other states that support concealed carry rights for law abiding citizens.
- I fully support enhancements to our schools which provide preventative and security measures that prevent school violence to include building and structure upgrades, technological security advancements and fulltime, P.O.S.T certified school resource officers stationed in individual schools.
- I fully support and have taken an oath to protect and honor the Constitution of the United States of America including the Second Amendment which reads; A well people to keep and bear arms, shall not be infringed.
- As a citizen of the United States of America and in my official capacity as the elected Sheriff, I will breathe my last breath defending this constitutional right that belongs to me, my family and all the people I serve from terrorism, both foreign and domestic, so help me God!!!
- I will not support any new legislation that infringes on the rights of law abiding citizens or in any way takes away their ability to defend themselves and their families from an imminent threat or act of violence.
- I will not support legislation that prohibits law abiding citizens from purchasing or which limits products and goods to include firearms, accessories and ammunition, or new legislation which punishes law abiding citizens for the criminal acts of a few.
- In my official capacity as Routt County Sheriff, I will defend our law abiding citizens against any unlawful or unconstitutional intrusion or enforcement action which clearly violates the constitutional rights of our citizens.

Over the past two hundred years, millions of Americans have died, many of them our own family members, defending this country in times of war, from terrorist attacks, and protecting our freedoms and constitutional rights afforded to every American citizen. To sit idle and do nothing while politically biased and agenda motivated individuals try to tear our US Constitution apart is not something we should allow to happen.

I share a common belief with the majority of Americans from both sides of the political aisle, that when it comes to human initiated acts of violence we should not blame the tool or piece of equipment used to conduct the horrible act but place the blame where it really belongs, on the "person" committing the act.

For instance; there are thousands of automobile related deaths every year in this country contributed to texting while driving. Have we seen legislation to ban cell phones, texting ability or vehicles? Hundreds of thousands of lives have been lost to automobile related deaths in this country related to DUI and DUID (pharmaceutical drugs and illegal drugs). Have we seen legislation requesting to ban alcohol, pharmaceutical drugs or vehicles? Were the jets blamed for 9/11? These questions seem ridiculous but the answers are "NO." Some people might argue that laws have been passed that prohibit drinking and driving, texting while driving and now we have strict security measures at airports. Yes, this is true but the fact is that people still use these common everyday things carelessly causing 100s of deaths around or nation. The common factor in all these scenarios is "Human behavior." That's right, human actions cause death and destruction. We as a society should hold humans accountable for their actions and not try to find blame in material objects. These beneficial tools are used every day for lawful purposes but unfortunately they are also used to cause accidents and planned acts of violence. Firearms, jets, cell phones, drugs and alcohol, and so on don't have minds of their own or decision making ability. They can't fire themselves, fly themselves, text themselves or digest themselves into someone's body. The fact is that humans and personal decisions are responsible for their use.

Regardless of the number of new laws we pass, it is impossible to prevent all human caused accidents or acts of violence. Horrible acts are committed around the globe every day by criminals, the mentally ill and evil minded people. To counter this evil, society has crafted laws to try to prevent bad things from happening to good people. Law abiding citizens typically honor and obey laws but most criminals see laws as nothing more than ink on a piece of paper. The creation of additional laws, as it relates to gun control, accomplishes nothing more than restricting the rights of law abiding citizens and provides a false sense of security for those who oppose gun rights. Criminals don't care how many laws are on the books as they have no intention of following them anyway. In fact, many criminals want more gun restrictions as this creates an easier, target rich environment of defenseless victims for them to rob, burglarize, rape and pillage. People do ignorant and evil things causing harm, destruction and death. We cannot and should not penalize millions of law abiding citizens for the horrible acts of just a few.

It is time to face the realization that none of these material objects can cause death or destruction without human manipulation.

The fact is: people kill people, let's hold humans responsible.

Garrett Wiggins

TABLE A5.1. RWE and gun laws

	Favors national database that includes a gun registry and performing background	Would participate in maintaining a gun registry and performing background checks
Right-wing extremism scale	−1.42**	−4.17**
	(0.35)	(0.87)
Population	2.26*	5.29*
	(0.97)	(2.54)
Office capacity	−0.02	1.19
	(0.83)	(2.10)
% Black	0.12	0.98
	(0.45)	(1.02)
% Rural	1.21**	2.24*
	(0.42)	(1.13)
% Biden 2020	−0.37	−1.01
	(0.49)	(1.18)
Sheriff ideology	−1.22**	−2.39*
	(0.37)	(0.95)
Republican sheriff	−0.12	−0.35
	(0.14)	(0.32)
Constant	2.40**	−0.09
	(0.57)	(1.44)
Observations	388	374
Pseudo R^2	0.1708	0.189

Note: Standard errors in parentheses

+ p<.1, * p<.05, ** p<.01

TABLE A5.2. RWE and red flag laws

	Would confiscate firearms from people flagged as a danger to themselves or other	Favors confiscating firearms from people flagged as a danger to themselves or others
Right-wing extremism scale	−2.82**	−0.97*
	(0.71)	(0.39)
Population	−0.14	0.39
	(1.88)	(1.08)
Office capacity	0.02	−0.10
	(1.61)	(0.92)
% Black	1.04	0.24
	(0.91)	(0.51)
% Rural	0.05	0.44
	(0.81)	(0.47)
% Biden 2020	−0.47	0.76
	(0.96)	(0.55)
Sheriff ideology	−0.72	−1.03*
	(0.73)	(0.42)
Republican sheriff	−0.28	0.03
	(0.27)	(0.16)
Constant	2.63*	3.65**
	(1.12)	(0.63)
Observations	390	389
Pseudo R^2	0.063	

Note: Standard errors in parentheses

+ $p<.1$, * $p<.05$, ** $p<.01$

TABLE A5.3. RWE and mask laws

	Enforce COVID mask mandate
Right-wing extremism scale	2.39**
	(0.84)
Population	0.17
	(4.12)
Office capacity	2.73
	(2.09)
% Black	−1.45
	(1.25)
% Rural	0.30
	(1.07)
% Biden 2020	−0.84
	(1.41)
Sheriff ideology	0.86
	(0.95)
Republican sheriff	−0.02
	(0.34)
COVID deaths	−3.53
	(3.43)
Republican governor	−0.49
	(0.31)
Constant	−0.30
	(1.45)
Observations	311
Pseudo R^2	0.086

Note: Standard errors in parentheses

+ $p<.1$, * $p<.05$, ** $p<.01$

TABLE A5.4. RWE and views of Jan 6 responsibility

	Trump responsible for Jan 6	Antifa responsible for Jan 6
Right-wing extremism scale	−2.49**	3.03**
	(0.86)	(0.74)
Population	0.90	−0.55
	(2.46)	(1.93)
Office capacity	−1.65	−2.85+
	(2.11)	(1.68)
% Black	0.43	−0.35
	(0.99)	(0.96)
% Rural	0.14	−1.10
	(1.09)	(0.84)
% Biden 2020	0.99	−0.31
	(1.15)	(1.00)
Sheriff ideology	−2.48*	0.87
	(0.98)	(0.75)
Republican sheriff	−0.69*	0.24
	(0.32)	(0.28)
Constant	2.14	−1.01
	(1.46)	(1.14)
Observations	390	390
Pseudo R^2	0.152	0.098

Note: Standard errors in parentheses

+ p<.1, * p<.05, ** p<.01

Notes

INTRODUCTION

1. Cain's biography also notes, "However, of the many titles and positions he has held throughout his career the one he is MOST proud of is 'PawPaw' . . . to granddaughters Alexis and Alyssa" (NSA, n.d.).

2. Buford Pusser was the sheriff of McNairy County, Tennessee; the movie *Walking Tall* is based on his life. Pusser is "one of Cain's heroes" (KaCo 2018). Sheriff David A. Clarke of Milwaukee County, Wisconsin, received the award the previous year. While sheriff, Clarke was criticized for deaths in his jail and alleged mistreatment of incarcerated people. He is now active in far-right politics as we discuss in chapter 5.

3. *The Guardian* named Kern County "American law enforcement's deadliest county," giving examples of deputies' violent behavior, including that "KCSO deputies have been caught rewarding colleagues for aggressive use of batons with a 'baby seal' prize for the best clubbing" (Swaine and Laughland 2015).

4. The ACLU report on cooperation between the California Central Valley counties and Immigration and Customs Enforcement (ICE) begins with a story of Erika, who was arrested after being falsely accused of stealing a bag of fruit. When she was released from KCSO custody, ICE agents were waiting to transfer her to a detention facility. She was held by ICE for six months, and during the first days of detention, her children thought she had been killed like their father had been by kidnappers in Mexico. Erika's detention by ICE prevented her from appearing at her court date, and she was arrested again and jailed for fifty-five days by KCSO for missing court. Youngblood disputed the allegations of the ACLU report (Desai 2022; ACLU 2022).

5. Even with the settlement, Sheriff Youngblood has defiantly opposed any omission of guilt. At the joint press conference announcing the settlement, he said, "I do not believe that the men and women in this organization have ever violated constitutional rights, have ever used excessive force that we didn't deal with punitively when we found [it]. That just doesn't happen in our organization" (Morgan 2020).

6. Sheriffs are elected in all states except Alaska (because the state has no counties), Connecticut (where they voted to abolish the office at the county level in 2000), Hawaii (there is a sheriffs' division in the state's Department of Public Safety, but it is not an elected office), and Rhode Island (where the office is appointed at the state level) and a few scattered counties across the country.

7. Ninety-eight percent of sheriffs are men, and 92 percent are white.

N.B.: Specs say lining figures for URLs, but show old-style, and they were used in samples; okay as done?

8. For example, Donald Trump's attorney general Jeff Sessions (2018) told the National Sheriffs' Association (NSA), "The office of sheriff is a critical part of the Anglo-American heritage of law enforcement." This was also the year that Sheriff Cain received the NSA's Sheriff of the Year award.

9. Cain went as far as to campaign for his successor, writing in an op-ed, "I love this Office, I spent my entire adult life here, and know I would NEVER mislead you in my thoughts of who should take up its mantle" (Cain 2022). Cain's preferred successor lost the election, which is uncharacteristic for these races, as we will discuss in chapter 2.

10. Sheriffs also try to cultivate a particular image in the minds of the public. During his time in office, Cain developed both a personal brand of a "10-gallon hat, blue jeans and cowboy boots [that] are as much a part of his persona as his five-point badge" (Foreman 2020) and one for his office: a kneeling knight with the Latin phrase *Inginio Vir Bellator Corde Servi*, or "skills of a warrior, heart of a servant." Youngblood and his deputies similarly developed a brand: Youngblood's campaign materials also feature him in a hat, on a horse, or alongside his mounted posse. The deputies in Youngblood's departments placed decals on their cars that read "We will kick your ass" (Swaine and Laughland 2015). Cain and Youngblood are not alone in their branding efforts. For example, in 1990, the Los Angeles Sheriff's Department reported that then "Sheriff Block initiated a contest to develop a department motto. Sgt. John Beaver won the contest and received $4,000 for his entry, 'A Tradition of Service.'"

11. In Kern County, sheriff deputies themselves have facilitated or engaged in the sexual assault of victims. In one circumstance, Kern County deputies offered a woman $1,500 to not sue the office after she was raped in jail (Laughland 2016; Laughland et al. 2015; Rocha 2017).

12. The Kern County Sheriff's Office did create a "Transparency" tab on their website in 2022 that details (among other pieces of information) that officers shot fourteen people in 2020, three in 2021, and five in 2022 and provides links to the officer's body camera footage for each "critical incident" (KCSO 2022).

13. In 2012, we also mailed every sheriff a postcard with a link to the survey.

14. The non-member price for the 2022 electronic directory was $1,250.

CHAPTER ONE

1. Sheriff Puckett told a local reporter that the jail's food is "not what mama cooks, but it's nutritious and dietician-approved" (Sheets 2021).

2. The executive director of the Alabama Sheriffs Association dismissed complaints over food by those incarcerated, saying, "You're never going to be able to satisfy them." Besides, "an inmate is not in jail for singing too loud in choir on Sunday" (Whitmire 2019).

3. Other Alabama sheriffs may have been acting similarly in 2018, but when reporters submitted open records requests to learn more, forty-nine (of the sixty-six) county sheriffs refused to hand over records (Whitmire 2018).

4. Voters in nearby Etowah County—home to its own nicknamed sheriff, Todd Entrekin, or the Beach House Sheriff, who reportedly bought a beach house after personally profiting $750,000 from the food fund (Sheets 2018)—passed local constitutional amendments to allow sheriffs to divert jail food funds again in 2020.

5. https://twitter.com/morgan_sheriff.

6. Yes, we are aware that the formation years do not align across the two sources. The Morgan County website discusses the formation of the county "with properties acquired from Cherokee and Chickasaw Indian tribes" and the site of the county as a "hotbed for the Civil War," with former enslaved persons in the county forming the 106th United States Colored Infantry (USCI), the only Black infantry unit raised in Alabama (Tabler 2014; "Morgan County About Us" 2022).

7. As described by civil rights activist C. T. Vivian (Brockell 2021), whom Clark punched in the face in front of television cameras on the Selma courthouse steps in 1965.

8. Sheriff Clark was later arrested for mail fraud and smuggling marijuana (Benn 2006; Fox 2007).

9. We focus on Alabama here in our opening to this chapter, but Alabama sheriffs are not unique in their incomplete and troubled histories, as we discuss further in the chapter. An interesting twist here is that Emily discovered (while writing this book, after spending more than a decade studying sheriffs) that her great-great-great grandfather was the sheriff of DeKalb county, Alabama for three terms in the nineteenth century. The DeKalb county website lists Sheriff P.M. Frazier as the first in their history, but provides no more details.

10. One North Carolina sheriff's office suggests sheriffs may go back even further, dating the office to the Bible and King Nebuchadnezzar of Babylon, based on a reference from the King James translation (1611) of the Book of Daniel 3:2–3 (OCSO 2022).

11. Scholars agree that the office originated in Saxon England "before during the reign of Edgar (944–975 AD)" (Wager 1928, 288; see also W. A. Morris 1918) and that the sheriff did not take the form that can be traced to the American office until the tenth century. The term *shire-reeve* existed prior to this point, but the office was more of a county commissioner than the current law enforcement officer (Chadwick 1905; W. A. Morris 1918).

12. In England, "the sheriff appears to almost never to have been a popular officer," as individuals bought the office from the Crown. Thus, a sheriff "was prone to exercise his functions solely as a means for fattening his purse" (Smith 1933, 39).

13. As B. Smith (1933, 43) notes, "The fact that the office was generally held by great landowners in the colonies, together with the scandals and peculations which too often characterized its conduct, also probably served to weaken the control which could be exercised by the colonial governors."

14. For example, in the New England colonies, the sheriff moved from being selected by a governor (who was, in turn, appointed by the Crown) to being the elected choice of town selectmen in 1691 (G. E. Howard 1889). In North Carolina, the colonial government changed the sheriff selection process from gubernatorial appointment to selection from a group of nominated individuals to direct election in the early 1700s (Wager 1928).

15. For example, South Carolina's 1776 constitution creates the office of the sheriff as an elected office: "sheriffs, qualified as by law directed, shall be chosen in like manner by the general assembly and legislative council, and commissioned by the president and commander-in-chief, for two years only."

16. Commonwealth v Martin (1898), 9 Kulp (Pennsylvania), 69, 73, 74.

17. Another New Jersey sheriff's office also skips from the "mid 1800s" to "before World War II" in the history of their office (Mercer County Sheriff's Office 2022).

18. "An act for the better ordering of slaves," vol 7, 343, clause I (1690).

19. Local sheriffs could (and would) abuse these privileges and arrest free Black persons because they could hold the prisoners in their jails and require labor from them while the individuals were assembling evidence of their free status. An 1822 South Carolina law ordered the Charleston sheriff to arrest and confine any free Black persons who were part of the crew of a ship in port and retain them in custody until the ship left. In 1843, Jim Jones, a free Black person on a British ship, was arrested, imprisoned, and assigned to sweep the jail where "he cursed the jailer villainously" in front of other Black prisoners and was beaten by guards (H. M. Henry 1914, 128).

20. For example, Pennsylvania's Fugitive Slave Act of 1826 directed sheriffs to "arrest and seize" any person accused of attempting to escape enslavement. Any Black person captured by a sheriff who could not provide a pass or evidence of their free status was viewed as a runaway. Sheriffs could financially benefit from this arrangement as any unclaimed enslaved person could be sold for costs (Leslie 1952).

21. For example, in Louisiana, sheriffs were automatically included in the rosters of slave patrols (E. R. Williams 1972).

22. For example, sheriffs in Florida were paid one dollar (to be paid by the enslaver) for whipping an enslaved person, and sheriffs received up to 30 percent of the value of any runaway enslaved individual sold at auction (J. F. Smith 1973).

23. In North Carolina, a report estimated "that 25 per cent of the poll taxes levied . . . was embezzled by the sheriffs" (Kay 1965, 441).

24. Crosby was reappointed sheriff following the arrival of federal troops but he was shot in the head by a white deputy in his office and was unable to fully recover and serve as sheriff (Crosby 2005).

25. For example, in Crenshaw County, Alabama, the sheriff recruited white men "known for their violence and recklessness in dealing with freedmen" to intimidate Black residents attempting to vote by crowding the polling place, jeering, and threatening the voters (Hahn 2005, 224).

26. Smead would later call Parker's murder one of the last "classic lynchings" in America (Smead 1988, 204).

27. Sheriff Ely rescued a Black prisoner from a lynch mob in 1916, spiriting the prisoner off to the State Hospital for the Criminally Insane when a white mob descended on the jail (Dray 2007). The mob eventually caught Ely and threatened to lynch the sheriff, beating him, breaking several ribs, and shredding his clothes. A Black newspaper heralded his actions, "Luckily, in the town of Lima there was a MAN WHO DARED DO HIS DUTY AS HE SAW IT . . . In the midst of the maelstrom of frenzy which had engulfed the citizens of Lima stood a pillar of manhood, Sheriff Sherman Ely, the hero of the hour . . . think of it! This is surely HEROISM if there ever was such . . . IN ALL TIMES LIKE THESE, GOD GAVE US MEN LIKE ELY" (Cleveland Advocate, 1916).

28. An example from journalist Douglas A. Blackmon: In 1908, Sheriff J. L. Walthall of Shelby County, Alabama, arrested Green Cottenham, a Black man, for vagrancy, the offense of not being able to prove one's employment that sheriffs selectively used

to arrest Black men. Sentenced to a term of hard labor, Cottenham was turned over to the Tennessee Coal, Iron & Railroad company to pay for trial expenses, which included fees paid to the sheriff. Cottenham, like many others facing the brutal and violent conditions in the mine, died malnourished and sick a few months after his arrest (Blackmon 2009).

29. Occasionally, a sheriff would get in legal trouble from the state or federal government for illegally kidnapping or imprisoning a Black member of their community (Novak 2014).

30. For example, see California State Statutes 1850, 1851, 1852, 1861.

31. Scholars note that the sheriff of the West is "novel" in comparison to the colonial or Anglo-Saxon sheriff, in that "their exploits as empire builders sometimes rank with those of the cattle kings and railroad magnates" (B. Smith 1933, 50). Some of the notoriety came from famed gunmen serving as sheriffs. For example, "Wild Bill" Hickok, elected as sheriff of Ellis County, Kansas, in 1869, publicly shot to death two men during his first month in office. He was also known as "an inveterate hater of Indian People" (Rosa 1994; Ashdown and Caudill 2020, 38). He served only two years in the position before losing his reelection bid to his deputy (Rosa 1994).

32. "The early American Sheriff was important to the security of the people, and was granted much power. Along the early frontier sheriffs administered punishment, not only conventional as we know it now, but also flogging, banishment, or execution by choking" (R. Scott, n.d.).

33. Occasionally mobs would hang or shoot sheriffs or deputies for killing a local citizen. For example, a mob hanged Sheriff Deputy Kerr in Pioneer, Arizona, in 1882 for shooting a citizen (McKanna 1997).

34. As one historian noted, "Undoubtably Henry Plummer, sheriff in Lewiston [Montana], was the principal in a gang of road agents. How many assaults and robberies they had committed was impossible to determine" (Franz 1969, 110).

35. For example, historians have noted participation in lynchings and vigilante "justice" by sheriffs in Omaha and Platte, Nebraska; Vernon County, Missouri; and Brown, Erath, and Walbarger, Texas (R. M. Brown 1969, 104).

36. Sheriffs often personally benefited from working with these companies. For instance, Logan County, West Virginia Sheriff Don Chafin received at least $50,000 annually in the form of bribes to supplement his annual salary of $3,500 in the early 1900s (Shogan 2004).

37. At one point, there were up to 326 men commissioned as deputy sheriffs in Huerfano County, Colorado.

38. Nearly forty years later, in 1973, a sheriff's deputy in Kern County, California, beat Nagi Daifullah, a Yemeni migrant farmworker and union organizer, to death for leading a grape strike (T. Hendricks 2002).

39. For example, one history of policing text notes, "The advent of Prohibition (1919–1933) only made the situation worse. The outlawing of alcohol combined with the fact that the overwhelming majority of urban residents drank and wished to continue to drink not only created new opportunities for police corruption but substantially changed the focus of that corruption" and goes on to detail the effects of Prohibition on several major cities (Potter 2013).

40. The year 2021 witnessed the highest rate of death for active-duty law enforcement since 1930, "with COVID-19 identified as the leading cause of death for the second year in a row" (Treisman 2022).

41. In some states, the temperance organizers successfully agitated to include constitutional amendments (in Maine, for example) or legislation that would allow state-level officials to discipline or even remove "delinquent sheriffs" who refused to enforce Prohibition (Cherrington 1920, 357).

42. In a 1967 federal report on crime and policing, sheriffs' constitutional status is specifically mentioned as an impediment to criminal justice reform as the office's "common-law powers cannot be removed or restricted with amending State constitutions" ("The Challenge of Crime in a Free Society" 1967, 123).

43. This message appears in the *Sheriff's Star*, the publication of the Florida Sheriffs' Association, of which Sheriff Genung served as president.

44. Moore also notes, "There are as many definitions of the American South as there are ways to cook barbecue" (1997, 51).

45. After his deputies beat Woodrow Wilson Daniels to death in front of his children, Sheriff Z. T. Matthews of Terrell County, Georgia, was quoted saying, "There's nothing like fear to keep n----- in line" (SPLC 2014b).

46. Ernest Thomas, Charles Greenlee, Walter Irvin, and Samuel Shepherd were posthumously exonerated by the state of Florida in 2021.

47. Bill Gale was a white supremacist who unsuccessfully ran for governor in Arkansas on the Constitution Party ticket to oppose Eisenhower's forceful desegregation efforts. Gale first coined the idea of the posse comitatus in 1957 (Levitas 2004).

48. Levitas (2004) argues that Beach plagiarized ideas from Gale in the early 1970s.

49. (95–1478), 521 US 898 (1997).

50. Los Angeles is one place where the sheriff is a department, not an office, a change that happened in the 1950s during the beginning of the professionalization movement. Many sheriffs assert that this language (with a preference for an office instead of a department) matters for understanding the authority and autonomy of the position.

51. The LASD timeline describes a piece of this as "federal authorities investigated allegations of inmate beatings and other misconduct by deputies in Los Angeles County Central Jail. The FBI paid a deputy $1,500 to smuggle a cell phone into Central Jail and given to an inmate, who was an FBI informant. This allowed the inmate to report directly to the agents when he observed deputies abusing inmates."

52. Among Sheriff Baca's many, many scandals while in office, his unique relationship with celebrities (and willingness to shield celebrities from the consequences of their illegal behavior) stands out—in particular, Sheriff Baca's attempt to suppress a video of Mel Gibson's arrest for drunk driving where Gibson engaged in an antisemitic rant (Weiner 2006). The incident made it into the sheriff's official timeline of 2006: "Actor Mel Gibson was arrested by Deputy James Mee for driving under the influence of alcohol. During the arrest, Gibson made negative remarks about Jews. A copy of the original report which contained the exact dialogue was leaked to the tabloid news TMZ. An investigation was conducted to determine how the information leaked out."

53. The LASD's history discusses the Kolts Commission Report as "assessing excessive force, officer involved shootings and risk management efforts by the Los Angeles County Sheriff's Department."

54. The LASD description: "The County Board of Supervisors formed the Citizens' Commission on Jail Violence to conduct a review of the nature, depth and cause of the problem of inappropriate deputy use of force in the jails, and to recommend corrective action as necessary. The task of the Commission was to restore public confidence in the constitutional operation of the jails."

CHAPTER TWO

1. One death in custody that received particular attention was the death of a baby born to a mentally ill woman who gave birth in a jail cell alone (Suarez 2022). County commissioners expressed frustration with the sheriff that they learned of the jail losing certification only from the local newspaper.

2. One officer described assaults, such as one that caused internal bleeding, a collapsed lung, and broken bones requiring surgery, as a "normal thing" in the Tarrant County jail (Manna 2022b).

3. Williams' controversy continued in his second term when he refused to drive new cars because they were Fords, not Chevys (the preferred car of his largest campaign donor), and later became convinced that his office was bugged.

4. See https://www.tarrantcountytx.gov/en/sheriff/about-us/former-sheriffs.html for a list of all sheriffs who have served in Tarrant County.

5. As we discuss in chapter 1, the first Black sheriff elected in the South post-Reconstruction was Lucius Amerson of Macon County, Alabama, in 1968. The first Black sheriff elected west of the Mississippi post-Reconstruction was John Lovick of Snohomish County, Washington, in 2007.

6. In a review of women as heads of policing agencies in 2001, Schulz (2004, 189) reported that "women make up 1 percent of the nation's sheriffs."

7. Two of the earliest women sheriffs were both appointed following their husbands' deaths in office: Emma Daugherty Banister was appointed sheriff of Coleman County, Texas, in 1918, and Clara Dunham Crowell was appointed in 1919 as the Lander County, Nevada sheriff. Florence Shoemaker Thompson, of Daviess county, Kentucky discussed in the first chapter, was the first woman to carry out an execution as a sheriff and was also appointed to finish her husband's term in office following his death.

8. In 1976, the New York Times profiled Martha Calbow, sheriff of Putnam County, Illinois, with the headline "Woman Is Sheriff but Her Husband Wears the Guns" (New York Times 1972). Calbow took over after her husband (the former sheriff) was termed out of office; he continued to retain the arrest powers and supervise deputies. Sheriff Calbow was the only woman to serve in Illinois at the time. In 2023, the state has zero women serving as sheriff—but five men named Jeff.

9. Mrs. Willie Clara Murphy was described as "a small woman with a smile on her lips and laughter in her voice" in her announcement as Desha County, Arkansas, sheriff (New York Times 1922).

10. From the *Salt Lake City Tribune* article about Rosie Rivera's election as Salt Lake City's sheriff: "She was a teen mother, a high school dropout and an onion-field worker—now she's Utah's first female sheriff" (Dobner 2017).

11. Tausanovitch and Warshaw (2013; 2022) pool together large surveys of the American public and use Bayesian Item-Response and multilevel regression and poststratification, which incorporates respondents' demographics and geography to estimate the ideological preferences of each county, even when counties have low populations or are not frequently surveyed.

12. The scale theoretically ranges from -5 (very conservative sheriff, very liberal county) to +5 (very liberal sheriff, very conservative county). In practice, the scale ranges from -3 to 1.4.

13. This sheriff also went on to note, "While I was in [a different county], I dealt with BLM and other ethnic protest groups. Their leaders were all very racist. They are Marxist in belief and hate America as a free nation. There is no middle ground to be had with these communists. History proves this over and over." Another sheriff refused to answer quite a few questions on the survey because "it is impossible to paint with a broad brush on complicated issues and our country has some extreme areas (on both sides), as well as many moderate areas, so it is impossible to pigeon hole our country as being one way or another on an issue" and then went on to say, "I, for example, do not want to 'go on record' as saying BLM is a threat (for example) despite the fact that some (maybe even many) of the members/leaders have supported violence against law enforcement."

14. This particular sheriff also noted, "And judging by some of your questions on this survey, I am beginning to wonder about TCU" (as the survey came from a TCU email address of one of the authors).

15. We draw on data from the Quinnipiac University Polling Institute, who conducted the poll in December of 2021.

16. Some cities (mostly in Virginia) elect a separate sheriff who is responsible only for their jail and courthouse security.

17. For example, Louisiana has a "jungle primary" system where the entire slate of candidates for the office face off in a general election, with a second run-off election for those elections where one candidate does not receive more than 50 percent of the vote. Voters prefer partisan to nonpartisan elections by a slight bit, but it is unclear whether this would translate into support for changing the political institution (Crawford 2022).

18. Sheriffs do not exist in Alaska and Connecticut, and Hawaii and Rhode Island appoint their sheriffs.

19. The National Sheriffs' Association notes, "The Office of Sheriff is not simply another 'department' of county government. The internal operation of an Office of Sheriff is the sole responsibility of the elected Sheriff. County department heads are subordinate to a county governing body, because a 'department' is truly only a division of county government. The Office of Sheriff is a statutory/constitutional office having exclusive powers and authority under state law and/or state constitution. These inherent powers are not subject to the dictates of a local county governing body."

20. Other states include a variety of clauses and stipulations that cast aspersions on the importance of the original constitutional origins of the office—for example, in

Maryland, the constitution designates that the sheriff should have "real and personal property in the State above the value of one thousand pounds current money" to be elected.

21. Per the National Sheriffs' Association, "The office was modified over a period of time to fit democratic ideals" (National Sheriffs' Association 2022).

22. As with many questions about sheriffs, we know very little about the effect of political competition on law enforcement outcomes (Evans, Ensley, and Carmines 2014).

23. Like other scholars and journalists, we draw on California data as the state regularly releases comprehensive data (California Elections Data Archive) on its elections, as opposed to other states where election data is less accessible as it is organized county by county. California data is particularly useful as candidates include ballot designations of prior experience/positions of candidates.

24. In 1993, a *Los Angeles Times* reporter called Loving County, Texas, "AMERICA STRIPPED bare" and the sheriff remarked, "People here don't need much sheriffing." (Meyer 1993).

25. The nickname Punk was derived from his family calling him "fat little punkin'" because he was such a chubby baby (Meyer 1993; M. B. Jones 2009).

26. When local lawyer Susan Hays heard the news about the judge's arrest, her response was, "You can't make this shit up" (S. Carroll 2022).

27. A third of the sheriffs on our 2021 survey also report family members in law enforcement, and many sheriffs reference their familial ties. From one sheriff: "I FOLLOWED IN MY UNCLE'S FOOTSTEPS. HE SERVED AS SHERIFF FOR 20 YEARS AND I BEGAN MY CAREER WITH HIM IN 1973."

28. Or candidates could come from other law enforcement agencies in the area, a pool that is very small in rural areas where the sheriff's office is the only law enforcement agency.

29. Neil, who switched to the Republican Party after his loss to McGuffey, said that his appearance at the Trump rally in 2016 was about the then-candidate's support for law enforcement: "I was very appreciative of Donald Trump's support of law enforcement. I was there merely to show appreciation of Donald Trump's support for law enforcement in the United States" (Noble 2016).

30. The deputy had been reprimanded in the past for posting extremist content on social media and was suspended for one day by the previous sheriff (Cheatham 2021a).

CHAPTER THREE

1. You can see K9 Deputy Mako sniffing lobsters on the MCSO office's Instagram: https://www.instagram.com/p/CR8HYm_LYZ4/?hl=en.

2. The office issues so many tickets that several law firms in the Keys specialize in helping people fight their tickets for illegal harvests.

3. He is also the target of a lawsuit by the Southern Poverty Law Center for his cooperation with ICE and illegally detaining (and mistreating) a US citizen that ICE mistakenly flagged as an unauthorized immigrant (SPLC 2018).

4. For example, the Florida 1887 constitution states, "The first election for County Judge, Clerk of the Circuit Court, Sheriff, Tax Assessor, Tax Collector, County Trea-

surer, County Superintendent of Public Instruction, County Surveyor, Justices of the Peace, Constables and all other elective County Officers shall be at the general election in 1888" (Article 18§10).

5. Clyde F. Snyder and Irving Howards, County Government in Illinois 78; Carbondale: U. of Ill. Pr. 1960.

6. Cnty. Of Edgar v. Middleton, 86 Ill. App. 3rd 502 (1899).

7. Some states further define this power—for example, California states that "the sheriff shall preserve peace, and to accomplish this object may sponsor, supervise, or participate in any project of crime prevention, rehabilitation of persons previously convicted of crime, or the suppression of delinquency" (CA Govt Code §26600 [2020]).

8. South Dakota Statute §11-15-03 (2015).

9. These grants are sometimes drawn from the state constitution, such as in Louisiana, where the state constitution notes, "The sheriff, except in the Parish of Orleans, shall be ex-officio collector of State and parish taxes. He shall give separate bonds for the faithful performance of his duty in each capacity. Until otherwise provided, the bonds shall be given according to existing laws. Sheriffs elected or appointed shall furnish bond within thirty days from the date of their commissions, in default of which the office shall be declared vacant, and the Governor shall appoint for the remainder of the term."

10. One example would be Travis County, Texas's Junior Deputy Summer Camp, where nine- to twelve-year-olds spend a week learning about the sheriff's office with presentations and "hands-on experience" from SWAT, K9, Estray, and Lake Patrol units.

11. These patterns may be particularly likely to happen in rural areas. As Weisheit and colleagues (1995, 39) note, rural sheriffs interact with their constituents in very different ways from sheriffs with large numbers of constituents: "The low levels of mobility and low population density means that rural law enforcement officers, such as sheriffs, are likely to personally know most offenders and their families. If a victim can identify a thief, for example, the sheriff is likely to know where to find the offender and to already know quite a bit about the offender and his or her family. Given this, a greater reliance on informal control in rural areas should be of no surprise."

12. In 2021, one of Ramsay's deputies was ticketed for taking six lobsters from a boat he had pulled over. A Facebook post about Ramsay charging his deputy with theft garnered 436 likes, 87 shares, and 187 comments, including the comment "Sheriff Ramsay for President."

13. You can see pictures of Hank, June Carter, BamBam, and other animals on the farm's Facebook page: https://www.facebook.com/KeysAnimalFarm.

14. A 2015 meta-analysis of research on "disordered policing" strategies found that they are "associated with an overall statistically significant, modest crime reduction effect. The strongest program effect sizes were generated by community and problem-solving interventions designed to change social and physical disorder conditions at particular places. Conversely, aggressive order maintenance strategies that target individual disorderly behaviors do not generate significant crime reductions" (Braga, Welsh, and Schnell 2015, 567). One of the most well-known examples of aggressive disordered policing, New York City's "stop and frisk" program, was deeply racist, with

Black and Latino men much more likely to be the subject of stop and frisk, even as those stops did not lead to higher instances of uncovering contraband materials, including firearms and drugs (Levchak 2021; Gelman, Fagan, and Kiss 2007).

15. Sheriff Ramsay repeats this often—for example, in the 2018 Monroe County Sheriff's Office annual report, he notes, "Many of you often see members of the Sheriff's Office picking up trash and covering graffiti. We do it, because I believe—and it's been proven by numerous studies—that cleaner streets means safer streets. I don't want to live surrounded by garbage and graffiti covered buildings and I know you don't either" (MCSO 2018).

16. On one occasion, this deputy wrote, "Words are insufficient in describing the extraordinary brilliance demonstrated by Sheriff Rick Ramsay and his magnificent team of officers, when it comes to their apprehending [a criminal breaking into cars]" (Donnelly 2018).

17. Pictures of the sheriff and his steed can be found on the sheriff's website: https://www.bhcso.org/ContentPage.aspx?id=122.

18. Appointed sheriffs oversee the New York City and the Miami-Dade County jails, although a sheriff will be elected in Miami-Dade County in 2024. An individual sheriff does not run the Southwest Virginia Regional Jail Authority in Virginia.

19. Average number of employees from LEMAS 2013.

20. In addition to the formal powers associated with running a jail, sheriffs also engage in a wide set of assumed powers: providing alternative incarceration programs, from work release to job training, as well as engaging in drug and alcohol rehabilitation and health care. As one sheriff noted, "Jails operate work release programs, boot camps, and other specialized services. They try to address educational needs, substance abuse needs, and vocational needs while managing inmate behavior. *Inmate idleness contributes to management problems*" (emphasis added).

21. South Dakota Statute §11-15-03 (2015).

22. Nevada Statute §211.030(1) (2015).

23. Arkansas Code §12-41-502 (2016).

24. The rate has increased from 68 people held per 100,000 in 1970 to 220 per 100,000 in 2013.

25. Other research from the 1980s articulated, "Given the invisibility of the local jail in public consciousness, public concern about the local prison is usually reaction to some event that has occurred in the jail such an escape or an accident which may have occurred under mysterious circumstances" (Handberg 1982).

26. Sheriffs also note challenges with "mental health challenged inmates in the county jail (inmates who should be in a mental health facility, not a jail)." In the sheriff's words, the jail provides "psychiatric services for those who are not necessarily criminal but we encounter on a regular basis and are forced to incarcerate."

27. This tracks with estimates of the prison population, where up to a quarter of the prison population have severe mental illnesses (K. Kim, Becker-Cohen, and Serakos 2015).

28. There was also a conflict over the sheriff's investigation of the county executive (which are called county judges in Kentucky) over the misuse of county funds: "Noble

has twice been arrested and charged with misuse of county funds, and it was Hollan's office which handled those investigations" (M. Berk 2020).

29. For example, in 2017, Lamoille County sheriff Roger Marcoux Jr. made $145,623, earning $67,951 from outside contracts alongside his $77,672 salary (Freese 2018). In 2005, Marion County, Indiana, sheriff Frank Anderson made $268,000 on fees collected from tax warrants, on top of his base pay of $102,000.

30. The sheriff office's annual report references the specific fees charged: "Fees charged in our facilities include: a $20 booking fee, an inmate subsistence fee of $1 per day per inmate, the inmate commissary which sells extra day-to-day necessities to inmates, indigent packs, mattress rentals, check writing fees, reading glasses, legal services and some medical services" (Monroe County Sheriff's Office 2020). These monies go into an "Inmate Welfare Fund" that pays for the sheriff's Animal Farm, for classes those in jail for domestic violence offenses, as well as a variety of wellness and mental health services.

31. Similarly, the US Marshals Service can request a hold and compensate the sheriff for holding someone with a federal warrant.

32. Sheriff Guida: "[Embridge] went around and traveled around prior to the pipeline ever being built and did a demonstration. That here's what the pipe that looks like in the ground . . . this is a replacement line. The line in 1960 was this and they showed us what the line today looks like. They showed us what the pipe today looks like. They showed us the different thicknesses where they're going to go onto the river and they're going to use this. They showed us all those things. And so they've got their story out to anybody that would want to listen" (Holtan 2021).

CHAPTER FOUR

1. Rowland faced trial for felony charges for aggravated assault and aggravated battery and a misdemeanor charge for the exhibition of a weapon for the November 2021 incident. As part of his defense, his attorney planned to call forty-seven sheriffs to testify on Rowland's behalf (Hines 2021). The judge allowed Rowland to stay in office as he awaited trial, despite the attorney general's request for him to take a leave of absence. The judge did confiscate his guns. The Bingham County Commissioners also called on Rowland to step down from his office, but they had no ability to force him to resign. The sheriff resigned after eight months of pressure to do so, writing that he had become a "distraction" (Olson 2022). The sheriff pled guilty to one count of aggravated assault and was sentenced to ten days in jail and three years on probation (KTVB Staff 2022).

2. We acknowledge the complexity of these problems: women are not the only victims of these crimes, these specific assaults are not the only forms of violence against women, and these acts are not identical in their effect on the lives of victims, how they are viewed by society, or how they are addressed by law enforcement. For a larger discussion of the history of law enforcement response to domestic violence, see Feder (1997).

3. *Thurman v. City of Torrington* 1985; *Bruno v. Codd* 1976; *Scott v. Hurt* 1976; *Thomas v. Los Angeles* 1979.

4. While awaiting trial for the criminal charges, a judge found the sheriff violated conditions of his release as he had repeatedly contact Altheimer or asked other law

enforcement to do so. The judge order Troyer to post a $100,000 bail and abide by the no-contact and anti-harassment orders (Brunner 2022a).

5. Babeu faced additional controversy when an ex-lover publicly reported allegations that he was threatened by the sheriff to be deported if he revealed their affair, but an investigation by the Arizona attorney general cleared Babeu of the allegations, explaining, "Although Orozco conducted himself in a manner that may constitute a violation of the law, there was no reasonable likelihood of conviction on anything more than a misdemeanor charge" (Sakal 2012). The Arizona attorney general's office later investigated Sheriff Babeu again, this time for "eyebrow-raising" mismanagement of racketeering funds, but again did not find proof of criminal activity, explaining that "one of the reasons is that record-keeping was so poor" (Anglen 2019).

6. Sheriffs do not actually have the legal authority to deport people. The American Civil Liberties Union has requested records relating to Coe's actions (Brnger 2022).

7. As of April 2023, Jenkins was indicted by a federal grand jury on five federal charges of conspiracy and false statements to acquire machine guns. He has pled not guilty, been ordered to surrender his firearm, and announced a leave of absence through the end of the trial but reinstated himself in August despite continuing to face charges.

8. In 2012, we also asked sheriffs to provide information about specific types of training; see Results appendix.

9. In a reported email, a spokesperson for the Plymouth Sheriff's Office wrote, "It would take a Jesuit scholar to debate whether or not Massachusetts taxpayers are benefiting from ICE detentions or bearing an additional burden" (McDonald 2020).

10. Four of five drug busts by the US Border Patrol are of US citizens (KQED 2013).

11. For example, the sheriff did not accept the measured weight of Willie Nelson's weed reported by the federal agents in his 2010 arrest. At the checkpoint, the weed weighed nearly seven ounces, but on scales in the sheriff's office, it weighed less than half of that, making Nelson conveniently eligible for a misdemeanor fine rather than felony charge. According to Sheriff West, when Nelson saw the sheriff's evidence room full of weed, he responded with dismay: "Whoa! Y'all got a lotta shit here. You don't need mine, give it back." Sheriff West did not (Reinart 2013).

12. https://dynamicwebdevelopment.net/revelation-dev.

CHAPTER FIVE

1. Songer's note claimed that he had sworn an oath before the "Supreme Judge of the Universe" (see Whitehead, Perry, and Baker 2018 for the Christian Nationalism origins of this phrasing) to uphold the Washington and US Constitution (Songer 2021).

2. The sheriffs' opposition to enforcing the state law prompted an open letter from the Washington attorney general. It reminded the sheriffs that local law enforcement is required to perform background checks. If they refuse to do so, and a crime results to someone who was sold or transferred a firearm because a background check was not conducted, the sheriff's office could be held liable (Ferguson 2019).

3. The term *posse comitatus* has its origins in Alfred the Great, who ruled England from AD 871–899, establishing the shire's militia, calling on a posse, or group of citizens, to maintain the peace on behalf of the king. In the United States, sheriffs may call

on a posse to help enforce the law. For instance, the Pitkin County, Colorado, sheriff called upon his local posse to recapture serial killer Ted Bundy, who had escaped jail in Aspen in 1977.

4. Beach's *Blue Book* provided information and pointed to places where the federal government had overstepped its bounds on education, the federal reserve, and the IRS. It also called individuals to form a Citizen's Posse (Kopel 2014a), where "every abled-bodied patriotic male of good character, who is interested in the preservation of law and order, becoming a member." Again, the sheriff plays a central role; posses are to work "directly with the County sheriffs" but should be prepared to "take steps to replace the Sheriff and get one in office that will represent the people by adhering to constitutional law, which they took an oath to do upon taking office."

5. These views were repeated in the *Posse's Blue Book*: "The County sheriff is the only legal law enforcement officer in the United States of America," adding that "he is elected by the people and is directly responsible for law enforcement in his County. It is his responsibility to protect the people of his County from unlawful acts on the part of anyone, including officials of government." In pointing out that the sheriff is responsible only to his citizens, Beach writes, "There is no lawful authority, for Judges and the Courts to direct the law enforcement activities of a County Sheriff."

6. Mack repeatedly endorsed *2000 Mules*, which makes the false claim that people were hired to stuff ballot boxes in key states in the 2020 election for Joe Biden's campaign. It has been thoroughly debunked by a variety of sources (Dreisbach 2022; Reuters Fact Check 2022); however, this has not dissuaded Mack from championing the movie (Stone 2022b; Eisler and Layne 2022).

7. Award names and years are inconsistent. Data compiled based on available information on the CSPOA website and other online sources.

8. CSPOA recently expanded its efforts to include county governments, with two rural Nevada county commissioners passing resolutions endorsing and paying to join the CSPOA in 2021.

9. For example, the 2021 CSPOA sheriff survey asks, "On December 1, 1955, Rosa Parks was arrested in Montgomery, Alabama for failing to give her seat to a white man. Knowing what we know now about equality and justice, if you were called back in time as the responding officer to this call, what would you have done? (choose one)" with the response options including A) "I would have to arrest her. It's not my job to pick and choose which laws to enforce. If it's on the books, I will enforce the law." B) "All laws must be enforced. The police don't make the laws, it is not for us to judge. Mrs. Parks would have to seek justice in the courts." C) "The police are not robots for the legislatures. I would never enforce such a stupid law. I would have sat down next to Mrs. Parks, would have shaken her hand, and made sure she got home safely and given her home extra patrol throughout the night." D) "I would have pretended to arrest her and then taken her home instead." Mack regularly implies that C is the acceptable answer for CSPOA members.

10. In 2022, Greene resigned over charges of misconduct, including making racist statements. Despite this resignation, voters again elected him to office. He resigned for a second time after taking office in early 2023.

11. The seven items hang together into a single scale (alpha=0.793) and load on a single factor.

12. This sheriff also listed "Understanding millennials" as one of their top concerns.

13. "I will stand and protect my rights, whatever it takes, to defend this valid ranch, the access for the public, and the policing power of the Clark County Sheriff" (SPLC 2014a).

14. The Instagram account is a combination of pictures of Lamb in uniform or dressed up in country-western finery with his wife (who has also written a book, *The Sheriff's Wife*).

CHAPTER SIX

1. The recording went on with the sheriff allegedly laughing while saying, "If they don't think I'll give the damn order to kill that motherfucker they're full of shit . . . Take him out." In another car pursuit, a recording caught Sheriff Shoupe as he seemed to instruct officers to lie after the fact about what happened (B. Hall 2018b).

2. For example, see accounts of sheriffs in colonial times, during slavery, and western vigilantism (Obert 2018; Hadden 2003; Wager 1928).

3. For example, the National Sheriffs' Association's elections position paper (previously discussed in chap. 2) argues for the importance of elections to sheriffs, including: "Under our republican form of government, 'voters' have the right to choose who is to 'serve' as their Sheriff, their local 'chief law enforcement officer'" (National Sheriffs' Association, n.d.).

4. Hampden County Sheriff's Department. 2022. "Retired Sheriff Michael J. Ashe, Jr." https://web.archive.org/web/20220205180421/http://hcsdma.org/sheriff-ashe -bio/.

5. In comparison, a white deputy with a history of accusations of sexual harassment was allowed to resign rather than face termination (Benson 2021).

6. Sheriffs are occasionally forced to create civilian oversight mechanisms as part of settlements after state or federal investigators identify civil rights violations. Sheriffs often pretend like they are adopting these mechanisms as a part of their broader interest in transparency (see Sheriff Youngblood in Kern County, California, as an example), but we do not see sheriffs voluntarily adopting these mechanisms as a form of oversight. In the Kern County Use of Force report, Sheriff Underwood wrote, "During my career as the Sheriff, transparency has been a priority for me. I have worked hard to achieve this goal. In 2020, the Community-wide Advisory Committee was founded to bring us closer to the people we serve and provide a credible voice the community can trust. Long before the committee, the Sheriff's Office held Community Academy's, hosted National Night Out events, and participated in many community events throughout our great county."

7. The National Association for Civilian Oversight of Law Enforcement, which tracks civilian oversight efforts and provides resources to boards and commissions, lists less than 15 oversight efforts over sheriff's office in their directory as of 2023.

8. Counties that appoint sheriffs include Denver County in Colorado; New York City (covering the cities' five counties); Nassau and Westchester counties in New York; Cuyahoga County, Ohio; and Northampton and Luzerne counties in Pennsylvania. Clark County, Washington moved to an appointed sheriff in 2022.

9. Similarly, in Broomfield, Colorado, the county has a county police department where the sheriff's duties are assigned to an appointed police chief. In St. Louis County, Missouri, the county transferred most of the sheriff's duties to a county police, and the court-appointed sheriff provides only court support.

10. Charter amendment 5 (appointment) and 6 (redefining the office's powers) passed with 55.6 percent and 62 percent of the vote.

11. https://twitter.com/SaveOur_Sheriff.

12. Although calls for defunding the police occupied a position in national political dialogues, particularly in the lead up to the 2020 election after the murder of George Floyd, local law enforcement agencies continue to enjoy large budgets, even in liberal cities (Weichselbaum and Lewis 2020; Sinclair, Love, and Gutiérrez-Vera 2021).

13. In *Elrod v. Burns* (1976), the US Supreme Court held that partisanship cannot be a condition in public employment, after the newly elected Democratic Cook County, Illinois, sheriff Richard Elrod dismissed Republican employees hired by the prior Republican sheriff, increasing protections for deputies.

14. One of the arguments that the Louisiana Sheriffs Association used to oppose marijuana legalization was that K9 dogs would be "null and void" if decriminalization passed (Karlin 2021).

15. For problems with professionalization, see Schrader (2019).

16. The bobble head is a play on Elf on the Shelf, a Christmas creature that moves around watching in someone's home and reports back to Santa whether the children have been naughty or nice. Some have argued that the Elf on the Shelf socializes children into accepting a surveillance state (Nosowitz 2019). Meanwhile, Sheriff Judd has adamantly opposed body cameras for his deputies because he argues they are an invasion of privacy (DaSilva 2021).

17. The photo essay included four photos of the sheriff slapping a Black woman with the caption "When woman from drunken party talks back to Lane he suddenly slaps her to the wall, gives her a piece of his mind."

18. The DOJ has limited capacity: they investigate fewer than 0.02 percent of the country's state and local law enforcement agencies each year (Rushin 2017).

19. New York State Executive Order 203, *New York State Police Reform and Reinvention Collaborative*.

20. Sheriff Osborne's "About Derek" section includes a childhood picture of the sheriff wearing a sheriff costume and the sheriff's philosophy: "When the public elects someone to the position of Sheriff, they are entrusting that person with their safety and the best quality of life possible. You deserve someone who will cherish that role and not waver, tire, or falter from their commitment to serving them."

21. The 8CantWait campaign was highly criticized as insufficient by abolitionists for overinflating its claims and undercutting more transformative demands.

22. For problems with (and opportunities from) federal grants, see "Reimagining Federal Grants for Public Safety and Criminal Justice Reform" by the Center for American Progress (CAP 2020).

23. Monitoring is allowed via Title VI of the Civil Rights Act of 1964 and Omnibus Crime Control and Safe Streets Act of 1968.

24. As we were finishing this chapter, news broke that Sheriff Kevin Clary of Mc-Curtain County, Oklahoma and other county officials were secretly recorded talking about killing reporters and lynching Black residents after a public meeting. The Oklahoma attorney general found no legal grounds to dismiss the sheriff.

25. Sheriff Stewart was one of the sheriffs that elected to speak to us and Maurice Chammah in follow-ups to our 2021 survey on the record.

26. When former president Obama designated the Bears Ears National Monument, Sheriff Vigil told the *Washington Times* that he was protesting because "this is about opposing so many thousands of acres that is going to create nothing more than a pathway for criminals to get into this country to do their criminal acts" (Boyer 2014). Sheriff Vigil also oversaw an office with sexual harassment between employees, concerns about budget irregularities, and issues with deputy retention (Litton 2018; Wesley 2016).

27. In discussing why she ran again, Sheriff Stewart posted, "It's a great distance, covered with countless details, between wanting to be the Sheriff and being the Sheriff" (K. Stewart 2022).

DATA AND METHODS APPENDIX

1. A staff member in a sheriff's office could complete the policy section of the survey, but they were asked to provide contact information for the sheriff so that the sheriff could complete the attitudes section. Of the surveys completed, 36 staff members completed the policy section; of those, 80 percent (or 29) of the sheriffs of those offices completed the attitudes section. The seven surveys completed only by the staff were dropped from the dataset.

References

8CantWait. 2022. "8 Can't Wait Research Basis." Campaign Zero.

ACLU. 2022. "Collusion in California's Central Valley: The Case for Ending Sheriff Entanglement with ICE." American Civil Liberties Union. Last modified February 9, 2022. https://www.aclunc.org/publications/collusion-californias-central-valley-case-ending-sheriff-entanglement-ice.

ACLU and Global Human Rights Clinic. 2022. "Captive Labor: Exploitation of Incarcerated Workers." University of Chicago. https://www.aclu.org/report/captive-labor-exploitation-incarcerated-workers.

Adams, Char. 2021. "Black Officers Say Washington Sheriff's Department Has a 'Culture of Animosity.'" *NBC News*. November 11, 2021. https://www.nbcnews.com/news/nbcblk/black-jail-officers-say-sheriffs-department-culture-animosity-rcna5334.

ADL. 2021. "The Constitutional Sheriffs and Peace Officers Association (CSPOA) and Richard Mack: How Extremists Are Successfully Infiltrating Law Enforcement." September 9, 2021. Anti-Defamation League. https://www.adl.org/resources/reports/the-constitutional-sheriffs-and-peace-officers-association-cspoa-and-richard-mack.

Adler, Jeffrey S. 2015. "Less Crime, More Punishment: Violence, Race, and Criminal Justice in Early Twentieth-Century America." *Journal of American History* 102 (1): 34–46.

Agar, John. 2020. "Sheriff Who Shared Stage with Militia Defends Their Rights but Not Alleged Governor Kidnapping Plot." Mlive. October 9, 2020. https://www.mlive.com/news/grand-rapids/2020/10/sheriff-who-shared-stage-with-militia-defends-their-rights-but-not-alleged-governor-kidnapping-plot.html.

Ahler, Douglas J., and David E. Broockman. 2018. "The Delegate Paradox: Why Polarized Politicians Can Represent Citizens Best." *Journal of Politics* 80 (4): 1117–33.

Ake, Jami, and Gretchen Arnold. 2017. "A Brief History of Anti-Violence against Women Movements in the United States." *Sourcebook on Violence Against Women, Thousand Oaks, CA: Sage*, 3–26.

Alabama Russell County Sheriff Statement on Shall Issue Permits. Last modified August 20, 2015. https://www.youtube.com/watch?v=Gjku2z_7pFE.

Alabama Sheriffs Association. n.d. "Sheriffs' History." Accessed August 28, 2023. https://www.alabamasheriffs.com/sheriffs-history.

Ambarian, Jonathan. 2020. "Broadwater County Sheriff to Hold Meetings on Public Safety Needs, Budget." *KTVH*. Last modified February 5, 2020. https://www.ktvh

.com/news/helena-news/broadwater-county-sheriff-to-hold-meetings-on-public
-safety-needs-budget.

American Sheriff Foundation. 2023. "ABOUT US." AS Foundation. Accessed October 9, 2023. https://www.americansherifffoundation.com/about-us.

Anania, Billie. 2020. "The Los Angeles Paper That Documented Police Brutality in the 1960s and '70s." *Hyperallergic*. Last modified June 11, 2020. http://hyperallergic .com/570172/los-angeles-free-press-police-protests-coverage.

Anglen, Robert. 2019. "Arizona Won't Prosecute Paul Babeu, Lando Voyles on Use of RICO Funds." *AZCentral*. https://www.azcentral.com/story/news/local/arizona -investigations/2019/04/10/paul-babeu-ex-pinal-sheriff-county-attorney-lando -voyles-prosecuted-rico-funds/3426837002/.

Ansell, Christopher K., and Arthur L. Burris. 1997. "Bosses of the City Unite! Labor Politics and Political Machine Consolidation, 1870–1910." *Studies in American Political Development* 11 (1): 1–43.

Anzia, Sarah F. 2011. "Election Timing and the Electoral Influence of Interest Groups." *Journal of Politics* 73 (2): 412–27.

———. 2013. *Timing and Turnout: How Off-Cycle Elections Favor Organized Groups*. Chicago: University of Chicago Press.

Anzia, Sarah F., and Rachel Bernhard. 2022. "Gender Stereotyping and the Electoral Success of Women Candidates: New Evidence from Local Elections in the United States." *British Journal of Political Science* 52 (4): 1544–63.

Archbold, Carol A. 2021. "Police Accountability in the USA: Gaining Traction or Spinning Wheels?" *Policing: A Journal of Policy and Practice* 15 (3): 1665–83.

Arellano, Gustavo. 2022. "Column: Is the Kern County Sheriff an out-of-Control Cowboy—or a Lost Cause?" *Los Angeles Times*, July 8, 2022. https://www.latimes.com /california/story/2022-07-08/column-donny-youngblood-kern-county-sheriff.

Arora, Ashna. 2018. "Too Tough on Crime? The Impact of Prosecutor Politics on Incarceration." Working paper. American Economics Association.

Ashdown, Paul, and Edward Caudill. 2020. *Imagining Wild Bill: James Butler Hickok in War, Media, and Memory*. Carbondale, IL: Southern Illinois University Press.

Associated Press. 2021a. "Florida Keys Officials Ready for 2-Day Lobster Mini-Season." *WTXL*, July 20, 2021. https://www.wtxl.com/news/local-news/florida-keys -officials-ready-for-2-day-lobster-mini-season.

———. 2021b. "Sheriff Contracts COVID-19, Still Plans to Fight Mandates." *The Seattle Times*, August 19, 2021. https://www.seattletimes.com/seattle-news/health /klickitat-county-sheriff-contracts-covid-19-still-plans-to-fight-mandates.

Assunção, Muri. 2020. "Openly Gay Woman Running for Sheriff in Ohio Wins Primary against Trump-Supporting Democrat; Gets 70% of Vote." *New York Daily News*, April 30, 2020. https://www.nydailynews.com/news/politics/ny-charmaine -mcguffey-hamilton-county-sheriff-ohio-wins-primary-20200430-i306eqw5fvhqtc gunzuefiwo6y-story.html.

Atlantic County Sheriff's Office. n.d. "History—Atlantic County Sheriff's Office." Accessed September 30, 2023. http://www.acsheriff.org/about/history.asp.

Avery, Dan. 2021. "Ohio's 1st Lesbian Sheriff on Her Rocky Journey to Becoming 'Proud and Fearless.'" *NBC News*, June 1, 2021. https://www.nbcnews.com/feature/nbc -out/ohio-s-1st-lesbian-sheriff-her-rocky-journey-becoming-proud-n1269156.

AZ Central. 2020. "Pinal County Sheriff Mark Lamb Founded a Charity. Its Spending Is a Mystery." *AZ Central*, August 31, 2020. https://www.azcentral.com/story/news

/politics/arizona/2020/08/31/pinal-county-sheriff-mark-lamb-charity-tax-filings
/5626026002.

Ba, Bocar A., Dean Knox, Jonathan Mummolo, and Roman Rivera. 2021. "The Role of Officer Race and Gender in Police-Civilian Interactions in Chicago." *Science* 371 (6530): 696–702.

Back, E. M. 2015. "South Polls: Judge Lynch Denied: Combating Mob Violence in the American South, 1877–1950." *Southern Cultures* 21 (2): 117–139.

Ballotpedia. 2021. "State Legislative Elections, 2020." Ballotpedia. Last modified January 11, 2021. https://ballotpedia.org/State_legislative_elections,_2020.

Ban, Charlie. 2020. "Civilian Review of Law Enforcement Remains Rare for Counties." National Association of Counties. Last modified June 22, 2020. https://www.naco
.org/articles/civilian-review-law-enforcement-remains-rare-counties.

Banda, Kevin K., and John Cluverius. 2023. "White American's Evaluations of the Alt-Right." *American Politics Research* 51 (4): 435–42.

Banks, Leo. 1995. "Arizona Sheriff Sticks to His Guns : Lawman Makes a Name for Himself by Attacking Brady Law and Backing Militia Groups. His Words Find Favor at Home." *Los Angeles Times*, May 2, 1995. https://www.latimes.com/archives/la-xpm
-1995-05-02-mn-61363-story.html.

Barker, Kim, Steve Eder, David D. Kirkpatrick, and Arya Sundaram. 2021. "How Police Justify Killing Drivers: The Vehicle Was a Weapon." *New York Times*, November 6, 2021. https://www.nytimes.com/2021/11/06/us/police-traffic-stops-shooting.html.

Barkun, Michael. 1997. *Religion and the Racist Right: The Origins of the Christian Identity Movement*. Chapel Hill, NC: UNC Press Books.

———. 2007. "Purifying the Law: The Legal World of 'Christian Patriots.'" *Journal for the Study of Radicalism* 1 (1): 57–70.

Barner, John R., and Michelle Mohr Carney. 2011. "Interventions for Intimate Partner Violence: A Historical Review." *Journal of Family Violence* 26 (3): 235–44.

Barnes, Kenneth C. 1998. *Who Killed John Clayton?: Political Violence and the Emergence of the New South, 1861–1893*. Durham, NC: Duke University Press.

Bartelme, Tony. 2020. "Suspended Colleton County Sheriff Andy Strickland Pleads Guilty to 3 Charges, Gets Probation." *Post and Courier*, October 23, 2020. https://
www.postandcourier.com/news/suspended-colleton-county-sheriff-andy
-strickland-pleads-guilty-to-3-charges-gets-probation/article_77cca50a-154b-11eb
-a5ef-37210765cfee.html.

Bateson, Regina. 2021. "The Politics of Vigilantism." *Comparative Political Studies* 54 (6): 923–55.

Baumgartner, Frank R., Derek A. Epp, and Kelsey Shoub. 2018. *Suspect Citizens*. New York: Cambridge University Press.

Becker, Andrew, and G. W. Schulz. 2013. "Minor Drug Busts at Border Checkpoint Breaking Texas County's Budget." *Reveal*, June 19, 2013. http://revealnews.org
/article/minor-drug-busts-at-border-checkpoint-breaking-texas-countys-budget.

Bell, Alex, dir. 2021. "Sheriff Youngblood Discusses Intention to Run for Re-Election in 2022." *KERO*. Bakersfield, CA. https://www.turnto23.com/news/local-news
/sheriff-donny-youngblood-on-re-election-yes-i-will-run.

Bell, Chanon. 2011. "History of County Term Limits." National Association of Counties. https://www.naco.org/sites/default/files/documents/County%20Term%20Limits.pdf.

Benegal, Salil D. 2018. "The Spillover of Race and Racial Attitudes into Public Opinion about Climate Change." *Environmental Politics* 27 (4): 733–56.

Benjamin, Andrea. 2017a. "Coethnic Endorsements, Out-Group Candidate Preferences, and Perceptions in Local Elections." *Urban Affairs Review* 53 (4): 631–57.
———. 2017b. *Racial Coalition Building in Local Elections: Elite Cues and Cross-Ethnic
Voting.* Cambridge University Press.
Benjamin, Andrea, and Alexis Miller. 2019. "Picking Winners: How Political Organizations Influence Local Elections." *Urban Affairs Review* 55 (3): 643–74.
Benn, Alvin. 2006. "Sheriff Jim Clark Died Believing He Did Right Thing." *Montgomery Advertiser*, 2006. https://www.montgomeryadvertiser.com/story/news/local
/selma50/2015/03/01/sheriff-jim-clark-died-believing-right-thing/24214459.
Benson, Riley. 2021. "Charleston County Sheriff Kristin Graziano Responds to Surveillance Criticism, Activists Moving Forward." *WCBD News 2*, October 1, 2021. https://
www.counton2.com/jamal-sutherland/charleston-county-sheriff-kristin-graziano
-responds-to-surveillance-criticism-activists-moving-forward/.
Berk, Michael. 2020. "Back to Work; Breathitt County Sheriff's Budget Passes." *WLEX*,
February 17, 2020. https://www.lex18.com/news/covering-kentucky/back-to-work
-breathitt-county-sheriffs-budget-passes.
Berk, Sarah Fenstermaker, and Donileen R. Loseke. 1980. "'Handling' Family Violence:
Situational Determinants of Police Arrest in Domestic Disturbances." *Law & Society
Review* 15 (2): 317–46.
Berlet, Chip, and Spencer Sunshine. 2019. "Rural Rage: The Roots of Right-Wing Popu-
lism in the United States." *Journal of Peasant Studies* 46 (3): 480–513.
Berlin, Ira. 2010. *The Making of African America: The Four Great Migrations.* Penguin.
Bernabo, Laurena. 2022. "Copaganda and Post-Floyd TVPD: Broadcast Television's
Response to Policing in 2020." *Journal of Communication* 72, no. 4 (August 2022):
488–96.
Bernhard, Rachel. 2022. "Wearing the Pants(Suit)? Gendered Leadership Styles, Par-
tisanship, and Candidate Evaluation in the 2016 U.S. Election." *Politics & Gender*
18 (2): 513–45.
Bernhard, Rachel, and Justin de Benedictis-Kessner. 2021. "Men and Women Candi-
dates Are Similarly Persistent After Losing Elections." *Proceedings of the National
Academy of Sciences* 118 (26): p.e2026726118.
Bernhard, Rachel, and Sean Freeder. 2020. "The More You Know: Voter Heuristics and
the Information Search." *Political Behavior* 42 (2): 603–23
Bernstein, Patricia. 2006. *The First Waco Horror: The Lynching of Jesse Washington and
the Rise of the NAACP.* Texas A&M University Press.
Bertram, Jacob. 2021. "Sheriff's Threats of Arrest Raise Concerns in Klickitat County."
Columbia Gorge News, June 30, 2021. https://www.columbiagorgenews.com/news
/sheriff-s-threats-of-arrest-raise-concerns-in-klickitat-county/article_c0d4fa98
-d91a-11eb-8040-a7d99db41f2a.html.
Berzon, Alexandra, and Nick Corasaniti. 2022. "2020 Election Deniers Seek Out Powerful Allies: County Sheriffs." *New York Times*, July 25, 2022. https://www.nytimes
.com/2022/07/25/us/politics/election-sheriffs-voting-trump.html.
Betz, Hans-Georg, and Carol Johnson. 2004. "Against the Current—Stemming the
Tide: The Nostalgic Ideology of the Contemporary Radical Populist Right." *Journal
of Political Ideologies* 9 (3): 311–27.
Bick, Caroline. 2020. "The Position of King County Sheriff Could Become an Appointed One. Here's Why That Matters." *South Seattle Emerald*, July 16, 2020.

https://southseattleemerald.com/2020/07/16/the-position-of-king-county-sheriff-could-become-an-appointed-one-heres-why-that-matters.

Blackmon, Douglas A. 2009. *Slavery by Another Name: The Re-Enslavement of Black Americans from the Civil War to World War II*. New York: Anchor Books.

Blakinger, Keri. 2023. "Former Sheriff Alex Villanueva Will Not Face Contempt Hearing for Defying Subpoenas, Judge Rules." *Los Angeles Times*, October 17, 2023. https://www.latimes.com/california/story/2023-10-17/former-sheriff-alex-villanueva-will-not-face-contempt-hearing-for-defying-subpoenas-judge-rules.

Blee, Kathleen M. 2009. *Women of the Klan: Racism and Gender in the 1920s*. Berkeley, CA: University of California Press.

Blee, Kathleen M., and Kimberly A. Creasap. 2010. "Conservative and Right-Wing Movements." *Annual Review of Sociology* 36 (1): 269–86.

Blocher, Joseph. 2013. "Firearm Localism." *Yale Law Journal*, 2013 (January): 82–146.

Blocher, Joseph, and Jacob D. Charles. 2020. "Firearms, Extreme Risk, and Legal Design: 'Red Flag' Laws and Due Process." *Virginia Law Review* 106 (6): 1285–1344.

Blum, Rachel M. 2020. *How the Tea Party Captured the GOP: Insurgent Factions in American Politics*. Chicago: University of Chicago Press.

Bock, Alan W. 1995. *Ambush at Ruby Ridge: How Government Agents Set Randy Weaver Up and Took His Family Down*. New York: Berkley Press.

Boggioni, Tom. 2016. "Idaho Sheriff Who Opposed New Rape Kit Law Apologizes for Saying Most Rapes Are 'Consensual.'" *Raw Story*. March 19, 2016. https://www.rawstory.com/2016/03/idaho-sheriff-who-opposed-new-rape-kit-law-apologizes-for-saying-most-rapes-are-consensual.

Bond, Julian. 1969. *Black Candidates: Southern Campaign Experiences*. Atlanta: Voter Education Project, Southern Regional Council.

Bonica, Adam, Jacob M. Grumbach, Charlotte Hill, and Hakeem Jefferson. 2021. "All-Mail Voting in Colorado Increases Turnout and Reduces Turnout Inequality." *Electoral Studies* 72 (August 2021): 102363.

Bostdorff, Denise M., and Steven R. Goldzwig. 2005. "History, Collective Memory, and the Appropriation of Martin Luther King, Jr.: Reagan's Rhetorical Legacy." *Presidential Studies Quarterly* 35 (4): 661–90.

Boyer, Dave. 2014. "Obama to Designate National Monument in New Mexico." *Washington Times*, May 19, 2014. https://www.washingtontimes.com/news/2014/may/19/obama-designate-national-monument-new-mexico.

Braga, Anthony A., Brandon C. Welsh, and Cory Schnell. 2015. "Can Policing Disorder Reduce Crime? A Systematic Review and Meta-Analysis." *Journal of Research in Crime and Delinquency* 52 (4): 567–88.

Brayne, Sarah. 2014. "Surveillance and System Avoidance: Criminal Justice Contact and Institutional Attachment." *American Sociological Review* 79 (3): 367–91.

Brevard Sheriff. 2023. "Wheel of Fugitive with Sheriff Wayne Ivey." February 7, 2023. https://www.youtube.com/watch?v=ajc3Gypk_F4&ab_channel=BrevardSheriff.

Briggs, William. 2017. "Police Oversight: Civilian Oversight Boards and Lessons Learned from Our Neighbors to the North." *Suffolk Transnational Law Review*, 40: 139.

Brnger, Garrett. 2022. "A Free Ride or De-Facto Deportation? Was It Legal for a Texas Sheriff to Drive Migrants to the Border?" *KSAT*, July 6, 2022. https://www.ksat.com/news/local/2022/07/07/a-free-ride-or-de-facto-deportation-was-it-legal-for-a-texas-sheriff-to-drive-migrants-to-the-border/.

Brockell, Gillian. 2021. "A Black Preacher, a White Sheriff and the Punch in the Face That Put Selma on the Map." *Washington Post*, February 21, 2021. https://www .washingtonpost.com/history/2021/02/21/ct-vivian-selma-punch-sheriff.

Bromley, Max L., and John K. Cochran. 1999. "A Case Study of Community Policing in a Southern Sheriff's Office." *Police Quarterly* 2 (1): 36–56.

Brown, Alleen. 2021a. "Pipeline Protesters Face Corporate Counterinsurgency in Minnesota." *The Intercept*, July 7, 2021. https://theintercept.com/2021/07/07/line-3 -pipeline-minnesota-counterinsurgency.

———. 2021b. "Minnesota Police Expected Pipeline Budget Boost to Fund New Weapons." *The Intercept*, July 22, 2021. https://theintercept.com/2021/07/22/minnesota -pipeline-line-3-police-budget-boost-enbridge.

Brown, Kailyn. 2022. "Sheriff Alex Villanueva Targets LA Times Journalist in Criminal Investigation." *Los Angeles Magazine*, April 26, 2022. https://www.lamag.com /citythinkblog/sheriff-alex-villanueva-targets-l-a-times-journalist-in-criminal -investigation.

Brown, Richard Maxwell. 1969. "The American Vigilante Tradition." In *Violence in America: Historical and Comparative Perspectives: A Report to the National Commission on the Causes and Prevention of Violence*, edited by Hugh Davis Graham and Ted Robert Gurr, 121–80. Washington, DC: US Government Printing Office.

Brunet, James R. 2015. "Goodbye Mayberry: The Curious Demise of Rural Police Departments in North Carolina." *Administration & Society* 47 (3): 320–37.

Brunner, Jim. 2022a. "Judge Orders Pierce County Sheriff Ed Troyer to Post $100,000 Bail, Finds Him 'a Substantial Danger' after Anti-Harassment Order." *Seattle Times*, July 1, 2022. https://www.seattletimes.com/seattle-news/law-justice/judge-orders -pierce-county-sheriff-ed-troyer-to-post-100000-bail-finds-him-a-substantial -danger-after-anti-harassment-order.

———. 2022b. "Pierce County Sheriff Ed Troyer Found Not Guilty of False Reporting." *Seattle Times*, December 14, 2022. https://www.seattletimes.com/seattle-news/law -justice/pierce-county-sheriff-ed-troyer-found-not-guilty-of-false-reporting/.

Brunner, Jim, and Lewis Kamb. 2021a. "Black Newspaper Delivery Driver Detained after Pierce County Sheriff Claims, Then Recants, Threat to Life." *Seattle Times*, March 18, 2021,. https://www.seattletimes.com/seattle-news/law-justice/black -newspaper-delivery-driver-detained-after-pierce-county-sheriff-claims-then -recants-threat-to-life.

———. 2021b. "Pierce County Investigation Report: Sheriff Ed Troyer Violated Policies in Encounter with Newspaper Carrier." *Seattle Times*, October 26, 2021. https:// www.seattletimes.com/seattle-news/pierce-county-investigation-report-sheriff-ed -troyer-violated-policies-in-encounter-with-newspaper-carrier/.

Brynelson, Troy. 2021. "Ahead of Washington Reopening, Klickitat County Sheriff Threatens Crusade If Pandemic Restrictions Return." *Oregon Public Broadcasting*, June 23, 2021. https://www.opb.org/article/2021/06/23/washington-covid-19 -reopening-klickitat-county-sheriff-bob-songer-pandemic-restrictions.

Bueno de Mesquita, Bruce, and Alastair Smith. 2017. "Political Succession: A Model of Coups, Revolution, Purges, and Everyday Politics." *Journal of Conflict Resolution* 61 (4): 707–43.

Bulman, George. 2019. "Law Enforcement Leaders and the Racial Composition of Arrests." *Economic Inquiry* 57 (4): 1842–58.

Bulman-Pozen, Jessica. 2012. "Federalism as a Safeguard of the Separation of Powers." *Columbia Law Review* 112: 459.

Burgess, Katherine. 2020. "'Defund Sheriff' Flyers, Paint Strewn around Shelby County Commissioners,' Sheriff's Homes." *Commercial Appeal*, July 29, 2020. https://www.commercialappeal.com/story/news/2020/07/29/defund-sheriff -flyers-paint-strewn-around-shelby-county-commissioners-homes/5535688002.

Burghart, Devin, and Leonard Zeskind. 2010. *Tea Party Nationalism: A Critical Examination of the Tea Party Movement and the Size, Scope, and Focus of Its National Factions*. Institute for Research & Education on Human Rights Kansas City, MO.

Burnett, John. 2006. "Larger-Than-Life Sheriff Rules Louisiana Parish." *NPR*, November 28, 2006. https://www.npr.org/2006/11/28/6549329/larger-than-life-sheriff -rules-louisiana-parish.

———. 2015. "At 'Checkpoint of the Stars,' Texas Sheriff Takes a Pass On Pot Cases." *NPR*, October 1, 2015. https://www.npr.org/2015/10/01/444780811/at-checkpoint -of-the-stars-texas-sheriff-takes-a-pass-on-pot-cases.

Burnett, Paull C. 1997. "A Historical Analysis of the Posse Comitatus Act and Its Implications for the Future." Air Force Inst of Tech Wright-Patterson AFB OH.

Burns, Peter F. 2006. *Electoral Politics Is Not Enough*. New York: SUNY Press.

Burns, Peter F., and Matthew Thomas. 2004. "Governors and the Development Regime in New Orleans." *Urban Affairs Review* 39 (6): 791–812.

———. 2015. *Reforming New Orleans: The Contentious Politics of Change in the Big Easy*. Ithaca, NY: Cornell University Press.

Buzawa, Eve, and Carl Buzawa. 1993. "The Impact of Arrest on Domestic Violence." *American Behavioral Scientist* 36 (5): 558–75.

Cain, Keith. 2022. "Letter to the Editor." *Owensboro Times*, May 16, 2022. https://www .owensborotimes.com/opinion/2022/05/letter-to-the-editor-cain-address-negative -social-media-comments-reinforces-support-of-smith-2/.

Campaign Zero. 2016. "Police Use of Force Policy Analysis." Campaign Zero.

Campbell, Angus, Philip E. Converse, Warren E. Miller, and Donald E. Stokes. 1960. *The American Voter*. Oxford, UK: John Wiley.

Campion, Kristy. 2019. "Australian Right Wing Extremist Ideology: Exploring Narratives of Nostalgia and Nemesis." *Journal of Policing, Intelligence and Counter Terrorism* 14 (3): 208–26.

CAP. 2020. "Reimagining Federal Grants for Public Safety and Criminal Justice Reform." *Center for American Progress*. October 7, 2020. https://www.american progress.org/article/reimagining-federal-grants-public-safety-criminal-justice -reform.

Carey, John, Richard Niemi, and Lynda Powell. 2000. *Term Limits in State Legislatures*. Ann Arbor, MI: University of Michigan Press.

Carey, John, Richard Niemi, Lynda Powell, and Gary Moncrief. 2006. "The Effects of Term Limits on State Legislatures: A New Survey of the 50 States." *Legislative Studies Quarterly* 31 (1): 105–34.

Carlson, Jennifer. 2020. *Policing the Second Amendment: Guns, Law Enforcement, and the Politics of Race*. Princeton, NJ: Princeton University Press.

Carpenter, Tim. 2022. "Kansans Pass Constitutional Amendment on Election, Removal of Sheriffs." *Kansas Reflector*. November 9, 2022. https://kansasreflector.com/2022 /11/08/kansans-pass-constitutional-amendment-on-election-removal-of-sheriffs.

Carroll, Heather. 2016. "Serious Mental Illness Prevalence in Jails and Prisons." Treatment Advocacy Center. https://www.treatmentadvocacycenter.org/evidence-and -research/learn-more-about/3695.

Carroll, Susan. 2022. "The Top Elected Official in Texas' Smallest County Has Been Charged with Cattle Theft." *NBC News*, May 21, 2022. https://www.nbcnews.com /news/us-news/loving-county-texas-cattle-theft-skeet-jones-rcna29719.

Carter, Jeff, and Timothy Nordstrom. 2017. "Term Limits, Leader Preferences, and Interstate Conflict." *International Studies Quarterly* 61 (3): 721–35.

Cary, Nathaniel. 2019. "How One SC County Seized More than $3.5 Million in Cash in 3 Years." *Greenville News*, February 3, 2019. https://www.greenvilleonline.com/in -depth/news/taken/2019/02/03/chuck-wright-spartanburg-county-sheriff-sc-civil -forfeiture/2459032002.

Cassese, Erin C., and Mirya R. Holman. 2019. "Playing the Woman Card: Ambivalent Sexism in the 2016 Presidential Race." *Political Psychology* 40 (1): 55–74.

Castle, Cerise. 2021. "A Tradition of Violence: The History of Deputy Gangs in the Los Angeles County Sheriff's Department." *Knock-LA*, March 22, 2021. https://knock-la .com/tradition-of-violence-lasd-gang-history.

Catalano, Shannan. 2009. "Female Victims of Violence." Bureau of Justice Statistics. https://www.bjs.gov/content/pub/pdf/fvv.pdf.

———. 2012. *Intimate Partner Violence, 1993–2010*. US Department of Justice, Office of Justice Programs, Bureau of Justice.

CAWP. 2018. "Current Numbers." New Brunswick, NJ: Center for American Women and Politics, Eagleton Institute of Politics, Rutgers University. http://www.cawp .rutgers.edu/current-numbers.

CBS 5 News. 2020. *Arizona's Top Prosecutor Launches Investigation into Pinal County Sheriff*. https://www.youtube.com/watch?v=U2YxI7SUokc.

CBS Sacramento. 2020. "Sacramento County Opens File On Death Of Unarmed Black Man Mikel McIntyre." May 28, 2020. https://sacramento.cbslocal.com/2020/05/28 /sacramento-county-opens-file-death-mikel-mcintyre.

CBS2 News. 2021. "Bingham County Commissioners Condemn 'drunk Indians' Remark from Sheriff." *KBOI*, December 16, 2021. https://idahonews.com/news/local /bingham-county-commissioners-condemn-drunk-indians-remark-from-sheriff.

CDC. 2021. "Law Enforcement Officer Motor Vehicle Safety." Washington, DC: Centers for Disease Control. https://www.cdc.gov/niosh/topics/leo/default.html.

Cenziper, Debbie, Madison Muller, Monique Beals, Rebecca Holland, and Andrew Ba Tran. 2021. "Under Trump, ICE Aggressively Recruited Sheriffs as Partners to Question and Detain Undocumented Immigrants." *Washington Post*, November 23, 2021. https://www.washingtonpost.com/investigations/interactive/2021/trump-ice -sheriffs-immigrants-287g.

Chadwick, Hector Munro. 1905. *Studies on Anglo-Saxon Institutions*. Cambridge, England: Cambridge University Press.

Chaloupka, William. 1996. "The County Supremacy and Militia Movements: Federalism as an Issue on the Radical Right." *Publius: The Journal of Federalism* 26 (3): 161–75.

Chammah, Maurice. 2020a. "The Rise of the Anti-Lockdown Sheriffs." *Searchlight New Mexico*. May 22, 2020. https://searchlightnm.org/the-rise-of-the-anti-lockdown -sheri.

———. 2020b. "The Sheriff's Race Pitting Trump Against Black Lives Matter." *The*

Marshall Project. September 19, 2020. https://www.themarshallproject.org/2020 /09/19/the-sheriff-s-race-pitting-trump-against-black-lives-matter.

———. 2022. "Progressive Sheriffs Are Here. Will They Win In November?" *The Marshall Project.* October 22, 2022. https://www.themarshallproject.org/2022/10/22 /progressive-sheriffs-are-here-will-they-win-in-november.

Chand, Daniel E. 2020. "Is It Population or Personnel? The Effects of Diversity on Immigration Policy Implementation By Sheriff Offices." *Public Performance & Management Review,* 43 (2): 304–33.

Cheatham, Craig. 2021a. "Deputy Investigated for Posting Far-Right Militia's Flag." *WCPO.* February 11, 2021. https://www.wcpo.com/news/local-news/i-team /hamilton-county-sheriff-investigates-deputy-who-had-three-percenter-flag-on -facebook-page.

———. 2021b. "Hamilton Co. Sheriff Fires Deputy for Social Media Posts." *WCPO.* February 19, 2021. https://www.wcpo.com/news/local-news/i-team/after -investigation-hamilton-co-sheriff-fires-deputy-with-3percenters-flag-on-facebook -profile.

Cherrington, Ernest Hurst. 1920. *The Evolution of Prohibition in the United States of America: A Chronological History of the Liquor Problem and the Temperance Reform in the United States from the Earliest Settlements to the Consummation of National Prohibition.* American Issue Press.

Christiani, Leah, Kelsey Shoub, Frank R. Baumgartner, Derek A. Epp, and Kevin Roach. 2021. "Better for Everyone: Black Descriptive Representation and Police Traffic Stops." *Politics, Groups, and Identities* 10(5), 807–16.

Clark, Cal, and Janet Clark. 1992. "Federal Aid to Local Governments in the West: An Irony of the Reagan Revolution." *Review of Policy Research* 11 (1): 91–99.

Clark, Jim. 1965. "Sheriff Clark Dissents." *New York Times,* September 13, 1965.

Clarke, Matthew. 2002. "Tarrant County (Texas) Jail's 'God Pod' Unconstitutional." *Prison Legal News,* January 15, 2002. https://www.prisonlegalnews.org/news/2002 /jan/15/tarrant-county-texas-jails-god-pod-unconstitutional.

Clear, Todd R., and Natasha A. Frost. 2013. *The Punishment Imperative.* New York: New York University Press.

Cleghorn, Reese. 1965. "The Two Faces of Sheriff Rainey." *New York Times,* February 21, 1965.

Clubb, Henry Stephen. 1856. *The Maine Liquor Law: Its Origin, History, and Results, Including a Life of Hon. Neal Dow.* New York: Published for the Maine Law Statistical Society by Fowler and Wells.

Cluverius, John, Kevin K. Banda, and Hannah Daly. 2020. "How the Alt-Right Label Informs Political Assessments." *Social Science Quarterly* 105 (5): 1699–1711.

Coalition of Sheriffs Organizations. 2014. "The Current Immigration Crisis Is Spiraling Out of Control." Coalition of Sheriffs Organizations.

Cobbina-Dungy, Jennifer, Soma Chaudhuri, Ashleigh LaCourse, and Christina DeJong. 2022. "'Defund the Police:' Perceptions among Protesters in the 2020 March on Washington." *Criminology & Public Policy* 21 (1): 147–74.

Cobbina-Dungy, Jennifer E., and Delores Jones-Brown. 2021. "Too Much Policing: Why Calls Are Made to Defund the Police." *Punishment & Society* 25, (1): 3–20.

Cochran, John, Max Bromley, and Lisa Landis. 1999. "Officer Work Orientations, Perceptions of Readiness and Anticipated Effectiveness of an Agency-Wide Community Policing Effort within a County Sheriff's Office." *Journal of Police and Criminal Psychology* 14 (1): 43–65.

Cochran, John K., Max L. Bromley, and Matthew J. Swando. 2002. "Sheriff's Deputies' Receptivity to Organizational Change." *Policing: An International Journal of Police Strategies & Management* 25 (3): 507–29.

Cohen, William. 1991. *At Freedom's Edge: Black Mobility and the Southern White Quest for Racial Control, 1861–1915.* Baton Rouge: Louisiana State University Press.

Cohn, Allen. 1978. *The Future of Policing.* Thousand Oaks, CA: Sage Press.

Collingwood, Loren, and Benjamin O'Brien Gonzalez. 2019. "Public Opposition to Sanctuary Cities in Texas: Criminal Threat or Immigration Threat?" *Social Science Quarterly* 100 (4): 1182–96.

Collins, Jonathan, Eddie Lucero, and Jessica Trounstine. 2020. "Will Concurrent Elections Reshape the Electorate?" *California Journal of Politics and Policy* 12 (1).

Colloff, Pamela. 1997. "Not-So-Loving County." *Texas Monthly*, October 1, 1997. https://www.texasmonthly.com/news-politics/not-so-loving-county.

Cook, Mike. 2022. "Sheriff Says She Is Running for Re-Election to Finish What She Has Started." *Las Cruces Bulletin*, March 22, 2022. https://www.lascrucesbulletin.com/stories/sheriff-says-she-is-running-for-re-election-to-finish-what-she-has-started,10719.

Coon, Michael. 2017. "Local Immigration Enforcement and Arrests of the Hispanic Population." *Journal on Migration and Human Security* 5 (3): 645–66.

Cooper, Cloee. 2019. "The National Sheriffs' Association Alignment with Far-Right Groups Undermines Public Safety." Political Research Associates. June 14, 2019. https://politicalresearch.org/2019/06/14/the-national-sheriffs-association-alignment-with-far-right-groups-undermines-public-safety.

Cope, Robert S. 1973. *Carry Me Back: Slavery and Servitude in Seventeenth Century Virginia.* Pikeville, KY: Pikeville College Press of the Appalachian Studies Center.

Cotterell, Bill. 2013. "Jury Acquits Florida Sheriff Who Freed Gun-Toting Man." *Reuters*, October 31, 2013. https://www.reuters.com/article/us-usa-florida-guns-idUSBRE99U13320131031.

County Sheriff Project, dir. 2012. *Sheriff Dave Mattis: CSPOA Lifetime Achievement Recipient.* https://www.youtube.com/watch?v=uSWZ9sGddg4.

Craig, Tim. 2022. "As Haitian Migration Routes Change, Compassion Is Tested in Florida Keys." *Washington Post*, April 9, 2022. https://www.washingtonpost.com/nation/2022/04/09/florida-keys-haitian-immigration/.

Cramer, Katherine J. 2016. *The Politics of Resentment: Rural Consciousness in Wisconsin and the Rise of Scott Walker.* Chicago: University of Chicago Press.

Cramer, Maria. 2020. "Woman Who Says She Was Fired for Being a Lesbian Is Elected Sheriff." *New York Times*, November 8, 2020. https://www.nytimes.com/2020/11/08/us/charmaine-mcguffey-sheriff-hamilton.html.

Crawford, Evan. 2022. "Who Prefers Nonpartisan Elections? The Role of Individual Party ID and County Partisanship." *Research & Politics* 9 (1): 20531680221083800.

CRO. 2007. "Congressional Record." Pages H10312–H10316 Volume 153 Issue 132. Washington, DC: Congressional Record Online. https://www.govinfo.gov/content/pkg/CREC-2005-11-16/html/CREC-2005-11-16-pt1-PgH10312.htm.

Crosby, Emilye. 2005. *A Little Taste of Freedom: The Black Freedom Struggle in Claiborne County, Mississippi.* Chapel Hill, NC: The University of North Carolina Press.

Crowder-Meyer, Melody. 2020. "Baker, Bus Driver, Babysitter, Candidate? Revealing the Gendered Development of Political Ambition Among Ordinary Americans." *Political Behavior* 42 (2): 359–84.

Crowder-Meyer, Melody, Shana Kushner Gadarian, and Jessica Trounstine. 2015. "Electoral Institutions, Gender Stereotypes, and Women's Local Representation." *Politics, Groups, and Identities* 3 (2): 318–34.

Crowder-Meyer, Melody, Shana Kushner Gadarian, Jessica Trounstine, and Kau Vue. 2020. "A Different Kind of Disadvantage: Candidate Race, Cognitive Complexity, and Voter Choice." *Political Behavior 42 (2): 509–30.*

CRS. 2021. "The 287(g) Program: State and Local Immigration Enforcement." Washington, DC: Congressional Research Service. https://crsreports.congress.gov /product/pdf/IF/IF11898.

CSPOA. 2014. "Resolution Of the Constitutional Sheriffs and Peace Officers Association." Constitutional Sheriff and Peace Officer Association. https://web.archive .org/web/20140307230552/http:/www.cspoa.org/docs/CSPOA_Resolution_Jan _2014.pdf.

———. 2016. "Sheriff Survey." Constitutional Sheriff and Peace Officer Association.

———. 2022a. "Join—Constitutional Sheriffs and Peace Officers Association." January 21, 2022. https://web.archive.org/web/20220121045350/https://cspoa.org/join.

———. 2022b. "Statement of Positions." Constitutional Sheriffs and Peace Officers Association. February 2, 2022. https://web.archive.org/web/20220201000000 /https://cspoa.org/sop.

Dalafave, Rachel. 2020. "An Empirical Assessment of Homicide and Suicide Outcomes with Red Flag Laws." *Loyola University Chicago Law Journal* 52: 867.

Dallas News. 2021. "21 People Died in the Tarrant County Jail Last Year. That's Unacceptable.," December 5, 2021. https://www.dallasnews.com/opinion/editorials /2021/12/06/21-people-died-in-the-tarrant-county-jail-last-year-thats -unacceptable.

Dallas News Editorial Team. 2021. "How Did 21 People Die in Tarrant County Jail? Here's What We Know." *Dallas News*, December 7, 2021. https://www.dallasnews .com/opinion/editorials/2021/12/07/how-did-21-people-die-in-tarrant-county-jail -heres-what-we-know/.

Darr, Joshua P., Matthew P. Hitt, and Johanna L. Dunaway. 2019. "Newspaper Closures Polarize Voting Behavior." *Journal of Communication* 68 (6): 1007–28.

DaSilva, Staci. 2021. "Body Camera Debate: Polk County Sheriff Grady Judd Remains Concerned as Other Agencies Buy Body Cameras." *WFLA.* May 27, 2021. https:// www.wfla.com/news/polk-county/body-camera-debate-polk-county-sheriff-grady -judd-remains-concerned-as-other-agencies-buy-bodycameras.

Davis, Angela Y, ed. 1998. "From the Prison of Slavery to the Slavery of Prison: Frederick Douglass and the Convict Lease System." In *The Angela Y. Davis Reader.* Malden, MA: Blackwell 74–95.

Davis, Mike. 2006. *City of Quartz: Excavating the Future in Los Angeles.* New York: Verso Books.

Davis, Mike, and Jon Wiener. 2021. *Set the Night on Fire: L.A. in the Sixties.* New York: Verso Books.

Day, Lucas. 2021. "Cayuga County Sheriff: 'No Wake Zone' on Area Waterways." *Finger Lakes Daily News.* August 20, 2021.

DEA. 2004. "Drug Enforcement Agency: History." Washington, DC: Drug Enforcement Agency.

de Benedictis-Kessner, Justin. 2017. "Off-Cycle and Out of Office: Election Timing and the Incumbency Advantage." *Journal of Politics* 80 (1): 119–32.

———. 2018. "How Attribution Inhibits Accountability: Evidence from Train Delays." *Journal of Politics* 80 (4): 1417–22.

———. 2021. "Strategic Partisans: Electoral Motivations and Partisanship in Local Government Communication." *Journal of Political Institutions and Political Economy* 2 (2): 227–48.

———. 2022. "Strategic Government Communication about Performance." *Political Science Research and Methods* 10 (3): 601–16.

de Benedictis-Kessner, Justin, and Michael Hankinson. 2019. "Concentrated Burdens: How Self-Interest and Partisanship Shape Opinion on Opioid Treatment Policy." *American Political Science Review* 113 (4): 1078–84.

de Benedictis-Kessner, Justin, John Sides, and Christopher Warshaw. 2022. "Criminal Justice and Voter Behavior in Local Elections." Working paper. Harvard Kennedy School.

de Benedictis-Kessner, Justin, and Christopher Warshaw. 2016. "Mayoral Partisanship and Municipal Fiscal Policy." *Journal of Politics* 78 (4): 1124–38.

———. 2020a. "Accountability for the Local Economy at All Levels of Government in United States Elections." *American Political Science Review*, 114 (3): 660–76.

———. 2020b. "Politics in Forgotten Governments: The Partisan Composition of County Legislatures and County Fiscal Policies." *Journal of Politics* 82 (2): 460–75.

Decadri, Silvia. 2021. "'What Have You Done for Me Lately?' Re-Thinking Local Representation." *Electoral Studies* 74 (December 2021): 102417.

Decker, Michele R., Charvonne N. Holliday, Zaynab Hameeduddin, Roma Shah, Janice Miller, Joyce Dantzler, and Leigh Goodmark. 2019. "'You Do Not Think of Me as a Human Being': Race and Gender Inequities Intersect to Discourage Police Reporting of Violence against Women." *Journal of Urban Health* 96 (5): 772–83.

Decker, Scott. 1979. "The Rural County Sheriff: An Issue In Social Control." *Criminal Justice Review* 4 (2): 97–111.

DeHart, Cameron. 2020. "The Rise (and Fall) of Elected Sheriffs." Working paper. Stanford University.

Deitch, Michele. 2009a. "Distinguishing the Various Functions of Effective Prison Oversight." *Pace Law Review*. 30: 1438.

———. 2009b. "Independent Correctional Oversight Mechanisms across the United States: A 50-State Inventory." *Pace Law Review* 30:1754.

———. 2020. "But Who Oversees the Overseers? The Status of Prison and Jail Oversight in the United States." *American Journal of Criminal Law* 47:207.

Delaware County Sheriff. n.d. "History of the Sheriff's Office." Accessed September 30, 2023. http://www.co.delaware.ny.us/departments/shrf/history.htm.

DeLoach, Zach. 2022. "Sheriff Discusses Personnel Shortage with County Commission." *Emporia Gazette*, July 17, 2022. https://www.emporiagazette.com/free/article_e84f8cea-ca0c-11eb-9d45-27ce93b71bf2.html.

Deng, Sally. 2020. "Revoked: How Probation and Parole Feed Mass Incarceration in the United States." Human Rights Watch. July 31, 2020. https://www.hrw.org/report/2020/07/31/revoked/how-probation-and-parole-feed-mass-incarceration-united-states.

Desai, Ishani. 2022. "ACLU Claims Kern County Misreported Individuals Transferred to ICE; Youngblood Denies Claims." *The Bakersfield Californian*, February 11,

2022. https://www.bakersfield.com/news/aclu-claims-kern-county-misreported-individuals-transferred-to-ice-youngblood-denies-claims/article_853a4fdc-8ba9-11ec-b8a1-77defe38bb24.html..

DeSante, Christopher D., and Candis Watts Smith. 2020a. "Fear, Institutionalized Racism, and Empathy: The Underlying Dimensions of Whites' Racial Attitudes." *PS: Political Science & Politics* 53 (4): 639–45.

———. 2020b. "Less Is More: A Cross-Generational Analysis of the Nature and Role of Racial Attitudes in the Twenty-First Century." *Journal of Politics* 82 (3): 967–80.

———. 2020c. *Racial Stasis*. Chicago, IL: University of Chicago Press.

Dexheimer, Eric, and St John Barned-Smith. 2021a. "Texas Police Search Thousands of Drivers and Find Nothing. Here's Where That Happens the Most." *Houston Chronicle*, November 4, 2021. https://www.houstonchronicle.com/politics/texas/article/Texas-police-search-thousands-of-drivers-and-find-16589982.php.

———. 2021b. "Dangling Air Fresheners and 'Faulty' Plates: These Texas Police Make the Most Minor Traffic Stops." *Houston Chronicle*, November 22, 2021. https://www.houstonchronicle.com/news/investigations/article/texas-police-most-minor-traffic-stop-investigation-16639125.php.

Dharmapala, Dhammika, Richard H. McAdams, and John Rappaport. 2022. "Collective Bargaining Rights and Police Misconduct: Evidence from Florida." *Journal of Law, Economics, and Organization* 38 (1): 1–41.

Dietrich, Bryce, Matthew Hayes, and Diana Z. O'Brien. 2019. "Pitch Perfect: Vocal Pitch and the Emotional Intensity of Congressional Speech on Women." *American Political Science Review* 113 (4): 941–62.

Dillon, John Forrest. 1911. *Commentaries on the Law of Municipal Corporations*. New York: Little, Brown.

Dilworth, Richardson. 2010. "The City in American Political Development." In *A History of the U.S. Political System*, edited by Richard Harris and Daniel J Tichenor. Santa Barbara, CA: ABC-CLIO, 175–89.

Dittmar, Kelly, Kira Sanbonmatsu, and Susan J. Carroll. 2018. *A Seat at the Table: Congresswomen's Perspectives on Why Their Presence Matters*. New York: Oxford University Press.

Dobchuk-Land, Bronwyn, and Kevin Walby. 2021. "Police Abolition as Community Struggle against State Violence." *Social Justice* 48 (1): 1–30.

Dobner, Jennifer. 2017. "She Was a Teen Mother, a High School Dropout and an Onion-Field Worker—Now She's Utah's First Female Sheriff." *Salt Lake City Tribune*, December 17, 2017. https://www.sltrib.com/news/2017/12/17/once-a-teenage-mom-and-high-school-dropout-rosie-rivera-utahs-first-female-sheriff-worked-hard-and-kept-at-it-to-blaze-the-trail-shes-on.

Dobratz, Betty A., and Stephanie L. Shanks-Meile. 2000. *The White Separatist Movement in the United States: "White Power, White Pride!"* Baltimore, MD: Johns Hopkins Press.

Doerner, William M., and William G. Doerner. 2010. "Collective Bargaining and Job Benefits: The Case of Florida Deputy Sheriffs." *Police Quarterly* 13 (4): 367–86.

DOJ. 2011. "Department of Justice Releases Investigative Findings on the Maricopa County Sheriff's Office." U.S. Department of Justice. December 15, 2011. https://www.justice.gov/opa/pr/department-justice-releases-investigative-findings-maricopa-county-sheriff-s-office.

———. 2013. "Justice Department Finds Unconstitutional Conditions of Confinement at Escambia County, Fla. Jail." U.S. Department of Justice. May 22. 2013. https://www.justice.gov/opa/pr/justice-department-finds-unconstitutional-conditions-confinement-escambia-county-fla-jail.

———. 2017. "Former Fentress County Sheriff Sentenced To Federal Prison." Middle District of Tennessee: U.S. Department of Justice. August 23, 2017. https://www.justice.gov/usao-mdtn/pr/former-fentress-county-sheriff-sentenced-federal-prison.

———. 2021. "Review of the Department's Administrative Enforcement of Title VI and the Safe Streets Act." September 15, 2021. https://www.justice.gov/asg/page/file/1433211/download.

Donnelly, John. 2018. "Sheriff Rick Ramsay—Detectives, Deputies & Staff Under His Command—Deliver Commendable Results." *The Blue Paper*, March 12, 2018. https://web.archive.org/web/20150515020858/http://thebluepaper.com/article/sheriff-rick-ramsay-detectives-deputies-staff-under-his-command-deliver-commendable-result/.

Doran, Will, and Avi Bajpai. 2022. "Gov. Cooper Vetoes Bill Forcing NC Sheriffs to Work with ICE." *News and Observer*, July 11, 2022. https://www.newsobserver.com/news/politics-government/article263289488.html.

Douglas, Stephanie. 2021. "$100K Donation from John Bushman Helping Ector Co. Sheriff's Office Buy Handguns, Vests." *CBS7*, September 16, 2021. https://www.cbs7.com/2021/09/16/100k-donation-john-bushman-helping-ector-co-sheriffs-office-buy-handguns-vests/.

Downing, Davia Cox, and William M Myers. 2020. "Federalism, Intergovernmental Relationships, and Emergency Response: A Comparison of Australia and the United States." *The American Review of Public Administration* 50 (6–7): 526–35.

Drago, Francesco, Roberto Galbiati, and Francesco Sobbrio. 2020. "The Political Cost of Being Soft on Crime: Evidence from a Natural Experiment." *Journal of the European Economic Association* 18 (6): 3305–36.

Dray, Philip. 2007. *At the Hands of Persons Unknown: The Lynching of Black America*. New York: Random House Publishing Group.

Dreisbach, Tom. 2022. "A Publisher Abruptly Recalled the '2,000 Mules' Election Denial Book. NPR Got a Copy." *NPR*, September 8, 2022. https://www.npr.org/2022/09/08/1121648290/a-publisher-abruptly-recalled-the-2-000-mules-election-denial-book-npr-got-a-cop.

Dries, Bill. 2020. "Sheriff to Address County Commission." *Daily Memphian*, June 15, 2020. https://dailymemphian.com/article/14837/floyd-bonner-county-commission-budget-state-of-the-shelby-county-sheriffs-office.

Dugdale, Emily Elena. 2021. "LA Inspector General Looks Into Allegations of Racist Policing by Sheriff's Deputies on School Grounds." *ProPublica*, November 1, 2021. https://www.propublica.org/article/la-inspector-general-looks-into-allegations-of-racist-policing-by-sheriffs-deputies-on-school-grounds.

Dujardin, Peter. 2020. "Virginia Lawmakers Pass Bill Giving Citizen Oversight Panels Actual Investigative Powers in Police Misconduct Complaints." *Daily Press*, October 17, 2020. https://www.dailypress.com/government/virginia/dp-nw-citizen-review-boards-20201017-mip35b3q5recfi4r2dpfmtmsdu-story.html.

Durham, Martin. 2006. *White Rage: The Extreme Right and American Politics*. London: Routledge (Taylor & Francis).

Dynes, Adam. 2022. "Procedural Obfuscation and Electoral Accountability in Local Politics." Working paper.

Edmondson, Aimee. 2019. *In Sullivan's Shadow: The Use and Abuse of Libel Law during the Long Civil Rights Struggle*. JSTOR.

Eisler, Peter, and Nathan Layne. 2022. "A Far-Right Sheriff Crusades to Prove Trump's Bogus Voter-Fraud Claims." *Reuters*, July 29, 2022. https://www.reuters.com /investigates/special-report/usa-elections-michigan-investigation.

Ekins, Emily. 2016. "Policing in America: Understanding Public Attitudes toward the Police. Results from a National Survey." Washington, DC: Cato Institute. https:// www.cato.org/survey-reports/policing-america-understanding-public-attitudes -toward-police-results-national.

Ellerbrock, Josh. 2023. "John Grismore Sworn in as Franklin County Sheriff; Vermont Begins Sheriff Reform Discussion on Same Day." *Saint Albans Messenger*, February 3, 2023. https://www.samessenger.com/news/john-grismore-sworn-in-as -franklin-county-sheriff-vermont-begins-sheriff-reform-discussion-on-same/article _26dbd1e4-a3e6-11ed-b978-fbb19be6cdbb.html.

Ellis, Rachel. 2019. "Attorney for Suspended Colleton Co. Sheriff Andy Strickland Says There's 'No Case'." *ABC4 News*, November 27, 2019. https://abcnews4.com/news /local/attorney-for-suspended-colleton-co-sheriff-andy-strickland-says-theres-no -case.

Epp, Charles R., Steven Maynard-Moody, and Donald P. Haider-Markel. 2014. *Pulled over: How Police Stops Define Race and Citizenship*. Chicago: University of Chicago Press.

Escobar, Edward J. 1993. "The Dialectics of Repression: The Los Angeles Police Department and the Chicano Movement, 1968–1971." *Journal of American History* 79 (4): 1483–1514.

Evans, Heather K., Michael J. Ensley, and Edward G. Carmines. 2014. "The Enduring Effects of Competitive Elections." *Journal of Elections, Public Opinion and Parties* 24 (4): 455–72.

Fairley, Sharon R. 2020. "Survey Says? U.S. Cities Double down on Civilian Oversight of Police despite Challenges and Controversy." *Cardozo Law Review De-Novo* 2020: 1–55.

Fairlie, John Archibald. 1920. *Local Government in Counties, Towns and Villages*. New York: Century Company.

Falcone, David N., and L. Edward Wells. 1995. "The County Sheriff as a Distinctive Policing Modality." *American Journal of Police* 14 (3/4): 123–49.

Farris, Emily M., and Mirya R. Holman. 2015. "Public Officials and a 'Private' Matter: Attitudes and Policies in the County Sheriff Office Regarding Violence Against Women." *Social Science Quarterly* 96 (4): 1117–35.

———. 2017. "All Politics Is Local? County Sheriffs and Localized Policies of Immigration Enforcement." *Political Research Quarterly* 70 (1): 142–54.

———. 2022. "Sheriffs, Right-Wing Extremism, and the Limits of U.S. Federalism during a Crisis." *Social Science Quarterly* 104 (2): 59–68.

———. 2023. "Local Gun Safety Enforcement, Sheriffs, and Right-Wing Political Extremism." *Urban Affairs Review*, OnlineFirst. https://doi.org/10.1177 /10780874231203681.

Farris, Emily M., Mirya R. Holman, and Miranda Sullivan. 2021. "Representation and Anti-Racist Policymaking in Cities during COVID-19." *Representation* 58 (2): 269–88.

Feder, Lynette. 1997. "Domestic Violence and Police Response in a Pro-Arrest Jurisdiction." *Women & Criminal Justice* 8 (4): 79–98.

Felson, Richard B., Steven F. Messner, Anthony W. Hoskin, and Glenn Deane. 2002. "Reasons for Reporting and Not Reporting Domestic Violence to the Police." *Criminology* 40 (3): 617–48.

Ferguson, Bob. 2019. "AG Ferguson Issues Open Letter to Law Enforcement on I-1639." Washington State Attorney General. https://www.atg.wa.gov/news/news-releases /ag-ferguson-issues-open-letter-law-enforcement-i-1639.

———. 2021. "Criminal Charges Filed against Pierce County Sheriff." Washington State Attorney General. https://www.atg.wa.gov/news/news-releases/criminal-charges -filed-against-pierce-county-sheriff.

Fernandez, Caleb. 2022. "Win a Custom AR-15 This Valentine's Day through Rifle Raffle." *KGUN 9*, February 10, 2022. https://www.kgun9.com/news/local-news/win-a -custom-ar-15-this-valentines-day-through-american-sheriff-rifle-raffle.

Fernandez, Lisa. 2022. "Protest at Santa Rita Jail over 'Inedible' Food and Rising Commissary Prices." *KTVU FOX 2*, January 19, 2022. https://www.ktvu.com /news/protest-at-santa-rita-jail-over-inedible-food-and-sheriffs-profit-on-rising -commissary-prices.

Fernández, Stacy. 2019. "Texas Sheriff at White House Briefing: If Criminal Immigrants Are Released, 'Drunks' Will 'Run over Your Children.'" *Texas Tribune*, October 10, 2019. https://www.texastribune.org/2019/10/10/texas-tarrant-county-sheriff-bill -waybourn-speaks-white-house.

Filindra, Alexandra, and Noah Kaplan. 2017. "Testing Theories of Gun Policy Preferences Among Blacks, Latinos, and Whites in America." *Social Science Quarterly* 98 (2): 413–28.

Fitch, John. 1915. "When a Sheriff Breaks a Strike." *The Survey*, August 7, 1915.

Flanagan, Anne. 2020. "This Tiny Louisiana Police Force Is a National Leader in Taking Guns From Abusers." *The Trace*, February 24, 2020. https://www.thetrace.org/2020 /02/guns-domestic-violence-lafourche-parish-valerie-martinez.

Florida Sheriffs' Association. 1957. "Bill to Kill Fee System Gets Sheriffs' Approval." *Sheriff's Star*, March 1957.

Foner, Eric. 1993. *Freedom's Lawmakers: A Directory of Black Officeholders During Reconstruction*. New York: Oxford University Press.

———. 2013. *Forever Free: The Story of Emancipation and Reconstruction*. New York: Knopf Doubleday.

Foreman, Kelly. 2016. "Preparing for the Future." *Kentucky Law Enforcement*, 2016. https://www.klemagazine.com/blog/2016/8/18/preparing-for-the-future.

———. 2020. "Daviess County Sheriff's Office." *Kentucky Law Enforcement*, 2020. https://www.klemagazine.com/blog/2020/3/16/daviess-county-sheriffs-office.

Fortner, Michael Javen. 2016. "Straight, No Chaser: Theory, History, and the Muting of the Urban State." *Urban Affairs Review* 52 (4): 591–621.

Fouirnaies, Alexander, and Andrew B. Hall. 2022. "How Do Electoral Incentives Affect Legislator Behavior? Evidence from US State Legislatures." *American Political Science Review* 116 (2): 662–76.

Fox, Margalit. 2007. "Jim Clark, Sheriff Who Enforced Segregation, Dies at 84." *New York Times*, June 7, 2007. https://www.nytimes.com/2007/06/07/us/07clark.html.

Fox News Staff. 2021. "Arizona Sheriff Goes Viral with Vow Not to Mandate Vaccines for His Officers." *Fox 10*, August 26, 2021. https://www.fox10phoenix.com/news/arizona-sheriff-goes-viral-with-vow-not-to-mandate-vaccines-for-his-officers.

Francis, Megan Ming. 2014. *Civil Rights and the Making of the Modern American State.* Cambridge University Press.

Francis, Megan Ming, and Leah Wright-Rigueur. 2021. "Black Lives Matter in Historical Perspective." *Annual Review of Law and Social Science* 17 (1): 441–58.

Franz, Joe. 1969. "The Frontier Tradition: An Invitation to Violence." In *Violence in America: Historical and Comparative Perspectives: A Report to the National Commission on the Causes and Prevention of Violence*, edited by Hugh Davis Graham and Ted Robert Gurr, 1–12. Washington, DC: U.S. Government Printing Office.

Fredericks, Pam. 2020. "Jared Rigby: Wasatch's Top Lawman." *Heber Valley Life*. February 21, 2020. https://hebervalleylife.com/jared-rigby.

Freese, Alicia. 2018. "For Vermont's Sheriffs, Policing Is a Lucrative Business." *Seven Days*, September 5, 2018. https://www.sevendaysvt.com/vermont/sheriff-inc/Content?oid=20070627.

Friedman, Lawrence M. 1994. *Crime and Punishment in American History*. New York: Basic Books.

Gale, Bill. 1971. "Guide for Volunteer Christian Posses." *Identity*, 1971.

Garcia, Justin. 2022. "Doña Ana County Sheriff Kim Stewart to Seek a Second Term." *Las Cruces Sun-News*, January 20, 2022. https://www.lcsun-news.com/story/news/2022/01/20/dona-ana-county-sheriff-kim-stewart-seek-second-term/6585325001/.

———. 2023. "'I'm Very Sorry.' DASO Sheriff Speaks to Media, Apologizes for Deputy's Sexual Assault." *Las Cruces Sun-News*, September 25, 2023. https://www.lcsun-news.com/story/news/crime/2023/09/25/daso-sheriff-speaks-to-media-apologizes-for-deputys-sexual-assault/70935766007/.

Gardner, Trevor, and Aarti Kohli. 2009. "The CAP Effect: Racial Profiling in the ICE Criminal Alien Program." The Chief Justice Earl Warren Institute on Race, Ethnicity, & Diversity. Berkeley, CA: Berkeley Law Center for Research and Administration.

Gathright, Jenny. 2020. "Prince William County Is Ending a Controversial Agreement with ICE." *WAMU*. June 18, 2020. https://wamu.org/story/20/06/18/prince-william-county-is-ending-a-controversial-agreement-with-ice.

Geller, William A., and Kevin J. Karales. 1981. "Shootings of and by Chicago Police: Uncommon Crises–Part I: Shootings by Chicago Police." *Journal of Criminal Law and Criminology* 72: 1813.

Gelman, Andrew, Jeffrey Fagan, and Alex Kiss. 2007. "An Analysis of the New York City Police Department's 'Stop-and-Frisk' Policy in the Context of Claims of Racial Bias." *Journal of the American Statistical Association* 102 (479): 813–23.

Gentzkow, Matthew, Jesse M. Shapiro, and Michael Sinkinson. 2011. "The Effect of Newspaper Entry and Exit on Electoral Politics." *American Economic Review* 101 (7): 2980–3018.

Gershowitz, Adam M. 2016. "Consolidating Local Criminal Justice: Should the Prosecutors Control the Jails." *Wake Forest Law Review*. 51: 677.

Gevitz, Norman. 1986. "Organized for Prohibition: A New History of the Anti-Saloon League." *JAMA* 255 (6): 825–26.

Gifford Law Center. 2022. "Lafourche Parish, LA." Gifford Law Center. https://www.preventdvgunviolence.org/community-spotlight/lafourche-parish-la.html.

Gildemeister, Glen Albert. 1977. "Prison Labor and Convict Competition with Free Workers in Industrializing America, 1840–1890." Northern Illinois University.

Gillette, Howard. 1973. "Philadelphia's City Hall: Monument to a New Political Machine." *The Pennsylvania Magazine of History and Biography* 97 (2): 233–49.

Glaser, Jack. 2006. "The Efficacy and Effect of Racial Profiling: A Mathematical Simulation Approach." *Journal of Policy Analysis and Management* 25 (2): 395–416.

Gleason, Karen. 2021. "NEWS—Militia Leader Says Group Will Stay until Kinney County Is 'Safe.'" October 19, 2021. https://830times.com/news-militia-leader-says -group-will-stay-until-kinney-county-is-safe.

Goffman, Alice. 2015. *On the Run: Fugitive Life in an American City*. Picador.

Goldendale Sentinel. 2022. "Songer Warns against ATF Intrusion." *Goldendale Sentinel.* August 3, 2022. https://web.archive.org/web/20230000000000*/https://www .goldendalesentinel.com/news/songer-warns-against-atf-intrusion/article_df11875e -0dcd-11ed-8651-7f6d2e5ff729.html.

Goldstein, Jared A. 2019. "A Group of Sheriffs Is Refusing to Enforce Gun Laws Based on a 1960s Constitutional Theory From the KKK." *Slate*, March 20, 2019. https:// slate.com/news-and-politics/2019/03/washington-constitutional-sheriffs-gun-ban -kkk.html.

Gonzalez, Christina. 2022. "Defund LA County Sheriff? What's Next for West Hollywood after Voting to Cut Deputy Funds." FOX 11 Los Angeles. June 29, 2022. https://www.foxla.com/news/defund-la-county-sheriff-whats-next-for-west -hollywood-after-voting-to-cut-deputy-funds.

Goodman, J. David. 2022. "Big Trouble in Little Loving County, Texas." *New York Times*, August 2, 2022. https://www.nytimes.com/2022/08/02/us/loving-county -texas.html.

Goodyear, Dana. 2022. "The L.A. County Sheriff's Deputy-Gang Crisis | The New Yorker." *The New Yorker*, May 30, 2022. https://www.newyorker.com/magazine /2022/06/06/the-la-county-sheriffs-deputy-gang-crisis.

Gordon, Linda. 2017. *The Second Coming of the KKK: The Ku Klux Klan of the 1920s and the American Political Tradition*. Liveright Publishing.

Gottschalk, Marie. 2006. *The Prison and the Gallows*. New York: Cambridge University Press.

———. 2016. *Caught: The Prison State and the Lockdown of American Politics*. Princeton, NJ: Princeton University Press.

Grant, Keneshia. 2019. *The Great Migration and the Democratic Party: Black Voters and the Realignment of American Politics in the 20th Century*. Philadelphia, PA: Temple University Press.

Gray, Callan. 2020. "Charter Commission Discussing Whether Ramsey County Sheriff Should Be Elected or Appointed." KSTP.Com Eyewitness News. September 14, 2020. https://kstp.com/kstp-news/top-news/charter-commission-discussing -whether-ramsey-county-sheriff-should-be-elected-or-appointed.

Greenberg, Martin Alan. 2005. *Citizens Defending America: From Colonial Times to the Age of Terrorism*. Pittsburgh: University of Pittsburgh Press.

Greene, Jody. 2021. "Good Afternoon, Columbus County Citizens." December 21, 2021. https://www.facebook.com/permalink.php?story_fbid=241003878168351&id= 100067762224665.

Grogger, Jeffrey, and Greg Ridgeway. 2006. "Testing for Racial Profiling in Traffic Stops from Behind a Veil of Darkness." *Journal of the American Statistical Association* 101 (475): 878–87.

Grumbach, Jacob M., and Charlotte Hill. 2022. "Rock the Registration: Same Day Registration Increases Turnout of Young Voters." *Journal of Politics* 84 (1): 405–17.

Guadalupe-Diaz, Xavier L., and Jana Jasinski. 2017. "'I Wasn't a Priority, I Wasn't a Victim' Challenges in Help Seeking for Transgender Survivors of Intimate Partner Violence." *Violence against Women* 23 (6): 772–92.

Guida, Daniel. 2018. "Dan Guida for Aitkin County Sheriff | Facebook." October 8, 2018. https://www.facebook.com/people/Dan-Guida-for-Aitkin-County-Sheriff /100069356643248/.

———. 2021. "Expenses Likely Reimbursed to Aitkin County." Aitkin County Sheriff Office. https://healingmnstories.files.wordpress.com/2021/11/guida-statement-line -3.pdf.

Gullion, Steven. 1992. "Sheriffs in Search of a Role." *NEW LJ* 142: 1156.

Gumprecht, Blake. 2018. "Kim Stewart Will Be First Openly Gay Sheriff in State History, First Woman Sheriff in County." *Las Cruces Sun-News*, November 7, 2018. https://www.lcsun-news.com/story/news/politics/elections/2018/11/07/kim -stewart-first-openly-gay-sheriff-new-mexico-history/1925051002/.

Gunderson, Anna. 2020. "Why Do States Privatize Their Prisons? The Unintended Consequences of Inmate Litigation." *Perspectives on Politics* 20 (1): 187–204.

Gunderson, Anna, and Laura Huber. 2022. "Blue First and Foremost: Female Descriptive Representation, Rape, and the Justice Gap." *Perspectives on Politics* (May): 1–16.

Hadden, Sally E. 2003. *Slave Patrols: Law and Violence in Virginia and the Carolinas.* Cambridge, MA: Harvard University Press.

Hafemeister, Thomas L. 2010. "If All You Have Is a Hammer: Society's Ineffective Response to Intimate Partner Violence." *Catholic University Law Review* 60 (1): 919–1002.

Hager, Eli. 2015. "Blue Shield: Did You Know Police Have Their Own Bill of Rights?" *The Marshall Project*, April 27, 2015. https://www.themarshallproject.org/2015/04 /27/blue-shield.

Hahn, Steven. 2005. *A Nation under Our Feet: Black Political Struggles in the Rural South from Slavery to the Great Migration.* Cambridge, MA: Harvard University Press.

Haines, Molly. 2018. "Citing Lack of Pay, Veteran Deputy Resigns." *Owenton News Herald*, July 3, 2018.

Halbrook, Stephen P. 2013. *That Every Man Be Armed: The Evolution of a Constitutional Right. Revised and Updated Edition.* Albuquerque, NM: University of New Mexico Press.

Hall, Andrew B., and James M. Snyder. 2015. "How Much of the Incumbency Advantage Is Due to Scare-Off?" *Political Science Research and Methods* 3 (3): 493–514.

Hall, Ben. 2017. "Woman Sues Sheriff Over Illegal Search." *New Channel 5 Nashville*, June 1, 2017. https://www.newschannel5.com/news/newschannel-5-investigates /woman-sues-sheriff-over-illegal-search.

———. 2018a. "Numerous Lawsuits Claim Aggressive Tactics by Sheriff." *WTVF*, February 23, 2018. https://www.newschannel5.com/news/newschannel-5-investigates /numerous-lawsuits-claim-aggressive-tactics-by-sheriff.

———. 2018b. "Sheriff Tells Deputies to Change Their Stories about What Happened after Pursuit." *WTVF*, December 17, 2018. https://www.newschannel5.com/news

/newschannel-5-investigates/nc5-investigates-sheriff-tells-deputies-to-change-their
-stories-about-what-happened-after-pursuit.

———. 2019. "Wrongly Arrested Man Files Federal Lawsuit against Former Sheriff."
WTVF, August 29, 2019. https://www.newschannel5.com/news/newschannel-5
-investigates/wrongly-arrested-man-files-federal-lawsuit-against-former-sheriff.

Hall, Daron. 2020. "Commentary: It's Time to Reallocate Law Enforcement Resources." *Tennessee Lookout*. July 6, 2020. https://tennesseelookout.com/2020/07
/06/commentary-its-time-to-reallocate-law-enforcement-resources.

Hall, M. L. 2008. "Professional Standards and Criteria to Hold the Office of Sheriff in
the State of Florida." Florida Department of Law Enforcement. https://www.fdle
.state.fl.us/FCJEI/Programs/SLP/Documents/Full-Text/Hall_MH.aspx.

Hamm, Mark S. 2002. *In Bad Company: America's Terrorist Underground*. Boston: University Press of Northeastern.

Hamm, Richard F. 1995. *Shaping the Eighteenth Amendment: Temperance Reform, Legal
Culture, and the Polity, 1880–1920*. Chapel Hill: University of North Carolina Press.

Hanchett, Ian. 2022. "AZ Sheriff Lamb: DC Would Go 'Berserk' If Migrant Deaths
Were a Shooting but They'll Be Ignored Because It 'Involves Illegal Immigration.'"
Breitbart News, June 28, 2022. https://www.breitbart.com/clips/2022/06/28/az
-sheriff-lamb-dc-would-go-berserk-if-migrant-deaths-were-a-shooting-but-theyll
-be-ignored-because-it-involves-illegal-immigration.

Handberg, Roger. 1982. "Jails and Correctional Farms: The Neglected Half of Rural Law
Enforcement." *Journal of Correctional Education (1974–)* 32 (4): 20–23.

———. 1984. "A Portrait of County Sheriffs in the United States." *American Journal of
Criminal Justice* 9 (1): 79–87.

Hanna, Jason, and Kaylee Hartung. 2018. "'I Love This S*** . . . I Thrive on It,' Tennessee Sheriff Says after Deadly Pursuit." *CNN*, February 11, 2018. https://www.cnn
.com/2018/02/10/us/tennessee-shooting-white-county-sheriff/index.html.

Hannaford, Alex. 2016. "Above the Law." *Texas Observer*, May 2, 2016. https://www
.texasobserver.org/above-the-law-pamela-elliott-sheriff/.

Harris, Allison P., Hannah L. Walker, and Laurel Eckhouse. 2020. "No Justice, No
Peace: Political Science Perspectives on the American Carceral State." *Journal of
Race, Ethnicity, and Politics* 5 (3): 427–49.

Harris, Carl V. 1972. "Reforms in Government Control of Negroes in Birmingham, Alabama, 1890–1920." *Journal of Southern History* 38 (4): 567–600.

Harris, David A. 2003. *Profiles in Injustice: Why Racial Profiling Cannot Work*. New Press.

———. 2020. "Racial Profiling: Past, Present, and Future?" *Criminal Justice* 34 (Winter): 10.

Harris, Julian. 1930. "Recent Lynchings Fail to Stir Georgia." *New York Times*, October 26, 1930.

Hawkins, Derek. 2017. "Tenn. Judge Reprimanded for Offering Reduced Jail Time in
Exchange for Sterilization." *Washington Post*, November 21, 2017. https://www
.washingtonpost.com/news/morning-mix/wp/2017/11/21/tenn-judge-reprimanded
-for-offering-reduced-jail-time-in-exchange-for-sterilization/.

Hayes, Jess G. 1968. *Sheriff Thompson's Day: Turbulence in the Arizona Territory*. University of Arizona Press.

Hayes, Matthew, David Fortunato, and Matthew V. Hibbing. 2021. "Race–Gender Bias
in White Americans' Preferences for Gun Availability." *Journal of Public Policy* 41
(4): 818–34.

Helms, Ronald. 2007. "The Impact of Political Context on Local Law Enforcement Resourcing: An Analysis of Deputy Employment Rates in US Counties." *Policing and Society* 17 (2): 182–206.

———. 2008. "Locally Elected Sheriffs and Money Compensation: A Quantitative Analysis of Organizational and Environmental Contingency Explanations." *Criminal Justice Review* 33 (1): 5–28.

Helms, Ronald, Ricky S. Gutierrez, and Debra Reeves-Gutierrez. 2016. "Jail Mental Health Resourcing: A Conceptual and Empirical Study of Social Determinants." *International Journal of Offender Therapy and Comparative Criminology* 60 (9): 1036–63.

Henderson, Thomas A. 1975. "The Relative Effects of Community Complexity and of Sheriffs upon the Professionalism of Sheriff Departments." *American Journal of Political Science* 19 (1): 107–32.

Hendricks, David. 2017. "Statement from Sheriff Rene 'Orta' Fuentes on Budget Cuts in Starr County #rgv." October 13, 2017. https://twitter.com/dmhj/status /918960189918924801.

Hendricks, Tyche. 2002. "Legacy of Yemeni Immigrant Lives on among Union Janitors / Farmworkers Organizer to Be Honored in S.F." *San Francisco Chronicle*, August 16, 2002. https://www.sfgate.com/bayarea/article/Legacy-of-Yemeni-immigrant-lives -on-among-union-2782183.php.

Henry, Howell Meadoes. 1914. *The Police Control of the Slave in South Carolina*. Nashville: Vanderbilt University Press.

Henry, Jason. 2021. "Oversight Commission Asks State to Review LA County Sheriff's Political Investigations." *Daily News*, September 23, 2021. https://www.dailynews .com/2021/09/23/oversight-commission-asks-state-to-review-l-a-county-sheriffs -political-investigations/.

Hernández, Kelly Lytle. 2017. *City of Inmates: Conquest, Rebellion, and the Rise of Human Caging in Los Angeles, 1771–1965*. Chapel Hill: The University of North Carolina Press.

Hessick, Carissa Byrn. 2018. "The Prosecutors and Politics Project: Study of Campaign Contributions in Prosecutorial Elections." UNC Chapel Hill.

Hessick, Carissa, and Michael Morse. 2020. "Local Prosecutor Elections, 2012–2017." UNC Dataverse.

Hines, Kalama. 2021. "Judge: Bingham County Sheriff Will Retain Position during Court Proceedings, Must Give up Guns." *East Idaho News*, December 29, 2021. https://www.eastidahonews.com/2021/12/bingham-county-sheriff-ordered-to -surrender-guns-at-initial-hearing.

Hinkley, Sara, and Rachel Weber. 2021. "Incentives and Austerity: How Did the Great Recession Affect Municipal Economic Development Policy?" *Urban Affairs Review* 57 (3): 820–55.

Hochschild, Arlie Russell. 2018. *Strangers in Their Own Land: Anger and Mourning on the American Right*. New York: New Press.

Hodges, Luther. 1956. Speech before the Annual North Carolina Sheriffs Association Convention.

Hoffman, Christopher. 2000. "Connecticut Voters Decide to Abolish Controversial Sheriff System." *The Middletown Press*, November 8, 2000. https://www .middletownpress.com/news/article/Connecticut-voters-decide-to-abolish -11939612.php.

Holman, Mirya, Erica Podrazik, and Heather Silber Mohamed. 2020. "Choosing Choice: How Gender and Religiosity Shape Abortion Attitudes among Latinos." *Journal of Race, Ethnicity and Politics* 5(2): 384–411.

Holman, Mirya R. 2015. *Women in Politics in the American City*. Philadelphia, PA: Temple University Press.

———. 2017. "Women in Local Government: What We Know and Where We Go from Here." *State and Local Government Review* 49 (4): 285–96.

Holman, Mirya R., and Nathan P. Kalmoe. 2021. "Partisanship in the #MeToo Era." *Perspectives on Politics* OnlineFirst: 1–18.

Holman, Mirya R., and J. Celeste Lay. 2021. "Are You Picking up What I Am Laying Down? Ideology in Low-Information Elections." *Urban Affairs Review* 57 (2): 315–41.

Holman, Mirya R., and Anna Mitchell Mahoney. 2023. "Take (Her) to the Limit: Term Limits Do Not Diminish Women's Overperformance in Legislative Office." *Legislative Studies Quarterly* 48(3): 681–94

Holt, James Clarke, George Garnett, and John Hudson. 2015. *Magna Carta*. New York: Cambridge University Press.

Holtan, Heidi. 2021. "Aitkin County Sheriff Dan Guida Says He Is Protecting All the People Involved with Line 3." *KAXE*, February 16, 2021. https://web.archive.org /web/20231030125424/https://www.kaxe.org/news/2021-02-16/aitkin-county -sheriff-dan-guida-says-he-is-protecting-all-the-people-involved-with-line-3

Homeland Security. 2022. "Operation Stonegarden (OPSG) Program." https://gohsep .la.gov/GRANTS/PREPAREDNESS-GRANTS/HSGP-OPSG.

Hopkins, Daniel J. 2018. *The Increasingly United States: How and Why American Political Behavior Nationalized*. University of Chicago Press.

Hopkins, Daniel J., and Katherine T. McCabe. 2012. "After It's Too Late: Estimating the Policy Impacts of Black Mayoralties in U.S. Cities." *American Politics Research* 40 (4): 665–700.

Hopkins, Daniel J., and Lindsay M. Pettingill. 2018. "Retrospective Voting in Big-City US Mayoral Elections." *Political Science Research and Methods* 6 (4): 697–714.

Hoppe, Susan J., Yan Zhang, Brittany E. Hayes, and Matthew A. Bills. 2020. "Mandatory Arrest for Domestic Violence and Repeat Offending: A Meta-Analysis." *Aggression and Violent Behavior* 53 (July): 101430.

Horwitz, Susan H., Despina Mitchell, Michelle LaRussa-Trott, Lizette Santiago, Joan Pearson, David M. Skiff, and Catherine Cerulli. 2011. "An inside View of Police Officers' Experience with Domestic Violence." *Journal of Family Violence* 26 (8): 617–25.

Howard, George Elliott. 1889. *An Introduction to the Local Constitutional History of the United States*. Baltimore, MD: Johns Hopkins University.

Hughlett, Mike. 2022. "Enbridge-Funded State Account Has Paid over $4.5M for Line 3 Policing." *Star Tribune*. January 12, 2022. https://www.startribune.com/enbridge -funded-state-account-has-paid-over-4-5m-for-line-3-policing-costs/600135174.

Huijsmans, Twan, Eelco Harteveld, Wouter van der Brug, and Bram Lancee. 2021. "Are Cities Ever More Cosmopolitan? Studying Trends in Urban-Rural Divergence of Cultural Attitudes." *Political Geography* 86 (April): 102353.

ICE. 2022. "Delegation of Immigration Authority Section 287(g) Immigration and Nationality Act." Immigration and Customs Enforcement. https://www.ice.gov /identify-and-arrest/287g.

ILRC. 2016. "Legal Issues with Immigration Detainers." Immigrant Legal Resource

Center. https://www.ilrc.org/sites/default/files/resources/detainer_law_memo_november_2016_updated.pdf.

Jackson, Sam. 2019a. "A Schema of Right-Wing Extremism in the United States." *ICCT Policy Brief* 2019 (October): 1–26.

———. 2019b. "Non-Normative Political Extremism: Reclaiming a Concept's Analytical Utility." *Terrorism and Political Violence* 31 (2): 244–59.

———. 2020. *Oath Keepers*. New York: Columbia University Press.

Jacobs, Emily. 2018. "Sheriff Loses Re-Election to His Deputy—Then Fires Him." *New York Post*. June 7, 2018. https://nypost.com/2018/06/07/sheriff-loses-re-election-to-his-deputy-then-fires-him.

Jardina, Ashley, and Spencer Piston. 2019. "Racial Prejudice, Racial Identity, and Attitudes in Political Decision Making." In *Oxford Research Encyclopedia of Politics*. New York: Oxford University Press.

Jarvie, Jenny. 2019. "Broke, a Sheriff in Appalachian Coal Country Struggles to Provide Law and Order." *Los Angeles Times*, March 4, 2019. https://www.latimes.com/nation/la-na-kentucky-sheriff-cuts-20190304-story.html.

Jefferson, Thomas. 1905. "Letter from Thomas Jefferson to Samuel Kerch (July 12, 1816)." In *The Works of Thomas Jefferson*, edited by Paul Leicester Ford. New York: G.P. Putnam's Sons, 39.

Jenner, Andrew. 2019. "A Day in the Life of Highland County's Sheriff." *WMRA and WEMC*, May 9, 2019. https://web.archive.org/web/20220801000000*/https://www.wmra.org/wmra-news/2019-05-09/a-day-in-the-life-of-highland-countys-sheriff.

Jet Magazine. 1959. "The Real Story behind Lynching of Mississippi Negro," May 14, 1959.

Jett, Terri, and Paul Gentle. 2018. "'Rollin' on the River': What Economic and Political Factors Caused Restoration of Service for the Gee's Bend Public Ferry?" *Geopolitics under Globalization* 2 (December): 45–54.

Jones, Hannah. 2020. "Tarrant County Jail Temporarily Decertified After Inmate Death, Unattended Inmate Birth." *NBC 5 Dallas-Fort Worth*. May 29, 2020. https://www.nbcdfw.com/news/local/tarrant-county-jail-temporarily-decertified-after-inmate-death-unattended-inmate-birth/2378489.

Jones, Mary Belle. 2009. "Loving County." https://sites.rootsweb.com/~txloving/loving-co-mary-jones.htm.

KaCo. 2018. "Keith Cain, 2018 National Sheriff of the Year." *County Line*, 2018. https://mydigitalpublication.com/article/Keith+Cain%2C+2018+National+Sheriff+of+the+Year/3257048/549586/article.html.

Kaiser-Schatzlein, Robin. 2022. "Opinion | The False Promise of a Progressive Sheriff." *New York Times*, November 3, 2022. https://www.nytimes.com/2022/11/03/opinion/progressive-sheriff-los-angeles.html.

Kalmoe, Nathan P., and Lilliana Mason. 2022. *Radical American Partisanship: Mapping Violent Hostility, Its Causes, and the Consequences for Democracy*. Chicago, IL: University of Chicago Press.

Kang-Brown, Jacob, and Ram Subramanian. 2017. "Out of Sight: The Growth of Jails in Rural America." Vera Institute. https://www.vera.org/downloads/publications/out-of-sight-growth-of-jails-rural-america.pdf.

Kanu, Hassan. 2022. "Texas Rangers as Investigators of Cops Is Dubious Plan."

Reuters, April 21, 2022. https://www.reuters.com/legal/government/texas-rangers -investigators-cops-is-dubious-plan-2022-04-21.

Karlin, Sam. 2021. "Rep. Fontenot warned that all the K9 dogs in Louisiana will be "null and void" if we legalize pot because they're trained to sniff out marijuana." In Twitter Thread that begins: "Louisiana Lawmakers Are Holding the First Hearing of a Committee Tasked with Exploring Legalizing Recreational Marijuana." December 16, 2021. https://twitter.com/samkarlin/status/1471560647867523083?lang=en.

Kass, Arielle. 2021. "Cobb, Gwinnett End 287(g) Immigration Programs, Work to Build Trust." *Atlanta Journal-Constitution*, February 2, 2021. https://www.ajc.com/news /atlanta-news/cobb-gwinnett-end-287g-immigration-programs-work-to-build -trust/TMT42MNZM5E4JCXSXYKBWUYAOU/.

Kaste, Martin. 2021. "When Sheriffs Won't Enforce the Law." *WAMU*, February 21, 2021. https://wamu.org/story/19/02/21/when-sheriffs-wont-enforce-the-law.

Kay, Marvin L. Michael. 1965. "Provincial Taxes In North Carolina During The Administrations Of Dobbs And Tryon." *North Carolina Historical Review* 42 (4): 440–53.

KCCI. 2021. "Central Iowa Deputies Rescue Injured Bald Eagle, Now Recovering." *K You TV*, August 17, 2021. https://www.kyoutv.com/2021/08/17/central-iowa -deputies-rescue-injured-bald-eagle-now-recovering.

KCSO. 2022. "Officer-Involved Shooting (OIS) Incidents." https://www.kernsheriff.org /Transparency/OfficerInvolvedShootings.

Keefe, Josh. 2021. "Sheriff Oversight Proposal Dies in Legislature." *Bangor Daily News*, June 12, 2021. http://bangordailynews.com/2021/06/12/politics/sheriff-oversight -proposal-dies-in-legislature.

Keefe, Josh, Erin Rhoda, and Callie Ferguson. 2021. "A Searchable Database of 5 Years of Punishments for County Officers in Maine." *Bangor Daily News*, January 12, 2021. https://bangordailynews.com/2020/12/02/mainefocus/a-searchable-database-of-5 -years-of-punishments-for-county-officers-in-maine.

Keenan, Kevin M., and Samuel Walker. 2004. "An Impediment to Police Accountability—An Analysis of Statutory Law Enforcement Officers' Bills of Rights." *Boston University Public Interest Law Journal* 14: 185.

Keith, Annisa. 2021. "Sheriff's Office Returns COVID Relief Funding." *Bonner County Daily Bee*, November 3, 2021. https://bonnercountydailybee.com/news/2021/nov /03/sheriffs-office-returns-covid-relief-funding.

Keller, Mary Grace. 2021. "Frederick Sheriff Settles ACLU Racial Profiling Lawsuit, Issues Apology." *Frederick News-Post*, January 21, 2021. https://web.archive.org /web/20230000000000*/https://www.fredericknewspost.com/news/crime_and _justice/cops_and_crime/frederick-sheriff-settles-aclu-racial-profiling-lawsuit -issues-apology/article_9b187c79-155b-509a-8704-737bc1a0d476.html.

Kelly, Amita. 2017. "President Trump Pardons Former Sheriff Joe Arpaio." *NPR*, August 25, 2017. https://www.npr.org/2017/08/25/545282459/president-trump -pardons-former-sheriff-joe-arpaio.

Kelly, Brian. 2001. *Race, Class, and Power in the Alabama Coalfields, 1908–21*. Urbana: University of Illinois Press.

Kenney, Andrew. 2022. "Why the El Paso County Sheriff Says He Couldn't Use Colorado's 'Red Flag' Law to Stop the Club Q Shooting." *Colorado Public Radio*, December 8, 2022. https://www.cpr.org/2022/12/08/club-q-shooting-el-paso -county-sheriff-red-flag-gun-law.

Kerodal, Ashmini G., Joshua D. Freilich, and Steven M. Chermak. 2016. "Commitment to Extremist Ideology: Using Factor Analysis to Move beyond Binary Measures of Extremism." *Studies in Conflict & Terrorism* 39 (7–8): 687–711.

Key, V. O. 1949. *Southern Politics in State and Nation.* New York: A. A. Knopf.

Kilgore, James. 2014. "Repackaging Mass Incarceration." *CounterPunch.Org*, June 6, 2014. https://www.counterpunch.org/2014/06/06/repackaging-mass-incarceration.

Kim, KiDeuk, Miriam Becker-Cohen, and Maria Serakos. 2015. "The Processing and Treatment of Mentally Ill Persons in the Criminal Justice System." Washington, DC: Urban Institute. https://www.urban.org/research/publication/processing-and-treatment-mentally-ill-persons-criminal-justice-system.

Kim, Mimi E. 2018. "From Carceral Feminism to Transformative Justice: Women-of-Color Feminism and Alternatives to Incarceration." *Journal of Ethnic & Cultural Diversity in Social Work* 27 (3): 219–33.

———. 2020. "The Carceral Creep: Gender-Based Violence, Race, and the Expansion of the Punitive State, 1973–1983." *Social Problems* 67 (2): 251–69.

Kim, Mi-son, Dongkyu Kim, and Natasha Altema McNeely. 2020. "Race, Inequality, and Social Capital in the US Counties." *Social Science Journal 2020 (1)*: 1–19.

Kindy, Kimberly. 2021. "Boosted by the Pandemic, 'Constitutional Sheriffs' Are a Political Force." *Washington Post*, November 2, 2021.

King, Desmond, and Rogers Smith. 2005. "Racial Orders in American Political Development." *American Political Science Review* 99 (1): 75–92.

King, Gilbert. 2018. *Beneath a Ruthless Sun: A True Story of Violence, Race, and Justice Lost and Found.* New York: Riverhead.

King, Jenna. 2021. "Josephine County Sheriff Prepares for Potential Budget Cuts." *KOBI-TV NBC5 / KOTI-TV NBC2*, April 17, 2021. https://kobi5.com/news/local-news/josephine-county-sheriff-prepares-for-potential-budget-cuts-149002/.

King, Joyce. 2017. "First African American Female Sheriff Is Woman Enough to Fill Big Boots." *Dallas News*, January 13, 2017. https://www.dallasnews.com/opinion/commentary/2017/01/13/first-african-american-female-sheriff-is-woman-enough-to-fill-big-boots.

King, William R. 2014. "Organizational Failure and the Disbanding of Local Police Agencies." *Crime & Delinquency* 60 (5): 667–92.

King County. 2022. "Executive Constantine Appoints Patti Cole-Tindall as King County Sheriff." May 3, 2022. https://kingcounty.gov/elected/executive/constantine/news/release/2022/May/03-KC-sheriff-selection.aspx.

Kirkland, Patricia A. 2021. "Representation in American Cities: Who Runs for Mayor and Who Wins?" *Urban Affairs Review* 58, no. 3 (October): 635–70.

KKIN. 2021. "Aitkin County Sheriff Dan Guida Monthly Update." May 3, 2021. https://web.archive.org/web/20210621041228/https://www.rjbroadcasting.com/2021/05/03/aitkin-county-sheriff-dan-guida-monthly-update-2/.

Klein, Joanne. 2014. "History of Police Unions." *Encyclopedia of Criminology and Criminal Justice.* New York: Springer, 2207–2217.

Kluckow, Rich, and Zhen Zeng. 2022. "Correctional Populations in the United States, 2020—Statistical Tables." Bureau of Justice Statistics. https://bjs.ojp.gov/library/publications/correctional-populations-united-states-2020-statistical-tables.

Kofman, Jeffrey. 2008. "Despite Criticism, 'America's Toughest Sheriff' Expects to Be Re-Elected." *ABC News*, October 20, 2008. https://abcnews.go.com/Politics/5050/story?id=6105331&page=1.

Kopel, David B. 2014. "The Posse Comitatus and the Office of Sheriff: Armed Citizens

Summoned to the Aid of Law Enforcement." *Journal of Criminal Law and Criminology* 104: 761.

KQED. 2013. "Four of Five Border Patrol Drug Busts Involve US Citizens, Records Show." *KQED*, March 26, 2013. https://www.kqed.org/news/92534/four-of-five -border-patrol-drug-busts-involve-us-citizens-records-show.

Kramer, Jillian. 2022. "'We're Making History': Louisiana's First Black Female Sheriff Sworn In." *Times-Picayune*, May 4, 2022.

Kreitzer, Rebecca J., Elizabeth A. Maltby, and Candis Watts Smith. 2023. "Fifty Shades of Deservingness: An Analysis of State-Level Variation and Effect of Social Constructions on Policy Outcomes." *Journal of Public Policy 42 (3): 436–64* .

Kreitzer, Rebecca J., and Tracy Osborn. 2019. "The Emergence and Activities of Women's Recruiting Groups in the U.S." *Politics, Groups, and Identities* 7 (4): 842–52.

Kreitzer, Rebecca J., and Tracy Osborn. 2020. "Women Candidate Recruitment Groups in the States," edited by Shauna L. Shames, Rachel Bernhard, Mirya R. Holman, and Dawn Langan Teele. Philadelphia, PA: Temple University Press, 183–192.

Kreitzer, Rebecca J., and Candis Watts Smith. 2018. "Reproducible and Replicable: An Empirical Assessment of the Social Construction of Politically Relevant Target Groups." *PS: Political Science & Politics* 51 (4): 768–74.

Krumholz, Sam. 2019. "The Effect of District Attorneys on Local Criminal Justice Outcomes." SSRN Scholarly Paper. Rochester, NY. https://doi.org/10.2139/ssrn .3243162.

KSAT 12, dir. 2022. *Kinney County Sheriff Defends Driving Immigrants Back to the Border.* https://www.youtube.com/watch?v=0c5zafkpPyU.

KTVB Staff. 2022. "Former Bingham County Sheriff Sentenced to 10 Days in Jail for Assault." *Ktvb.com*, October 7, 2022. https://localnews8.com/news/crime-tracker /2022/10/25/former-bingham-sheriff-sentenced-to-10-days-in-jail/.

KTVU. 2021. "Solano County Sheriff Releases New Video from Traffic Stop That Led to Federal Lawsuit." *KTVU FOX 2*, August 23, 2021. https://www.ktvu.com/news /solano-county-sheriff-releases-new-video-from-traffic-stop-that-led-to-federal -lawsuit.

Lacy, Akela. 2019. "Progressive Candidates Run for County Sheriff's Offices." *The Intercept*, October 7, 2019. https://theintercept.com/2019/10/07/county-sheriff -elections-virginia-louisiana.

LaFrance, C., and S. Lee. 2010. "Sheriffs' and Police Chiefs' Differential Perceptions of the Residents They Serve: An Exploration and Preliminary Rationale." *Law Enforcement Executive Forum* 10: 125–36.

LaFrance, T. Casey. 2012. "The County Sheriff's Leadership and Management Decisions in the Local Budget Process Revisited." *International Journal of Police Science & Management* 14 (2): 154–65.

Lartey, Jamiles. 2018. "Tennessee Sheriff Taped Saying 'I Love This Shit' after Ordering Suspect's Killing." *The Guardian*, February 6, 2018. https://www.theguardian .com/us-news/2018/feb/06/tennessee-sheriff-caught-on-tape-killing-suspect -lawsuit.

Lau, Maya. 2018. "Alex Villanueva, Who Beat Long Odds in Historic Election Upset, Sworn in as L.A. County Sheriff." *Los Angeles Times*, December 3, 2018. https:// www.chicagotribune.com/la-me-sheriff-swearing-in-20181203-htmlstory.html.

———. 2019. "L.A. County Supervisors Admonish Sheriff Alex Villanueva for Rehiring Deputy Accused of Abusing and Stalking Woman." *Los Angeles Times*, January 30,

2019. https://www.latimes.com/local/lanow/la-me-losangeles-supervisors-sheriff
-villanueva-20190129-story.html.

Laughland, Oliver. 2016. "California's Kern County Settles for $1m over Sexual Assault
by Sheriff's Deputy." *The Guardian*, May 9, 2016. https://www.theguardian.com/us
-news/2016/may/09/kern-county-california-deputy-sexual-assault-settlement.

Laughland, Oliver, Jon Swaine, Mae Ryan, and Guardian US Interactive Team. 2015.
"The County: Sexual Assault and the Price of Silence." *The Guardian*, December 8,
2015. http://www.theguardian.com/us-news/2015/dec/08/the-county-kern-county
-california-sexual-assault-secret-payoffs.

Lausen, Marcia. 2008. *Design for Democracy: Ballot and Election Design*. Chicago: University of Chicago Press.

Leddy, Edward. 1985. "The National Rifle Association: The Evolution of a Social
Movement." PhD diss., Fordham University. https://www.proquest.com/docview
/303390135/abstract/27C85A9BE6714DE6PQ/1.

LEMAS. 2013. "Law Enforcement Management and Administrative Statistics (LEMAS),
2013." Washington, DC: United States Department of Justice.

———. 2016. "Law Enforcement Management and Administrative Statistics (LEMAS),
2016." Washington, DC: Department of Justice.

———. 2020. "Sheriffs' Offices Personnel, 2020." Law Enforcement Management and
Administrative Statistics. Washington, DC: Department of Justice, Bureau of Justice
Statistics.

LEOKA. 2019. "Law Enforcement Officer Deaths." Federal Bureau of Investigation.

Lerman, Amy E., and Vesla Weaver. 2014a. "Staying out of Sight? Concentrated Policing and Local Political Action." *The ANNALS of the American Academy of Political
and Social Science* 651 (1): 202–19.

Lerman, Amy E., and Vesla M. Weaver. 2014b. *Arresting Citizenship*. Chicago: University of Chicago Press.

Lerten, Barney. 2021. "Federal Jury Awards Fired DCSO Deputy over $1 Million in
Lawsuit against County, Sheriff Nelson." *KTVZ*, August 24, 2021. https://ktvz.com
/news/crime-courts/2021/08/23/federal-jury-awards-fired-dcso-deputy-over-1
-million-in-lawsuit-against-county-sheriff-nelson.

Leslie, William R. 1952. "The Pennsylvania Fugitive Slave Act of 1826." *The Journal of
Southern History* 18 (4): 429–45.

Levchak, Philip J. 2021. "Stop-and-Frisk in New York City: Estimating Racial Disparities in Post-Stop Outcomes." *Journal of Criminal Justice* 73 (March): 101784.

Levin, Sam. 2020. "Los Angeles Sheriff's Department Faces a Reckoning after Another
Police Shooting." *The Guardian*, July 1, 2020. https://www.theguardian.com/us
-news/2020/jul/01/los-angeles-sheriffs-department-reckoning-police-shootings.

———. 2021. "California Opens Civil Rights Inquiry into LA County Sheriff's Department." *The Guardian*, January 22, 2021. https://www.theguardian.com/us
-news/2021/jan/22/california-los-angeles-county-sheriffs-department-civil-rights
-investigation.

Levitas, Daniel. 2004. *The Terrorist Next Door: The Militia Movement and the Radical
Right*. New York: Macmillan.

Levitt, Steven D., and Catherine D. Wolfram. 1997. "Decomposing the Sources of Incumbency Advantage in the U. S. House." *Legislative Studies Quarterly* 22 (1): 45–60.

LIFE Magazine. 1950. "LIFE Visits Sheriff 'Buckshot' Lane A Texan Keeps the Peace—
and Writes About It." July 17, 1950.

Lindberg, Staffan I. 2004. "The Democratic Qualities of Competitive Elections: Participation, Competition and Legitimacy in Africa." *Commonwealth & Comparative Politics* 42 (1): 61–105.

Littman, Aaron. 2021. "Jails, Sheriffs, and Carceral Policymaking." *Vand. L. Rev.* 74: 861.

Litton, Andra. 2018. "Doña Ana County Undersheriff Retains Job, despite Sexual Harassment Allegations." *KTSM 9 News*, January 26, 2018. https://www.ktsm.com /local/las-cruces-news/dona-ana-county-undersheriff-retains-job-despite-sexual -harassment-allegations.

Louisiana State Legislature. 2018. "CCRP 1003." Baton Rouge, LA. https://www.legis.la .gov/legis/Law.aspx?d=1106500.

Lowe, John. 2019. "Financial Future for Martin County Sheriff's Office Looking Brighter." *WSAZ News Channel*, July 17, 2019. https://www.wsaz.com/content /news/Martin-County-Sheriffs-Office-suffering-more-setbacks-512857511.html.

Lowery, David, and Lee Sigelman. 1981. "Understanding the Tax Revolt: Eight Explanations." *American Political Science Review* 75 (4): 963–74.

Lublin, David, and Sarah E. Brewer. 2003. "The Continuing Dominance of Traditional Gender Roles in Southern Elections." *Social Science Quarterly* 84 (2): 379–96.

Lucas, Jack. 2022. "Do 'Non-Partisan' Municipal Politicians Match the Partisanship of Their Constituents?" *Urban Affairs Review* 58 (1): 103–28.

Lynch, Kellie R., T. K. Logan, and Dylan B. Jackson. 2018. "'People Will Bury Their Guns before They Surrender Them': Implementing Domestic Violence Gun Control in Rural, Appalachian versus Urban Communities." *Rural Sociology* 83 (2): 315–46.

MacManus, Susan A., and Nikki R. VanHightower. 1989. "Limits of State Constitutional Guarantees: Lessons from Efforts to Implement Domestic Violence Policies." *Public Administration Review* 49 (3): 269–78.

Macon Republican. 1853. "Alabama Sheriff Advertises Planned Sale of Enslaved Black Man." December 22, 1853. https://calendar.eji.org/racial-injustice/dec/22.

Mai, Chris, Mikelina Belaineh, Ram Subramanian, and Jacob Kang-Brown. 2019. "Broken Ground: Why America Keeps Building More Jails and What It Can Do Instead." Report. Vera Institute.

Mancini, Matthew J. 1996. *One Dies, Get Another: Convict Leasing in the American South, 1866–1928*. University of South Carolina Press.

Manna, Nichole. 2022a. "Protest Planned over Tarrant County Jail Deaths, Alleged Policy Violations." *Fort Worth Star-Telegram*, May 10, 2022. https://www.star-telegram .com/news/local/fort-worth/article261257067.html.

———. 2022b. "Lawsuit Alleges an Inmate Beaten By Tarrant County Jailers Was Left in Cell for 2 Days." *Star Telegram*, July 19, 2022. https://www.star-telegram.com /news/local/fort-worth/article263615643.html.

Manza, Jeff, and Christopher Uggen. 2008. *Locked Out: Felon Disenfranchisement and American Democracy*. New York: Oxford University Press.

Marmor, Theodore R., and Karyn C. Gill. 1989. "The Political and Economic Context of Mental Health Care in the United States." *Journal of Health Politics, Policy and Law* 14 (3): 459–75.

Marohn, Kirsti. 2022. "Defendants Seek Dismissal of Line 3 Protest Charges." *MPR News*, July 18, 2022. https://www.mprnews.org/story/2022/07/18/defendants-seek -dismissal-of-line-3-protest-charges.

Marshall Project. 2022. "About Us." The Marshall Project. 2022. https://www .themarshallproject.org/about.

Martin, Mark K., and Paul Katsampes. 2007. *Sheriff's Guide to Effective Jail Operations.* US Department of Justice, National Institute of Corrections Washington, DC.

Martinez, Laura. 2021. "Second Employee Files Federal Lawsuit against Cameron County Sheriff Eric Garza." *MyRGV.Com,* May 11, 2021. https://myrgv.com/featured /2021/05/11/second-employee-files-federal-lawsuit-against-cameron-county-sheriff -eric-garza.

Marvar, Alexander. 2018. "The Two Faces of Lummie Jenkins." Topic. November 2018. https://web.archive.org/web/20230628213937/https://www.topic.com/the-two -faces-of-lummie-jenkins.

Maryland Sheriffs' Association. n.d. "Office of Sheriff." Accessed September 30, 2023. https://www.mdsheriffs.org/office-of-sheriff.

Mason, Lilliana. 2018. *Uncivil Agreement: How Politics Became Our Identity.* Chicago: University of Chicago Press.

Massey, Douglas S., Jorge Durand, and Nolan J. Malone. 2003. *Beyond Smoke and Mirrors: Mexican Immigration in an Era of Economic Integration.* Thousand Oaks, CA: Russell Sage Foundation.

Mattick, Hans Walter. 1971. "The Contemporary Jails of the United States: An Unknown and Neglected Area of Justice." University of Chicago Law School.

Maveety, Nancy. 2018. *Glass and Gavel: The U.S. Supreme Court and Alcohol.* New York: Rowman & Littlefield.

Mayhew, David R. 1974. *Congress: The Electoral Connection.* New Haven, CT: Yale University Press.

McBrayer, Markie, and Robert Lucas Williams. 2022. "The Second Sex in the Second District: The Policy Effects of Electing Women to County Government." *Political Research Quarterly* 76 (2): 825–40..

McCarthy, Michelle, Claire Bates, Paraskevi Triantafyllopoulou, Siobhan Hunt, and Karen Milne Skillman. 2019. "'Put Bluntly, They Are Targeted by the Worst Creeps Society Has to Offer': Police and Professionals' Views and Actions Relating to Domestic Violence and Women with Intellectual Disabilities." *Journal of Applied Research in Intellectual Disabilities* 32 (1): 71–81.

McCarty, William P., and Stacy Dewald. 2017. "Sheriff's Deputies and Police Officers: Comparing Their Views." *Policing: An International Journal of Police Strategies & Management* 40 (1): 99–111.

McDonald, Danny. 2020. "In Recent Years, Four Mass. Jails Got $164 Million in Federal Money to House ICE Detainees." *Boston Globe,* January 28, 2020. https://hls .harvard.edu/clinic-stories/legal-policy-work/in-recent-years-four-mass-jails-got -164-million-in-federal-money-to-house-ice-detainees/.

McDowell, Meghan G., and Luis A. Fernandez. 2018. "'Disband, Disempower, and Disarm': Amplifying the Theory and Practice of Police Abolition." *Critical Criminology* 26 (3): 373–91.

Mcfeely, Mike. 2022. "North Dakota Sheriff Says He'll Deputize Citizens against U.S. Government." InForum, February 3, 2022. https://www.inforum.com/opinion /mcfeely-north-dakota-sheriff-says-hell-deputize-citizens-against-u-s-government.

McGahan, Jason. 2022. "Sheriff Villanueva Slams WeHo Vote to Defund Him." *Los Angeles Magazine.* July 1, 2022. https://www.lamag.com/citythinkblog/sheriff -villanueva-slams-weho-vote-to-defund-him-exclusive.

McGirr, Lisa. 2015. *The War on Alcohol: Prohibition and the Rise of the American State.* New York: W. W. Norton.

McGrath, Roger D. 1987. *Gunfighters, Highwaymen, and Vigilantes: Violence on the Frontier*. Berkeley: University of California Press.

McGregor, Shannon C. 2018. "Personalization, Social Media, and Voting: Effects of Candidate Self-Personalization on Vote Intention." *New Media & Society* 20 (3): 1139–60.

McGregor, Shannon C., Regina G. Lawrence, and Arielle Cardona. 2017. "Personalization, Gender, and Social Media: Gubernatorial Candidates' Social Media Strategies." *Information, Communication & Society* 20 (2): 264–83.

McGuffey, Charmaine, dir. 2020. *Meet Charmaine McGuffey for Sheriff*. https://www.youtube.com/watch?v=RZcVVW6MboE.

McHarris, Philip V., and Thenjiwe McHarris. 2020. "Opinion | No More Money for the Police." *New York Times*, May 30, 2020. https://www.nytimes.com/2020/05/30/opinion/george-floyd-police-funding.html.

McKanna, Clare V. 1994. "Seeds of Destruction: Homicide, Race, and Justice in Omaha, 1880–1920." *Journal of American Ethnic History* 14 (1): 65–90.

———. 1995. "Death in the Colorado Coal Country: Homicide and Social Instability in Las Animas County, 1880–1920." *Western Legal History*. 8: 163.

———. 1997. *Homicide, Race, and Justice in the American West, 1880–1920*. Tucson, AZ: University of Arizona Press.

MCSO. 2018. "The Monroe County Sheriff's Office Annual Report." Monroe County, FL: Monroe County Sheriff's Office.

———. 2022. "Monroe County Sheriff's Office Annual Report 2020/2021." Monroe County Sheriff's Office. https://www.keysso.net/pdf/MCSO%202020%20Annual%20Report.pdf.

McWhorter, Diane. 1989. "Since Mississippi Burned." *People Magazine*, January 9, 1989. https://people.com/archive/since-mississippi-burned-vol-31-no-1.

Meeks, Lindsey. 2020. "Undercovered, Underinformed: Local News, Local Elections, and US Sheriffs." *Journalism Studies* 21 (12): 1609–26.

Meier, Kenneth J., and Jill Nicholson-Crotty. 2006. "Gender, Representative Bureaucracy, and Law Enforcement: The Case of Sexual Assault." *Public Administration Review* 66 (6): 850–60.

Melendez, Pilar. 2021. "This State's Rogue Sheriff Problem Somehow Just Got Worse." *Daily Beast*, December 14, 2021. https://www.thedailybeast.com/marlboro-county-sheriff-charles-lemon-and-ex-deputy-david-andrew-cook-indicted-for-tasing-in-south-carolina.

Mencimer, Stephanie. 2021. "He Was a Board Member of the Oath Keepers. Now He's Holding State-Approved Trainings for Law Enforcement in Texas." *Mother Jones*. October 29, 2021. https://www.motherjones.com/politics/2021/10/oath-keepers-texas-richard-mack-profile-sheriff.

Mercer County Sheriff's Office. 2022. "History | Mercer County, NJ." 2022. https://www.mercercounty.org/government/sheriff/history.

Merchant, John. 2017. "Brown Co Readies For Eclipse Crowds." *MSCNews*, August 14, 2017.

Meskell, Matthew W. 1998. "An American Resolution: The History of Prisons in the United States from 1777 to 1877." *Stanford Law Review* 51: 839.

Meyer, Richard. 1993. "West of Pecos : There Ain't Many Folks in Loving County, but Durned Near Everyone's a Character." *Los Angeles Times*, January 31, 1993. https://

web.archive.org/web/20220728000000*/https://www.latimes.com/archives/la
-xpm-1993-01-31-tm-848-story.html.

Mickey, Robert. 2015. *Paths Out of Dixie: The Democratization of Authoritarian Enclaves
in America's Deep South, 1944–1972*. Princeton, NJ: Princeton University Press.

Modrich, Stefan. 2021. "County Unveils Portrait of County's First Black Sheriff." *Fort
Bend Star*, March 2, 2021. https://www.fortbendstar.com/countynews/county
-unveils-portrait-of-county-s-first-black-sheriff/article_1d80a940-7b79-11eb-b008
-43ebfa0658d4.html.

Mojica, Adrian. 2022. "Lawsuit Claims Tennessee Man Killed by Deputy Was Unarmed,
Holding Wallet." *WZTV*, January 7, 2022. https://fox17.com/news/local/lawsuit
-claims-tennessee-man-killed-by-deputy-was-unarmed-holding-wallet-crime
-alertnest-police-shooting-white-county-nashville.

Moley, Raymond. 1929. "The Sheriff and the Constable." *The ANNALS of the American
Academy of Political and Social Science* 146 (1): 28–33.

Monahan, Heather, and Staci DaSilva. 2021. "'Grinch' with 'Eggnog for Brains' Accused
of Stealing Christmas Gifts from Single Mom's Lakeland Home." *WFLA*, December 21, 2021. https://www.wfla.com/news/polk-county/eggnog-for-brains-search
-underway-for-grinch-who-stole-christmas-gifts-from-lakeland-familys-home.

Monroe County Sheriff's Office. 2020. "Annual Report." Monroe County, FL: Monroe
County Sheriff's Office.

Moore, Evan. 2001. "Sheriff Keeps Doors Open." *Chronicle*, March 25, 2001. https://
www.chron.com/news/houston-texas/article/Sheriff-keeps-doors-open-2013018
.php.

Moore, Kimberly. 2022. "Part 1: Polk County Sheriff Grady Judd Marks 50 Years in
Law Enforcement." *LkldNow*. July 21, 2022. https://www.lkldnow.com/part-1-polk
-county-sheriff-grady-judd-marks-50-years-in-law-enforcement/.

Moore, Toby. 1997. "Race and the County Sheriff in the American South." *International
Social Science Review* 72 (1/2): 50–61.

Moran, Brian, and Amanda McDowell. 2021. "Pierce County Council Authorized In-
vestigation." Orrick, Herrington & Sutcliffe LLP. https://www.piercecountywa.gov
/DocumentCenter/View/109150/Moran-Investigation-Oct-2021-findings?fbclid=
IwAR2Q8L-uxvZjipNtiKfGU6uMlVD9RMUFUsVFYYDSD93s-JoDigoZbOufTv4.

Moreno-Jaimes, Carlos. 2007. "Do Competitive Elections Produce Better-Quality Governments?: Evidence From Mexican Municipalities, 1990–2000." *Latin American
Research Review* 42 (2): 136–53.

"Morgan County About Us." 2022. https://web.archive.org/web/20220201000000*
/http://www.co.morgan.al.us/aboutus.htm.

Morgan County Sheriff's Office. 2020. "Facebook." September 1, 2020. https://www
.facebook.com/MorganSheriffOffice/posts/do-you-know-the-history-of-the-office
-of-sheriff-also-known-as-the-keeper-of-the/3224864480924413.

Morgan, Sam. 2020. "UPDATED: Kern County Sheriff's Office Enters into 'Major Settlement' with Department of Justice Following Civil Rights Investigation." *Bakersfield Californian*, December 23, 2020. https://web.archive.org/web
/20220201000000*/https://www.bakersfield.com/news/updated-kern-county
-sheriffs-office-enters-into-major-settlement-with-department-of-justice-following
-civil/article_99b492da-4490-11eb-b48f-4be7e77ce825.html.

Morlin, Bill. 2017. "ACT's Anti-Muslim Message Fertile Ground for Oath Keepers."

Southern Poverty Law Center. June 12, 2017. https://www.splcenter.org/hatewatch /2017/06/12/act%E2%80%99s-anti-muslim-message-fertile-ground-oath-keepers.

Morris, Kevin. 2021. "Turnout and Amendment Four: Mobilizing Eligible Voters Close to Formerly Incarcerated Floridians." *American Political Science Review* 115 (3): 805–20.

Morris, Scott. 2021. "Pressure Grows for Oversight of Solano County Sheriff's Office." *Vallejo Sun*, October 29, 2021. https://www.vallejosun.com/pressure-grows-for -oversight-of-solano-county-sheriffs-office.

Morris, W. A. 1918. "The Office of Sheriff in the Early Norman Period." *The English Historical Review* 33 (130): 145–75.

Morse, Janice. 2013. "Sheriffs Say Border Security Should Be Priority." *USA Today*, August 14, 2013. http://www.usatoday.com/story/news/nation/2013/08/14/ohio -sheriffs-say-border-security-should-be-priority/2657979.

Mudde, Cas. 2019. *The Far Right Today*. New York: John Wiley & Sons.

Mughan, Siân, Danyao Li, and Sean Nicholson-Crotty. 2020. "When Law Enforcement Pays: Costs and Benefits for Elected Versus Appointed Administrators Engaged in Asset Forfeiture." *American Review of Public Administration* 50 (3): 297–314.

Muhammad, Khalil Gibran. 2011. *The Condemnation of Blackness: Race, Crime, and the Making of Modern Urban America*. Cambridge, MA: Harvard University Press.

Muller, Christopher, and Daniel Schrage. 2021. "The Political Economy of Incarceration in the Cotton South, 1910–1925." *American Journal of Sociology* 127 (3): 828–866.

Mullin, Megan. 2008. "The Conditional Effect of Specialized Governance on Public Policy." *American Journal of Political Science* 52 (1): 125–41.

Musgrave, Paul. 2020. "Bringing the State Police In: The Diffusion of U.S. Statewide Policing Agencies, 1905–1941." *Studies in American Political Development* 34 (1): 3–23.

Mutpfay, Patricia. 1997. "Domestic Violence Legislation and the Police." *Women & Politics* 18 (2): 27–53.

NAACP. 1919. *Thirty Years of Lynching in the United States, 1889–1918*. National Association for the Advancement of Colored People.

Narea, Nicole. 2020. "New Democratic Sheriffs in Georgia and South Carolina Have Vowed to Cut Ties with ICE." *Vox*, November 17, 2020. https://www.vox.com/2020 /11/17/21558400/sheriff-ice-north-carolina-georgia-287g.

National Commission on Law Observance and Enforcement. 1931. "Report on the Enforcement of the Prohibition Laws of the United States." Washington, DC: January 7, 1931.

National Sheriffs' Association. 2013. "National Sheriffs' Association Position Paper on Comprehensive Immigration Reform." Charlotte, NC: National Sheriffs Association. http://www.sheriffs.org/sites/default/files/uploads/documents/GovAffairs /NSA%20CIR%202013%20FINAL.pdf.

———. 2022. "The Office of the Sheriff." 2022. https://web.archive.org/web /20230000000000*/https://www.sheriffs.org/about-nsa/history/roots.

———. n.d. "The Elected Office of the Sheriff." Washington, DC: National Sheriffs' Association.

Navajo County, AZ. 2022. "Sheriff Biography." https://navajocountyaz.gov/Departments /Sheriff.

NBC News. 2004. "Alabama Deputy Discovers Civil Rights Era Artifacts," July 23, 2004. https://www.nbcnews.com/id/wbna5499858.

NCSA. 2022. "History of the Sheriff." *North Carolina Sheriffs' Association*. https://ncsheriffs.org/about/history-of-the-sheriff.

NCSL. 2021. "State Trends in Law Enforcement Legislation." National Conference of State Legislatures. https://www.ncsl.org/civil-and-criminal-justice/law-enforcement-legislation-significant-trends-2021.

Neiwert, David. 2016. "'Constitutional' Oregon Sheriff Under Investigation for Malheur Role Hired 70 'Special Deputies.'" *Southern Poverty Law Center*, March 23, 2016. https://www.splcenter.org/hatewatch/2016/03/23/constitutional%E2%80%99-oregon-sheriff-under-investigation-malheur-role-hired-70-%E2%80%98special-deputies%E2%80%99.

Nelson, Michael J. 2010. "Uncontested and Unaccountable—Rates of Contestation in Trial Court Elections." *Judicature* 94: 208.

Nemerever, Zoe. 2021. "Contentious Federalism: Sheriffs, State Legislatures, and Political Violence in the American West." *Political Behavior* 43 (1): 247–70.

Nemerever, Zoe, and Melissa Rogers. 2021. "Measuring the Rural Continuum in Political Science." *Political Analysis* 29 (3): 267–86.

News8000. 2020. "Federal Complaint Filed against Trempealeau County Sheriff's Department." *WKBT*, September 8, 2020. https://www.news8000.com/federal-complaint-filed-against-trempealeau-county-sheriffs-department.

New York Times. 1915. "Fees of $400,000 to Five Sheriffs. Commissioner Wallstein Reports Collections Made by the Officials in Nine Years. In Favor of Bill Which Proposes to Limit Income of the Office to a Salary." *New York Times*, February 25, 1915.

———. 1933. "Alabama Mob Kills 2 Indicted Negroes," August 14, 1933. https://timesmachine.nytimes.com/timesmachine/1933/08/14/99918324.html?zoom=15.67&pageNumber=1.

———. 1922. "WOMAN SHERIFF ON JOB," August 3, 1922.

———. 1926. "Smith Names Mrs. Clara Senecal as Sheriff To Succeed Her Husband in Clinton County," April 10, 1926.

———. 1929. "Sheriff and Chief Convicted in Alabama," April 29, 1929.

———. 1953. "Sheriff in Alabama Kills Opposing Negro Witness," December 29, 1953.

———. 1960. "Alabama Forming Race-Riot Posses," April 10, 1960.

———. 1965. "The Sheriff Is Uncertain," February 17, 1965.

———. 1970. "Ex-Sheriff Convicted," April 26, 1970.

———. 1972. "Woman Is Sheriff, But Her Husband Wears the Guns," December 3, 1972.

Nichanian, Daniel. 2018. "Sheriff Race in Doña Ana, New Mexico Puts Spotlight on Operation Stonegarden." The Appeal Political Report, October 4, 2018. https://theappeal.org/politicalreport/dona-ana-nm-sheriff.

Nichols, Scott. 2020. "A Message from the Sheriff Regarding the Latest Executive Order." April 1, 2020. https://www.facebook.com/permalink.php?story_fbid=3472476659447896&id=878512678844320.

Nielsen, Rasmus Kleis. 2015. *Local Journalism: The Decline of Newspapers and the Rise of Digital Media*. New York: Bloomsbury Publishing.

Niskanen, William A. 1975. "Bureaucrats and Politicians." *Journal of Law and Economics* 18 (3): 617–43.

Noble, Greg. 2016. "Sheriff Apologizes for Attending Trump Rally." *WCPO*, March 14, 2016. https://www.wcpo.com/news/political/local-politics/democratic-leader-criticizes-hamilton-county-sheriff-jim-neil-for-appearing-at-donald-trump-rally.

Norton, Jack, and Jacob Kang-Brown. 2018. "Federal Farm Aid for the Big House." Vera

Institute. https://www.vera.org/in-our-backyards-stories/federal-farm-aid-for-the-big-house.

Nosowitz, Dan. 2019. "How Elf on the Shelf Became a Surveillance State Apparatus." *VICE*, December 24, 2019. https://www.vice.com/en/article/5dmpbz/how-elf-on-the-shelf-became-a-surveillance-state-apparatus.

Nossiter, Adam. 2009. "As His Inmates Grew Thinner, a Sheriff's Wallet Grew Fatter." *New York Times*, January 9, 2009. https://www.nytimes.com/2009/01/09/us/09sheriff.html.

Nourse, Victoria F. 1996. "Where Violence, Relationship, and Equality Meet: The Violence against Women Act's Civil Right Remedy." *Wisconsin Women's Law Journal* 11: 1.

Novak, Daniel A. 2014. *The Wheel of Servitude: Black Forced Labor after Slavery*. Lexington, KY: University Press of Kentucky.

Novisky, Meghan A., and Robert L. Peralta. 2015. "When Women Tell: Intimate Partner Violence and the Factors Related to Police Notification." *Violence against Women* 21 (1): 65–86.

NPR. 2008. "The Untold History of Post-Civil War 'Neoslavery,'" March 25, 2008. https://www.npr.org/templates/story/story.php?storyId=89051115.

———. 2021. "With the Latest Payout, Former Sheriff Joe Arpaio Has Cost Arizona Taxpayers $100M," October 29, 2021. https://www.npr.org/2021/10/29/1050490391/joe-arpaio-legal-costs-100-million-arizona-sheriff.

NSA. n.d. "Keith Cain Daviess County Sheriff's Office Kentucky." https://www.sheriffs.org/sites/default/files/Cain_Bio.pdf.

Obert, Jonathan. 2018. *The Six-Shooter State: Public and Private Violence in American Politics*. New York: Cambridge University Press.

OCSO. 2022. "Sheriffs Office History Detail." Orange County Sheriff's Office. https://www.ocsonc.com/history-detail.

Oliver, Ned. 2020. "Virginia Lawmakers Pass Bill Limiting Pretextual Traffic Stops, barring Searches Based on Smell of Marijuana." *Virginia Mercury*, October 2, 2020. https://www.virginiamercury.com/2020/10/02/virginia-lawmakers-pass-bill-banning-pretextual-traffic-stops-and-searches-based-on-the-smell-of-marijuana.

Olson, Alndrea. 2022. "Bingham County Sheriff Submits Letter of Resignation." *East Idaho News*, July 25, 2022. https://www.eastidahonews.com/2022/07/bingham-county-sheriff-submits-letter-of-resignation.

Ondercin, Heather L. 2017. "Who Is Responsible for the Gender Gap? The Dynamics of Men's and Women's Democratic Macropartisanship, 1950–2012." *Political Research Quarterly* 70 (4): 749–77.

Ondercin, Heather L., and Mary Kate Lizotte. 2021. "You've Lost That Loving Feeling: How Gender Shapes Affective Polarization." *American Politics Research* 49 (3): 282–92.

Orren, Karen. 1998. "'A War Between Officers': The Enforcement of Slavery in the Northern United States, and Of the Republic for Which It Stands, Before the Civil War." *Studies in American Political Development* 12 (2): 343–82.

Orren, Karen, and Stephen Skowronek. 2004. *The Search for American Political Development*. Cambridge University Press.

Osborn, Tracy. 2012. *How Women Represent Women: Political Parties, Gender and Representation in the State Legislatures*. New York: Oxford University Press.

Osborne, Derek. 2022. "The Issues." Osborne4sheriff. https://web.archive.org/web/20221007145626/https://www.osborne4sheriff.com/platfor.

Oshinsky, David M. 1997. *Worse Than Slavery*. New York: Simon and Schuster.

Oxford, Andrew. n.d. "Charity Founded by Pinal County Sheriff Mark Lamb Has $18,000 in Unaccounted Spending." Arizona Republic. Accessed April 14, 2022. https://www.azcentral.com/story/news/politics/arizona/2020/08/31/pinal -county-sheriff-mark-lamb-charity-tax-filings/5626026002.

Page, Joshua, and Joe Soss. 2021. "The Predatory Dimensions of Criminal Justice." *Science* 374 (6565): 291–94.

Palmer, Ken. 2020. "New Guidelines: Lansing Police Won't Stop Drivers Solely for Minor Violations." *Lansing State Journal*, July 1, 2020. https://www.lansingstatejournal .com/story/news/local/2020/07/01/new-guidelines-lansing-police-wont-stop -drivers-solely-minor-violations/5357206002.

Pantucci, Raffaello, and Kyler Ong. 2021. "Persistence of Right-Wing Extremism and Terrorism in the West." *Counter Terrorist Trends and Analyses* 13 (1): 118–26.

Parfitt, Jamie. 2019. "Report: Calls for Help Often Went Unanswered in Josephine County after 2012 Funding Cuts." *KDRV*, December 4, 2019. https://web.archive.org /web/20211012045205/https://www.kdrv.com/content/news/Report-Crime-gun -permits-spike-in-Josephine-County-after-2012-funding-cuts-565811602.html.

Parham, Wayne. 2022. "FL Sheriff's Office Deploys Mobile Video Game Theater for Kids." *Police Mag*, July 6, 2022. https://www.policemag.com/640462/fl-sheriffs -office-deploys-mobile-video-game-theater-for-kids.

Parnas, Raymond I. 1967. "The Police Response to the Domestic Disturbance." *Wisconsin Law Review* 2: 914–60.

Paterson, Leigh. 2019. "Months before Controversial Gun Law Takes Effect, Colorado Sheriffs Continue To Resist." Guns and America. https://gunsandamerica.org/story /19/07/02/months-before-controversial-gun-law-takes-effect-colorado-sheriffs -continue-to-resist.

Patten, Ryan, Jonathan W. Caudill, Stephanie E. Bor, Matthew O. Thomas, and Sally Anderson. 2015. "Managing a Criminal Justice Crisis: An Organizational Justice Understanding of Change in a Sheriff's Office." *American Journal of Criminal Justice* 40 (4): 737–49.

Patty, John W., and Ian R. Turner. 2021. "Ex Post Review and Expert Policy Making: When Does Oversight Reduce Accountability?" *Journal of Politics* 83 (1): 23–39.

Paul, John. 2020. "Sheriff Tony Guy's Campaign Ads May Cost Taxpayers $25,000— Commissioners Voting Next Week." *BeaverCountian.Com*, September 3, 2020. https://beavercountian.com/content/beaver-county-government/sheriff-tony -guys-campaign-ads-may-cost-taxpayers-25000-commissioners-voting-next-week.

Pearson-Merkowitz, Shanna, and Joshua J. Dyck. 2017. "Crime and Partisanship: How Party ID Muddles Reality, Perception, and Policy Attitudes on Crime and Guns." *Social Science Quarterly* 98 (2): 443–54.

Pegram, Thomas R. 2008. "Hoodwinked: The Anti-Saloon League and the Ku Klux Klan in 1920s Prohibition Enforcement." *The Journal of the Gilded Age and Progressive Era* 7 (1): 89–119.

Perez, Nicholas Michael, Max Bromley, and John Cochran. 2017. "Organizational Commitment among Sheriffs' Deputies during the Shift to Community-Oriented Policing." *Policing: An International Journal of Police Strategies & Management* 40 (2): 321–35.

Perliger, Arie. 2012. "Challengers from the Sidelines: Understanding America's Violent Far-Right." West Point: Combating Terrorism Center.

Perry, David M. 2018. "How to Beat ICE in Your Hometown? Run for Sheriff." *Pacific Standard*, October 11, 2018. https://psmag.com/social-justice/how-to-beat-ice-in -your-hometown-run-for-sheriff.

Peters, B. Guy, Jon Pierre, and Desmond S. King. 2005. "The Politics of Path Depen- dency: Political Conflict in Historical Institutionalism." *The Journal of Politics* 67 (4): 1275–1300.

Petrohilos, Dylan. 2021. "Leaked: Sheriff Chuck Jenkins Speaks Ahead of the Capitol Riot." *Medium*. January 28, 2021. https://dpetrohilos.medium.com/leaked-sherriff -chuck-jenkins-speaks-ahead-of-the-capitol-riot-70d178c12838.

Perez, Thomas E. 2011. "United States' Investigation of the Maricopa County Sheriff's Office." Letter, Perez, U.S. Department of Justice, Civil Rights Division, to Bill Montgomery, County Attorney, December 15, 2011. https://www.justice.gov/sites /default/files/crt/legacy/2011/12/15/mcso_findletter_12-15-11.pdf.

Pfeiffer, Eric. 2014. "Arizona Sheriff Defends His Rallying of Anti-Immigration Pro- testers: 'I'm Not the Villain.'" Yahoo News. 2014. https://web.archive.org/web /20140901000000*/https://www.yahoo.com/news/arizona-sheriff-defends -rallying-anti-immigration-protests---i-m-not-the-villain-192634199.html.

Phillips, Patrick, and Jared Kofsky. 2020. "Probation but No Jail Time for Former Colle- ton Co. Sheriff after Guilty Pleas." *WCSC*, October 23, 2020. https://www.live5news .com/2020/10/23/suspended-colleton-county-sheriff-face-judge-friday.

Pickett, Mike. 2021. "Cain Reflects on Nearly Five Decades in Law Enforcement in Daviess County." *WEHT/WTVW*, November 30, 2021. https://www.tristatehomepage.com /news/local-news/cain-reflects-on-nearly-five-decades-in-law-enforcement-in -daviess-county/.

Pierson, Emma, Camelia Simoiu, Jan Overgoor, Sam Corbett-Davies, Daniel Jenson, Amy Shoemaker, Vignesh Ramachandran, et al. 2020. "A Large-Scale Analysis of Racial Disparities in Police Stops across the United States." *Nature Human Be- haviour* 4 (7): 736–45.

Pinto, Pablo M., and Jeffrey F. Timmons. 2005. "The Political Determinants of Eco- nomic Performance: Political Competition and the Sources of Growth." *Compara- tive Political Studies* 38 (1): 26–50.

Pishko, Jessica. 2019. "Are Sheriffs Necessary?" *The Appeal*, April 24, 2019. https:// theappeal.org/are-sheriffs-necessary.

———. 2021. "He Calls Himself the 'American Sheriff.' Whose Law Is He Following?" *POLITICO*, October 15, 2021. https://www.politico.com/news/magazine/2021/10 /15/mark-lamb-arizona-constitutional-sheriff-elections-republicans-514781.

Piston, Spencer. 2018. *Class Attitudes in America: Sympathy for the Poor, Resentment of the Rich, and Political Implications*. New York: Cambridge University Press.

Placide, MaCherie M., and Casey LaFrance. 2014. "The County Sheriff in Films: A Portrait of Law Enforcement as a Symbol of Rural America." *International Journal of Police Science & Management* 16 (2): 101–12.

Planalp, Brian. 2021. "Ohio Senate Passes Concealed Carry Bill over Objections of Law Enforcement Groups." *Fox19.com*. Last modified December 15, 2021. https://www .fox19.com/2021/12/15/ohio-senate-passes-bill-allowing-general-concealed-carry -guns/.

Porter, Kirk Harold. 1922. *County and Township Government in the United States*. Mac- millan.

"Our History." 2022. Sun Lakes Sheriff's Posse. Accessed September 30, 2023. http://www.sunlakesposse.org/our-history.html.

Potter, Gary. 2013. *The History of Policing in the United States*. Lexington, KY: University of Kentucky.

Powell, Lawrence. 2006. "Centralization and Its Discontents in Reconstruction Louisiana." *Studies in American Political Development* 20 (2): 105–31.

Powers, Ashley. 2018. "The Renegade Sheriffs." *The New Yorker*, April 23, 2018. https://www.newyorker.com/contributors/ashley-powers.

Prassel, Frank Richard. 1972. *The Western Peace Officer: A Legacy of Law and Order*. Norman, OK: University of Oklahoma Press.

Puente, Mark. 2023. "Calls Grow Louder to Restore Cuyahoga County Sheriff to an Elected Post." The Marshall Project. February 13, 2023. https://www.themarshallproject.org/2023/02/13/calls-grow-louder-to-restore-cuyahoga-county-sheriff-to-an-elected-post.

Ramirez, Quixem. 2022. "3 Black Officers Win $1 Million in Racism, Sexism Lawsuit against Pierce County Jail." King5.Com. June 2, 2022. https://www.king5.com/article/news/local/3-black-women-win-1-million-racism-sexism-lawsuit-pierce-county-jail/281-0644a6e0-7d9a-425c-b7ac-fe1e40f4d8ef.

Reed, Zeke. 2023. "LA Sheriff Vows an End to 'Us vs. Them' Department Mentality." *KCRW*, March 29, 2023. https://www.kcrw.com/news/shows/greater-la/la-sheriff/robert-luna.

Reid, Herbert O. 1956. "The Supreme Court Decision and Interposition." *Journal of Negro Education* 25 (2): 109–17.

Reilly, Ryan. 2016. "An Inmate Died of Thirst in a Jail Run by a Loudly Pro-Trump Sheriff." *HuffPost*, September 19, 2016. https://www.huffpost.com/entry/david-clarke-jail-death-terrill-thomas_n_57e03580e4b04a1497b5f12e.

Reinart, Al. 2013. "The Best Little Checkpoint in Texas." *Texas Monthly*, July 15, 2013. https://www.texasmonthly.com/articles/the-best-little-checkpoint-in-texas.

Remkus, Ashley. 2018. "Prosecutor Sues Alabama Sheriff over Inmate Food Money." *AL.com*, December 21, 2018. https://www.al.com/news/2018/12/prosecutor-sues-alabama-sheriff-who-loaned-jail-food-money-to-car-lot.html.

Reuters Fact Check. 2022. "Fact Check—Does '2000 Mules' Provide Evidence of Voter Fraud in the 2020 U.S. Presidential Election?" *Reuters*, May 27, 2022. https://www.reuters.com/article/factcheck-usa-mules-idUSL2N2XJ0OQ.

Rhee, Foon. 2021. "Watching the Sheriff." *Sacramento News & Review*, February 8, 2021. https://sacramento.newsreview.com/2021/02/08/watching-the-sheriff.

Rhoda, Erin. 2021. "A Maine Sheriff Didn't Punish a Top Officer Investigated for Targeting Employees." *Bangor Daily News*, February 16, 2021. http://bangordailynews.com/2021/02/16/mainefocus/a-maine-sheriff-didnt-punish-a-top-officer-investigated-for-targeting-employees/.

Riley County Police Department. 2021. "History." https://www.rileycountypolice.org/188/History.

Riley, Rachel. 2020. "Budget Proposal Prompts Calls to Defund Sheriff's Office." *HeraldNet.com*, June 11, 2020. https://www.heraldnet.com/news/budget-proposal-prompts-calls-to-defund-sheriffs-office/.

Ring, Kelly. 2022. "Polk County Sheriff Grady Judd Says Grabbing Public Attention Helps Him Keep the Community Safe." *FOX 13 News*, March 21, 2022. https://

www.fox13news.com/news/polk-county-sheriff-grady-judd-says-grabbing-public
-attention-helps-him-keep-the-community-safe.

Ritchie, Andrea J. 2017. *Invisible No More: Police Violence against Black Women and Women of Color*. Boston: Beacon Press.

Roberts, Lacey. 2020. "'I Am Just One Member of It': Breathitt County Sheriff Lays Off Entire Staff Because Budget Was Not Approved in Time." *WYMT*, February 13, 2020. https://www.wymt.com/content/news/Breathitt-County-Sheriff-lays-off -entire-staff-because-2020-budget-was-not-approved-567839351.html.

Robinson, Amanda L., and Meghan S. Chandek. 2000. "The Domestic Violence Arrest Decision: Examining Demographic, Attitudinal, and Situational Variables." *Crime & Delinquency* 46 (1): 18–37.

Rocha, Veronica. 2017. "Kern County Sheriff's Deputy Arrested in Connection with Domestic Violence Incident." *Los Angeles Times*, June 29, 2017. https://www.latimes .com/local/lanow/la-me-ln-kern-sheriffs-deputy-arrested-domestic-violence -20170629-story.html.

Rodden, Jonathan A. 2019. *Why Cities Lose: The Deep Roots of the Urban-Rural Political Divide*. New York: Basic Books.

Rodriguez, Christina, A. Chishti Muzaffar, and Kimberly Nortman. 2010. "Legal Limits of Immigration Enforcement." In *Taking Local Control: Immigration Policy Activism in U.S. Cities and States*, 31–50. Palo Alto, CA: Stanford University Press.

Rogers, Brad. 2014. "My Trip to the Cliven Bundy Ranch in Bunkerville, Nevada." April 21, 2014. https://www.facebook.com/notes/394152504923956/.

Rogers, William Warren, and James Denham. 2001. *Florida Sheriffs: A History, 1821– 1945*. Tallahassee, FL: Sentry Press.

Rogers, William Warren, and Ruth Rogers Pruitt. 2005. *Alabama's Outlaw Sheriff, Stephen S. Renfroe*. Tuscaloosa, AL: University of Alabama Press.

Romero, Mary, and Marwah Serag. 2004. "Violation of Latino Civil Rights Resulting from Ins and Local Police's Use of Race, Culture and Class Profiling: The Case of the Chandler Roundup in Arizona." *Cleveland State Law Review* 52: 75.

Rosa, Joseph G. 1994. *The West of Wild Bill Hickok*. University of Oklahoma Press.

Roth, Max. 2016. "Piute County Sheriff Threatens Arrest of Forest Service Personnel." *KSTU*, February 24, 2016. https://www.fox13now.com/2016/02/23/piute-county -sheriff-threatens-arrest-of-forest-service-personnel.

Rowhani-Rahbar, Ali, M. Alex Bellenger, Lauren Gibb, Heather Chesnut, Madison Lowry-Schiller, Emma Gause, Miriam J. Haviland, and Frederick P. Rivara. 2020. "Extreme Risk Protection Orders in Washington." *Annals of Internal Medicine* 173 (5): 342–49.

Rubado, Meghan E., and Jay T. Jennings. 2020. "Political Consequences of the Endan- gered Local Watchdog: Newspaper Decline and Mayoral Elections in the United States." *Urban Affairs Review* 56 (5): 1327–56.

Run for Something. 2018. "Why We Run: Dave 'Hutch' Hutchinson." *Why We Run (And You Can, Too!)*. September 6, 2018. https://medium.com/why-we-run-young -people-in-government/why-we-run-dave-hutch-hutchinson-9838a5dbd316.

Rushin, Stephen. 2013. "Federal Enforcement of Police Reform." *Fordham Law Review*. 82: 3189.

———. 2016. "Police Union Contracts." *Duke Law Journal* 66 (6): 1191–1266.

———. 2017. *Federal Intervention in American Police Departments*. Cambridge: Cam- bridge University Press.

Ryan, Jacob. 2020. "Police Must Detail Seizures or Lose Training Money under Proposed Bill." *89.3 WFPL News Louisville*, January 15, 2020. https://wfpl.org/police-must-detail-seizures-or-lose-training-money-under-proposed-bill/.

Sakal, Mike. 2012. "Babeu Exonerated in Case Involving Illegal Immigrant He Had a Relationship With." *East Valley Tribune*, September 3, 2012. https://www.eastvalleytribune.com/local/cop_shop/babeu-exonerated-in-case-involving-illegal-immigrant-he-had-a-relationship-with/article_52f92898-f399-11e1-8c48-001a4bcf887a.html.

Sanbonmatsu, Kira, and Kelly Dittmar. 2020. "Are You Ready to Run? Campaign Trainings and Women's Candidacies in New Jersey." In *Good Reasons to Run: Women and Political Candidacy*, edited by Shauna L. Shames, Rachel Bernhard, Mirya R. Holman, and Dawn Langan Teele. Philadelphia, PA: Temple University Press, 193–203.

Santucci, Jack. 2018. "Maine Ranked-Choice Voting as a Case of Electoral-System Change." *Representation* 54 (3): 297–311.

Santucci, Jack, and Jamil Scott. 2021. "Do Ranked Ballots Stimulate Candidate Entry?" SSRN Scholarly Paper. Rochester, NY. https://doi.org/10.2139/ssrn.3956554.

Saslow, Eli. 2014. "Going It Alone." *Washington Post*, August 9, 2014. https://www.washingtonpost.com/sf/national/2014/08/09/going-it-alone/.

Sattler, T. 1992. "The High Sheriff in England Today: The Invisible Man?" *Sheriff* 44 (4): 20–23.

Sawers, Brian. 2017. "The Poll Tax before Jim Crow." *American Journal of Legal History* 57 (2): 166–97.

"'Scarborough Country' for June 19." 2006. NBC News. June 20, 2006. https://www.nbcnews.com/id/wbna13438766.

Schaeffer, Katherine. 2019. "Racial, Ethnic Diversity Increases yet Again with the 117th Congress." *Pew Research Center*. 2019. https://www.pewresearch.org/fact-tank/2021/01/28/racial-ethnic-diversity-increases-yet-again-with-the-117th-congress.

Schaffner, Brian F., Jesse H. Rhodes, and Raymond J. La Raja. 2020. *Hometown Inequality: Race, Class, and Representation in American Local Politics*. New York: Cambridge University Press.

Schechter, Susan. 1982. *Women and Male Violence: The Visions and Struggles of the Battered Women's Movement*. South End Press.

Schnedler, Jack. 2021. "Uproar in Chicot County." *Arkansas Online*, December 5, 2021. https://www.arkansasonline.com/news/2021/dec/05/uproar-in-chicot-county.

Schneider, Anne, and Helen Ingram. 1993. "Social Construction of Target Populations: Implications for Politics and Policy." *American Political Science Review* 87 (2): 334–47.

Schneider, Monica C., and Angela L. Bos. 2014. "Measuring Stereotypes of Female Politicians." *Political Psychology* 35 (2): 245–66.

Schneider, Monica C., Mirya R. Holman, Amanda B. Diekman, and Thomas McAndrew. 2016. "Power, Conflict, and Community: How Gendered Views of Political Power Influence Women's Political Ambition." *Political Psychology* 37 (4): 515–31.

Schneider, Roger. 2011. "Middlebury Dairy Farmer, Sheriff Stand up to FDA." *Goshen News*, December 17, 2011. https://goshennews.com/news/middlebury-dairy-farmer-sheriff-stand-up-to-fda/article_b07a8430-9897-5504-9820-d943d60149f6.html.

Schroeer, Jordan. 2022. "Deputy who ran against Cass Co. Sheriff not re-appointed to department." *Valley News Live*, November 17, 2022. https://www.valleynewslive

.com/2022/11/17/deputy-who-ran-against-cass-co-sheriff-not-re-appointed
-department/.

Schrader, Stuart. 2019. "To Protect and Serve Themselves: Police in US Politics since
the 1960s." *Public Culture* 31 (3): 601–23.

Schulz, Dorothy Moses. 2004. *Breaking the Brass Ceiling: Women Police Chiefs and Their
Paths to the Top.* New York: Greenwood.

Schweers, Jeffrey. 2016. "Man Freed by Sheriff Nick Finch Accused of Murder." *Tallahassee Democrat*, September 27, 2016. https://www.tallahassee.com/story/news
/2016/09/26/bristol-man-accused-second-degree-murder-killing-53-year-old
/91132564.

Scott, Michael S. 2009. "Progress in American Policing? Reviewing the National Re-
views." *Law & Social Inquiry* 34 (1): 169–85.

Scott, Roger. n.d. "ROOTS: A Historical Perspective of the Office of Sheriff." National
Sheriffs' Association.

Sessions, Jeff. 2018. "Attorney General Sessions Delivers Remarks to the National Sheriffs' Association Annual Conference." June 18, 2018. https://www.justice.gov/opa
/speech/attorney-general-sessions-delivers-remarks-national-sheriffs-association
-annual.

Shah, Paru R., Eric Gonzalez Juenke, and Bernard L. Fraga. 2022. "Here Comes Everybody: Using a Data Cooperative to Understand the New Dynamics of Representation." *PS: Political Science & Politics* 55 (2): 300–02.

Shapira, Harel. 2013. *Waiting for José.* Princeton University Press. https://press.princeton
.edu/books/hardcover/9780691152158/waiting-for-jose.

Sharpe, Richard. 2016. "The Earliest Norman Sheriffs." *History* 101 (347): 485–94.

Shaun Attwood, dir. 2010. *Sheriff Joe Arpaio Brags His Tent City Jail Is a Concentration
Camp.* https://www.youtube.com/watch?v=D7reZOp2Qco.

Sheet, Connor. 2019. "How Nine Sheriffs Who Lost Reelection Made Life Harder
for Their Successors." *ProPublica*, June 12, 2019. https://www.propublica
.org/article/alabama-sheriffs-accusations-impeding-successors?token=
QWMHNu1frTkwNtZ9tn8UvtoO9Qq1EbGO.

Sheets, Connor. 2018. "Etowah Sheriff Pockets Jail Food Funds, Buys $740k Home."
AL.com, March 13, 2018. https://www.al.com/news/birmingham/2018/03/etowah
_sheriff_pocketed_over_7.html.

———. 2021. "'It Looks Like Just Slop.' After Landing Last Two Morgan County Sheriffs in Court, Inmates Say Jail Food Woes Continue." *AL.com*, June 25, 2021. https://
www.al.com/news/2021/06/it-looks-like-just-slop-after-landing-last-two-morgan
-county-sheriffs-in-court-inmates-say-jail-food-woes-continue.html.

———. 2022. "L.A. Democrats Failed to Mount United Campaign against Sheriff Villanueva despite Anger." *Los Angeles Times*, June 2, 2022. https://www.latimes.com
/california/story/2022-06-02/la-sheriff-race-democrats.

Sheriff Civilian Oversight Commission. 2023. "Report Regarding Deputy Gangs and
Deputy Cliques in the Los Angeles County Sheriff's Department." Sheriff Civilian
Oversight Commission.

"Sheriff Clarence Strider." n.d. *American Experience.* Accessed August 3, 2022. https://
www.pbs.org/wgbh/americanexperience/features/emmett-biography-sheriff
-clarence-strider.

Sherman, Lawrence W., and Richard A. Berk. 1984. "The Specific Deterrent Effects of
Arrest for Domestic Assault." *American Sociological Review* 49 (2): 261–72.

Sherman, Lawrence W., Janell D. Schmidt, Dennis P. Rogan, Douglas A. Smith, Patrick R. Gartin, Ellen G. Cohn, Dean J. Collins, and Anthony R. Bacich. 1992. "The Variable Effects of Arrest on Criminal Careers: The Milwaukee Domestic Violence Experiment." *The Journal of Criminal Law and Criminology* 82 (1): 137–69.

Shields, Leah, and Chad Darnell. 2018. "Re-Elected Graves County Sheriff Redmon Speaks on Camera While Facing Charges." *WPSD Local 6*, November 7, 2018. https://www.wpsdlocal6.com/news/re-elected-graves-county-sheriff-redmon -speaks-on-camera-while-facing-charges/article_ca33a447-e3ee-55ab-930e -6611da4e7778.html.

Shofner, Jerrell H. 1981. "Judge Herbert Rider and the Lynching at Labelle." *Florida Historical Quarterly* 59 (3): 292–306.

Shogan, Robert. 2004. *The Battle of Blair Mountain: The Story of America's Largest Labor Uprising*. Boulder, CO : Westview Press.

Shoub, Kelsey. 2022. "Comparing Systemic and Individual Sources of Racially Disparate Traffic Stop Outcomes." *Journal of Public Administration Research and Theory* 32 (2): 236–51.

Shoub, Kelsey, and Leah Christiani. 2022. "Context Matters: The Conditional Effect of Black Police Chiefs on Policing Outcomes." *Urban Affairs Review* 59 (6): 2043–2056.

Shoub, Kelsey, Derek A. Epp, Frank R. Baumgartner, Leah Christiani, and Kevin Roach. 2020. "Race, Place, and Context: The Persistence of Race Effects in Traffic Stop Outcomes in the Face of Situational, Demographic, and Political Controls." *Journal of Race, Ethnicity and Politics* 5 (3): 481–508.

Shoub, Kelsey, Katelyn E. Stauffer, and Miyeon Song. 2021. "Do Female Officers Police Differently? Evidence from Traffic Stops." *American Journal of Political Science* 65 (3): 755–69.

Silber Mohamed, Heather. 2017. *The New Americans?: Immigration, Protest, and the Politics of Latino Identity*. Lawrence, KS: University Press of Kansas.

Simard, François. 2004. "Self-Interest in Public Administration: Niskanen and the Budget-Maximizing Bureaucrat." *Canadian Public Administration* 47 (3): 406–11.

Sinclair, J. Andrew, Maya Love, and María Gutiérrez-Vera. 2021. "Federalism, Defunding the Police, and Democratic Values: A Functional Accountability Framework for Analyzing Police Reform Proposals." *Publius: The Journal of Federalism* 51 (3): 484–511.

Sitton, Thad. 2000. *The Texas Sheriff Lord of the County Line*. Norman, OK: University of Oklahoma Press.

Sledge, Matt. 2020. "Orleans Parish Sheriff Marlin Gusman Tells Court It's Time to Run His Own Jail Again." *Nola.com*, May 2020. https://www.nola.com/news/courts /orleans-parish-sheriff-marlin-gusman-tells-court-its-time-to-run-his-own-jail -again/article_c3d1c230-9fd2-11ea-a1a4-2307a2df746f.html.

Smead, Howard. 1988. *Blood Justice: The Lynching of Mack Charles Parker*. Oxford University Press, USA.

Smith, Beth. 2020. "Sheriff's Deputy Shortage in Henderson County Prompts Look at Pay Increase." *The Gleaner*, December 11, 2020. https://www.thegleaner.com/story /news/2020/12/11/sheriffs-deputy-shortage-prompts-close-look-at-pay-increase /3877601001.

Smith, Brad W. 2003. "The Impact of Police Officer Diversity on Police-Caused Homicides." *Policy Studies Journal* 31 (2): 147–62.

Smith, Bruce. 1933. *Rural Crime Control*. New York: Institute of Public Administration, Columbia University.

Smith, Julia Floyd. 1973. *Slavery and Plantation Growth in Antebellum Florida*. Gainesville, FL: University of Florida Press.

Smith, Tracey. 2015. "Know Your Sheriff: Mitchell County." WFXL. July 23, 2015. https://wfxl.com/news/local/know-your-sheriff-mitchell-county.

Songer, Bob. 2021. "Greetings from Sheriff Bob Songer of Klickitat County, Washington." *Local News*. June 17, 2021. https://gorgenewscenter.com/2021/06/18/greetings-from-sheriff-bob-songer-of-klickitat-county-washington.

Soss, Joe, and Vesla Weaver. 2017. "Police Are Our Government: Politics, Political Science, and the Policing of Race–Class Subjugated Communities." *Annual Review of Political Science* 20: 565–91.

Soss, Joe, Richard C. Fording, and Sanford F. Schram. 2011. *Disciplining the Poor: Neoliberal Paternalism and the Persistent Power of Race*. University of Chicago Press.

South Dakota Sheriffs' Association. 2022. "Brown County Sheriff Mark Milbrandt." https://web.archive.org/web/20190817000212/https://www.southdakotasheriffs.org/county/brown.html.

South Seattle Emerald. 2022. "Local Leaders, Activists React to What They Need in New King County Sheriff." *South Seattle Emerald*, April 26, 2022. https://southseattleemerald.com/2022/04/26/local-leaders-activists-react-to-what-they-need-in-new-king-county-sheriff.

Southwell, Priscilla L. 2009. "Analysis of the Turnout Effects of Vote by Mail Elections, 1980–2007." *The Social Science Journal* 46 (1): 211–17.

Spectrum News Staff. 2019. "Feud Between ICE and Sheriff McFadden Heats up Again." *Spectrum News*, September 27, 2019. https://spectrumlocalnews.com/nc/charlotte/news/2019/09/27/feud-between-ice-and-sheriff-mcfadden-heats-up-again.

Speri, Alice. 2018. "A County Sheriff's Election in North Carolina Has Become a Referendum on ICE's Deportation Machine." *The Intercept*, April 27, 2018. https://theintercept.com/2018/04/27/ice-287g-mecklenburg-county-sheriff-election.

SPLC. 2013. "'Sheriff of the Year' Says Government Is Greater Threat than Terrorists." *Southern Poverty Law Center*, August 22, 2013. https://www.splcenter.org/fighting-hate/intelligence-report/2013/%E2%80%98sheriff-year%E2%80%99-says-government-greater-threat-terrorists.

———. 2014a. "War in the West: The Bundy Ranch Standoff and the American Radical Right." *Southern Poverty Law Center*. https://www.splcenter.org/20140709/war-west-bundy-ranch-standoff-and-american-radical-right.

———. 2014b. "The 'Forgotten.'" *Southern Poverty Law Center*. https://www.splcenter.org/news/2015/07/27/forgotten.

———. 2018. "SPLC Brings First Lawsuit Challenging Florida Sheriffs' Latest Collaboration Agreements to Detain People for ICE." *Southern Poverty Law Center*, December 3, 2018. https://www.splcenter.org/news/2018/12/03/splc-brings-first-lawsuit-challenging-florida-sheriffs%E2%80%99-latest-collaboration-agreements.

———. 2023. "Federation for American Immigration Reform." *Southern Poverty Law Center*. https://www.splcenter.org/fighting-hate/extremist-files/group/federation-american-immigration-reform.

Stenglein, Christine, and Kamarck. 2019. "How Many Undocumented Immigrants Are

in the United States and Who Are They?" *Brookings*. November 12, 2019. https://
www.brookings.edu/policy2020/votervital/how-many-undocumented-immigrants
-are-in-the-united-states-and-who-are-they.

Stevens and Hildenbrand vs US. No. 91-10227. Kentucky (1991).

Stewart, Kim. 2022. "Stewart 4 Sheriff." Facebook. July 22, 2022.

Stewart, Shannon. 2021. "On the Porch with the Sheriff—Arvin West." *Hudspeth County
Herald*. May 14, 2021.

Stock, Catherine McNicol. 1996. *Rural Radicals: Righteous Rage in the American Grain*.
2nd ed. Ithaca, NY: Cornell University Press.

Stoker, Gerry. 1996. "Redefining Local Democracy." In *Local Democracy and Local Government*, edited by Lawrence Pratchett and David Wilson, 188–209. Government
Beyond the Centre. London: Macmillan Education UK.

Stoltze, Frank. 2023. "With Focus on Deputy Gangs, LA Sheriff Luna Elevates Role of
Constitutional Policing Advisor." *LAist*, February 15, 2023. https://laist.com/news
/criminal-justice/la-sheriff-luna-will-again-elevate-the-role-of-constitutional
-policing-advisor-focusing-on-deputy-gangs-and-more.

Stone, Peter. 2022a. "MyPillow Chief Spends Tens of Millions in Fresh Crusade to Push
Trump's Big Lie." *The Guardian*, August 4, 2022. https://www.theguardian.com/us
-news/2022/aug/04/mypillow-mike-lindell-trump-big-lie-election-fraud.

———. 2022b. "Rightwing Sheriffs' Groups Ramp up Drives to Monitor US Midterm
Elections." *The Guardian*, August 17, 2022. https://www.theguardian.com/us-news
/2022/aug/17/rightwing-sheriffs-trump-midterm-elections-voting-arizona.

Streb, Matthew J., Brian Frederick, and Casey LaFrance. 2007. "Contestation, Competition, and the Potential for Accountability in Intermediate Appellate Court Elections." *Judicature* 91: 70.

Struckhoff, DR. 1994. *The American Sheriff*. Joliet, IL: Justice Research Institute.

Suarez, Miranda. 2020. "Tarrant County Sheriff's Race Homes In on Safety at County
Jail." *KERA News*, October 22, 2020. https://www.keranews.org/government/2020
-10-22/tarrant-county-sheriffs-race-hones-in-on-safety-at-county-jail.

———. 2022. "A Woman Gave Birth Alone in a Tarrant County Jail Cell. A Federal
Lawsuit Says It's the Jail's Fault." *KERA News*, January 14, 2022. https://www
.keranews.org/news/2022-01-14/a-woman-gave-birth-alone-in-a-tarrant-county
-jail-cell-a-federal-lawsuit-says-its-the-jails-fault.

Subramanian, Ram, and Leah Skrzypiec. 2017. "To Protect and Serve: New Trends in
State-Level Policing Reform, 2015–2016." Vera Institute.

Sullivan, Francis X. 1999. "The Usurping Octopus of Jurisdictional/Authority: The
Legal Theories of the Sovereign Citizen Movement." *Wisconsin Law Review* 785.

Swaine, Jon, and Oliver Laughland. 2015. "The County: Where Deputies Dole Out
Rough Justice." *The Guardian*, December 4, 2015. http://www.theguardian.com/us
-news/2015/dec/04/the-county-kern-county-california-deputies-tactics.

Swenson, Steve. 2010. "Sheriff's Department Gets Nearly $1 Million from Drug Case
Seizure." *Bakersfield Californian*, May 26, 2010. https://www.bakersfield.com/news
/sheriffs-department-gets-nearly-1-million-from-drug-case-seizure/article_ff23f2b8
-cf4a-5cc5-a7de-df8968243c11.html.

Tabler, Dave. 2014. "New Exhibit: The Civil War in Morgan County, AL." *Appalachian
History*. September 23, 2014. https://www.appalachianhistory.net/2014/09/new
-exhibit-civil-war-morgan-county-al.html.

Taft, Molly. 2021. "Cops Are Using Facebook to Target Line 3 Protest Leaders, New

Documents Reveal." *Gizmodo*, June 10, 2021. https://gizmodo.com/cops-are-using
-facebook-to-target-line-3-pipeline-prote-1847063533.

Taft, Philip, and Philip Ross. 1969. "American Labor Violence Its Causes, Character,
and Outcome." In *Violence in America: Historical and Comparative Perspectives: A
Report to the National Commission on the Causes and Prevention of Violence*, edited
by Hugh Davis Graham and Ted Robert Gurr. Washington, DC: U.S. Government
Printing Office.

Tanner, Chuck. 2021. "Klickitat County Sheriff Aligns with Far-Right Groups." *Institute
for Research and Education on Human Rights*. June 29, 2021. https://www.irehr.org
/2021/06/28/klickitat-county-sheriff-aligns-with-far-right-groups.

———. 2022. "'Constitutional Sheriffs' and the 'Election Fraud' Conspiracy Posse ★
Institute for Research and Education on Human Rights." *Institute for Research and
Education on Human Rights*. June 14, 2022. https://www.irehr.org/2022/06/14
/constitutional-sheriffs-and-the-election-fraud-conspiracy-posse.

Tausanovitch, Chris, and Christopher Warshaw. 2013. "Measuring Constituent Policy
Preferences in Congress, State Legislatures, and Cities." *The Journal of Politics* 75
(2): 330–42.

———. 2022. "Mass Ideology of U.S. Geographies from 2000–2022." Dataset. https://
dataverse.harvard.edu/file.xhtml?fileId=6690214&version=1.0.

Taylor, Kirstine. 2018. "Sunbelt Capitalism, Civil Rights, and the Development of
Carceral Policy in North Carolina, 1954–1970." *Studies in American Political Development* 32 (2): 292–322.

Tchekmedyian, Alene. 2021a. "L.A. County Sheriff's Unit Accused of Targeting Political Enemies, Vocal Critics." *Los Angeles Times*, September 23, 2021. https://www
.latimes.com/california/story/2021-09-23/sheriff-alex-villanueva-secret-police.

———. 2021b. "Sheriff Villanueva and Top Aide Defy Watchdog Subpoenas." *Los Angeles Times*, October 22, 2021. https://www.latimes.com/california/story/2021-10-21
/sheriff-villanueva-undersheriff-murakami-defy-subpoenas.

Templeton, Amelia. 2013. "Loss of Timber Payments Cuts Deep in Oregon." *NPR*,
May 21, 2013. https://www.npr.org/2013/05/21/185839248/loss-of-timber-payments
-cuts-deep-in-oregon.

Thacher, David. 2020. "How Law Shapes Policing: The Regulation of Alcohol in the
U.S., 1750–1860." *Policing and Society* 30 (10): 1171–90.

"The Challenge of Crime in a Free Society." 1967. Washington, DC: President's Commission on Law Enforcement and Administration of Justice.

The Dana Show. 2022. "ATF's Unconstitutional Searches—HOW TO RESPOND." The
First TV. July 26, 2022. https://www.thefirsttv.com/watch/sheriff-bob-songer-atfs
-unconstitutional-searches.

The Editorial Board. 2016. "Should Sheriff Be Elected or Appointed? A Well-Timed
Question: Editorial." Oregonlive. Last modified July 12, 2016. https://www
.oregonlive.com/opinion/2016/07/should_sheriff_be_elected_or_a.html.

The National Sheriffs' Association. 2015. "PRESERVE THE OFFICE OF SHERIFF BY
CONTINUING THE ELECTION OF OUR NATION'S SHERIFFS." The National Sheriffs'
Association. https://www.sheriffs.org/sites/default/files/tb/Preserving_the_Office
_of_Sheriff_Through_Election.pdf.

Thompson, Daniel M. 2020. "How Partisan Is Local Law Enforcement? Evidence from
Sheriff Cooperation with Immigration Authorities." *American Political Science Review* 114 (1): 222–36.

Thompson, Gabriel. 2016. *America's Social Arsonist: Fred Ross and Grassroots Organizing in the Twentieth Century*. Berkeley, CA: University of California Press.

Thompson, Joel A. 1986. "The American Jail: Problems, Politics, Prospects." *American Journal of Criminal Justice* 10 (2): 205–21.

Thoreau, Henry David. 1849. *Civil Disobedience*. New York: Broadview.

Thornton, J. Mills. 1978. *Politics and Power in a Slave Society: Alabama, 1800–1860*. Baton Rouge, LA: LSU Press.

Tjaden, Patricia Godeke, and Nancy Thoennes. 2000. *Full Report of the Prevalence, Incidence, and Consequences of Violence against Women: Findings from the National Violence Against Women Survey*. US Department of Justice, Office of Justice Programs, National Institute of Justice.

Tobar, Hector. 2011. "Finally, Transparency in the Ruben Salazar Case." *Los Angeles Times*, August 5, 2011. https://www.latimes.com/local/la-xpm-2011-aug-05-la-me-0805-tobar-20110805-story.html.

Tobson, Kevin. 2021. "SC Sheriffs' Association President Offers Perceptive on National Police Reform." South Carolina Sheriffs' Association.

Tocqueville, Alexis de. 1835. *Democracy in America*. New York: Adlard and Saunders.

Toohey, Grace. 2021. "Orange Sheriff Declines Advisory Board's Advice to Limit Deputies' Social Media Posts." *Orlando Sentinel*, August 13, 2021. https://www.orlandosentinel.com/news/crime/os-ne-orange-sheriff-social-media-20210813-a54mvayozjcadegtzhdty6u7am-story.html.

Treisman, Rachel. 2022. "COVID Was Again the Leading Cause of Death among U.S. Law Enforcement in 2021." *NPR*, January 12, 2022. https://www.npr.org/2022/01/12/1072411820/law-enforcement-deaths-2021-covid.

Tripodi, Francesca Bolla. 2021. "ReOpen Demands as Public Health Threat: A Sociotechnical Framework for Understanding the Stickiness of Misinformation." *Computational and Mathematical Organization Theory* 28 (August): 321–334.

Tripp, Drew. 2019. "Colleton Sheriff Suspended by Governor after Domestic Violence Indictment." November 21, 2019. https://www.abccolumbia.com/2019/11/21/colleton-sheriff-suspended-by-governor-after-domestic-violence-indictment.

Trounstine, Jessica. 2008. *Political Monopolies in American Cities: The Rise and Fall of Bosses and Reformers*. Chicago: University of Chicago Press.

———. 2011. "Evidence of a Local Incumbency Advantage." *Legislative Studies Quarterly* 36 (2): 255–80.

———. 2013. "Turnout and Incumbency in Local Elections." *Urban Affairs Review* 49 (2): 167–89.

———. 2018. *Segregation by Design Local Politics and Inequality in American Cities*. New York: Cambridge University Press.

Trump, Donald. 2020. "Campaign Press Release—48 Sheriffs Endorse President Trump in Tampa, Florida | The American Presidency Project." July 31, 2020. https://www.presidency.ucsb.edu/documents/trump-campaign-press-release-48-sheriffs-endorse-president-trump-tampa-florida.

Tsai, Robert L. 2017. "The Troubling Sheriffs' Movement That Joe Arpaio Supports." *POLITICO Magazine*, September 1, 2017. https://www.politico.com/magazine/story/2017/09/01/joe-arpaio-pardon-sheriffs-movement-215566.

Turner, George A. 2002. "The Lattimer Massacre: A Perspective from the Ethnic Community." *Pennsylvania History: A Journal of Mid-Atlantic Studies* 69 (1): 11–30.

Turner, Ian R. 2018. "Reviewing Procedure vs. Judging Substance: The Scope of Review and Bureaucratic Policymaking." *Journal of Political Institutions and Political Economy* 2 (4): 569–96.

Tyler, Tom R., Jonathan Jackson, and Avital Mentovich. 2015. "The Consequences of Being an Object of Suspicion: Potential Pitfalls of Proactive Police Contact." *Journal of Empirical Legal Studies* 12 (4): 602–36.

Tyler, Tom R., Kenneth A. Rasinski, and Kathleen M. McGraw. 1985. "The Influence of Perceived Injustice on the Endorsement of Political Leaders." *Journal of Applied Social Psychology* 15 (8): 700–25.

Ulloa, Jazmine. 2020. "All the President's Sheriffs." *Boston Globe*, January 20, 2020. https://www.bostonglobe.com/news/politics/2020/01/20/all-president-sheriffs-how-one-law-enforcement-group-became-ardent-trump-supporters/YvqIHMRszFqljvoq2oIZpI/story.html.

US Census Bureau. 2020. "Latest City and Town Population Estimates." Washington, DC: US Census Bureau.

U.S. Customs and Border Patrol. 2022. "Drug Seizure Statistics." U.S. Customs and Border Protection. https://www.cbp.gov/newsroom/stats/drug-seizure-statistics.

Van Sickler, Michael. 2018. "How a Florida Sheriff Took on Rick Scott, Beat Him, and Inspired an Alt-Right Movement." *Tampa Bay Times*, April 27, 2018. https://www.tampabay.com/florida-politics/buzz/2018/04/27/how-a-liberty-county-sheriff-took-on-rick-scott-beat-him-and-inspired-an-alt-right-movement/.

Vankin, Jonathan. 2021. "Civilian Sheriff's Oversight Is Now Law in California. Will It Make a Difference?" *California Local*, July 25, 2021. https://californialocal.com/localnews/statewide/ca/article/show/571-sheriffs-oversight-law-ab-1185.

———. 2022. "Will California Embrace Progressive Sheriffs? State Starts Leaning Toward Reform." *California Local*, July 12, 2022. https://californialocal.com/localnews/statewide/ca/article/show/8451-california-sheriffs-progressive.

Vardalis, James J., and Shannon N. Waters. 2010. "An Analysis of Texas Sheriffs' Opinions Concerning Domestic Terrorism: Training, Equipment, Funding and Perceptions Regarding Likelihood of Attack." *Journal of Homeland Security and Emergency Management* 7 (1): 1–17.

Varsanyi, Monica W. 2010. *Taking Local Control: Immigration Policy Activism in US Cities and States*. Palo Alto, CA: Stanford University Press.

Vaughan, Jessica, and James R. Edwards. 2009. *The 287(g) Program: Protecting Home Towns and Homeland*. Center for Immigration Studies.

Vazquez, By Maegan. 2018. "Sessions Invokes 'Anglo-American Heritage' of Sheriff's Office | CNN Politics." CNN, February 12, 2018. https://www.cnn.com/2018/02/12/politics/jeff-sessions-anglo-american-law-enforcement/index.html.

Vera Institute. 2022. "What Jails Cost: Daviess County." Vera Institute of Justice. https://www.vera.org/publications/what-jails-cost-statewide/kentucky/daviess-county.

Vitale, Alex S. 2017. *The End of Policing*. New York: Verso.

Vogel, Bob. 2001. *Fighting to Win*. Paducah, KY: Turner.

Wager, Paul Woodford. 1928. *County Government and Administration in North Carolina*. Chapel Hill, NC: University of North Carolina Press.

Wagner, Peter, and Alexi Jones. 2019. "State of Phone Justice." Prison Policy Initiative. https://www.prisonpolicy.org/phones/state_of_phone_justice.html.

Walker, Hannah L. 2014. "Extending the Effects of the Carceral State: Proximal Contact, Political Participation, and Race." *Political Research Quarterly* 67 (4): 809–22.

———. 2020. "Targeted: The Mobilizing Effect of Perceptions of Unfair Policing Practices." *The Journal of Politics* 82 (1): 119–34.

Walker, Samuel. 1977. *A Critical History of Police Reform.* Lexington, MA: Lexington Books.

Walker, Samuel, and Charles Katz. 1992. *The Police in America: An Introduction.* New York: McGraw-Hill.

Walker, Tim. 2021. "House Panel Hears about Public Safety Concerns in Greater Minnesota." *Minnesota House of Representatives,* January 29, 2021. https://www.house .leg.state.mn.us/sessiondaily/Story/15531.

Ward, Geoff. 2018. "Living Histories of White Supremacist Policing: Towards Transformative Justice." *Du Bois Review: Social Science Research on Race* 15 (1): 167–84.

Warshaw, Christopher, and Jonathan Rodden. 2012. "How Should We Measure District-Level Public Opinion on Individual Issues?" *Journal of Politics* 74 (1): 203–19.

Washington, Robin. 2018. "About the 'Anglo-American Heritage of Law Enforcement.'" *The Marshall Project,* February 13, 2018. https://www.themarshallproject.org/2018 /02/13/about-the-anglo-american-heritage-of-law-enforcement.

Washington Times. 2022. "Sheriffs, Jails Brace for Cuts." *Washington Times,* 2022. https://www.washingtontimes.com/news/2009/feb/3/sheriffs-jails-brace-for-cuts.

Waslin, Michele. 2010. "Immigration Enforcement by State and Local Police: The Impact on the Enforcers and Their Communities." In *Taking Local Control: Immigration and Policy Activism in US Cities and States,* 97–114. Palo Alto, CA: Stanford University Press.

Waybourn, Bill, dir. 2016. *Chuck Norris Says Vote Bill Waybourn!* https://www.youtube .com/watch?v=L6nMkfZLL4Q.

Weaver, Vesla M., and Amanda Geller. 2019. "De-Policing America's Youth: Disrupting Criminal Justice Policy Feedbacks That Distort Power and Derail Prospects." *The ANNALS of the American Academy of Political and Social Science* 685 (1): 190–226.

Weaver, Vesla, Gwen Prowse, and Spencer Piston. 2019. "Too Much Knowledge, Too Little Power: An Assessment of Political Knowledge in Highly Policed Communities." *Journal of Politics* 81 (3): 1153–66.

———. 2020. "Withdrawing and Drawing In: Political Discourse in Policed Communities." *Journal of Race, Ethnicity, and Politics* 5 (3): 604–47.

Weber, Christopher R., Howard Lavine, Leonie Huddy, and Christopher M. Federico. 2014. "Placing Racial Stereotypes in Context: Social Desirability and the Politics of Racial Hostility." *American Journal of Political Science* 58 (1): 63–78.

Weichselbaum, Simone, and Nicole Lewis. 2020. "Support for Defunding the Police Department Is Growing. Here's Why It's Not a Silver Bullet." *The Marshall Project,* June 29, 2020.

Weiner, Allison Hope. 2006. "Mel Gibson: The Speed of Scandal." *New York Times,* August 1, 2006. https://www.nytimes.com/2006/08/01/business/media/01gibson .html.

Weisheit, Ralph, David N. Falcone, and L. Edward Wells. 1994. "Crime and Rural Policing." National Institute of Justice Research in Action. Washington, DC: U.S. Department of Justice.

———. 1995. "Crime and Policing in Rural and Small Town America." Washington, DC: National Institute of Justice.

Weizel, Richard. 2000. "High Noon for Sheriffs." *New York Times,* April 30, 2000. https://www.nytimes.com/2000/04/30/nyregion/high-noon-for-sheriffs.html.

Wells, L. Edward, and David N. Falcone. 2006. *Crime and Policing in Rural and Small-Town America*. Prospect Heights, IL: Waveland.

Wesley, Lashay. 2016. "Doña Ana County Sheriff's Dispute with County Grows." *KDBC*, January 26, 2016. https://cbs4local.com/news/local/doa-ana-county-sheriffs-dispute-with-county-grows.

Westera, Nina J., Mark R. Kebbell, and Becky Milne. 2016. "Want a Better Criminal Justice Response to Rape? Improve Police Interviews with Complainants and Suspects." *Violence against Women* 22 (14): 1748–69.

White, Ariel. 2019. "Misdemeanor Disenfranchisement? The Demobilizing Effects of Brief Jail Spells on Potential Voters." *American Political Science Review* 113 (2): 311–24.

White, Ismail K., and Chryl N. Laird. 2020. *Steadfast Democrats: How Social Forces Shape Black Political Behavior*. *Steadfast Democrats*. Princeton, NJ: Princeton University Press.

Whitehead, Andrew L., Samuel L. Perry, and Joseph O. Baker. 2018. "Make America Christian Again: Christian Nationalism and Voting for Donald Trump in the 2016 Presidential Election." *Sociology of Religion* 79 (2): 147–71.

Whitlock, Craig. 2016. "How a High-Profile Texas Sheriff Is Tied to a Rogue Navy Unit Facing a Criminal Probe." *Washington Post*, September 30, 2016. https://www.washingtonpost.com/investigations/how-a-high-profile-texas-sheriff-is-tied-to-a-rogue-navy-unit-facing-a-criminal-probe/2016/09/30/35c7d120-8585-11e6-a3ef-f35afb41797f_story.html.

Whitmire, Kyle. 2018. "49 Alabama Sheriffs Hide Jail Food Funds, Flout Open Records Law." *AL.com*, March 21, 2018. https://www.al.com/opinion/2018/03/49_alabama_sheriffs_flout_open.html.

———. 2019. "Move Over Beach House Sheriff. Meet Sheriff Scratch-Off." *AL.com*, August 28, 2019. https://www.al.com/news/2019/08/move-over-beach-house-sheriff-meet-sheriff-scratch-off.html.

Who Leads Us. 2019. "Tipping the Scales: Challengers Take on the Old Boys Club of Elected Prosecutors." Campaign for Reflective Democracy. https://wholeads.us/research/tipping-the-scales-elected-prosecutors/.

———. 2020. "Confronting the Demographics of Power: America's Sheriffs." Campaign for Reflective Democracy.

Wickser, Philip J. "Grover Cleveland: His Character, Background and Legal Career." *American Bar Association Journal* 33 (4): 327–330.

Wiener, Jonathan M. 1979. "Class Structure and Economic Development in the American South, 1865–1955." *The American Historical Review* 84 (4): 970–92.

Wiita, Tommy. 2022. "Hennepin County Investigating after FOX 9 Revelations about Sheriff Hutchinson." *Bring Me the News*, July 12, 2022. https://bringmethenews.com/hennepin-news/hennepin-county-investigating-series-of-revelations-by-fox-9-about-sheriff-dave-hutchinson.

Williams, Brady. 2021. "Gov. Pritzker Signs Police and Criminal Justice Reform Bill into Law." 14news.com, February 24, 2021. https://www.14news.com/2021/02/25/gov-pritzker-signs-police-criminal-justice-reform-bill-into-law.

Williams, E. Russ. 1972. "Slave Patrol Ordinances of St. Tammany Parish, Louisiana, 1835–1838." *Louisiana History: The Journal of the Louisiana Historical Association* 13 (4): 399–412.

Wilson, Chris. 2022. "Nostalgia, Entitlement and Victimhood: The Synergy of White Genocide and Misogyny." *Terrorism and Political Violence* 34 (8):1810–25.

Wimmer, Andreas. 2002. *Nationalist Exclusion and Ethnic Conflict: Shadows of Modernity.* New York: Cambridge University Press.

Winter, Margaret. 2014. "Notorious Sheriff Baca Finally Retires." American Civil Liberties Union. January 9, 2014. https://www.aclu.org/blog/national-security /notorious-sheriff-baca-finally-retires.

Winton, Richard. 2018. "Kern County Sheriff Is Caught on Tape Saying It Costs Less to Kill Suspects than to Wound Them." *Los Angeles Times*, April 10, 2018. https://www .latimes.com/local/lanow/la-me-kern-county-sheriff-tape-20180410-story.html.

Woldoff, Rachael A., Robert C. Litchfield, and Angela Sycafoose Matthews. 2017. "Unpacking Heat: Dueling Identities and Complex Views on Gun Control among Rural Police." *Rural Sociology* 82 (3): 444–72.

Wood, Betty. 2007. *Slavery in Colonial Georgia, 1730–1775.* University of Georgia Press.

Wood, Kim Swindell. 2022. "Page to Serve Second Term as Sheriff, Robinson Re-Elected White County Executive." *Sparta Live*, May 5, 2022. https://spartalive .com/stories/page-to-serve-second-term-as-sheriff-robinson-re-elected-county -executive,43956.

Wright, John. 2018. "Judge Refuses to Reinstate Law Enforcement Duties for Redmon." *Murray Ledger and Times*, November 8, 2018. https://www.murrayledger .com/news/local/judge-refuses-to-reinstate-law-enforcement-duties-for-redmon /article_51c9ab62-e2ff-11e8-a881-63464ff1fc29.html.

Wright, Stuart A. 2007. *Patriots, Politics, and the Oklahoma City Bombing.* New York: Cambridge University Press.

Wrightson, Margaret. 1986. "Interlocal Cooperation and Urban Problems: Lessons for the New Federalism." *Urban Affairs Quarterly* 22 (2): 261–75.

WTOK. 2019. "Former Sheriff Sentenced in Sumter County." Last modified January 9, 2019. https://www.wtok.com/content/news/Former-sheriff-sentenced-in-Sumter -County-504120641.html.

WTVF. 2020. "Body Cam Video Shows TN Deputy Ordering Dog to Bite Woman Who Had Verbally Surrendered." *WLEX*, July 16, 2020. https://www.lex18.com/news /america-in-crisis/body-cam-video-shows-tn-deputy-ordering-dog-to-bite-woman -who-had-verbally-surrendered.

WTVG, dir. 2021. "Ohio AG Files Lawsuit to Stop Vaccine Mandate for Federal Contractors." ABC 13. https://www.13abc.com/2021/11/04/ohio-ag-files-lawsuit-stop -vaccine-mandate-federal-contrators.

Wu, Nicholas, and Marianne Levine. 2021. "Police Reform Talks Stalling as Law Enforcement Groups Bristle." *POLITICO*, June 10, 2021. https://www.politico.com /news/2021/06/10/police-reform-talks-stalling-as-law-enforcement-groups-bristle -493220.

Yanochik, Mark Andrew. 1997. *Essays on the Economics of Slavery.* Auburn University.

Yardley, Jim. 2001. "New York's Sewage Was a Texas Town's Gold." *New York Times*, July 27, 2001. https://www.nytimes.com/2001/07/27/us/new-york-s-sewage-was-a -texas-town-s-gold.html.

Yardley, Rosemary. 1991. "Who Owns Congress, You or the NRA?" *Greensboro News and Record*, May 1991. https://greensboro.com/who-owns-congress-you-or-the-nra /article_0936c79b-7208-5aca-9a4c-877a27e2b664.html.

Yntiso, Sidak. 2022. "Does Prosecutor Partisanship Exacerbate the Racial Charging Gap? Evidence from District Attorneys in Three States." Working paper. Harris School of Public Policy, University of Chicago.

Youngentob, Dana. 2021. "Rep. Cuellar Announces $2,392,000 in Federal Funding to Support Border Security in Starr County." US Representative Henry Cuellar. Last modified November 23, 2021. https://cuellar.house.gov/news/documentsingle.aspx?DocumentID=406735.

Zaitz, Les. 2016. "Oregon Justice Department Opens Investigation of Grant County Sheriff." Oregonlive. March 17, 2016. https://www.oregonlive.com/oregon-standoff/2016/03/oregon_justice_department_open.html.

Zatz, Noah D. 2020. "Get to Work or Go to Jail: State Violence and the Racialized Production of Precarious Work." *Law & Social Inquiry* 45 (2): 304–38.

Zeng, Zhen, and Todd D. Minton. 2021. "Census of Jails, 2005–2019—Statistical Tables." Bureau of Justice Statistics. https://bjs.ojp.gov/library/publications/census-jails-2005-2019-statistical-tables.

Zielbauer, Paul. 2001. "Hartford Report Details Financial Abuses by County Sheriffs." *New York Times*, July 11, 2001. https://www.nytimes.com/2001/07/11/nyregion/hartford-report-details-financial-abuses-by-county-sheriffs.html.

Zimring, Franklin E., and Gordon Hawkins. 1995. *Incapacitation: Penal Confinement and the Restraint of Crime*. New York: Oxford University Press.

———. 1999. *Crime Is Not the Problem: Lethal Violence in America*. New York: Oxford University Press.

Zoorob, Michael. 2019a. "Blue Endorsements Matter: How the Fraternal Order of Police Contributed to Donald Trump's Victory." *PS: Political Science & Politics* 52 (2): 243–50.

———. 2020. "Going National: Immigration Enforcement and the Politicization of Local Police." *PS: Political Science & Politics* 53 (3): 421–26.

———. 2022. "There's (Rarely) a New Sheriff in Town: The Incumbency Advantage for County Sheriffs." Electoral Studies 80 (2022): 102550.

Zucchino, David. 2012. "North Carolina Town Split over Sheriff's Treatment of Latinos." *Los Angeles Times*, November 23, 2012. http://articles.latimes.com/2012/nov/23/nation/la-na-sheriff-20121124.

Printed in the USA
CPSIA information can be obtained
at www.ICGtesting.com
JSHW050911210524
63509JS00011B/27